Everyday
Greatness

Inspiration for a Meaningful Life

Everyday Greatness

INSIGHTS AND COMMENTARY BY

Stephen R. Covey

Compiled by David K. Hatch

THOMAS NELSON
Since 1798

NASHVILLE DALLAS MEXICO CITY RIO DE JANEIRO BEIJING

Published by Rutledge Hill Press, a Division of Thomas Nelson, Inc.,
P.O. Box 141000, Nashville, Tennessee 37214.

Rutledge Hill Press books may be purchased in bulk for
educational, business, fund-raising, or sales promotional use.
For information, please e-mail SpecialMarkets@ThomasNelson.com.

Library of Congress Cataloging-in-Publication Data

Covey, Stephen R.
Inspiration for a meaningful life : everyday greatness / Steven R. Covey
and Readers's Digest / Compiled by David K. Hatch.
p. cm.
Includes bibiographical references.
ISBN-13: 978-1-4016-0241-3 (hardcover)
ISBN-13: 978-1-4016-0356-4 (IE)
1. Conduct of life. I. Hatch, David K., 1958–
II. Readers' Digest Association. III. Title.
BJ1531.C69 2006
170'.44—dc22
2006019786

Printed in the United States of America
08 09 10 — 7 6 5 4 3

CONTENTS

OVERCOMING ADVERSITY

BLENDING THE PIECES

INTRODUCTION

DR. STEPHEN R. COVEY

I feel blessed.

In a world where turmoil dominates the evening news and words of discouragement often prevail, I feel blessed to meet daily with individuals around the globe whose lives convince me that there is an abundance of good among us.

In a day when we hear so much of corporate scandals and ethical breaches, I feel blessed to associate with leaders of nations, heads of business, and first time supervisors whose lives are filled with integrity and moral fortitude.

In a time when echoes of crime, war, natural disasters, and disease are common, I feel blessed to work with law enforcers, military experts, civic administrators, and medical professionals who sacrifice much and whose intentions are honorable.

In an age when parenthood and family ties are being challenged as perhaps never before, I feel blessed to know strong fathers and noble mothers who by day and night do their best to provide sustenance and nurturance for their children.

And, in an era when schools and youths are being bombarded with negativism and sensitive social dilemmas, I feel blessed to be familiar with dedicated teachers and talented youths who are rich in character and committed to make a difference—each in their own unique way.

Indeed, I feel blessed to encounter people from all walks of life and all parts of the world who are genuinely good and who do so much to contribute to the world around them. They inspire me.

Probabilities are high that you are such a person.

A COLLECTION FOR OUR TIMES

Yes, I believe that the majority of people in this world are good people doing good things, and that we should not let the noise of the negative minority drown out the steady sound of good that is around us.

But let me also say this. While so many of us are up to good things and probably deserve more credit than we give ourselves, most of us know that the *good* we are doing does not always represent our *best*. And so in our quieter moments, we sense there is still more we can be getting out of life, more we can be giving.

Isn't that true for you?

I like to approach life with the belief that my most important work is always ahead of me, not behind me, and my personal motto is "Live life in crescendo." As a result, I feel a persisting desire to stretch myself in new directions, to look for worthy ways to make a difference. And when I personally experience the desire for life enhancement, I find it valuable to have a resource such as this collection available for reading and reflection. Gathered by *Reader's Digest* from decades of classic "success" literature and from many of the most currently respected people around the globe, it is a true treasury of timeless principles and practical insights for optimizing life—a collection for our times.

For you, I hope this collection will have at least three outcomes. First, I hope you will be able to sit back, relax, and enjoy your reading. Let's face it. Life is not easy. The world is in commotion and all forecasts point toward more turbulence ahead. So much of what we hear and read these days is discomforting, even rattling. As such, it is increasingly rare to be able to sit down and enjoy an uplifting reading experience such as this. May you find it to be a refuge from the storm, a haven of hope.

Second, I hope this collection will provide you with inspiration as to how you personally can get a little more out of life—and, yes, give a little more, too. For more than eighty years, *Reader's Digest* has been a fountain of insights for effective living. We are so fortunate to have literally hundreds of their most inspiring stories and insights brought together in this one collection. My desire is that some piece of what you read will provide the nudge you may be seeking to advance you from doing good to doing your best, both today and in your pathways ahead.

Third, I hope this collection will arouse within you a greater passion for being a transition person. A transition person is one who breaks the flow of bad—the negative traditions or harmful practices that get passed from generation to generation, or from situation to situation, whether in a family, a workplace, a community, or wherever. Transition persons transcend their own needs and tap into the deepest, most noble impulses of human nature. In times of darkness, they are lights, not judges; models, not critics. In periods of discord, they are change catalysts, not victims; healers, not carriers. Today's world needs more transition persons. Trust yourself to become one of the best, and watch your influence grow.

Everyday Greatness

Occasionally, the world witnesses a heroic feat or discovers a person with rare talent. Every now and then, a scientist makes a pivotal discovery or an engineer designs a revolutionary device. Each decade or so, a pair of politicians sign a bold peace initiative. Annually, extravagant affairs tout the year's best actors, musicians, athletes, and salespeople, while hometown festivals crown the person who can eat the most chili peppers or sound the best yodel.

Such singular events and accomplishments often appear in sizzling media headlines under the banner of "greatness." And in most cases they do represent a type of greatness that is deserving of attention and applause. For many of them represent achievements that move society forward in significant, progressive ways, while others simply add a much needed measure of spice and humor to life.

But most people know there is another type of greatness that tends to be more quiet by nature, one that generally escapes the headlines. Yet, it is a greatness that in my opinion is deserving of higher honor, even more respect. I call it "Everyday Greatness."

Everyday Greatness is what I have called, in other settings, "primary greatness." It has to do with character and contribution, as distinguished from "secondary greatness," which has to do with notoriety, wealth, fame, prestige, or position. Everyday Greatness is a way of living, not a one-time event. It says more about who a person is than what a person has, and is portrayed more by the goodness that radiates from a face than the title on a business card. It speaks more about people's motives than about their talents; more about small and simple deeds than about grandiose accomplishments. It is humble.

When asked to describe Everyday Greatness, people typically respond with descriptions of individuals they know personally, such as a farmer who year in and year out weathers the storms of life, provides for family, and helps neighbors. Or a mother who knows she is not perfect but who perseveres in doing her everyday best to exhibit unconditional love to a challenging child. They describe a grandparent, a teacher, a work colleague, a neighbor, or a friend who is always dependable, honest, hardworking, and respectful of others. Above all, they describe someone who is within reach of emulation, sensing that they do not have to be the next Gandhi or Abraham Lincoln or Mother Teresa to exhibit Everyday Greatness.

Yes, the type of people they describe when trying to define Everyday Greatness are the same caliber of people I described in the opening lines of this Introduction—people who, despite the negative noise in the world, still somehow find ways to step up and do their part to make a positive contribution. The key is that it is all part of who they are every day.

THREE EVERY DAY CHOICES

So what leads to Everyday Greatness? What is at its roots?

I am convinced that the answer lies in three every day choices, choices that each of us make every day of our life, whether we are consciously aware of them or not.

#1—THE CHOICE TO ACT

The first choice we make each and every day is, *Will we act upon life, or will we merely be acted upon?*

Clearly we cannot control everything that happens to us. Life hits like the waves of the ocean as one event rolls in after another. Some events are incidental, causing us little or no impact. Others virtually pummel us. But each day we make the choice: Will we be as driftwood that passively floats with the tides and currents of the day, or will we instead take proactive responsibility for determining our actions and destinations?

On the surface, the choice is an easy one. After all, who would not prefer to act upon life rather than be acted upon? But at the end of the day, only our actions provide the truest answers. For many people say they want to be in charge of their life, but then they turn their evening schedules over to their television sets to determine when and what they will do. Others say they have lofty career dreams and goals, but then they turn responsibility for their skill development over to their employers. Still others say they want to stand by firm values, but then they let their integrity shrivel under the slightest bit of opposition. So, yes, many people say they want to act upon life, but at the end of the day it appears more that life is acting upon them.

To the contrary, each and every story in this collection represents a person who chooses to act. They are people who recognize that while we cannot always choose what happens to us, we can choose our responses. Some of the people are well known by name, most are not. Some make choices heroic in nature, most do not. Some make choices in public settings, most do not. Most are common people making common choices in everyday private ways. I challenge you to explore their lives and the choices they make. See if you do not observe the same theme that I observe—that those who get the most out of life and those who give the most are those who make the choice to act.

We can and we should become the creative force of our own lives—and of our own futures.

#2—THE CHOICE OF PURPOSE

But plenty of us have made the choice to act, only to find that we made poor choices—choices that turned out to be of no value to ourselves or to others, some perhaps even harmful. So, alone, the choice to act is not sufficient.

And so the second choice we make each and every day is of great significance: *To what ends, or purposes, will our daily choices lead?*

We each want to be of value—to know our life matters. We do not want to just be busy, we want to be busy pursuing worthwhile purposes. But, in today's rush, rush world, it is easy to pass through each day without even thinking about the purposes we are pursuing, much less pausing long enough to reflect on the purposes we would most *like* to pursue. And thus we see so many people hurriedly running from place to place, yet really going nowhere.

But not the people in this collection. From John Baker to Maya Angelou, from Luba Gercak to Joe Paterno, from a man who makes wheel chairs to a family that rallies around a disabled child, all make proactive choices to pursue meaningful and honorable purposes— sometimes even at great risk or personal sacrifice.

In fact, the origins of this collection stem from two individuals who made the choice of purpose—the late DeWitt and Lila Wallace— founders of *Reader's Digest*. In 1922, they started the magazine as newlyweds trying to make ends meet. But their goals extended well beyond making money, as they set their sights on a quest DeWitt had written down as a young boy: "Whatever my occupation may be, I intend to do as much good in the world as possible." Together they chose to "help people help themselves" by filling each issue with stories, anecdotes, humor—*much humor*—and practical insights that reinforced the principles of effective living they admired most, among them courage, charity, integrity, quality, respect, and unity.

Today, printed in twenty-one languages, *Reader's Digest* promotes those same principles and continues to strike a common chord in what has become a community of eighty million readers worldwide— it is the world's most widely read magazine.

So it was that the Wallaces—page by page, issue by issue—chose to live lives of purpose. So too the people in this collection—step by step, day by day—similarly have made choices to pursue worthy ends. I hope you enjoy reading of the purposes they pursued and take the opportunity to reflect on your own efforts to fill your life with meaning and contribution.

#3—The Choice for Principles

But, of course, none of this happens by magic or luck. While I believe in the power of positive thought, I do not believe that you or I can simply psyche ourselves into success or peace of mind. Rather, enjoying a life rich in meaning and progress—a life of Everyday Greatness—comes only as we live in harmony with timeless, universal principles.

And so the third choice we make each and every day is, *Will we live our lives in accordance with proven principles, or will we suffer the consequences of not doing so?*

To partially explain what I mean, let me share a favorite anecdote from the December 1983 edition of *Reader's Digest*. Though intended as humor, I believe it vividly illustrates the power of principles and how they impact our lives and choices.

One foggy night at sea the captain of a ship saw what looked like the lights of another ship heading toward him. He had his signalman contact the other ship by light. The message was: "Change your course ten degrees to the south."

The reply came back: "Change your course ten degrees to the north."

Then the captain answered: "I am a captain, so you change your course ten degrees to the south."

Reply: "I am a seaman first class—change your course ten degrees to the north."

This last exchange really infuriated the captain, so he signaled back: "I am a battleship—change your course ten degrees to the south."

Reply: "And I am a lighthouse. Change your course ten degrees to the north!" (Contributed by Dan Bell)

Though lighthearted, the message is straightforward: Neither the size of the vessel nor the rank of the helmsman mattered. The lighthouse was not going to change its course. It was permanent, fixed. Only the captain had the choice of whether or not to course correct.

The lighthouse is like a principle. Principles are immovable; they are timeless and universal. They do not change. They are no respecters of age, race, creed, gender, or status—everyone is equally subject to them. Like the lighthouse, principles provide permanent markers against which people can set their direction in times of both storm and calm, darkness and light.

Thanks to the Einsteins and Newtons of the world, many such principles, or *natural laws*, have been discovered in scientific domains. Pilots, for example, are governed by the four principles of flight—gravity, lift, thrust, and drag. Farmers must learn to master similar principles, or laws of the harvest. Gymnasts and engineers work within principles of physics, including laws of opposing forces. But neither the pilots nor the farmers nor the gymnasts nor the engineers invented the principles, nor can they alter them. Instead, like the ship's captain, they can only choose whether or not they will set their courses by them, or suffer the consequences. For while values drive behaviors, principles govern consequences.

As with science, I am convinced that similar lighthouse principles exist within the human realm, several of which are brought together in this collection. Principles such as *vision, innovation, humility, quality, empathy, magnanimity, perseverance,* and *balance*. All are principles that can mobilize us toward greater personal effectiveness and increased life satisfaction. If you doubt this, consider living life based on their opposites, such as lack of vision, laziness, vanity, sloppiness, closed mindedness, revenge, lack of determination, or imbalance. Hardly the ingredients for success.

Some of the entries contained in this collection were written decades ago. But the very fact that they are based upon principles is what makes them timeless and timely—applicable both today and twenty years from now. Therefore, as you read the accounts and insights of the people in this collection, do not dwell on the time-frames when they transpired or the names involved. Rather, focus on the principles and how the people applied the principles to their lives. Even more important, consider how you personally might more fully use the lighthouse principles as beacons by which to chart your path, measure your progress, and make course adjustments in your own journey toward Everyday Greatness.

What About You?

So there you have the three choices that provide the foundation for Everyday Greatness. In a sense, the choice to act represents the energy we bring to life—our will power. The choice of purpose represents our destination—where we choose to go in life, what we choose to accomplish. The choice for principles then determines the means for how we will get there—how we will attain our goals.

I believe that the people I mentioned at the start of this Introduction—the people who exhibit Everyday Greatness in today's world—distinguish themselves through their responses to these three choices. I also believe that the people you will read about in this collection have set themselves apart at various points of their lives by responding positively to these same three choices.

But this collection is not about those people. It's about you. In other words, it is not intended to highlight what others have done or said, but rather to encourage you to examine your own life. What you contribute on a daily basis. How you treat people. How you use your time. Whether you are doing good or doing your best.

And so I ask:

- Is your life like driftwood being tossed to and fro, or are you instead making your own waves and going in directions you—by choice—want to go?

- To what ends, or purposes, are your daily choices leading? To what ends, or purposes, would you like them to lead?

- Is your life in harmony with timeless, universal principles?

These are tough questions. If you are unsure about or displeased with any of your answers, I hope you take advantage of this collection. For each entry is a reminder that your life does matter and that your days—regardless of what transpires in the world around you—can be rich in meaning and progress.

You will note that the entries have been divided into seven categories, each containing three principles. Within each of the twenty-one principles is a series of stories that illustrate the principle, followed by supporting quotes and anecdotes. Brief commentary and insights that I have contributed are interspersed to provide narration and make application to today's world. One of the things that makes the book's format so friendly is that you can pick it up at any page and find inspiration. A prior chapter's understanding is not required to benefit from a later chapter.

I can envision many uses of this material. I can see parents and teachers gleaning from it thoughts or stories to inspire youth. I can visualize professional speakers and business leaders using it as a content resource. I can imagine work teams discussing and applying the principles to various work efforts. But most of all, I can see individuals like you using it to discover inspiring, mind-expanding insights and solutions to specific personal challenges. Therefore, I challenge you to tap your conscience. Highlight specific quotes or principles that you feel—if applied better—will help you toward your goals. As you do, consider the suggestions provided in the Afterword to generate a realistic go-forward plan for enhancing your capacity for Everyday Greatness.

In Conclusion

I want to conclude with an expression of both gratitude and respect for those involved in bringing this collection together, as well as to offer a final word of encouragement.

First, I wish to pay tribute to *Reader's Digest*—from the Wallaces to the present-day team. Every entry in this collection was previously published by *Reader's Digest*. Each entry is a compliment to them and the purposes they pursue. I greatly admire their ongoing success in staying so relevant and in being such an influential voice in today's reality.

Second, I applaud the comprehensive efforts of David K. Hatch in compiling this work. It was David who initiated this project as he was scouring for stories and quotes to use in his profession as a leadership consultant. The more he organized the material, however, the more he felt that it should be shared with a larger audience. His eye in meticulously sifting through the more than one thousand issues of *Reader's Digest* has proven invaluable, as has his vision of the potential for good this collection can have in the lives of people like you.

Third, I express gratitude for the tremendous wealth of wisdom offered by the many authors, philosophers, and common heroes cited in this collection—a number of whom I know and admire personally. Each is an inspiration in his or her own way. They, like all of us, are not perfect, but they have aspired to honorable deeds and thereby help to build the confidence within us that we too can make a difference.

Finally, I offer my respect to you as a unique individual. I believe that you are one of the people I spoke of in the beginning—one who is already up to good things in a world that shouts so much of turmoil. You have experiences and talents exclusive to you. Trust them. Use them to improve upon the many insights in this collection. But above all, make the three choices. Act upon life. Attach yourself to meaningful, uplifting purposes. Live in accordance with timeless, universal principles. As you do, I have firm confidence that you will find greater joy, more peace of mind, and an enhanced feeling of worth that comes through living a life of Everyday Greatness.

SEARCHING FOR MEANING

I have Immortal longings in me.
—WILLIAM SHAKESPEARE

Within each individual lies the need for meaning—the longing to be of value. This craving for purpose propels us to make the choices that will bring us the most joy and satisfaction from life. But in a busy world, it is so easy to become diverted by lesser choices—choices that in the long run are of little value or meaning. And so to gain the peace of mind and sense of accomplishment that we desire, we must pause momentarily to develop a clear image of the dreams, priorities, and goals that we believe will have the most lasting meaning, both for us and for others.

Principles that help us in our search for meaning include

- Contribution

- Charity

- Attention

I

CONTRIBUTION

All men should strive to learn before they die,
what they are running from, and to, and why.
—JAMES THURBER

In our most reflective moments, each of us wants to make a difference—a contribution. Call it a cause or call it a mission, we want be a part of something meaningful. Detecting what our contribution will be on a daily basis, however, is not always easy, especially when we are so tangled up with the little things of life. Yet there comes a point when each individual should strive to clarify what he or she will stand for and what purposes he or she will choose to pursue.

The following stories highlight three individuals who each came to a point of choice in life—a time when each was forced to decide whether he or she was to act upon life by stepping forward and making a contribution, or simply sit back and be acted upon. The first story tells of a young man by the name of John Baker. A gifted runner with Olympic aspirations, John's sense of meaning and contribution is tested like never before. As you read of the choices he made and the purposes he chose to pursue, reflect on what you will do with your life over the next weeks, months, and year. What contributions will you make?

JOHN BAKER'S LAST RACE

William J. Buchanan

The future looked bright to twenty-four-year-old John Baker in the spring of 1969. At the peak of an astonishing athletic career, touted by sportswriters as one of the fastest milers in the world, he had fixed his dreams on representing the United States in the 1972 Olympic Games.

Nothing in Baker's early years had hinted at such prominence. Light of build, and inches shorter than most of his teenage Albuquerque pals, he was considered "too uncoordinated" to run track in high school. But something happened during his junior year that changed the course of his life.

For some time, the Manzano High track coach, Bill Wolffarth, had been trying to induce a tall, promising runner named John Haaland—who was Baker's best friend—to join the track team. Haaland refused. "Let me join the team," Baker suggested one day. "Then Haaland might, too." Wolffarth agreed, and the maneuver worked. And John Baker had become a runner.

SURGE OF ENERGY

The first meet that year was a 1.7-mile cross-country race through the foothills east of Albuquerque. Most eyes were focused on Albuquerque's reigning state cross-country champion, Lloyd Goff. Immediately after the crack of the gun, the field lined up as expected, with Goff setting the pace and Haaland on his heels. At the end of four minutes, the runners disappeared one by one behind a low hill inside the far turn of the course. A minute passed. Two. Then a lone figure appeared. Coach Wolffarth nudged an assistant. "Here comes Goff," he said. Then he raised his binoculars. "Good grief!" he yelled. "That's not Goff! It's Baker!"

Leaving a field of startled runners far behind, Baker crossed the finish line alone. His time—8:03.5—set a new meet record.

What happened on the far side of that hill? Baker later explained. Halfway through the race, running well back of the leaders, he had asked himself a question: *Am I doing my best?* He didn't know. Fixing his eye on the back of the runner immediately in front of him, he closed his mind to all else. Only one thing mattered: catch and pass that runner, and then go after the next one. An unknown reserve of energy surged through his body. "It was almost hypnotic," Baker recalled. One by one he passed the other runners. Ignoring the fatigue that tore at his muscles, he maintained his furious pace until he crossed the finish line and collapsed in exhaustion.

Had the race been a fluke? As the season progressed, Wolffarth entered Baker in a number of other events, and always the result was the same. Once on the track, the modest, fun-loving teenager became a fierce, unrelenting competitor—a "heart" runner who simply wouldn't be beat. By the end of his junior year Baker had broken six state track records, and during his senior year he was proclaimed the finest miler ever developed in the state. He was not yet eighteen.

"Upset John"

In the fall of 1962, Baker entered the University of New Mexico in Albuquerque and stepped up his training. Each morning at dawn, spray can in hand to ward off snapping dogs, he ran through city streets, parks, and golf courses—twenty-five miles a day. The training told. Soon, in Abilene, Tulsa, Salt Lake City, wherever the New Mexico Lobos competed, "Upset John" Baker was confounding forecasters by picking off favored runners.

In the spring of 1965, when Baker was a junior, the most feared track team in the nation belonged to the University of Southern California. So, when the mighty Trojans descended on Albuquerque for a dual meet, sportscasters predicted doom for the Lobos. The mile, they said, would fall to U.S.C.'s "Big Three"—Chris Johnson, Doug Calhoun, and Bruce Bess, in that order. All had better times for the mile than Baker.

Baker led for one lap, then eased purposely back to fourth position. Rattled, Calhoun and Bess moved uneasily into the forfeited lead. Johnson, wary, held back. In the far turn of the third lap, at the same moment, Baker and Johnson moved for the lead—and collided. Fighting to stay on his feet, Baker lost precious yards, and Johnson moved into the lead. With 330 yards to go, Baker kicked into his final sprint. First Bess, then Calhoun, fell back. On the final turn it was Johnson and Baker neck and neck. Slowly, Baker inched ahead. With both hands above his head in a V-for-Victory sign, he broke the tape—a winner by three seconds. Inspired by Baker's triumph, the Lobos swept every following event, handing the demoralized Trojans their third-worst defeat in sixty-five years.

A COACH WHO CARED

Upon graduation, Baker considered his options. There were college coaching offers, but he had always planned to work with children. There was also his running. Was he, he wondered, Olympic material? In the end, he accepted a job that would allow him to pursue both ambitions—he became a coach at Aspen Elementary School in Albuquerque, and at the same time renewed his rigorous training with an eye to the 1972 Games.

At Aspen, another facet of Baker's character emerged. On his playing fields there were no stars, and no criticism for lack of ability. His only demand was that each child do his or her best. This fairness, plus an obviously sincere concern for his students' welfare, triggered a powerful response. Youthful grievances were brought first to Coach Baker. Real or fancied, each was treated as if at the moment it was the most important matter in the world. And the word spread: "Coach cares."

Early in May 1969, shortly before his twenty-fifth birthday, Baker noticed that he was tiring prematurely during workouts. Two weeks later, he developed chest pains, and one morning near the end of the month he awoke with a painfully swollen groin. He made an appointment to see a doctor.

To urologist Edward Johnson, Baker's symptoms were ominous, requiring immediate exploratory surgery. The operation confirmed Johnson's fears. A cell in one of Baker's testicles had suddenly erupted in cancerous growth, and the mass was already widespread. Though Dr. Johnson didn't say it, he estimated that even with a second operation, Baker had approximately six months to live.

At home recuperating for the second operation, Baker confronted the grim reality of his world. There would be no more running, and no Olympics. Almost certainly, his coaching career was ended. Worst of all, his family faced months of anguish.

EDGE OF THE PRECIPICE

On the Sunday before the second operation, Baker left home alone for a drive in the mountains. He was gone for hours. When he returned that evening, there was a marked change in his spirits. His habitual smile, of late only a mask, was again natural and sincere. What's more, for the first time in two weeks, he spoke of future plans. Late that night, he told his sister Jill what had happened that clear June day.

He had driven to Sandia Crest, the majestic two-mile-high mountain peak that dominates Albuquerque's eastern skyline. Seated in his car near the edge of the precipice, he thought of the extended agony his condition would cause his family. He could end that agony, and his own in an instant. With a silent prayer, he revved the engine and reached for the emergency brake. Suddenly a vision flashed before his eyes—the faces of the children at Aspen Elementary, the children he had taught to do their best despite the odds. What sort of legacy would his suicide be for them? Shamed to the depths of his soul, he switched off the ignition, slumped in the seat and wept. After a while he realized that his fears were stilled, that he was at peace. *Whatever time I have left,* he told himself, *I'm dedicating to the kids.*

In September, following extensive surgery and a summer of treatments, Baker re-immersed himself in his job and to his already full schedule he added a new commitment—sports for the handicapped. Whatever their infirmity, children who had once stood idle on the sidelines now assumed positions as "Coach's Time Keeper" or "Chief Equipment Supervisor" all wearing their official Aspen jerseys, all eligible to earn a Coach Baker ribbon for trying hard. Baker made the ribbons himself, at home in the evening, from material purchased with his own money.

SILENT SUFFERING

By Thanksgiving, letters in praise of Baker from grateful parents were arriving almost daily at Aspen (more than five hundred would be received there and at the Baker residence before a year had passed). "My son was a morning monster" one mother wrote. "Getting him up, fed, and out the door was hardly bearable. Now he can't wait for school. He's the Chief Infield Raker."

"Despite my son's assertions, I could not believe that there was a Superman at Aspen," wrote another mother. "I drove over secretly to watch Coach Baker with the children. My son was right." And this from two grandparents: "In other schools, our granddaughter suffered terribly from her awkwardness. Then, this wonderful year at Aspen, Coach Baker gave her an 'A' for trying her best. God bless this young man who gave a timid child self-respect."

In December, during a routine visit to Dr. Johnson, Baker complained of a sore throat and headaches. Tests confirmed that the malignancy had spread to his neck and brain. For four months, Johnson now recognized, Baker had been suffering severe pain in silence, using his incredible power of concentration to ignore the pain just as he had used it to ignore fatigue when he ran. Johnson suggested painkilling injections. Baker shook his head. "I want to work with the kids as long as I'm able," he said. "The injections would dull my responsiveness."

"From that moment," Johnson later remarked, "I looked upon John Baker as one of the most unselfish persons I've ever known."

CUPS FOR DASHERS

Early in 1970, Baker was asked to help coach a small Albuquerque track club for girls from elementary through high school age. Its name: the Duke City Dashers. He agreed on the spot and, like the children of Aspen, the girls on the Dashers responded to the new coach with enthusiasm.

One day Baker arrived at a practice session carrying a shoebox. He announced that it held two awards, one for the girl who, though never a winner, wouldn't quit. When Baker opened the box, the girls gasped. Inside were two shiny gold trophy cups. From then on, deserving Dashers received such cups. Months later, Baker's family would discover that the trophies were his, from his racing days, with his own name carefully burnished away.

By summer, the Duke City Dashers were a club to contend with, breaking record after record at meets throughout New Mexico and bordering states. Proudly, Baker made a bold prediction: "The Dashers are going to the national AAU finals."

But now a new problem plagued Baker. His frequent chemotherapy injections brought on severe nausea, and he could not keep food down. Despite steadily decreasing stamina, however, he continued to supervise the Dashers, usually sitting on a small hill above the training area, hollering encouragement.

One afternoon in October, following a huddle on the track below, one of the girls ran up the hill toward Baker. "Hey Coach!" she shouted. "Your prediction's come true! We're invited to the AAU finals in St. Louis next month."

Elated, Baker confided to friends that he had one remaining hope—to live long enough to go along.

WALKING TALL

But it was not to be. On the morning of October 28, at Aspen, Baker suddenly clutched his abdomen and collapsed on the playground. Examination revealed that the spreading tumor had ruptured, triggering shock. Declining hospitalization, Baker insisted on returning to school for one last day. He told his parents that he wanted the children to remember him walking tall, not lying helpless in the dirt.

Sustained now by massive blood transfusions and sedation, Baker realized that for him the St. Louis trip was impossible. So he began telephoning Dashers every evening and didn't stop until he had urged each girl to do her best at the finals.

In the early evening of November 23, Baker collapsed again. Barely conscious as attendants loaded him into an ambulance, he whispered to his parents, "Make sure the lights are flashing. I want to leave the neighborhood in style." Shortly after dawn on November 26, he turned on his hospital bed to his mother, who was holding his hands and said, "I'm sorry to have been so much trouble." With a final sigh, he closed his eyes. It was Thanksgiving Day of 1970, eighteen months after John Baker's first visit to Dr. Johnson. He had beaten the odds against death by twelve months.

Two days later, with tears streaming down their cheeks, the Duke City Dashers won the AAU championship in St. Louis—"for Coach Baker."

That would be the end of the John Baker story except for a phenomenon which occurred after his funeral. A few of the children of Aspen began calling their school "John Baker School" and the change of name spread like wildfire.

Then a movement began to make the new name official. "It's our school," the kids said, "and we want to call it John Baker." Aspen officials referred the matter to the Albuquerque school board, and the board suggested a voter referendum. In early spring of 1971, 520 families in the Aspen district voted on the question. There were 520 votes for, none against.

That May, in a ceremony attended by hundreds of Baker's friends and all of his children, Aspen School officially became John Baker Elementary. It stands today as a visible monument to a courageous young man who, in his darkest hours, transformed bitter tragedy into an enduring legacy.

John Baker did not choose to have cancer, but he did choose his response. He chose to make a contribution. By focusing his last energies on the hearts and spirits of the children, he left a lasting legacy in the lives of those he touched. And in so doing, surely he experienced the inner rewards that accompany a life of meaning.

Like John Baker, Mary Clarke, too, faced a choice point. With her children out of the nest, her husband gone, and so much of life behind her, would she choose to sit back and be a "spectator" or choose instead to make a contribution?

ANTONIA'S MISSION
Gail Cameron Wescott

A riot was raging through La Mesa prison in Tijuana, Mexico. Twenty-five hundred fed-up prisoners, packed into a compound built for six hundred, angrily hurled broken bottles at police, who fired back with machine guns.

Then, at the peak of the pandemonium, came a startling sight: A tiny, five-foot-two, sixty-three-year-old woman in an immaculate nun's habit calmly strolled into the battle, hands outstretched in a simple gesture of peace. Ignoring the shower of bullets and flying bottles, she stood quietly and ordered everyone to stop. Incredibly, they did. "No one else in the world but Sister Antonia could have done that," said Robert Cass, a former inmate, now rehabilitated. "She has changed thousands of people's lives."

In Tijuana, when Sister Antonia walks along a sidewalk, traffic in the street routinely stops; people there affectionately claim her as their own Mother Teresa. For the past quarter-century, she has lived, by choice, in a ten-foot concrete cell at La Mesa, without hot water, surrounded by murderers, thieves, and drug lords, all of whom she lovingly calls her "sons." She attends to their needs round the clock, procuring antibiotics, distributing eyeglasses, counseling the suicidal, washing bodies for burial. "I live on the premises," she explained with no hint of complaint, "in case someone is stabbed in the middle of the night."

It is a world away from the plush precincts of Beverly Hills where Sister Antonia—then, Mary Clarke—grew up. Her father, from humble beginnings, owned a prosperous office-supply company. "He always said that it's easier to suffer when you are rich," she remembered. He also told her that once a Beverly Hills girl, always a Beverly Hills girl. She believed him.

"I was a romantic," she said, "and still am, really—always looking at the world through rose-colored glasses." Clarke grew up during the heyday of Hollywood—big stars tap-dancing down the stairs—and also during World War II. A vibrant beauty by her teens, she spent her weekend evenings dancing with young soldiers at the canteen and dreaming about the future. Her dream included a husband, many children, and a picture-book house.

It all came true. After graduating from high school, Clarke married and raised seven children in an airy Granada Hills home. Twenty-five years later, the marriage ended in divorce, a subject that remains painful for her and which she declined to discuss. "Because a dream ends doesn't mean that it didn't come true once," she said. "What matters now is my second life."

With her marriage over and her children, with whom she stays in close touch, grown, she turned instinctively to helping the less fortunate. The suffering of others had always affected her profoundly. "I walked out of *Mutiny on the Bounty* because I couldn't stand seeing men tied to the mast and lashed," she said. She had kept her father's business going for seventeen years following his death, but had no desire to expand it. "It takes the same amount of energy to make business calls as it does to make calls to get beds donated to hospitals in Peru," she pointed out. "There comes a time when you can't just be a spectator. You have to step outside the lines."

In her case, she took a giant leap. In the mid-'60s she began traveling across the Mexican border with a Catholic priest to take medicines and supplies to the poor. "At the time," she noted, "the only Mexicans I knew were gardeners." Now she found herself deeply drawn to the people.

Her second life began the day she and the priest got lost in Tijuana. Looking for the local jail, they wound up by mistake at La Mesa. She was instantly moved by what she saw. "In the infirmary, men were desperately sick, yet would stand when you entered." Soon she was spending nights there, sleeping on a bunk in the women's section, learning Spanish, assisting the inmates and their families in any way she could.

In 1977, convinced that she had found God's true purpose for her, Mary Clarke became Sister Antonia. La Mesa prison became her permanent home, the place she chooses to spend even Christmas Eve. "Her children understand her priorities," said her friend Noreen Walsh-Begun. "They realize that she cared for them, and now it's her turn to care for others."

"I don't know how anyone keeps up with her," said Cass, the former inmate who recently named his newborn daughter after Sister Antonia. "She's always rushing, yet always has time for you. She's not loved without reason."

Love, said Sister Antonia, is what she offers everyone. "I'm hard on crime but not the criminal," she said. "Just this morning, I talked to a young man, nineteen years old, who had stolen a car. I asked him if he had any idea what a car means to a family, how long it takes to buy one. I said, 'I love you, but I don't sympathize with you. Do you have a girlfriend? Well, maybe someone will steal her while you're in here.' Then I hugged him." She hugs everyone, including the guards, whom she also instructs and counsels.

For years, Sister Antonia zipped around Tijuana in what was once a New York Checker cab, repainted royal blue. "One day I backed into a police car," she said, laughing boisterously, "and my immediate thought was, *Oh, thank God,* which I realize is not a typical response, but I love the police and they love me."

A charismatic speaker, she has attracted a whole network of supporters who contribute everything from mattresses to medicines to money. A local dentist has provided thousands of sets of false teeth at cost for prisoners who had never seen a toothbrush. "You have to be able to smile in order to get a job," snapped Sister Antonia. Sister Antonia said she's the most fortunate person on the planet. "I live in a prison," she said, "but I have not experienced one day of depression in twenty-seven years, never felt hopeless. And I have never once felt there wasn't something I could do to make things better."

The message from Sister Antonia is not that a person must abandon country, home, or lifestyle to make a contribution. Rather, it is that each person—regardless of age or status—will at various times encounter points when they must choose whether to step forward and make a difference or sit back and be a "spectator." Sister Antonia chose to get out of her spectator chair and engage herself in a life of meaning, doing her part "to make things better."

Vedran Smailovic also faced a profound moment of choice. Witnessing the ravages of war, he had every reason to remain securely indoors and keep to himself. Yet when life called out to him, he answered the call—by doing what he did best.

THE CELLIST OF SARAJEVO

Paul Sullivan

As a pianist, I was invited to perform with cellist Eugen Friesen at the International Cello Festival in Manchester, England. Every two years a group of the world's greatest cellists and others devoted to that unassuming instrument—bow makers, collectors, historians—gather for a week of workshops, master classes, seminars, recitals, and parties. Each evening the six hundred or so participants assemble for a concert.

The opening-night performance at the Royal Northern College of Music consisted of works for unaccompanied cello. There on the stage in the magnificent concert hall was a solitary chair. No piano, no music stand, no conductor's podium. This was to be cello music in its purest, most intense form. The atmosphere was supercharged with anticipation and concentration.

The world-famous cellist Yo-Yo Ma was one of the performers that April night in 1994, and there was a moving story behind the musical composition he would play.

On May 27, 1992, in Sarajevo, one of the few bakeries that still had a supply of flour was making and distributing bread to the starving, war-shattered people. At 4 p.m. a long line stretched into the street. Suddenly, a mortar shell fell directly into the middle of the line, killing twenty-two people and splattering flesh, blood, bone, and rubble.

Not far away lived a thirty-five-year-old musician named Vedran Smailovic. Before the war he had been a cellist with the Sarajevo Opera, a distinguished career to which he patiently longed to return. But when he saw the carnage from the massacre outside his window, he was pushed past his capacity to absorb and endure any more. Anguished, he resolved to do the thing he did best: make music. Public music, daring music, music on a battlefield.

For each of the next twenty-two days, at 4:00 p.m., Smailovic put on his full, formal concert attire, took up his cello and walked out of his apartment into the midst of the battle raging around him. Placing a plastic chair beside the crater that the shell had made, he played in memory of the dead Albinoni's *Adagio in G minor,* one of the most mournful and haunting pieces in the classical repertoire. He played to the abandoned streets, smashed trucks, and burning buildings, and to the terrified people who hid in the cellars while the bombs dropped and bullets flew. With masonry exploding around him, he made his unimaginable courageous stand for human dignity, for those lost to war, for civilization, for compassion, and for peace. Though the shellings went on, he was never hurt.

After newspapers picked up the story of this extraordinary man, an English composer, David Wilde, was so moved that he, too, decided to make music. He wrote a composition for unaccompanied cello, "The Cellist of Sarajevo," into which he poured his own feelings of outrage, love, and brotherhood with Vedran Smailovic.

It was "The Cellist of Sarajevo" that Yo-Yo Ma was to play that evening.

Ma came out on stage, bowed to the audience and sat down quietly on the chair. The music began, stealing out into the hushed hall and creating a shadowy, empty universe, ominous and haunting. Slowly it grew into an agonized, screaming, slashing furor, gripping us all before subsiding at last into a hollow death rattle and, finally, back to silence.

When he had finished, Ma remained bent over his cello, his bow resting on the strings. No one in the hall moved or made a sound for a long time. It was as though we had just witnessed that horrifying massacre ourselves.

Finally, Ma looked out across the audience and stretched out his hand, beckoning someone to come to the stage. An indescribable electric shock swept over us as we realized who it was: Vedran Smailovic, the cellist of Sarajevo!

Smailovic rose from his seat and walked down the aisle as Ma left the stage to meet him. They flung their arms around each other in an exuberant embrace. Everyone in the hall erupted in a chaotic, emotional frenzy—clapping, shouting, and cheering.

And in the center of it all stood these two men, hugging and crying unashamedly. Yo-Yo Ma, a suave, elegant prince of classical music, flawless in appearance and performance; and Vedran Smailovic, dressed in a stained and tattered leather motorcycle suit. His wild long hair and huge mustache framed a face that looked old beyond his years, soaked with tears and creased with pain.

We were all stripped down to our starkest, deepest humanity at encountering this man who shook his cello in the face of bombs, death, and ruin, defying them all.

Back in Maine a week later, I sat one evening playing the piano for the residents of a local nursing home. I couldn't help contrasting this concert with the splendors I had witnessed at the festival. Then I was struck by the profound similarities. With his music the cellist of Sarajevo had defied death and despair, and celebrated love and life. And here we were, a chorus of croaking voices accompanied by a shopworn piano, doing the same thing. There were no bombs and bullets, but there was real pain—dimming sight, crushing loneliness, all the scars we accumulate in our lives—and only cherished memories for comfort. Yet still we sang and clapped.

It was then I realized that music is a gift we all share equally. Whether we create it or simply listen, it's a gift that can soothe, inspire, and unite us, often when we need it most—and expect it least.

Today's world is covered with battlefields—some literal, others social, emotional, or spiritual. Indeed, we all know of people whose lives are for whatever reason in various levels of despair. Perhaps their livelihoods are threatened. Maybe they have concerns about a family member. Possibly their health is waning. When Vedran Smailovic saw people in need, he left the security of his home and "resolved to do what he did best," and that was to play music.

~

WRAP UP

John Baker, Sister Antonia, and Vedran Smailovic each faced pivotal choice points. John Baker's occurred on Sandia Crest. Sister Antonia's followed the departure of her husband and children. Vedran Smailovic's happened as he peered through his window and saw devastation. But while each of those pivotal choice points was significant, the truly life-changing decisions they faced took place each and every day as they chose anew to abandon their "spectator" seats and make a contribution. And that is what Everyday Greatness is—an everyday way of living, an every day choice, not a one-time event.

So what about you? Based on the past week, are you more of a spectator or a contributor? Are you satisfied with your present contributions? If not, I suggest you train yourself to ask on a daily basis, What is life asking of me? Then listen to the still, small voice of conscience for the answer.

REFLECTIONS

- John Baker found Sandia Crest to be a secluded location for pondering his future and the contribution he wished to make. Where is your Sandia Crest? Do you go there often enough?

- How *would* you choose to spend the next year if you knew it was your last? How *will* you spend your next year, month, or day?

- Sister Antonia gave up a Beverly Hills lifestyle and chose daily to sleep instead in a prison. What comforts are you willing to give up to make a more significant contribution?

- Vendran Smailovic resolved to do what he did best—make music. His example inspired the story's author, Paul Sullivan, to play the piano for nursing home patients. "Best" in their cases did not mean "better than anyone else," but rather their best personally. What do you do best?

FURTHER INSIGHTS ON
Contribution

~

THE SEARCH FOR MEANING

People who search for meaning in life are those who have formed their thoughts and actions around a purpose that makes their life of most worth.

When I was a kid, only Batman had a cell phone. He had a car phone. I was like: Man, can you imagine having a car phone? But technology has not altered our lives, other than perhaps how we go about them. We are still in the position of waking up and having a choice: Do I make the world better today somehow, or do I not bother?

—TOM HANKS

■ ■ ■

It is not enough to be industrious; so are the ants. What are you industrious about?

—JAMES THURBER

■ ■ ■

Some can't distinguish between being busy and being productive. They are human windmills, flailing at work, but actually accomplishing little.

—CAROLINE DONNELLY,
MONEY

■ ■ ■

In all strong characters, when one listens behind the scenes, one hears echoes of strife and contention. Nevertheless, far from being at loose ends within themselves, such persons have organized their lives around some supreme values and achieved a powerful concentration of purpose and drive.

—HARRY EMERSON FOSDICK,
ON BEING A REAL PERSON

He who has a why to live for can bear almost any how.

—FRIEDRICH NIETZSCHE

▉ ▉ ▉

While it is well enough to leave footprints on the sands of time, it is even more important to make sure they point in a commendable direction.

—JAMES BRANCH CABELL

▉ ▉ ▉

Nothing is more liberating than to fight for a cause larger than yourself, something that encompasses you but is not defined by your existence alone.

—JOHN MCCAIN,
FAITH OF MY FATHERS

THE POWER OF ONE

We may feel we have nothing to contribute. But the lessons
of history are full of examples of the power that can come
from the daily choices of a solitary individual.

We ourselves feel that what we are doing is just a drop in the ocean. But the
ocean would be less because of that missing drop.

—MOTHER TERESA

■ ■ ■

No man is so poor as to have nothing worth giving: as well might the mountain
streamlets say they have nothing to give the sea because they are not rivers. Give
what you have. To someone it may be better than you dare to think.

—HENRY WADSWORTH LONGFELLOW

■ ■ ■

We all have something to give. So if you know how to read, find someone
who can't. If you've got a hammer, find a nail. If you're not hungry, not
lonely, not in trouble—seek out someone who is.

—GEORGE H. W. BUSH

■ ■ ■

It may seem to you conceited to suppose that you can do anything important
toward improving the lot of mankind. But this is a fallacy. You must believe
that you can help bring about a better world. A good society is produced
only by good individuals, just as truly as a majority in a presidential election
is produced by the votes of single electors.

—BERTRAND RUSSELL
"A PHILOSOPHY FOR YOU IN THESE TIMES"

■ ■ ■

Even a small star shines in the darkness.

—FINNISH PROVERB

■ ■ ■

I have always held firmly to the thought that each one of us can do a little to
bring some portion of misery to an end.

—ALBERT SCHWEITZER

INDIVIDUAL UNIQUENESS

The Cellist of Sarajevo "resolved to do the thing he did best—make music." What is unique about you that you can contribute?

Whoever you are, there is some younger person who thinks you are perfect. There is some work that will never be done if you don't do it. There is someone who would miss you if you were gone. There is a place that you alone can fill.

—JACOB M. BRAUDE,
*BRAUDE'S SOURCE BOOK
FOR SPEAKERS AND WRITERS*

■ ■ ■

When I was around seven, we moved to New York. I was already studying the cello, and a couple of years later my parents signed me up to take lessons from Leonard Rose. Leonard was a great cellist, and a renowned teacher. Fortunately, he was also patient, because I was a very shy boy.

When I listened to Leonard play, I thought, "How can you make such a gorgeous sound? How can anyone do that?" But that's not what music is about. Which he knew. What Leonard said was, "I've taught you many things, but now you have to go off and learn on your own." Because in fact the worst thing you can do is say to yourself, "I want to be just like somebody else." You have to absorb knowledge from someone else, but ultimately you have to find your own voice.

—YO-YO MA

■ ■ ■

Man's earthly task is to realize his created uniqueness. As a Hasidic rabbi called Zusya put it on his deathbed: "In the world to come they will not ask me, 'Why were you not Moses?' They will ask me, 'Why were you not Zusya?'"

—MARTIN BUBER,
TIME

■ ■ ■

We relish news of our heroes, forgetting that we are extraordinary to somebody too.

—HELEN HAYES,
OUR BEST YEARS

PERSONAL MISSIONS

Some of our most thought provoking moments occur when we find time to record what we feel is the essence of our existence in a succinct statement. Such statements can become a personal constitution—the framework for making life-directing decisions. Consider the following examples:

I want to be thoroughly used up when I die, for the harder I work the more I love. I rejoice in life for its own sake. Life is no brief candle to me; it is a sort of splendid torch which I've got a hold of for the moment and I want to make it burn as brightly as possible before handing it on to future generations.

—GEORGE BERNARD SHAW
IN *GEORGE BERNARD
SHAW, HIS LIFE AND WORKS*

To laugh often and much; to win the respect of intelligent people and the affection of children; to earn the appreciation of honest critics and endure the betrayal of false friends; to appreciate beauty, to find the best in others; to leave the world a bit better, whether by a healthy child, a garden patch or a redeemed social condition; to know even one life has breathed easier because you lived. This is to have succeeded.

—RALPH WALDO EMERSON

I shall pass through this life but once.
Any good, therefore, that I can do
Or any kindness I can show to any fellow creature,
Let me do it now.
Let me not defer or neglect it,
For I shall not pass this way again.

—ETIENNE DE GRELLET

Lord, make me a channel of Thy peace,
That where there is hatred I may bring love;
That where there is wrong I may bring the spirit of forgiveness;
That where there is discord I may bring truth;
That where there is doubt I may bring faith;
That where there is despair I may bring hope;
And where there are shadows I may bring Thy light;
That where there is sadness I may bring joy;
Lord grant that I may seek rather to comfort than be comforted,
To understand than be understood,
To love than be loved;
For it is by giving that one receives,
It is by self-forgetting that one finds,
It is by forgiving that one is forgiven,
It is by dying that one awakens to eternal life.

—ST. FRANCIS OF ASSISI

I want it said of me by those who knew me best, that I always plucked a
thistle and planted a flower where I thought a flower would grow.

—ABRAHAM LINCOLN

2

CHARITY

What do we live for if not to make
the world less difficult for each other?
—GEORGE ELIOT

Though some people may attempt to live life from a purely selfish, self-centered perspective, it is in giving of ourselves to others that we find our greatest sense of meaning. And so, as we search for meaning, one of the best places to look is outward—toward others—using the principle of charity.

Too often the meaning of charity is reduced to the act of giving alms or donating sums of money to those who are economically disadvantaged. But charity in its purest forms involves so much more. It includes the giving of our hearts, our minds, and our talents in ways that enrich the lives of all people—regardless of whether they are poor or rich. Charity is selflessness. It is love in work clothes. A poignant example is found in the story of "The Man on the Train." Recalled by distinguished author Alex Haley, it is the true story of a man Alex never met, but one to whom he came to give great honor and credit. As you read his account, resist the temptation to reduce the story to that of a kind man offering a handout.

THE MAN ON THE TRAIN
Alex Haley

Whenever my brothers, sister, and I get together we inevitably talk about Dad. We all owe our success in life to him—and to a mysterious man he met one night on a train.

Our father, Simon Alexander Haley, was born in 1892 and reared in the small farming town of Savannah, Tennessee. He was the eighth child of Alec Haley—a tough-willed former slave and part-time sharecropper—and of a woman named Queen.

Although sensitive and emotional, my grandmother could be tough-willed herself, especially when it came to her children. One of her ambitions was that my father be educated.

Back then in Savannah a boy was considered "wasted" if he remained in school after he was big enough to do farm work. So when my father reached the sixth grade, Queen began massaging grandfather's ego.

"Since we have eight children," she would argue, "wouldn't it be prestigious if we deliberately *wasted* one and got him educated?" After many arguments, grandfather let Dad finish the eighth grade. Still, he had to work in the fields after school.

But Queen was not satisfied. As eighth grade ended, she began planting seeds, saying grandfather's image would reach new heights if their son went to high school. Her barrage worked. Stern old Alec Haley handed my father five hard-earned ten dollar bills, told him never to ask for more and sent him off to high school. Traveling first by mule cart and then by train—the first train he had ever seen—Dad finally alighted in Jackson, Tennessee, where he enrolled in the preparatory department of Lane College. The black Methodist school offered courses up through junior college.

Dad's fifty dollars was soon used up, and to continue in school, he worked as a waiter, a handyman, and a helper at a school for wayward boys. And when winter came, he'd arise at 4:00 a.m., go into prosperous white families' homes and make fires so the residents would awaken in comfort.

Poor Simon became something of a campus joke with his one pair of pants and shoes, and his droopy eyes. Often he was found asleep with a textbook fallen into his lap.

The constant struggle to earn money took its toll. Dad's grades began to founder. But he pushed onward and completed senior high. Next he enrolled in A&T College in Greensboro, North Carolina, a land-grant school where he struggled through freshman and sophomore years.

One bleak afternoon at the close of his second year, Dad was called into a teacher's office and told that he'd failed a course—one that required a textbook he'd been too poor to buy.

A ponderous sense of defeat descended upon him. For years he'd given his utmost, and now he felt he had accomplished nothing. Maybe he should return home to his original destiny of sharecropping.

But days later, a letter came from the Pullman Company saying he was one of twenty-four black college men selected from hundreds of applicants to be summertime sleeping-car porters. Dad was ecstatic. Here was a chance! He eagerly reported for duty and was assigned a Buffalo-to-Pittsburgh train.

The train was racketing along one morning about 2:00 a.m. when the porter's buzzer sounded. Dad sprang up, jerked on his white jacket, and made his way to the passenger berths. There a distinguished-looking man said he and his wife were having trouble sleeping, and they both wanted glasses of warm milk. Dad brought milk and napkins on a silver tray. The man handed one glass through the lower-berth curtains to his wife and sipping from his own glass, began to engage Dad in conversation.

Pullman Company rules strictly prohibited any conversation beyond "Yes, sir" or "No, ma'am," but this passenger kept asking questions. He even followed Dad back into the porter's cubicle.

"Where are you from?"

"Savannah, Tennessee, sir."

"You speak quite well."

"Thank you, sir."

"What work did you do before this?"

"I'm a student at A&T College in Greensboro, sir," Dad felt no need to add that he was considering returning home to sharecrop.

The man looked at him keenly, finally wished him well, and returned to his bunk.

The next morning, the train reached Pittsburgh. At a time when fifty cents was a good tip, the man gave five dollars to Simon Haley, who was profusely grateful. All summer, he had been saving every tip he received, and when the job finally ended, he had accumulated enough to buy his own mule and plow. But he realized his savings could also pay for one full semester at A&T without his having to work a single odd job.

Dad decided he deserved at least one semester free of outside work. Only that way would he know what grades he could truly achieve.

He returned to Greensboro. But no sooner did he arrive on campus than he was summoned by the college president. Dad was full of apprehension as he seated himself before the great man.

"I have a letter here, Simon," the president said.

"Yes, sir."

"You were a porter for Pullman this summer?"

"Did you meet a certain man one night and bring him warm milk?"

"Yes, sir."

"Well, his name is Mr. R. S. M. Boyce, and he's a retired executive of the Curtis Publishing Company, which publishes *The Saturday Evening Post*. He has donated five hundred dollars for your board, tuition, and books for the entire school year."

My father was astonished. The surprise grant not only enabled dad to finish A&T, but to graduate first in his class. And that achievement earned him a full scholarship to Cornell University in Ithaca, New York.

In 1920 Dad, then a newlywed, moved to Ithaca with his bride, Bertha. He entered Cornell to pursue his master's degree, and my mother enrolled at the Ithaca Conservatory of Music to study piano. I was born the following year.

One day decades later, editors of *The Saturday Evening Post* invited me to their editorial offices in New York to discuss the condensation of my first book, *The Autobiography of Malcom X.* I was so proud, so happy, to be sitting in those wood-paneled offices on Lexington Avenue. Suddenly I remembered Mr. Boyce, and how it was his generosity that enabled me to be there amid those editors, as a writer. And then I began to cry. I just couldn't help it.

We children of Simon Haley often reflect on Mr. Boyce and his investment in a less fortunate human being. By the ripple effect of his generosity, we also benefited. Instead of being raised on a sharecrop farm, we grew up in a home with educated parents, shelves full of books, and with pride in ourselves. My brother George is chairman of the U.S. Postal Rate Commission, Julius is an architect, Lois a music teacher, and I'm a writer.

Mr. R. S. M. Boyce dropped like a blessing into my father's life. What some may see as a chance encounter, I see as the working of a mysterious power for good.

And I believe that each person blessed with success has an obligation to return part of that blessing. We must all live and act like the man on the train.

Yes, Mr. Boyce did help pay for Simon's education, but his charity extended well beyond giving money. He also gave time in visiting with young Simon and in contacting the university president. He gave vision by spotting potential in a young man where others saw only a servant and a glass of milk. He gave confidence by complimenting Simon's communication skills. He gave hope to a young man high in aspirations but low in resources. In so doing, his charity stretched far beyond its original intent, as it spread down the generations to Simon's children, including Alex. Indeed, no one ever fully knows the ongoing potential of a single act of charity.

Deeply embedded in charity is the concept of selflessness. Consider the outcomes that continue even today thanks to the moment when a desperate individual decided to stop thinking only of himself and instead started to focus outwards—on others.

THE LAW OF UNSELFISHNESS

Fulton Oursler

A man we'll call Bill Wilkins, a Wall Street broker, woke up one morning in a hospital for drunkards. Despondently he peered up at the house physician and groaned, "Doc, how many times have I been in this joint?"

"Fifty! You're now our half-century plant."

"I suppose liquor is going to kill me?"

"Bill," replied the doctor solemnly, "it won't be long now."

"Then," said Bill, "how about a little snifter to straighten me out?"

"I guess that would be all right," agreed the doctor. "But I'll make a bargain with you. There's a young fellow in the next room in a pretty bad way. He's here for the first time. Maybe if you showed yourself as a horrible example, you might scare him into staying sober for the rest of his life."

Instead of resentment, Bill showed a flicker of interest. "Okay," he said. "But don't forget that drink when I come back."

The boy was certain that he was doomed, and Bill, who considered himself an agnostic, incredulously heard himself urging the lad to turn to some higher power.

"Liquor is a power outside yourself that has overcome you," he urged. "Only another outside power can save you. If you don't want to call it God, call it truth. The name isn't important."

Whatever the effect on the boy, Bill greatly impressed *himself.* Back in his own room, he forgot his bargain with the doctor. He never did collect the promised drink. Thinking of someone else at long last, he had given the law of unselfishness a chance to work on him. It worked so well that he lived to become a founder of a highly effective movement in healing faith—Alcoholics Anonymous.

William Griffith Wilson was Bill's real name, though in keeping with Alcoholics Anonymous tradition, most knew him simply as Bill W. How could he have ever imagined what worldwide good would eventually come about as a result of the moment he shifted his focus from being selfish to selfless? It is in forgetting ourselves and investing in others that we often reap the greatest dividends.

Core to the principle of charity is the principle of sacrifice. Sacrifice involves giving up something of personal value in exchange for something that is of benefit to others, as exhibited by Antonio Seay.

BROTHERLY LOVE

By Tom Hallman, Jr.

Antonio Seay sat on the edge of his bed and tipped the photograph back and forth in his hands. The portrait had been taken a few years earlier when he was up North in college. He touched his image, wiping away a layer of dust.

Forget the past, he told himself, letting the photograph fall to the blue bedspread. He turned his attention to the day's mail, a stack of bills and paperwork officials required before they'd consider deferring payments on his $20,000 college loan. He sighed and tossed the envelopes to the far side of the bed, then flopped back on his pillow and stared at the ceiling.

Two of his college buddies had recently called. They had solid careers and fat paychecks. One was getting married. Antonio wanted those things too. He'd planned to go to law school or become a cop. Instead, at age 25, he was trapped in a housing project in a run-down neighborhood in Miami. Cockroaches skittered across the kitchen counter. The appliances were older than he was. The floors, even in the bedroom, were ancient linoleum, worn and chipped. The walls, grimy with sections of peeling paint, revealed decades of hard living.

Antonio glanced again at the photo of the young man full of dreams. Then he swung his legs off the bed and walked outside the bunker-like house into the night air.

The thump-thump-thump of rap music blared from somewhere in the dark. Up the street, someone shouted. Tires squealed. He went down a pathway littered with trash and turned and studied his home. The very place he'd vowed to escape. He closed his eyes and heard his mother's voice. She'd asked him to drive her to the store that day. That's where this journey of his had begun—four years ago on a trip to the store.

It was a hot August afternoon in 2002 when Antonio rolled down the car windows and pulled away from the curb. He hardly noticed the bleak neighborhood where he and four younger brothers and sisters lived with their mother, Dorothea. In his mind he was already living in the future.

The first in his family to go to college, in ten months he would graduate from St. Peter's College in New Jersey, with a major in business management and a minor in criminal justice.

He glanced at his mother, who sat quietly in the front seat looking out the window. She was his inspiration, the strength in a family absent a father. She'd never complained. All she wanted was kids smart enough to avoid her mistakes.

"Sweetie," she said softly, "I got something to tell you."

Antonio's stomach tightened. When his mother talked like that, he knew it was something serious.

"I know I should've told you," she said. "But I didn't know how." She paused, searching for the words. "I'm letting you know, from mother to son, I've got HIV."

Antonio was silent. He gripped the steering wheel with both hands.

"Sweetie," his mother said, "I'm going to die."

He returned to college, and each week he and his mother talked by phone.

Antonio learned a man she'd trusted and loved had infected her. By the time she got sick, tests revealed the virus had developed into full-blown AIDS. She was alive, though, when her son graduated and returned home in May. Two months later she was admitted to the hospital and soon afterward, a hospice.

Her death would rip the family apart. Antonio could escape, but only if he left behind his sisters, Shronda, 15, Keyera, 13, and his 14-year-old twin brothers, Torrian and Corrian.

Aunts and uncles lived nearby. Others were out of state. But none offered to care for the kids. They'd become wards of the state and sent to foster homes under the supervision of the Florida Department of Children & Families.

Then he got this crazy idea. What if he gained legal custody? He'd never heard of such a thing, but why not? He talked it over with friends. Some admired his guts. Others said if he had any sense he'd run and not look back. He knew his siblings would be a burden. He'd have to postpone any thought of a better life for eight years until his baby sister turned 21. A home in a nice neighborhood? Forget it. Law school? Out. He figured he could get some government assistance, but he had no job and no way to support himself and four children.

Maybe it would be better for everyone if the family split up. They could all start clean. The choice was clear—abandon them, or his dreams. He prayed he'd do the right thing.

A legal aid attorney helped him prepare for court. She asked questions and filled out paperwork. Antonio was in her office the day in August 2003, just a year after his mother had told him the news, when a hospice nurse called. Dorothea had died.

Hours later he gathered his brothers and sisters in the living room and talked bluntly about the future. "We have to be strong," he said through tears. "It's not the end of the world because Mom's gone. We're still a family, still going on, no matter what. We have to be here for each other."

A week after the funeral, after mourners stopped bringing meals to the house, Antonio was on his own. He waited for a court date, hoping that the judge wouldn't think he was a fool, but a man who wanted to be a father figure the best he knew how.

At the hearing, the judge had Antonio and his brothers and sisters stand. "You look young," she told Antonio. "How old are you?"

"Twenty-three," he answered.

"This is a big responsibility," the judge said. "Most men might not take care of their own child, and you come in here to get legal responsibility of your brothers and sisters."

The judge studied the paperwork provided by Legal Aid.

"I respect you," the judge told him, before turning her attention to his siblings. "Do you want to stay with him?"

"Yes," they answered.

Five minutes later the hearing ended. Antonio signed papers and drove his family home to start a new life.

"Homework?" Antonio asked.

"Ain't got none," Keyera said. Antonio frowned. "I mean," she said quickly, "I don't have any tonight."

He spotted Corrian and asked him how he'd done in school.

"I had to find a way home this afternoon," his brother grumbled. "I didn't have bus fare 'cause I had to pay $15 for that book bag I lost. I'm still short. How about it?"

Antonio raised his hand. "Your responsibility," he said. "You lost it, why should I bail you out? Instead of taking the bus, you walk for a while. Each step, you'll learn to be more careful."

Antonio turned away to make sure his brother and sister couldn't see him smile. He remembered how naive he'd been when he first took charge of the family. He'd wanted to be liked, and made few demands. But the family started falling apart. The grades were terrible, homework missing and no one helped out at home. And so one night, he closed the door to his room and evaluated his brothers and sisters as if he were a cold-hearted boss sent in to turn around a failing company.

Shronda's grades were lousy because no one pushed her to do better. Corrian was a follower who got in trouble because his friends manipulated him. His twin, Torrian, liked to be sneaky and never feared being caught. Keyera worried too much and didn't believe in herself.

That night Antonio called a family meeting. Everyone found a seat on a dilapidated sectional sofa that relatives had given to the family. He stood in front of them, pacing the floor, making sure they got his message. "We're all we have in the world," he said. "We're going to succeed in life. That would make Mom happy."

He began writing on four pieces of paper. Then he walked to the kitchen and taped the papers to the refrigerator. "Chores," he called out. "Your chores." His brothers and sisters moaned and hustled to the kitchen. Clean the dishes, the bathroom and the kitchen. Take out the trash. Clean the living room. Everyone had tasks, and on Saturday everyone worked together.

They grumbled and said he was too strict. But he was just warming up. He imposed a curfew. Homework would be done on time. He'd read every paper and help figure out every math problem his mother had been unable to do. And if his siblings thought the teachers were demanding, wait until they dealt with Antonio. He planned to bring a little college home to Miami.

And he demanded each of them find a passion, a hobby, a sport, something that would make them see the world was bigger than this neighborhood. Their future would not be the streets, or falling in with drug dealers who claimed turf up the block. They'd go to college, just like he had.

In time, Shronda went from C's and D's to A's. She made the honor roll, as did the twins. Corrian played on the football team. Torrian discovered he liked to sing and joined the school choir. Keyera and her sister joined the dance team at church.

One day, the girls brought home two bumper stickers that said: "I'm the proud parent of an honor student." The stickers went on the front door to let everyone in the neighborhood know who lived in this house.

In December 2003, Antonio got a job as a youth counselor for a non-profit agency, making a salary of $31,000 a year. The job had regular hours, allowing him to be home every day to make dinner for the kids. He attended their football games, church performances, and parent/teacher meetings. And every month he put a little money in savings accounts for each of them.

Tonight, another hot Miami evening in 2006 with the old photograph and the bills lying on the bed, Antonio stopped short on the littered sidewalk outside his house. Down the street he saw Corrian talking with some boys. Around here—in a neighborhood of single mothers—Antonio is known as the strict man who doesn't tolerate people hanging around or traipsing in and out of his house without a reason.

Out of the corner of his eye, he could see a copper-colored $50,000 Hummer slowly making its way down the street. "I don't know who that is," Antonio said to himself. "Hey, you all get over here by the house," he called to Corrian and his friends.

Arms crossed, Antonio stared straight ahead as the Hummer stopped. Fifteen seconds passed before the vehicle moved up the block to where drug dealers lived. "You all stay by the house," Antonio said. "You hear me?"

Satisfied for the moment, Antonio walked inside and stood next to a display cabinet. His mother's ashes are in a white box on the cabinet. "Mama, we love U always," one of her children had written on the outside of the box. A small snapshot of Dorothea Seay was tucked in one edge, making it appear as though she is looking down, watching her family.

The man of the house yawned and rubbed his face. He had to be up at 5:30 to wake everyone and get them breakfast before he took them to school. From there he'd go to the counseling office. Grab groceries for dinner on his lunch break. Tight, but doable. He sat on the edge of his bed. The bills were still there and the photo of the kid with the dreams.

He heard laughter out on the stoop. "Is everything cool out there?" Antonio asked his brothers. "Don't want no problems."

Everything was cool.

A fat paycheck, a chance at graduate school, a home in a nice neighborhood, and perhaps a new car to go along with some fancy clothes, all these dreams and more were placed aside by Antonio to wait for a later day. His thoughts instead were fixed on something of greater value to him, his family. So he scarcely hesitated when it came to deciding what he would do. In a society where too many people make family a disposable commodity, Antonio's determination in choosing family over his other dreams provides a touching example of sacrifice and charity. The seeds of charity are planted and rooted in the home, so there it is also that they ought to bear the richest of fruits.

~

WRAP UP

Charity is found in our words and deeds, but mostly in our motives. Mr. Boyce did not do what he did because he thought a future child of the young train servant would become famous and write about him. Bill W. preferred to remain anonymous, so notoriety could not have been his motive in starting Alcoholics

Anonymous. And neither of the two instructors received more pay for excelling beyond their job titles, so wealth surely was not their motive. Rather, all of these people held motives that were unselfish, as they looked outside themselves and chose to enhance the lives of others.

In your own search for meaning, the best place to start is outside yourself—by thinking of others and exhibiting acts of charity, however small they might be. Whether through a simple act of kindness, the offering of hope, a well-timed compliment, or through lighting another's darkened path, opportunities for charity that extend beyond giving money are around every corner, every day.

REFLECTIONS

- Mr. Boyce saw potential in young Simon and determined to help. Are there any "boys on a train" that you can influence through charitable acts? Neighbors, work colleagues, friends?

- The individuals in these stories all gave more than money. They gave of their time, vision, encouragement, and wisdom to benefit others. What do you have to share—talents, humor, hobbies, belongings, hope, compliments?

- Bill W. preferred to stay anonymous. Do you ever keep your charitable acts anonymous? What motives are behind "what you do" for others?

- Antonio postponed his dreams in behalf of his siblings. What sacrifices are you willing to make that would allow your family members to feel your acts of charity?

FURTHER INSIGHTS ON
Charity

~

GIVING OF OURSELVES

Charity is more than giving money to the poor. It is the giving of our hearts, time, talents, and energies to lighten the lives of others, rich or poor.

If you haven't any charity in your heart, you have the worst kind of heart trouble.

—BOB HOPE

■ ■ ■

I hear people say: "Oh, if I were only rich, I would do great things to help people." But we all can be rich in love and generosity. Moreover, if we give with care, if we find out the exact wants of those who need our help most, we are giving our own loving interest and concern, which is worth more than all the money in the world.

—ALBERT SCHWEITZER

■ ■ ■

Nowadays we think of a philanthropist as someone who donates big sums of money, yet the word is derived from two Greek words, philos (loving) and anthropos (man): loving man. All of us are capable of being philanthropists. We can give of ourselves.

—EDWARD LINDSEY,
GUIDEPOSTS

■ ■ ■

It is in spending oneself that one becomes rich.

—SARAH BERNHARDT

■ ■ ■

The dead take to the grave, clutched in their hands, only what they have given away.

—DEWITT WALLACE

■ ■ ■

I find life an exciting business—and most exciting when it is lived for others.

—HELEN KELLER

■ ■ ■

If you want others to be happy, practice compassion. If you want to be happy, practice compassion.

—DALAI LAMA

■ ■ ■

True heroism is remarkably sober, very undramatic. It is not the urge to surpass all others at whatever cost, but the urge to serve others at whatever cost.

—ARTHUR ASHE

■ ■ ■

On the day after Mrs. Fosdick died, I saw Harry Emerson Fosdick's religious faith, and I shall never forget it. My husband and I went to call on him. He was 86, and we expected to find him shattered by the loss of the wife he had cherished for more than 60 years. Instead, he met us with a smile. "Florence enjoyed good health, you know, right to the end," he said. "I'm the one who had ailments, and I was afraid I'd die first and leave her alone. Now she's gone, and I will be the one to face loneliness. I'm so thankful for that. This is something I can do for Florence."

—NARDI REEDER CAMPION

SACRIFICING SELF-INTERESTS

As Antonio demonstrated, acts of charity require a level of sacrifice—forgoing self interests in order that others may benefit.

The mass of men worry themselves into nameless graves while here and there a great unselfish soul forgets himself into immortality.

—RALPH WALDO EMERSON

◾ ◾ ◾

To a woman who wrote me of the boredom that came into her life when her children were grown and gone from home, I replied: "In the past, your immediate family needed most of your time and strength. Now you can extend the range of your love. There are children in your neighborhood who need understanding and friendship. There are aged people near you who are starved for companionship, blind people who cannot even enjoy the television you find so boring. Why not get out and find the joy of helping others?" Weeks later, she wrote again: "I tried your prescription. It works! I have walked from night into day!"

—THE REV. BILLY GRAHAM

◾ ◾ ◾

The ultimate test of man's conscience may be his willingness to sacrifice something today for future generations whose words of thanks will not be heard.

—GAYLORD NELSON
IN THE *NEW YORK TIMES*

◾ ◾ ◾

Seldom can a heart be lonely if it seeks a lonelier still, self-forgetting, seeking only emptier cups to fill.

— FRANCES RIDLEY HAVERGAL

◾ ◾ ◾

To ease another's heartache is to forget one's own.

—ABRAHAM LINCOLN

LITTLE ACTS OF KINDNESS

Charity does not require a large deed. It often takes little acts
of kindness in the form of a warm smile or a kind word.

One kind word can warm three winter months.

—JAPANESE PROVERB

■ ■ ■

Kind words can be short and easy to speak, but their echoes are
truly endless.

—MOTHER TERESA

■ ■ ■

Kindness is a language which the deaf can hear and the blind can read.

—MARK TWAIN

■ ■ ■

One can pay back the loan of gold, but one dies forever in debt to those who
are kind.

—MALAYAN PROVERB

■ ■ ■

A warm smile is the universal language of kindness.

—WILLIAM ARTHUR WARD

■ ■ ■

Always try to be a little kinder than is necessary.

—JAMES M. BARRIE

■ ■ ■

A letter from Abraham Lincoln to General Rosecrans, commander of the Army of the Southwest, concerned the proposed execution of a Confederate officer: "I have examined personally all the papers in the Lyons case, and I cannot see that it is a matter for executive interference. So I turn it over to you with full confidence that you will do what is just and right; only begging you, my dear General, to do nothing in reprisal for the past—only what is necessary to ensure security for the future; and remind you that we are not fighting against a foreign foe, but our brothers, and that our aim is not to break their spirits but only to bring back their old allegiance. Conquer by kindness—let that be our policy. Very truly yours, A. Lincoln."

Kindness is more important than wisdom, and the recognition of this is the beginning of wisdom.

—THEODORE ISAAC RUBIN, MD,
ONE TO ONE

■ ■ ■

The ideals which have lighted my way, and time after time have given me new courage to face life cheerfully, have been kindness, beauty and truth.

—ALBERT EINSTEIN,
IDEAS AND OPINIONS

■ ■ ■

Let no one ever come to you without leaving better and happier.

—MOTHER TERESA

HOPE

Mr. Boyce gave young Simon hope. And, indeed, one of the most charitable gifts we can give another is a slice of optimism.

What we must do for our young people is challenge them to put hope in their brains rather than dope in their veins. What difference does it make whether the doors swing wide open if our young people are too dizzy to walk through them?

—THE REV. JESSE JACKSON
IN THE *NEW YORK TIMES MAGAZINE*

■ ■ ■

The natural flights of the human mind are not from pleasure to pleasure but from hope to hope.

—SAMUEL JOHNSON

■ ■ ■

I know the world is filled with troubles and many injustices. But I think it is just as important to sing about beautiful mornings as it is to talk about slums. I just couldn't write anything without hope in it.

—OSCAR HAMMERSTEIN II

■ ■ ■

Popular artist-illustrator Norman Rockwell once explained why his art is almost always an upbeat experience for the viewer: "When I grew up and found the world wasn't always the pleasant place I had thought it would be, I unconsciously decided that if it wasn't an ideal world, it should be. And so I painted it that way."

—LENA TABORI FRIED,
IN *GOOD HOUSEKEEPING*

3

ATTENTION

It is more noble to give yourself completely to one individual
than to labor diligently for the salvation of the masses.
—DAG HAMMARSKJÖLD

Sometimes people mistakenly think that finding meaning in life requires making a huge contribution that impacts millions. But often the most meaningful and lasting contributions or acts of charity are those that occur in small, one-on-one ways when attention is given to a solitary individual.

In fact, when I ask audiences to identify a person who has been greatly influential in their life, typically they do not respond with a person who performed some great act of courage or excelled in a particular talent. Rather, they describe people who took time out of their busy schedules to focus their attention on them as individuals—to make them feel important by including them in their life, if only for a moment. As you read the following stories, consider individuals who might benefit by receiving a little more one-on-one attention from you.

THE BOY WHO COULDN'T READ

Tyler Currie

I learn Rommel can't read on the first day of class at Mildred Green Elementary School. I've handed out an assignment, which I call "All About You." For the kids, it's a series of fun questions. ("If you could be any flavor of ice cream, which would it be? Explain.") For me, it's a peek at my new students' skills.

After I lead a parade of twenty-seven fourth-graders to the cafeteria for lunch, I go back to my room to read a pile of surveys. I learn that my class is filled with aspiring football players, singers, and would-be tubs of mint chocolate chip ice cream. Then I find a survey that is blank. No birth date, no favorite color, and apparently this Rommel Sales does not want to be ice cream. Rommel's blank page alarms me because usually every kid acts like an angel on the first day of school.

I go down to the cafeteria and search for Rommel. Which child is he? There are so many. Yes, there. The ten-year-old without a school uniform. He's lean and healthy looking, about the height of a light switch, with closely clipped hair. "Can I speak with you for a second?" I ask him.

"Uh-huh," he says.

He follows me down the hall. When he walks, he bounces.

"How was your summer?" I ask.

"Okay."

"What'd you do?" He says he doesn't remember. He's jittery. "Don't worry, it's nothing bad," I assure him. "I'm just wondering, how's your reading?"

"Umm, not so good," he says. "I'm working on it."

I take out the kind of book a child should be reading at the end of first grade. "Let's see," I say, opening to the first page.

Rommel handles the first word, *the,* just fine. After that, the book might as well be written in Aramaic. He can't read another word.

In his defense, he says that he knows the word c-a-t, which his mother taught him.

"That's really good," I say.

"How about this one?" I point to the letter "r." He knows that one—it's the initial sound of his name, which is pronounced ro-*mel.*

We chat for a minute. "I'm special ed," he tells me, making the term sound like a lower social caste. He says he doesn't like sports. Not crazy about music either. He likes art. He shows me a book of his drawings, done in the style of Japanese animation. His ninja-like figures are tall and muscular. They shoot fireballs from their hands and have eccentric hairdos.

I admire Rommel's work, but I wonder what I'm going to do with him. This kid shouldn't be in fourth grade.

It's September 5, 2000, and this is my second year teaching at Mildred Green, a brick school in southeast Washington, the heart of the inner city. I'd earned an English degree from the University of Michigan and signed up for Teach for America, which places newly minted college grads in low-income urban classrooms across the country.

Most of the kids read and write relatively well. One girl is reading Stephen Crane's *The Red Badge of Courage,* but even the stragglers are light years ahead of Rommel. His special ed teacher, sober and sorrowful, tells me that "Rommel will never read."

For a long time, I don't challenge that devastating pronouncement. I'm too busy keeping order, soothing tempers, and teaching the rest of the class.

So I push Rommel to the side, literally. During language arts, when the class reads literature, Rommel listens to recorded stories in a corner. Or I have him draw his assignments since he can't write them.

Yet he's not stupid. When I teach math, he has no problem keeping up. So why hasn't Rommel learned to read? I ask this question often because there's one part of the day—actually two—when Rommel truly shines: story time. I read books to my students—first thing in the morning and after recess—that most of them couldn't manage on their own. For Rommel, of course, that means any book.

Nonetheless, he's transfixed by the stories. He'll chuckle at subtle humor that the others miss, or he'll blurt out "no fair" when a character acts treacher-ously. He answers questions, defends his opinions, and challenges the interpre-tations of his classmates. When I read Tolkien's *The Hobbit,* Rommel goes around hissing like the creature Gollum.

But when story time ends, Rommel's transformation is sudden. Like a wizard drained of his magic, he loses his animation. Once again, he's the child who can't read.

After the Christmas holidays, I develop a plan for helping Rommel. I name it Pinching Words.

Rommel and I spend ten minutes a day reading *Harry Potter and the Chamber of Secrets,* just the two of us. It's a story he absolutely loves. I do most of the reading. Rommel is responsible for one or two preselected words. These are the pinching words.

"Rommel, today the pinching word is *off.*" I write o-f-f. Then I begin the story. Eventually I'll come to a sentence like this: "And the old man hugged Mr. Dursley around the middle and walked—" Rommel is supposed to recognize the next word as the pinching word. If he says "off," I continue reading. If he doesn't, I pinch him on the arm.

So word by word, I'm pinching the illiteracy out of Rommel. My method is untested, unorthodox, probably illegal, but heck, Rommel likes both the attention and the story. Besides, I don't pinch that hard.

But weeks later, Rommel's still not reading. I've been promising him that we'll do some serious work, but he gets in a fight, and he's suspended.

It's not the first time.

He returns to school in a week with his mother, Zalonda Sales. Florine Bruton, Green's tireless assistant principal, and I take turns flinging platitudes at Rommel. Practice self-control. Fighting doesn't solve anything. Ask your teacher for help. Blah, blah, blah.

I snap to attention when Ms. Sales brings up her son's reading. Rommel hangs his head. His mother is on the verge of tears. She pleads with him: "If you would just listen to your teacher, Rommel. You can learn to read. Pay attention to Mr. Currie. He'll teach you."

I don't want to tell Ms. Sales that her son's not the problem. It's us.
The teachers, who should have taught Rommel to read. The administrators, who passed him along. All of us have failed this skinny boy who's slumped here in self-disgust.

The school year is coming to a close, and I finish reading *Harry Potter and the Chamber of Secrets* to Rommel. He asks if he can borrow the 341-page novel. The request puzzles me.

"No, Rommel, it's not like you can even . . ." I stop myself before pointing out the obvious. "Rommel, it's my only copy."

Finally, after more fruitless pleas, Rommel returns to his desk and takes out a sheet of drawing paper.

At the end of the day, I go home. I take off my shoes, rub my sore feet, and look around my little apartment. Books are piled in teetering stacks, monuments to the joy of literacy.

I put my shoes back on, walk to the bookstore, and buy *Harry Potter and the Chamber of Secrets* on cassette tape. The next day, when I give Rommel the tape and the book, his eyes bug out in astonishment.

"Keep them, Rommel. They're yours."

"Aw, man, thanks!"

"Excuse me?" He's not supposed to call me "man."

"Sorry. I mean thank you, Mr. Currie." He slings his backpack over his shoulder, accidentally knocking it into his desk. Out tumble dozens and dozens of drawings on crumpled pieces of notebook paper.

He stuffs them in the trash can by the armful. What a waste. Not of paper, of a year.

That night I make a decision: I'm going to teach Rommel to read.

I could kiss Mrs. Bruton. She's blessed my unconventional idea for tackling Rommel's illiteracy and even given me a little classroom, the former band room. Rommel and I will spend nine hours there each week. I won't be responsible for any other students, and I won't be paid, which is okay because my new job waiting tables in the evenings more than covers my old salary.

On September 4, 2001, Rommel and I sit down for the first time in our little classroom. "Welcome to the Douglass Literacy Project," I say. I've named our venture after Frederick Douglass, the great writer and statesman who, like Rommel, grew up in the same area and who also struggled to read as a youth.

I pull out a phonics book. "Okay. Let's get to work."

Rommel doesn't know letter sounds, so we start with "A."

We learn one vowel sound and one consonant sound per week. Rommel devises his own mnemonic system. For every new sound, he creates a character. Alex the Apple Axeman. Iggy the Idiot Iguana. Oscar the Octopus. Dingo Dog.

He's drawn cartoons of these characters, covering an entire wall of our room. When he forgets a sound, he looks at the wall. Slowly, he learns to blend these sounds into words.

Weeks later Rommel and I go to Mrs. Bruton's office, which is filled with students. "Children, excuse me for a moment, please," she says.

Rommel sits beside her. He clears his throat and opens Dr. Seuss's *The Foot Book*. Like a solemn minister he begins to read: "Left foot, left foot Right foot, right Feet in the morning Feet at night."

For a week, he's been preparing for his meeting with Mrs. Bruton. When he finishes, she hugs him. "I'm so proud," she says.

Rommel plays like it's no big thing. But then Mrs. Bruton says: "I'm going to call your mother and tell her." Rommel can't contain himself any longer. His face breaks into the giddiest grin I've ever seen.

As the holidays approach, Rommel is learning to read at an astounding pace. We are saturated with letters and sounds and stories, and he absorbs it all like a starved, desiccated sponge. But in all the hoopla of reading instruction, I've forgotten its equally important twin: writing. I give Rommel a journal after Christmas and tell him we will begin each session by writing in it.

Rommel's first entry—his first self-authored sentence—reads: "I like pasta." By the time he returns from spring break, he's bragging that he's reading *Harry Potter and the Prisoner of Azkaban,* the third book in the series. I ask him to write about it in his journal: "In chapter two, Harry chose to run away from home. He chose to run away because he blew up his aunt Marge. The consequences were that he met Fudge and they had a talk. I think he made the right choice because if he'd stayed he'd be in trouble."

For a long time, I believed the word around school—that Rommel would never learn to read. But what none of us understood was just how much this kid wanted to read.

It's not that Rommel couldn't learn. We simply never taught him.

Not enough school teachers receive the applause (or attention) they deserve. How many lives have been touched by a noble teacher who, despite the obstacles and lack of resources, finds ways to provide individual attention? In this instance, the mere act of using his lunch hour to go in search of Rommel in the cafeteria speaks volumes about Mr. Currie and the importance he places on individual attention.

———————

Of course, schoolteachers are not alone in recognizing the value of attention. I have been fortunate to work with many individuals whom I consider to be great leaders. One thing that always sets these people apart—that lifts them above the others—is that, regardless of the size or nature of their organizations, they never forget the worth of the individual. Consider the following leader—a leader of millions—who never lost sight of what even a little attention can mean to an individual.

POPE JOHN PAUL II

Peggy Noonan

In June 2000, I was granted an audience with the Holy Father in Rome, along with about thirty others. The day before, on the phone, I had been told by a woman with an Italian accent to "go to the bronze doors of the Vatican, and wait." No address, just the "bronze doors." So I went and waited. I was ushered into a room. The others chatted quietly. There was a buzz of excitement.

Suddenly it was silent, as if an unheard signal had been given, and we all turned our heads in the same direction. The doors in the corner opened, and the Pope shuffled in, using a cane. People burst into applause. A group of dark-haired young nuns in blue, on the left, spontaneously broke into joyful song.

The Pope, moving slowly, stopped in front of them. His head went back a little, and he took his cane and shook it toward them comically and said, in a rich baritone, "Philippines?"

The Filipino nuns exploded in joy. Some of them bent to their knees as he passed them.

Next he looked at another group and shook his cane and said, "Brah-*sill!*" The group of Brazilians applauded and started to cry.

The Pope walked on, more quickly now. He approached an extraordinary-looking young man with thick, coal-black hair. He was slim, Asian, dressed like a seminarian. He looked dreamy, happy, his hands held in prayer. The Pope held his cane toward him and said, "China!" The young man slid to his knees, went to kiss the Pope's shoe. But the Pope caught him in an embrace. It was so honest and impromptu that my eyes actually filled with tears.

Finally the Pope came closer to me. I tried to think what to say. About how I had yearned for years to meet this man who ministered to millions around the world, who was born of humble circumstances and became the most famous man in the world. Then suddenly, there he was, inches from me. I'd run out of time to think, but it didn't matter. He came closer, and his face was before me. I touched his left hand with my hands. Then I sort of curtsy-bowed. As I held his hand, I leaned forward and kissed his thick knuckles. I think I said, "Papa" or "Hello, Papa."

He looked at me and pressed into my hand a soft brown plastic envelope. It was two inches square and bore an imprint of the papal seal. When I opened it later, I saw white plastic rosary beads and a silver cross.

I still have the photo of our meeting. I never saw anyone take it and was surprised to receive it from the cardinal's office. I look happy, transported.

The last in the room to meet the Pope was a Canadian heavy-metal rocker. When the Pope approached him, the young man bowed and kissed his hand. He said, "I have written music for you." He had a sheet of music, beautifully hand drawn. It had a title like "A Song for John Paul II."

The Pope said, "You wrote?"

And the rocker said, "Yes, for you."

The Pope took it, walked over to a big brown table, and signed the sheet music in a flourish, Ioannes Paulus pp. II. He came back and gave it to the rocker. Then he walked on, and out of the room. There was silence until the rocker said softly, "This is the greatest moment of my life."

People were weeping, laughing, as we left the room. I felt lighter than air. I went into the streets of Rome, hailed a cab, told the driver my hotel, and was still so excited that I left my glasses behind on the seat. But my rosary I remembered.

I still have it.

Within a matter of minutes and inside of a very short walking distance, Pope John Paul II—leader of millions—presented through his actions a masterful sermon on the worth of attention. Even the largest of organizations are made up of "ones"— solitary individuals who crave to know they matter. The key to the many is the one.

It has been said that "often we hurt the most those we love the most." Another way of saying it is that "often we ignore the most those we love the most." The following husband found a way to change that by offering a generous portion of undivided attention to his wife and family.

HOW LOVE CAME BACK

Tom Anderson

I made a vow to myself on the drive down to the vacation beach cottage. For two weeks I would try to be a loving husband and father. Totally loving. No ifs, ands, or buts.

The idea had come to me as I listened to a commentator on my car's tape player. He was quoting a Biblical passage about husbands being thoughtful of their wives. Then he went on to say, "Love is an act of will. A person can *choose* to love." To myself, I had to admit that I had been a selfish husband—that our love had been dulled by my own insensitivity. In petty ways, really: chiding Evelyn for her tardiness; insisting on the TV channel *I* wanted to watch; throwing out day-old newspapers that I knew Evelyn still wanted to read. Well, for two weeks all that would change.

And it did. Right from the moment I kissed Evelyn at the door and said, "That new yellow sweater looks great on you."

"Oh, Tom, you noticed," she said, surprised and pleased. Maybe a little perplexed.

After a long drive, I wanted to sit and read. Evelyn suggested a walk on the beach. I started to refuse, but then I thought, *Evelyn's been alone here with the kids all week and now she wants to be alone with me.* We walked on the beach while the children flew their kites.

So it went. Two weeks of not calling the Wall Street investment firm where I am a director; a visit to the shell museum, though I usually hate museums (and I enjoyed it); holding my tongue while Evelyn's getting ready made us late for a dinner date. Relaxed and happy, that's how the whole vacation passed. I made a new vow to keep on remembering to *choose* love.

There was one thing that went wrong with my experiment, however. Evelyn and I still laugh about it today. On the last night at our cottage, preparing for bed, Evelyn stared at me with the saddest expression.

"What's the matter?" I asked her.

"Tom," she said, in a voice filled with distress, "do you know something I don't?"

"What do you mean?"

"Well . . . that checkup I had several weeks ago . . . our doctor . . . did he tell you something about me? Tom, you've been so good to me . . . am I dying?"

It took a moment for it all to sink in. Then I burst out laughing.

"No, honey," I said, wrapping her in my arms, "you're not dying; I'm just starting to live!"

Tom "chose to love" by setting aside his Wall Street worries and personal interests to focus undivided attention on his family, chiefly Evelyn. What resulted provides further evidence that in focusing on individuals—particularly those we love the most—we often make the most meaningful and lasting impact. In Evelyn's case, she was so surprised by the attention that she was receiving that she thought something must be wrong—even had thoughts that she might be dying. She turned out to be just fine, but there are many people in the world who are dying for a little attention. See if you can find them and cure them of what ails them.

～

Wrap Up

To me, knowing that there are teachers who remember the worth of the "one" is reassuring. Knowing that there are leaders who take time out to give individual attention is soothing. Because each of us is ultimately a one. So to know that there are people in the world who recognize the value of individual attention is heartwarming. We all need to be reminded from time to time that we are individually important—unique persons of worth. So in your search for meaning, one of your first considerations might well be to pause and ask yourself, What individuals would most benefit from an increased measure of attention from me? Never underestimate the power of individual attention.

REFLECTIONS

- You do not need to dedicate your entire life to a person to give attention. Sometimes all that is required is a few minutes, or time enough to share a compliment. Does some "one" you know need attention—today?

- Was there ever a person who during a critical stage in your life offered you the undivided attention you needed? Are you that type of person for someone?

- Though a leader of many, Pope John Paul II found ways to give individual attention. If you are a leader, such as a business leader, a parent, a teacher, a coach, what have you found to be successful ways of giving individual attention?

FURTHER INSIGHTS ON
Attention

∼

INDIVIDUAL ATTENTION

All people desire individual attention. For while we are all a part of the masses, each of us is also ultimately a one.

My advice to salesmen is this: pretend that every single person you meet has a sign around his or her neck that says, "Make me feel important." Not only will you succeed in sales, you will succeed in life.

—MARY KAY ASH

■ ■ ■

I do not agree with the big way of doing things. Love needs to start with an individual.

—MOTHER TERESA,
SIMPLE PATH

■ ■ ■

The greatest gift you can give another is the purity of your attention.

—RICHARD MOSS, M.D.

■ ■ ■

As the old man walked the beach at dawn, he noticed a young man ahead of him picking up starfish and flinging them into the sea. Finally catching up with the youth, he asked him why he was doing this. The answer was that the stranded starfish would die if left until the morning sun.

"But the beach goes on for miles and there are millions of starfish," countered the other. "How can your effort make any difference?"

The young man looked at the starfish in his hand and then threw it to safety in the waves. "It makes a difference to this one," he said.

—MINNESOTA LITERACY COUNCIL

TEACHING AND INSPIRING

As Mr. Currie demonstrated, one of the most effective ways to give individuals attention is to inspire them by sharing insights and revealing to them their own potential.

The dream begins most of the time with a teacher who believes in you, who tugs and pushes and leads you on to the next plateau, sometimes even poking you with a sharp stick called truth.

—DAN RATHER,
THE CAMERA NEVER BLINKS

■ ■ ■

A leader takes people where they want to go. A great leader takes people where they don't necessarily want to go, but ought to be.

—ROSALYNN CARTER

■ ■ ■

To do our fellow men the most good in our power, we must lead where we can, follow where we cannot and still go with them, watching always the favorable moment for helping them to another step.

—THOMAS JEFFERSON

■ ■ ■

If you have knowledge, let others light their candles at it.

—MARGARET FULLER

■ ■ ■

There are two ways of spreading light; to be the candle or the mirror reflecting it.

—EDITH WHARTON

■ ■ ■

Education is more than filling a child with facts. It starts with posing questions.

—D. T. MAX,
THE *NEW YORK TIMES*

LOVE

> Of course the highest form of giving attention is to accept and love a person for who they are.

A young sociology professor sent his class out to a Baltimore slum to interview two hundred boys and predict their chances for the future. The students, shocked by slum conditions, predicted that about 90 percent of the boys they interviewed would someday serve time in prison.

Twenty-five years later, the same professor assigned another class to find out how the predictions had turned out. Of 190 of the original boys located, only four had ever been to jail.

Why had the prediction been so wrong? More than 100 of the men remembered one high-school teacher, a Miss O'Rourke, as having been an inspiration in their lives. After a long search, Sheila O'Rourke, more than seventy years old, was found. But when asked to explain her influence over her former students, she was puzzled. "All I can say," she finally decided, "is that I loved every one of them."

—JOHN KORD LAGEMANN

■ ■ ■

I felt approaching footsteps. I stretched out my hand, as I supposed, to my mother. Someone took it, and I was caught up and held close in the arms of her who had come to reveal all things to me, and, more than all things else, to love me.

—HELEN KELLER,
IN *GUIDEPOSTS*

■ ■ ■

The supreme happiness of life is the conviction that one is loved; loved for oneself, or better yet, loved despite oneself.

—VICTOR HUGO

■ ■ ■

We are not held back by the love we didn't receive in the past, but by the love we're not extending in the present.

—MARIANNE WILLIAMSON

BEYOND GAMES

Professional athletes are known for receiving attention, but
the true beauty of the athlete is revealed when the attention
is turned outward in one-on-one ways.

The Boston Bruins were playing the New York Rangers, and I was in charge
of the penalty box. Directly behind me on a special ramped section, I spotted
a boy of four or five seated in a wheelchair, frantically waving a Bruin banner.

After the pre-game warm-ups, Ranger Phil Esposito caught sight of the
boy and stopped to chat. "If you're still here at the end of the game, you've
got my stick," I heard him say.

I could see how excited the boy was, and he stayed that way throughout
the game. I hoped that the pro would remember.

The final buzzer sounded, and in seconds Esposito was up at the ramp,
handing the lad his stick and offering words of encouragement.

That night the Rangers lost the game, but Phil Esposito won two lifetime
fans.

—JOHN HOLLINGSWORTH

Recalling the one moment that stood out most during her husband's
illustrious twenty-six-year baseball career:

Inevitably, sometime during a game Nolan would pop up out of
the dugout and scan the stands behind home plate, looking for me. He
would find my face and grin at me, maybe snapping his head up in a
quick nod as if to say, There you are; I'm glad.

It was a simple moment, never noted in record books or career
summaries.

—RUTH RYAN,
COVERING HOME

Grambling football coach Eddie Robinson cared for every individual on his
team. When they built a new stadium they placed a huge marker at the
entrance: Robinson Stadium: "Where Everybody Is Somebody."

—JEROME BRONDFIELD,
EDDIE ROBINSON'S GAME PLAN FOR LIFE

TAKING
CHARGE

Even if you're on the right track,
you'll get run over if you just sit there.
—WILL ROGERS

The search for meaning inspires us to create a blueprint for the contributions we want to make in life, a daily standard against which we can chart our course and measure progress. But the reality is that nothing of substance will happen until we take charge of our life and accept responsibility for bringing our dreams to fruition. These efforts require fearless discipline and focused energy on what matters most.

Principles that enable us to take charge of life include

- Responsibility

- Courage

- Discipline

4

RESPONSIBILITY

I believe that every right implies a responsibility;
every opportunity, an obligation, every possession, a duty.
—NELSON ROCKEFELLER

When life does not go our way or we inadvertently make a mistake, it is so easy to make excuses, place blame on others, or argue that circumstances were against us. But we only progress in life to the extent that we take responsibility for our actions and attitudes, and put forth the initiative necessary to create our own circumstances.

The following autobiographical accounts relate instances when three well-known individuals were forced to determine the level of responsibility they would take for their lives. They include former First Lady Betty Ford, author Maya Angelou, and action film star Chuck Norris. All three faced the decision of whether they themselves would take charge or allow external factors to govern their choices. We begin with Betty Ford's brave and revealing description of her battle with addiction, which took place at a time when such personal confessions were rarely publicly disclosed.

I INTEND TO MAKE IT!

Betty Ford with Chris Chase

It wasn't until after we had left the White House and retired to private life that my family realized I was in trouble. For fourteen years I'd been on medications—for a pinched nerve, arthritis, muscle spasms in my neck, and in 1974 for relief during my recovery from a radical mastectomy. I'd built up a tolerance to the drugs prescribed for me. And just one drink, taken on top of so much medication, would make me groggy.

In the fall of 1977, I went to Moscow to narrate *The Nutcracker* ballet for television. Later, there were comments about my "sloe-eyed, sleepy-tongued" performance. Jerry and the children were worried, but I had no idea what was happening to me or how much I had changed. Only now do I realize that after the trip to Russia I began to suffer lapses of memory.

Finally my daughter Susan discussed my condition with our doctor. He recommended direct intervention. The thinking used to be that a person chemically addicted to either alcohol or pills had to hit bottom, then decide he or she *wanted* to get well, before recovery could begin. But it has now been demonstrated that a sick person's family, along with others important to the patient, can intervene to help. With this new intervention method, the recovery rate has increased significantly.

CONFRONTATION

While Jerry was in the East on a speaking tour, the doctor, along with Susan and my secretary, Caroline Coventry, marched into my sitting room and confronted me. They started talking about my giving up all medication and liquor. I got very angry, and was so upset that after they left I called a friend and complained about the terrible invasion of my privacy. (I don't remember that call; the friend has since told me about it.)

On the morning of April 1—it was a Saturday—I was thinking about phoning my son Mike and his wife, Gayle, in Pittsburgh, when the front door opened and in they came, along with the entire family. I was thrilled, thinking they'd gathered because I wasn't feeling well. We hugged and kissed and went into the living room—where they all proceeded to confront me a second time. And they meant business. They had brought along Captain Joe Pursch, the navy doctor who is head of the Alcohol and Drug Rehabilitation Service at Long Beach.

I was in shock. Mike and Gayle spoke of wanting children, and wanting those children's grandmother to be healthy and in charge of her own life. Jerry mentioned times when I'd fallen asleep in the chair, and times when my speech had slurred, and Steve brought up a recent weekend when he and a girlfriend had cooked dinner for me and I wouldn't come to the table on time. "You just sat in front of the TV," Steve said, "and had one drink, two drinks, three drinks. You hurt me."

Well, he hurt me back. They all hurt me. I collapsed in tears. But I still had enough sense to realize that they hadn't come around just to make me cry; they were there because they loved me and wanted to help me.

Yet I resisted any suggestion that liquor had contributed to my illness; all I would confess to was overmedication. Captain Pursch told me it didn't matter. He gave me the book *Alcoholics Anonymous* and told me to read it, substituting the words "chemically dependent" for "alcoholic." Since a tranquilizer or a dry martini each brings the same relief, you can use the same book for drugs and alcohol. And when I say drugs, I'm talking about legal medications, prescribed by doctors.

At first I was bitter toward the medical profession for all those years of being advised to take pills rather than wait for the pain to hit. I took pills for pain and pills to sleep, and I took tranquilizers. Today, many doctors are beginning to recognize the risks in these medications, but some of them used to be all too eager to write prescriptions. (The odd thing is that I had already tapered myself off one medication and was beginning to work on letting go of another when the intervention started.)

FIRST STEPS

Two days after my sixtieth birthday, I entered the hospital at Long Beach. I could have gone to a private facility, but I decided that it was better to seek treatment publicly rather than to hide behind a silk sheet. A statement which said I'd been overmedicating myself was to be released to the press once I was safely ensconced.

Captain Pursch met me on the fourth floor and escorted me to a room with four beds. I balked. I'd expected privacy. I was not going to sign in; I was not going to release my statement. Captain Pursch handled the situation perfectly. "If you insist on a private room," he said, "I will have all these women move out . . ." He put the ball right in my court.

"No, no, I won't have that," I said, quickly and self-consciously. An hour later, I was settled in with three roommates and my statement was being read to reporters.

On April 15, at the end of my first week in Long Beach, my son Steve—caught by a reporter outside the hospital—said I was fighting the effects not only of pills but of alcohol as well. I wasn't enchanted; I wasn't yet prepared to admit that. All week I had been talking about medications, and everyone had nodded respectfully.

Five days later there was a meeting in Captain Pursch's office. Jerry and I were there, along with several doctors. Now they told me that I should make a public statement admitting that I was also an alcoholic. I refused. "I don't want to embarrass my husband," I said.

"You're trying to hide behind your husband," Captain Pursch said. "Why don't you ask him if it would embarrass him if you say you're an alcoholic?"

I started to cry, and Jerry took my hand. "There will be no embarrassment to me," he insisted. "You go ahead and say what should be said."

With that, my crying got worse. When Jerry took me back to my room, I was still sobbing so hard I couldn't get my breath. I hope I never have to cry like that again. It was terrifying. But once it was over, I felt a great relief.

That night, propped up in bed, I scrawled yet another public statement: "I have found that I am not only addicted to the medications I have been taking for my arthritis, but also to alcohol. I expect this treatment and fellowship to be a solution for my problems, and I embrace it not only for me, but for all the others who are here to participate." It was a big step for me to write that, but it was only the first of many steps that I would have to take.

BATTLE STATIONS

The reason I had rejected the idea that I was an alcoholic was that my addiction wasn't dramatic. So my speech had become deliberate and I forgot a few telephone calls. So I fell in the bathroom and cracked three ribs. But I never drank to ease a hangover, and I hadn't been a solitary drinker, either. I'd never hidden bottles in chandeliers or toilet tanks. There had been no broken promises (Jerry never came to me and said, "Please quit") and no drunken driving. And I never wound up in a strange part of town with a bunch of sailors.

Until Long Beach.

I loved the sailors at Long Beach. We were all on a first-name basis—everywhere I went, people called "Hi, Betty!"—and as we struggled with our dependencies and our terrors, each of us held out his hands to the others.

Each day the alarm clock went off at 6:00 a.m. I got up, made my bed, fixed myself a cup of tea, and then answered the shout "Muster!" which meant roll call. (I was in the navy, after all.) Cleaning detail came next, each of us being given a housekeeping task. Frequently there was an 8:00 a.m. "Doctors' Meeting." This was a period in which patients interacted with visiting doctors, most of them naval officers. These doctors were being trained to recognize addiction and not to push medication to solve people's problems.

LIFELINES

On mornings when I didn't have a Doctors' Meeting, I had group therapy at eight forty-five, and there was always a second group-therapy session right before lunch. After lunch there would be a lecture or a film, then another class. Each group is composed of six or seven patients and one counselor. In these groups you begin to feel the support, the warmth, and comradeship that will be your lifeline back to sobriety. In my group were a twenty-year-old sailor (a jet mechanic who'd been drinking since he was eight years old), a young officer (twice married, twice divorced) and a clergyman (addicted to drugs and drink, living on the thin edge of his nerves).

At first, I loathed these sessions. I was uncomfortable, unwilling to speak up. Then one day another woman said she didn't think that her drinking was a problem. I became very emotional and got to my feet. "I'm Betty," I said. "I'm an alcoholic, and I know my drinking has hurt my family." I heard myself, and couldn't believe it. I was trembling; another defense had cracked.

Nothing you hear is to be repeated outside the group. You can freely admit to having wrecked your car and your liver, broken your teeth and your marriage and your dreams. Your group-mates will nod and say yes, but you're not alone, and after all it could be worse. You could still be conning yourself or cursing your genes or your doctors.

In the end, what it comes down to is that you have to take the responsibility for yourself. Never mind that your wife kept a dirty house, or your mother didn't like you, or your husband can't remember your wedding anniversary. Everybody's had disappointments, and anyone can rationalize his actions. But none of that matters. Blaming other people for your condition is a total waste of time.

After I entered the hospital, flowers and bags of mail from well-wishers followed. So many kind people were pulling for me. The *Washington Post* ran an editorial recalling that my candor in discussing my mastectomy had given heart "to countless other victims and prospective victims of breast cancer." And the paper praised me for revealing my addiction to pills and alcohol: "Whatever combination of emotional and psychological stress and physical pain brought her to this pass, she is, characteristically, determined to overcome it. And she is unafraid and unembarrassed to say so."

I thank the *Post*, but I don't deserve the accolade. I've been both afraid and embarrassed. I've gone through loneliness, depression, anger, discouragement. Here, for example, is the April 21 notation from a diary I kept at Long Beach:

Now to bed. These damn scratchy wool blankets. Little did I know when I signed in that it was going to be so rough, and I don't mean just the blankets, either. It's a good program, but mighty hard for someone who turned 60 a couple of weeks ago. What in hell am I doing here? I've even started talking like the sailors. I could sign out, but I won't let myself do that. I want it too badly. Guess I'll just cry.

POINT OF NO RETURN

You get better when you least expect to, when you're not even trying, when you're down, or by the coffee machine kibitzing with two card-playing seamen. In my everyday life, I would never have met these men, but they and I helped to heal one another.

Toward the end of my month at Long Beach, I tried to tell my group—we were Group Six and called ourselves the Six Pack—what they had meant to me, but I couldn't express it in words. I started to cry, and one of the fellows handed me some tissues and said, "Now we know you're going to get better."

Serenity is hard won, but I'm making progress. I don't want to drink anymore, and it's been a great relief to stop. Eisenhower Hospital, in Palm Springs, is planning an active program for chemically addicted patients, and I hope to participate to help others, which is the best possible therapy.

There are plenty of chemically dependent people like me, women who aren't recognized as problem drinkers until confrontation is forced on them or they crack. I've heard stories about women who are business successes and leaders of their communities—but the iced tea in their hands or the coffee at their desks is laced with vodka just to keep them going. It's crucially important to realize how easy it is to slip into such dependency on pills or alcohol. And how hard it is to admit that dependency.

I'm grateful to Captain Pursch and the rest of the believers at Long Beach for their skills and for their caring. I'm grateful to thousands of strangers for their kindness and encouragement.

I've learned a lot about myself. As I continue to study and learn and work toward an aware future, I'm sure more will be revealed to me, and I'm looking forward to that. I intend to make it!

Since her days in Long Beach, Betty Ford has done much more than "intend to make it." Her everyday efforts to help people fight addiction and her campaigns to aid women in the battle against breast cancer are widely praised. One prominent theme of all she has accomplished is the lesson she came to know for herself, that "In the end, what it comes down to is that you have to take responsibility for yourself." And, now, through her openness, genuineness, and example, thousands of people have followed her footsteps and "made it" as well.

———————

Removed from her parents as a toddler, violently abused at age eight, and exposed to a biased education system, Maya Angelou had every reason to abandon her dreams and blame her unfavorable circumstances. But as you read "Maya's Journey Home," observe the turning point that occurs on graduation day when Maya recognizes that by taking responsibility for her life she can transform herself from victim to victor.

Maya's Journey Home

Maya Angelou

During the last days of school in 1940, the black children in Stamps trembled visibly with anticipation. Large classes were graduating from both the grammar school and the high school. The junior students, moving into the graduation classes' vacated chairs, strutted through the school exerting pressure on the lower grades. The graduating classes themselves were the nobility. Even teachers were respectful of the now quiet and aging seniors.

Unlike the white high school in Stamps, Lafayette County Training School distinguished itself by having neither lawn, nor hedges, nor tennis court. Its two buildings (housing the main classrooms, the grade school, and home economics) were set on a dirt hill. A large expanse to the left of the school was used alternately as a baseball diamond and a basketball court. Rusty hoops on the swaying poles represented the permanent recreational equipment.

Over this rocky area, relieved by a few shady persimmon tress, the high-school senior class walked. They seemed not ready to give up the old school, the familiar paths, and classrooms. Only a small percentage would be continuing on to college—one of the South's agricultural and mechanical schools, which trained Negro youths to be carpenters, farmers, handymen, masons, maids, cooks, and baby nurses. Their future rode heavily on their shoulders and blinded them to the collective joy that had pervaded the lives of the students in the grammar-school graduating class.

At home I was the person of the moment. The birthday girl. The center. The girls in my class were wearing yellow-piqué graduation dresses, and Momma (my grandmother) smocked the yoke on mine into tiny crisscrossing puckers; then shirred the rest of the bodice. I was going to be lovely, and it didn't worry me that I was only twelve years old and merely an eighth-grader graduating from grammar school.

My academic work had won me a top place, and I was going to be one of the first called in the graduating ceremonies. But Henry Reed, a small boy with hooded eyes, was class valedictorian. Each term he and I had vied for the best grades. Most often he bested me, but instead of being disappointed I was pleased that we shared top places between us. He was courteous to elders, but on the playground he chose to play the roughest games. I admired him. Anyone, I reckoned, sufficiently able to operate at a top level with both adults and children was admirable.

The weeks until graduation were filled with heady activities. A group of small children were to be presented in a play about buttercups and daisies and bunny rabbits. They could be heard throughout the building practicing their hops and their little songs. The older girls were assigned the task of making refreshments for the night's festivities. A tangy scent of ginger, cinnamon, nutmeg, and chocolate wafted around the home-economics building. In the workshop, axes and saws split timber as the woodshop boys made sets and stage scenery.

When the great day finally dawned, I sprang out of bed and threw open the back door to see it more clearly. Sunlight was itself still young, and the day had none of the insistence maturity would bring it in a few hours. In my robe and barefoot in the backyard, I gave myself up to the gentle warmth and thanked God that no matter what evil I had done in my life he had allowed me to live to see this day.

My older brother, Bailey, came out and gave me a box wrapped in Christmas paper. He said he had saved his money for months to pay for it. It was a soft-leather-bound copy of a collection of poems by Edgar Allan Poe. I turned to "Annabel Lee" and we walked up and down the garden rows, the cool dirt between our toes, reciting the beautifully sad lines.

Momma made a Sunday breakfast although it was only Friday. After we finished the blessing, I opened my eyes to find a Mickey Mouse watch on my plate. It was a dream of a day. Everything went smoothly. Near evening I put on my dress. It fit perfectly, and everyone said that I looked like a sunbeam in it.

In front of the school, I joined my fellow "greats," the graduating class. Hair brushed back, legs oiled, new dresses and pants pressed to a military slickness, fresh pocket handkerchiefs and little handbags, all home-sewn. Oh we were up to snuff, all right.

The school band struck up a march, and all classes filed in to the crowded auditorium as had been rehearsed. We stood in front of our assigned seats and sang the national anthem, after which we recited the Pledge of Allegiance.

We remained standing to sing the song every black person I knew called the "Negro National Anthem." But suddenly the choir director and the principal signaled to us, rather desperately I thought, to take our seats. As we fumbled for our chairs, I was overcome with a presentiment of worse things to come.

The principal welcomed "parents and friends" and asked the Baptist minister to lead us in prayer. When the principal came back to the dais, his voice had changed. He said a few vague things about the friendship of kindly people to those less fortunate than themselves. With that his voice nearly faded away. But he cleared his throat and said, "Our speaker tonight came from Texarkana to deliver the commencement address, but due to the irregularity of the train schedule, he's going to, as they say, 'speak and run.' I give you Mr. Edward Donleavy."

Not one but two white men came through the door offstage. The shorter one walked to the speaker's platform, and the tall one, who was never introduced, moved over to the center seat—our principal's seat—and sat down. The principal bounced around for a long breath or two. Finally, the Baptist minister gave him his chair and with more dignity than the situation deserved, walked off the stage.

Donleavy told us of the wonderful changes we children in Stamps had in store. The Central School (naturally, the white school was Central) had a well-known artist coming from Little Rock to teach art to them. They were going to have the newest microscopes and chemistry equipment for their laboratory. Mr. Donleavy didn't leave us long in the dark over who made these improvements available to Central High. Nor were we to be ignored in the general betterment scheme he had in mind.

He said he had pointed out to people at a very high level that one of the first-line football tacklers at Arkansas Agricultural, Mechanical, and Normal College had graduated from good old Lafayette County Training School. He went on to say how he had bragged that "one of the best basketball players at Fisk University sank his first ball at Lafayette County Training School."

So that was it. The white kids were going to have a chance to become Galileos and Madame Curies and Edisons and Gauguins, and our boys (the girls weren't even in on it) would try to be Jesse Owenses and Joe Louises. Owens and the Brown Bomber were great heroes in our world, but what school official in the white-goddom of Little Rock had the right to decide that those two men must be our only heroes? Who decided that for Henry Reed to become a scientist he had to work, like George Washington Carver, a bootblack, to buy a lousy microscope?

Donleavy was running for election, and assured our parents that if he won we could count on having the only paved playing field for coloreds in that part of Arkansas. Also, we were bound to get some new equipment for the home-economics building and the workshop.

The man's dead words fell like bricks around the auditorium. To my left and right the proud graduating class of 1940 had dropped their heads. Every girl in my row had found something new to do with her handkerchief. Some folded the tiny squares into love knots, some into triangles, but most were wadding them. And then pressing them flat on their yellow laps.

On the dais, our principal sat rigid, a sculptor's reject. His large, heavy body seemed devoid of will or willingness, and his eyes said he was no longer with us.

Graduation, the hush-hush magic time of frills and gifts and congratulations and diplomas, was finished for me before my name was called. My accomplishment was nothing. The meticulous maps, drawn in three colors of ink, learning and spelling decasyllabic words, memorizing the whole of "The

Rape of Lucrece"—it was for nothing. Donleavy had exposed us. We were maids and farmers, handymen and washerwomen, and anything higher that we aspired to was farcical and presumptuous.

There was rustling around me, and then Henry Reed was giving his valedictory address, "To Be or Not to Be." The English teacher had helped him to create a sermon winging through Hamlet's soliloquy. To be a man, a doer, a builder, a leader, or to be a tool, an unfunny joke, a crusher of funky toadstools. I marveled that Henry could go through with the speech, as if we had a choice.

I had been listening and silently rebutting each sentence with my eyes closed; then there was a hush. I looked up and saw Henry turn his back to the audience and turn to us, the proud graduating class of 1940, and sing, nearly speaking.

> "Lift ev'ry voice and sing
> Till earth and heaven ring
> Ring with the harmonies of
> Liberty . . ."

It was the Negro National Anthem. Out of habit we of the graduating class began singing too. Our parents stood and joined the hymn of encouragement. Then the small children chimed in, the buttercups and daisies and bunny rabbits.

> "Stony the road we trod
> Bitter the chastening rod
> Felt in the days when hope, unborn, had died.
> Yet with a steady beat
> Have not our weary feet
> Come to the place for which our fathers sighed?"

Every child I knew had learned that song with his ABCs. But I personally had never heard the words, despite the thousands of times I had sung them. Never thought they had anything to do with me. And now I heard, really for the first time:

> "We have come over a way that
> With tears has been watered,

We have come, treading our path
Through the blood of the slaughtered. "

While echoes of the song shivered in the air, Henry Reed returned to his place in the line. The tears that slipped down many faces were not wiped away in shame.

We were on top again. As always, again. We had survived. The depths had been icy and dark, but now a bright sun spoke to our souls.

Following that and other graduation days, Dr. Angelou went on to teach modern dance in Israel and Italy, to appear in *Porgy and Bess* on a twenty-two-nation tour, and to direct the play *Moon on a Rainbow* in London. She became a magazine editor in Egypt and an administrator at the University of Ghana's School of Music. Fluent in six languages, she conducted an occasional orchestra and starred in Alex Haley's television drama *Roots*. Her writings produced a Pulitzer Prize nomination, while her Broadway debut earned a Tony Award nomination.

Certainly these and Maya's many other accomplishments can be attributed in part to the inspiration she received from the graduation day's Negro anthem that recalled to her how her ancestors had traveled along their stony roads to achieve their dreams. The lyrics ignited an unconquerable determination in Maya to take responsibility for her life and find success in her everyday pursuits—in spite of what circumstances and Mr. Donleavy would send her way. The key is in our decisions, not our conditions.

Anyone who has ever witnessed film star Chuck Norris's action-packed martial arts skills has seen the very model of a person who takes life into his own hands. But by his own admission, in his youth he was not always so bold—at least not until he began to pack groceries.

Create Your Own Breaks

Chuck Norris

I was sixteen and found a job packing groceries at a Boys Market in Gardena, a Los Angeles suburb. It was the 1950s, and in those days grocery stores used boxes for the heavier items.

I thought everything was fine, until the end of the first day, when the manager told me not to return. I wasn't sacking fast enough.

I was a painfully shy kid, and I surprised even myself when I blurted out, "Let me come back tomorrow and try one more time. I know I'll do better!" Speaking up went against my very nature, but it worked. I got a second chance, moved a lot faster, and for the next year and a half boxed groceries from four to ten on weekdays for $1.25 an hour and sometimes all day on Saturday or Sunday.

That moment when I spoke up is burned in my memory, and so is the lesson: If you want to accomplish anything in life, you can't just sit back and hope it will happen. You've got to make it happen.

I was not a natural athlete when I began studying karate, but I trained harder than anyone else and was a world middleweight karate champion for six years. Later, when I decided to become an actor, I was thirty-six and had no experience. There were maybe sixteen thousand unemployed actors in Hollywood, and I'd be competing against guys who had already been in movies or on TV. If I had said, "I don't stand a chance," one thing is clear: I wouldn't have.

People whine, "I haven't succeeded because I haven't had the breaks." You create your own breaks.

Undeniably, the day-to-day circumstances we encounter influence the opportunities that come our way. But in the final analysis, as Chuck Norris pointed out, we create our own breaks as we take responsibility for our life—and that includes working hard and speaking up for ourselves.

~

WRAP UP

In the years that I have been consulting with organizations and making presentations in front of audiences, no topic has stimulated more interest or more discussion than that of taking responsibility for your life. It's the notion that despite what happens to us, we have the capacity to choose our responses — our attitudes, thoughts, and actions. It's the concept that suggests that on the climb up any ladder of success there is no room for just sitting back and idly hoping for luck or woefully waiting for better circumstances. The best way to predict our futures is to create them. As such, the principle of responsibility is one of the most powerful, life enhancing, life changing principles we have at our disposal if we just learn how to master and channel it toward worthwhile purposes.

REFLECTIONS

- It gave Betty Ford no advantage to blame others for her problems or make excuses. Do you ever catch yourself blaming your problems or limitations on others, genetics, or your environment?

- Maya Angelou did not allow adverse circumstances to dictate her life and attitudes. Do you let circumstances drive what you do in life, or do you create your own circumstances?

- Chuck Norris showed initiative and created his own break by standing up for himself and promising to do better. What level of initiative do you demonstrate when times are tough?

FURTHER INSIGHTS ON
Responsibility

~

TAKING THE REINS

The more we accept responsibility for who we are and who we can become, the greater will be our progress and contribution.

I don't believe for a minute that everything that happens to you is your doing or your fault. But I do believe the ultimate quality of your life and your happiness is determined by your courageous and ethical choices and your overall attitude. You may get shipped some bad bricks and weak steel, but you are still the general contractor.

—LAURA SCHLESSINGER,
HOW COULD YOU DO THAT?

■ ■ ■

The tragic truth is that the language of "victimization" is the true victimizer—a great crippler of young minds and spirits. To teach young people that their lives are governed—not by their own actions, but by socioeconomic forces or government budgets or other mysterious and fiendish forces beyond their control—is to teach our children negativism, resignation, passivity, and despair.

—LOUIS W. SULLIVAN

■ ■ ■

I call it the New Obscenity. It's not a four-letter word, but an oft-repeated statement that strikes at the very core of our humanity. The four words are: "I can't help myself."

This philosophy sees man as an organism being acted upon by biological and social forces, rather than as an agent with a free will. It views offenders not as sinful or criminal but as "sick." By ignoring the idea that people face temptations that can—and should—be resisted, it denies the very quality that separates us from the animals.

—WILLIAM LEE WILBANKS, PROFESSOR OF LAW,
VITAL SPEECHES OF THE DAY

STOPPING THE BLAME GAME

When problems arise, the easy route is to play the blame game or make excuses. But the most successful people avoid scapegoating, choosing instead to accept responsibility when the responsibility is theirs to own.

People are always blaming their circumstances for what they are. I do not believe in circumstances. The people who get on in this world are the people who get up and look for the circumstances they want, and if they cannot find them, make them.

—GEORGE BERNARD SHAW

▦ ▦ ▦

The only thing blame does is to keep the focus off you when you are looking for external reasons to explain your unhappiness or frustration. You may succeed in making another feel guilty of something by blaming him, but you won't succeed in changing whatever it is about you that is making you unhappy.

—WAYNE W. DYER,
YOUR ERRONEOUS ZONES

▦ ▦ ▦

The fault is not in our stars, but in ourselves.

—SHAKESPEARE

▦ ▦ ▦

Only the weak blame parents, their race, their times, lack of good fortune, or the quirks of fate. Everyone has it within his power to say, This I am today; that I will be tomorrow.

—LOUIS L'AMOUR,
THE WALKING DRUM

▦ ▦ ▦

He who cannot dance puts the blame on the floor.

—HINDI PROVERB

▦ ▦ ▦

The search for a scapegoat is the easiest of all hunting expeditions.

— DWIGHT D. EISENHOWER

HAPPINESS IS AN INSIDE JOB

Happiness in life comes from the inside. It does us little
good to sit back and wait for it to come from outside sources.

Happiness doesn't depend on outward conditions. It depends on inner
conditions.

—DALE CARNEGIE,
HOW TO WIN FRIENDS AND INFLUENCE PEOPLE

■ ■ ■

Many popular songs on the radio carry the message "You make me happy; I
would be lost without you; you are my world." This way of thinking takes
away all the responsibility to make yourself happy and gives it to someone
else. That is an enormous amount of pressure to put on another person.

—RICHARD AND KRISTINE CARLSON,
DON'T SWEAT THE SMALL STUFF IN LOVE

■ ■ ■

On starting out a gloomy day: First you must realize that it is the day that is
gloomy, not you. If you want to be gloomy, too, that's all right, but it's not
mandatory.

—NORA GALLAGHER

■ ■ ■

If we make up our minds that this is a drab and purposeless universe,
it will be that, and nothing else. On the other hand, if we believe that the
world is ours, and that the sun and the moon hang in the sky for our delight,
there will be joy because the Artist in our souls glorifies creation.

—HELEN KELLER,
PERSONALITY

■ ■ ■

Though we travel the world over to find the beautiful, we must carry it with
us or we find it not.

—RALPH WALDO EMERSON

A MATTER OF ATTITUDE

Our willingness to take responsibility and to exhibit initiative depends on our thoughts and attitudes.

We who have lived in concentration camps can remember the men who walked through the huts comforting others, giving away their last piece of bread. They may have been few in number, but they offer sufficient proof that everything can be taken from man but one thing: the last of the human freedoms—to choose one's attitude in any given set of circumstances—to choose one's own way.

—VIKTOR FRANKL,
MAN'S SEARCH FOR MEANING

■ ■ ■

Good thoughts bear good fruit, bad thoughts bear bad fruit—and man is his own gardener.

—JAMES ALLEN

■ ■ ■

The greatest discovery of my generation is that a human being can alter his life by altering his attitude.

—WILLIAM JAMES

■ ■ ■

The unconscious is a great dynamo, but it is also a computer that has to be properly programmed. If fear thoughts, worry thoughts, failure thoughts are constantly channeled into the unconscious, nothing very constructive is going to be sent back. But if a clear, purposeful goal is steadfastly held in the conscious mind, the unconscious will eventually accept it and begin to supply the conscious mind with plans, ideas, insights, and the energies necessary to achieve that goal.

—NORMAN VINCENT PEALE

■ ■ ■

When it comes to staying young, a mind-lift beats a face-lift any day.

—MARTY BUCELLA

PREPARING FOR LUCK

Occasionally opportunity is thrust upon us or luck bounces in our direction. But most often opportunity and luck come only after a steady dose of preparation.

Luck is a matter of preparation meeting opportunity.

—OPRAH WINFREY

■ ■ ■

Chance favors the prepared mind.

—LOUIS PASTEUR

■ ■ ■

I was once asked if there were such a thing as luck in trial law. "Yes," I replied, "but it only comes in the library at three o'clock in the morning." That holds true for me to this day. You'll still find me in the library looking for luck at three o'clock in the morning."

— LOUIS NIZER,
ATTORNEY AND AUTHOR
AT THE AGE OF 82

■ ■ ■

No man ever was wise by chance.

—SENECA

■ ■ ■

Nowadays some people expect the door of opportunity to be opened with a remote control.

—M. CHARLES WHEELER

■ ■ ■

When I was 15, I had lucky underwear. When that failed, I had a lucky hairdo, then a lucky race number, even lucky race days. After 15 years, I've found the secret to success is simple. It's hard work.

—MARGARET GROOS,
MARATHON RUNNER,
RUNNER'S WORLD

TAKING ACTION

As Maya Angelou learned on graduation day, you cannot wait upon the world for success. You must take action, go out and hunt it down, exhibiting initiative every step of the way.

Duty is a very personal thing. It is what comes from knowing the need to take action and not just a need to urge others to do something.

—MOTHER TERESA

■ ■ ■

I don't wait for moods. You accomplish nothing if you do that. Your mind must know it has got to get down to work.

—PEARL S. BUCK

■ ■ ■

People say to me: "You're a roaring success. How did you do it?" I go back to what my parents taught me. Apply yourself. Get all the education you can, but then, by God, do something! Don't just stand there, make something happen.

—LEE IACOCCA,
IACOCCA

■ ■ ■

If you want to leave footprints in the sands of time, don't drag your feet.

—ARNOT L. SHEPPARD

■ ■ ■

Success isn't a result of spontaneous combustion. You must set yourself on fire.

—ARNOLD H. GLASOW

■ ■ ■

A man would have to keep his mouth open a long, long time before a roasted pheasant flies into it.

—IRISH PROVERB

■ ■ ■

The times are bad. Very well, you are there to make them better.

—THOMAS CARLYLE

■ ■ ■

If your ship doesn't come in, swim out to it!

—JONATHAN WINTERS

■ ■ ■

To reach the port of heaven, we must sail sometimes with the wind and sometimes against it—but we must sail, and not drift, nor lie at anchor.

—OLIVER WENDELL HOLMES
THE AUTOCRAT OF THE BREAKFAST TABLE

■ ■ ■

God gives every bird his worm, but he does not throw it into the nest.

—SWEDISH PROVERB

5

COURAGE

Courage is being scared to death—and saddling up anyway.
—JOHN WAYNE

Those familiar with actor John Wayne can imagine the steel in his eyes, the swagger in his stance, and the drawl in his voice as he made the statement above. While saddling up in the face of fear required John Wayne to step up, courage most often requires us to step out—out from our comfort zones, out from our doubts, and out into uncharted waters.

Courage is not the absence of fear, but the awareness that something else is more important. Courage can be displayed in heroic, visible ways, or in quiet, private battles we fight when attempting to conquer inner fears. These different ranges of courage are displayed in the following three accounts. Luba Gercak's courage is heroic in nature as she stands up to her Nazi captors to protect children. Lee Maynard's courage is less intense as he learns from his mother not to run from his fears. And Reba McEntire's is even more subtle as she develops the self-confidence to be herself. As you read these accounts, consider how much courage you display daily in overcoming personal doubts and fears, and how strong you are in standing by your principles.

A HEROINE IN HELL

Lawrence Elliott

A ragged band of children stood in an open area in the Bergen-Belsen concentration camp, shivering in the wind. It was the first week of December 1944, and these few dozen Jewish waifs from Holland, having managed to survive four and a half years of war and many months of imprisonment, were now desperately alone.

They had watched mutely as their fathers and older brothers were loaded aboard a convoy of SS trucks and driven away. No one said where they were going, but some had heard the whispered names of the death camps: Auschwitz, Treblinka, Chelmno.

After the men had disappeared, the trucks came for the mothers and older sisters. After they had been taken away, the children were driven to the women's compound, where they were ordered off the trucks. As the trucks took off, eleven-year-old Gerard Lakmaker discovered that his last few belongings, wrapped in a yellow blanket, were gone.

Now huddling together in the black emptiness, the older children tried to comfort the crying babies.

In the darkness of a nearby barrack, a woman named Luba Gercak shook her neighbor awake. "Do you hear that? That child crying?"

"There's nothing," was the reply. "You're having bad dreams again." Luba clamped her eyes tight, trying to shut away terrible memories.

She had grown up in a *shtetl*, a Jewish community in Poland. Still in her teens, she married a cabinet maker, Hersch Gercak, and they were blessed with a son, Isaac. They looked forward to more children and a calm life. But then war broke out, and they were stuck into its deadly undertow. Nazis loaded what seemed like all of the region's Jews onto horse-drawn wagons for a nightmare trek to Auschwitz-Birkenau, the most murderous concentration camp in the German system.

As Luba entered its gates, she held Isaac tightly in her arms. But within minutes SS guards tore the three-year-old away. His cries rang in her ears "Mama! Mama!" as they threw him up on a truck with others too young or too old to work. Soon the truck rolled away to the gas chamber. Blurred black days followed and then came the moment she saw a truck dragging the lifeless body of her husband. She felt that she didn't want to live.

But an inner toughness would not let Luba give in. Maybe God had some purpose for her. Her scalp shaven, the number 32967 tattooed on her arm, she talked her way into a job working in the Auschwitz hospital, a building where the sick were left to die.

Endless days and phantom-filled nights passed. Luba learned German and kept an ear to the ground. One day she heard that nurses were being sent to a camp in Germany. Luba volunteered to go. In December of 1944 she was sent to Bergen-Belsen. There were no gas chambers at this camp, but malnutrition, disease, and summary execution made it a gruesomely efficient extermination center.

With the Allied forces closing in and order breaking down, already wretched conditions had worsened. Endless transports brought ever more starving souls to be jammed into jerry-built, vermin-infested barracks.

Tossing restlessly, Luba again heard the sounds of a crying child. This time, she bounded for the door, then stopped, dumbfounded by the spectacle of a rabble of terrified, shivering children. Luba beckoned them to come closer, and a few cautiously approached her.

"What happened?" she whispered. "Who left you here?"

In halting German, an older boy named Jack Rodri explained that SS guards had brought them there without telling them where they were going. The oldest of the fifty-four children, Hetty Werkendam, was fourteen. She was holding Stella Degen, two and a half. Others were even younger. Taking Jack by the hand, Luba gestured for the rest to follow.

Some of the women tried to stop her from bringing the children into the barracks. They knew how little it took to provoke the SS to get a bullet in the back of the head.

But Luba was driven—certain that this was meant to be. She shamed the women by asking, "If this were your children, would you tell me to turn them away? Listen to me, they're somebody's children." And she led the ragged band inside.

In the morning Jack Rodri told Luba their story. Initially, they had been spared the worst of the Nazi atrocities because their fathers made up the backbone of Amsterdam's diamond industry, and the Germans needed their skills in diamond cutting. The cutters and their families were sent to Bergen-Belsen. There the parents were eventually taken from the children who were abandoned where Luba found them.

Luba's heart soared in gratitude to God for bringing the children to her. He had given meaning to her life again. Her son had been murdered, but she was going to save these children from that fate.

Knowing she could not hide dozens of children, she told an SS officer at the camp what had happened. "Let me take care of them," she said, putting a hand on his arm. "They will never be a problem. I promise."

"You're a nurse, what do you want with this Jewish trash?" he replied.

"Because I am a mother too," she said. "Because I lost my own child in Auschwitz."

Taking this in, the SS officer suddenly realized that her hand was still on his arm. Prisoners did not touch Germans. He struck her full in the face with his fist, knocking her to the ground.

Luba got up, her lip bleeding. But she did not back away. "You're old enough to be a grandfather," she said. "Why do you want to harm innocent children? Babies? They will all die without someone to look after them."

Maybe he was moved. Or maybe he just didn't want to decide what to do with all these children. "Keep them," he muttered. "To hell with them."

But Luba wasn't finished. "They need something to eat. Let me get some bread." He gave her a note authorizing two loaves.

Food became the focus of each day, an unending anxiety. The stipulated ration, one slice of dark bread and half a bowl of thin soup, barely warded off starvation. So every morning Luba set off on her rounds—the storehouse, the kitchen, the bakery—and begged, bartered, and stole food. The children crowded to the door when they saw her in the distance. "She's coming! And she has food for us!"

They cherished her as they had their own lost mothers, for it was Luba who scavenged necessities, nursed them when they fell ill, and sang lullabies through their long, dark nights. The Dutch-speaking children didn't understand her words. But they understood her love.

Weeks and months marched by. Bergen-Belsen's inmates knew the Allies were closing in. And as the awful winter inched toward the spring of 1945, the Germans tried to dispose of the corpses that littered the camp. But it was a losing battle. Dysentery spread, leaving the children dehydrated, limp with exhaustion, and vulnerable to the raging fever and headaches of Typhus.

In a nearby barrack another child from Amsterdam, Anne Frank, succumbed. In their own barracks, a number of Luba's children fell ill. She went from child to child, feeding those who could eat, touching their foreheads with her lips to gauge their temperatures and doling out precious aspirins to the sickest. She prayed for a miracle to save them.

It came on Sunday, April 15, 1945, when a British tank column rolled into Bergen-Belsen. Loudspeakers boomed "You are free! You are free!" in a half a dozen languages.

The Allies brought medicine and doctors, but it was too late for many. There were thousands of corpses lying unburied in the camp and of the other sixty thousand inmates, nearly a quarter died after liberation.

But fifty-two of Luba's children, all but two of the group she had found eighteen weeks before, lived. When they were strong enough to travel, a British military plane took them home. Luba was also on board, looking after them on the way. A Dutch official later wrote: "It is thanks to her that these children survived. As Dutchmen, we owe her much for what she has done."

Temporary shelter was found for the children while they awaited reunion with their mothers, nearly all of whom survived. At the request of the International Red Cross, Luba then accompanied forty war-orphaned children from numerous other camps to Sweden, where they would begin new lives.

Luba began a new life too. In Sweden she met Sol Frederick, another Holocaust survivor. They married and moved to the United States, where they had two children. But Luba never forgot the others.

Wherever they settled, almost all of Luba's "children" blossomed. Jack Rodri made his way eventually to Los Angeles, where he became a successful businessman. Hetty Werkendam went into real estate in Australia and was voted the country's most successful immigrant. Gerard Lakmaker prospered as a manufacturer. Stella Degen-Fertig had no recollection of Bergen-Belsen. But as she grew up, her mother told her how much she owed to a woman named Luba—Stella wondered where her protector was.

Others decided to seek Luba. Jack Rodri managed to talk his way on to TV to tell Luba's story. "If anybody knows where she is," Jack pleaded, "please call this station."

"I do," said a caller from Washington, D.C. "She lives here in the city."

Jack called Luba on the spot. Within the week he was standing in her apartment and holding Luba in his arms. Both wept unashamedly.

Some time later, Gerard Lakmaker, who lived in London, set about organizing a tribute to Luba. The handful who were already in touch began an assiduous search for the others.

On a shining April afternoon in 1995, on the fiftieth anniversary of their liberation, some thirty men and women, nearly all of whom had last seen one another as children, gathered in the Amsterdam city hall to honor Luba.

His voice charged with emotion, the deputy lord mayor, on behalf of Queen Beatrix, bestowed on Luba the Netherlands' Silver Medal of Honor for Humanitarian Services. Luba was shaken.

After the ceremony Stella Degen-Fertig approached. "I have thought of you all my life," Stella said, struggling to keep her voice steady. "My mother always told me that she had given birth to me, but that I owed my life to a woman named Luba. She said that I was never to forget it." Crying freely, she took Luba into her arms and whispered, "I never will."

Luba clung to her and looked at the others through misty eyes. For this was her real reward: to be with "her children," to know again the love that saved them—and her—from the shadow of the death camps.

While Luba saw fear in the eyes of the children the night she met them, the children found a source of hope and refuge in her courageous eyes. For Luba knew what values and principles she stood for and had the boldness to hold fast to them even at the risk of her life.

———————

While occasionally courage is displayed in life-threatening situations, more often it arises in the much smaller occurrences of our everyday lives. But even then it is up to us to determine if we will run away from our fears or have the courage to run to something that is better.

THE RUNAWAY

Lee Maynard

I get off the airplane and rush through wet, drab streets to the hospital, and now I sit by my mother's bed in the big white room. Her gray hair is neatly combed. Her eyes are closed, but now and then I see a tiny movement there, as though secret things are going on in her mind. I watch her breathe softly, thinly. I wonder if my mother knows I am here. I wonder if my mother knows I am her son.

There is much to say, and no one to say it to. I have waited far too long. And so I wait, again.

Her shoulder twitches and I take her hand, press my face against her arm, breathe in the scent that says, even after all these years, she is my mother. In my hand, I feel her fingers move.

I reach under the front of my parka and touch the old, flat brown button that is sewn on the inside, just above my heart. The button has been sewn inside every parka I have ever owned. I can see the day I got the button, as though it were yesterday.

We live deep within Appalachia, a small family just surviving. My father works two jobs and has to travel into the next county.

I am a child filled with little knowledge and a vivid imagination, and I feel that I do not belong here. At every opportunity I run away. But there is nowhere to run to—only into the brooding hills or down along the muddy river. But that does not stop me. And I ran away again.

This time, I ran to the woods because of some imagined slight. My ingenuous, rigid sense of right and wrong made me do it. I would show her. I'd make her sorry.

But now I am cold and hungry, so I come crashing down out of the woods and run, stumbling, through the chill evening light to the ramshackle clapboard house on the riverbank—but she is gone.

Mothers are supposed to be there.

I charge through the small rooms. There is no fire in the stove; the house is chilled. I run outside, circle the house, my feet thumping on the hard-packed clay. Stiff little tines of brush whip my face as I head along the riverbank to a neighbor's house a quarter mile away.

"No, boy, your ma's not here. Come by when it was full light, left your sister here. Said . . . well, didn't say much that I can recall. Just left your sister here. Run off in a hurry, like."

Run off? Why? How could she do that to me?

Maybe she has wanted to run away for a long time. What is she doing in our clan, anyway? What is she doing out here in this place, where there is no piano to play, where no one sings, where no one can hear the lilt of her voice? And why did she leave me here alone?

Wandering back to the river, I sit on the bank and throw clods of dirt into the water and the willows. And then I see, dangling from one of the willows, my mother's ragged coat.

I crash down through the cane stubble to the coat. And the thought hits me like lightning: *She has run off. Gone across the river into Kentucky.*

Sweeping willow branches aside, I storm out into the river yelling, "Momma!" Yelling until my voice grows hoarse. Exhausted, I climb up the slimy bank and find the coat again—that ragged sign of her abandonment. And I start to tear it to shreds, flailing it against the brush and stomping it into the earth. A large, flat, brown button rips off in my hand. Finally I fling the coat into the river.

I don't want to go inside the house. So I find a tattered horse blanket in the shed and sit wrapped against the cold, wet darkness—trying to melt the ice that plugs my heart.

I am still waiting there in the morning when the bleak light seeps over the ridge into the valley, and my mother comes down the dirt lane toward the house. She walks with the grace that none of us will ever have, light glistening in her red hair, a shawl around her shoulders.

When she sees me, she says nothing. I can tell she is angry with me for running away yesterday.

After the stove is fired and the house is warming, I slink into the kitchen and sit on the woodbox in the corner. She is talking, as though to herself, but I know she is talking to me. "An upriver neighbor lady was ill," she says. She went to help.

"But I seed your coat down on the riverbank."

"You saw my coat. I gave it to the neighbor girl. I have a shawl, and she didn't have a coat. You know she isn't quite . . . right. I expect she never even got home with it."

Mother looks at me and knows what I have been thinking: that she ran away.

"Strong people don't run away from," she says. "That isn't the way to live your life. But strong people can run away to. If there's something that's better."

She feeds me breakfast: biscuits and bacon and hand-churned butter, and I know that I am forgiven. I never tell her what I did to her coat.

Years tumble and fall. And I am sitting in the big white room, holding my mother's hand. I finger the old flat button inside my parka. In the thousand times of my life when I have wanted to run away from, I have felt the button. And I have changed my direction.

I squeeze the button, and I know that wherever she's running, she is running to . . .

Having a deeper yes burning inside us gives us the courage not to run away from our fears but rather to run away to "something better," including our dreams and the principles we stand for.

———————

One of the most subtle, yet challenging, forms of courage is self-confidence. In fact, many people wage civil wars within themselves, fighting to feel proud of who they are. Country music star Reba McEntire fought such a battle until she created a style of her own.

A STYLE OF MY OWN

Reba McEntire, as told to Alanna Nash

On September 17, 1977, I was standing in the wings of the Grand Ole Opry in Nashville, about to sing two songs in my first appearance at the mother church of country music. I was twenty-two and had dreamed of being a star ever since first grade back in Kiowa, Oklahoma. Growing up on my family's cattle ranch, I'd competed in rodeos and sang in a trio with my older brother Pake and my little sister Susie. It seemed like every day had brought me one step closer to this moment.

I was wearing a patchwork skirt, a denim shirt, and a handkerchief around my neck. And though I was nervous as a thin-skinned calf on branding day, I was ready. Then a man walked up to me and said, "Reba, we're going to have to cut you down to one song."

I asked, "Why?"

And he said, "Well, Dolly's just made a surprise appearance."

My knees buckled. "Dolly Parton's in the building?" I said. Just then, she came floating by, wearing this beautiful black chiffon pantsuit with rhinestone butterflies on it and her hair all big. Man, she was just what a star ought to be. After that, I didn't care if I sang or not. I'd just seen Dolly Parton in the flesh.

Dolly wasn't just the reigning queen of Nashville—she was my hero. I've been a fan since I first heard her on *The Porter Wagoner Show* back in 1967. So many of the songs she'd written—"Coat of Many Colors," "My Blue Ridge Mountain Boy," and "Gypsy, Joe, and Me"—brought back so many childhood memories. When I went to basketball camp and entertained the kids, I sang those songs.

They say that imitation is the highest form of flattery, and, boy, I was shameless with Dolly. I studied her. She can get real soft and very emotional, then louder to prove her point. I tried to imitate her trills. And the way she played the guitar! Dolly was also a businesswoman who branched out into movies and television. Looking back, I see she was a model for me even there.

She was a strong woman who'd had a rough childhood in East Tennessee. Her family was poor, but she was always striving to overcome hardships and improve her life. She wanted to see just what all she could do if she worked real hard—and I did too.

I guess you could say I lived and breathed Dolly Parton. But sooner or later, I had to break away from copying her and learn to be Reba. That was the hardest thing.

In high school, we had a country-western band, and Mama would get after me. She'd say, "Reba, there's only one Dolly Parton. You've got to find your own style of singing. Dolly would be the first to tell you that."

Momma was right. You can still hear a lot of Dolly on my first records, but I worked hard to get her sound out of my voice. It was impossible to get her entirely out of my thoughts, though—especially when it came to the way I dressed. I'd always heard Dolly say she wanted stuff that was shiny, so I wanted shiny stuff too. I even hired her designer, Tony Chase, to create clothes for me. He made me dresses that were all rhinestones and sequins, beaded from top to bottom. And guess what? It didn't work. It just wasn't me. Like my mama told me, Dolly wouldn't have worn something she wasn't comfortable in either.

When it comes down to it, I guess I'm a lot more like Annie Oakley than Dolly, and it took some time, and a lot of trial and error, to realize how to dress like my own self.

For years, I had people telling me what to wear. I would go with what they said, but when I walk out in front of somebody, if I'm not comfortable, I'm inhibited. If I put on clothes that I feel sassy and spunky in, the at-ease Reba comes out. Then I'm at my best.

So now I have my own style and know what I like. I like bright colors, nothing that emphasizes my stomach, none of those big bold prints for a skirt and a jacket.

And, still following Dolly a little, I've turned my style into a business—a clothing line called Reba. I worked hard to get the line right, making sure things don't pinch and bind, and, yes, I would wear everything in it. I don't want to be performing one day and feel like I want to cringe when somebody in the front row stands up and says, "Hey, I'm wearing Reba."

But back to Dolly. She can be a real cutup; the first time I called her on the phone, she answered and said, "Is this really Reba McEntire or some squirrel who thinks she's Reba McEntire?" Well, I am the real Reba. Even if it took me a little while, I finally know who Reba is. Just between us, though, I'm also still Dolly's biggest fan.

When asked what she would do if her superstar status suddenly disappeared, Reba's idol, Dolly Parton, said: "I would always have applause and attention. If I had a club, I'd be Miss Kitty, or if I were a cafe waitress, I would be Flo. I would be the one stirring up the most commotion. I would make people happy by giving of myself. I'd be making cookies and presents. I'd make people laugh. I might start at the bottom, but I'd be running things soon if I wanted to." Dolly unmistakably possesses the form of courage we call self-confidence. And by developing a style of her own, Reba was able to come out of Dolly's shadows and fashion her own unshakable self-confidence.

~

WRAP UP

Whether facing large, life-threatening choices such as those encountered by Luba or facing the more common small occurrences that rattle our everyday tranquility, we too must be willing to step out of our comfort zones and step up to our convictions through dignified acts of courage. Such attempts to develop courage and self-confidence are daily journeys that everyone makes—a life process from which no one is exempt. But as we mature, the trend should be for us to pick up more and more self-confidence as we go, becoming more and more our own selves as opposed to mimics of others. As we do, then we, like Reba, expand our capacity to overcome inner doubts and are at ease with who we are no matter our audience. Again, the key to developing all types and levels of courage is in recognizing that courage is not the absence of fear, but the awareness that something else is more important.

REFLECTIONS

- Think of a specific situation in which you are currently involved that requires courage. If you were to visualize yourself being courageous in that situation, what are some specific words you might use or actions you might see yourself exhibiting?

- What are some of your more common fears? How often do you come up against them? What from Luba's, Lee's, or Reba's example might you learn to overcome such fears?

- The essence of maturity is the ability to balance courage with consideration. Is your courage tempered with good judgment and tact, or do people find your boldness obnoxious?

- It is all too easy to dwell on our weaknesses or use them as sticks to beat down our self-esteem. Do you dwell more on your weaknesses or your strengths, your failures or your successes?

FURTHER INSIGHTS ON
Courage

THE BOLDNESS CONNECTION

Courage is the companion to every other principle of Everyday Greatness. It is a boldness that is found even within our smallest moments.

Courage is not simply one of the virtues, but the form of every virtue at the testing point.

—C. S. LEWIS

Life shrinks or expands in proportion to one's courage.

— *THE DIARY OF ANAÏS NIN*

What you can do, or dream you can, begin it:
Boldness has genius, power and magic in it.

—GOETHE

Courage is the virtue on which all the other virtues mount.

—CLARE BOOTH LUCE

There's a fine line between courage and foolishness. Too bad it's not
a fence.

—JIM FIEBIG

Courage is contagious. When a brave man takes a stand, the spines of others are stiffened.

—THE REV. BILLY GRAHAM

THE RISK OF RISKLESS LIVING

Courage requires accepting a measure of reasonable risk. Think of how many lives would have been left unfulfilled if Luba had not faced risk head on.

Too much caution is bad for you. It is usually wiser to stand up to a scary-seeming experience and walk right into it, risking the bruises or hard knocks. You are likely to find it is not as tough as you had thought. Or you may find it plenty tough, but also discover you have what it takes to handle it.

—NORMAN VINCENT PEALE,
DYNAMIC IMAGING

■ ■ ■

A ship in harbor is safe—but that is not what ships are for.

—JOHN A. SHEDD

■ ■ ■

Far better it is to dare mighty things, to win glorious triumphs, even though checkered by failure, than to take rank with those poor spirits who neither enjoy much nor suffer much, because they live in the gray twilight that knows not victory nor defeat.

—THEODORE ROOSEVELT

■ ■ ■

By embracing risk, you will accomplish more than you ever thought you could. In the process you will transform your life into an exciting adventure that will constantly challenge, reward and rejuvenate you.

—ROBERT J. KRIEGEL
AND LOUIS PATLER,
IF IT AIN'T BROKE, BREAK IT

■ ■ ■

Many things are lost for want of asking.

—ENGLISH PROVERB

CONQUERING FEARS

The largest opponent to courage is fear—fear of the unknown,
fear of failure, fear of others. Successful people acknowledge
fears, but work to conquer them.

Of all the liars in the world, sometimes the worst are your own fears.

—RUDYARD KIPLING

■ ■ ■

Courage is about the management of fear, not the absence of fear.

—RUDY GIULIANI

■ ■ ■

I have not ceased being fearful, but I have ceased to let fear control me. I have
accepted fear as a part of life—specifically fear of change and fear of the
unknown; and I have gone ahead despite the pounding in the heart that says;
turn back, turn back, you'll die if you venture too far.

—ERICA JONG,
IN *VOGUE*

■ ■ ■

Don't let the sensation of fear convince you that you're too weak to have
courage. Fear is the opportunity for courage, not proof of cowardice.

—JOHN McCAIN,
WHY COURAGE MATTERS

■ ■ ■

If bravery is a quality which knows not fear, I have never seen a brave man.
All men are frightened. The more intelligent they are, the more they are
frightened. The courageous man is the man who forces himself, in spite of his
fear, to carry on.

—GENERAL GEORGE S. PATTON, JR.

■ ■ ■

We must constantly build dikes of courage to hold back the flood of fear.

—MARTIN LUTHER KING, JR.

Inner Confidence

Often the greatest adversity we face is the opposition that takes place inside of us—our own self doubts.

It isn't always others who enslave us. Sometimes we let circumstances enslave us; sometimes we let routine enslave us: sometimes we let things enslave us: sometimes, with weak wills, we enslave ourselves.

—Richard L. Evans

He who gains a victory over other men is strong, but he who gains a victory over himself is all-powerful.

—Lao-tse

Do not let what you cannot do interfere with what you can do.

—John Wooden

I seldom think about my limitations, and they never make me sad. Perhaps there is just a touch of yearning at times; but it is vague, like a breeze among flowers. The wind passes, and the flowers are content.

—Helen Keller,
Personality

What many of us need most is a good vigorous kick in the seat of the can'ts.

—Ame Babcock

Trust thyself.

—Ralph Waldo Emerson's creed

Some of us have more fears than others, but the one fear we must all guard against is the fear of ourselves.

—JOHN McCAIN,
WHY COURAGE MATTERS

■ ■ ■

Even when I was in the orphanage, when I was roaming the street trying to find enough to eat, even then I thought of myself as the greatest actor in the world. I had to feel the exuberance that comes from utter confidence in yourself. Without it, you go down to defeat.

—CHARLIE CHAPLIN

■ ■ ■

No one can make you feel inferior without your consent.

—ELEANOR ROOSEVELT

6

DISCIPLINE

Life is tons of discipline.
—ROBERT FROST

Taking charge of your life requires discipline. Yes, tons of it. But discipline is neither readily attained nor easily maintained. It demands the mental stamina to overcome empty passions and faulty habits. It also requires the fortitude to resist the pull of so many temptations that otherwise might lure us toward meaningless sideshows. But more than anything, it demands a relentless focus on what matters most.

The following individuals all had destinies they wanted to attain. And by far the most daunting obstacles they faced were internal in the form of opposing choices—choices that in their eyes were lesser in true value, but oh, so tempting. The first vivid example is demonstrated by Joe Paterno in "The Man Who Said No to $1 Million." One of collegiate sport's most accomplished coaches, certainly much of Joe Paterno's success can be attributed to the discipline he requires from his athletes, both on and off the field. But those who know him best know that an even greater portion of his success is to be attributed to the discipline he demands of himself.

THE MAN WHO SAID NO
TO $1 MILLION

Joe Paterno with Bernard Asbell

I remember the day I was forced to decide who I am. All night I lay awake wrestling with my past, trying to make sense of my future. It was December 1972. I had been head football coach at Pennsylvania State University for almost seven years, and I thought I was content.

Then that unexpected phone call had come—an offer to make me a rich man if I left the school I loved. The man on the phone was Bill Sullivan, former president and principal owner of the New England Patriots. "I want to meet with you to talk about coaching my team," he said.

I told Sullivan I'd had other offers and wasn't much interested in the pros. Then he hit me with his package—$1.3 million, plus part ownership of the franchise and a $100,000 bonus for signing.

At Penn State my pay was a grand total of $35,000. The money had always satisfied my family—but Sullivan's offer made me dizzy. In the end, I told my wife, "I have to take the job."

"Joe, whatever you want to do will be fine with me," Sue replied.

I called Sullivan and told him we had a deal. When Sue and I went to bed that evening, I said, "Okay, kid. Tonight you get to sleep with a millionaire."

At 2:00 a.m., Sue was sitting in her rocking chair nursing our baby. I'm sure she thought I was asleep. She had never said she didn't want to go to Boston. But now tears were slipping down her face.

I lay there thinking about the life I was leaving. I saw the school where I had met my wife, the only home our five kids had ever known. I saw the students, the granite statue of our mascot, the Nittany Lion, and my thick-necked, fragile-hearted football players.

What had made me tell Sullivan I'd come? Yes, Boston was a great city. It was a new challenge. But it was . . . the *money*.

Suddenly I knew what it was I had to do, what it was I *wanted* to do.

In the morning, I told Sue, "You went to bed with a millionaire, but you woke up with me. I'm not going." Her first thought she later told me, was *Oh, thank God.*

From the moment of that nighttime revelation, I knew what college football means to me—and what pro football never could mean. I love winning games as much as any coach does, but I know there's something that counts more than victory or defeat. I get to watch my players grow—in their personal discipline, in their educational development, and as human beings. That is a deep, lasting reward that I could never get in pro ball.

Years have passed since that choice in 1972. Many players have come and gone; many championships have been won. Coaching salaries have soared. And today Joe Paterno remains at the helm of the Penn State Nittany Lions doing what he loves the most, helping players succeed both on and off the field. Through it all, not only has he become one of college football's all-time winningest coaches, but he has also always enjoyed one of the highest player graduation rates in college sports. And though several of his players have joined the ranks of professional football, far more have enjoyed successful careers in business, teaching, and the like, all the while giving much of the credit to Joe and the lessons of life he taught them. All this comes as the result of an extraordinary show of discipline to purpose that Joe and Sue exhibited not just in the silence of that moonlit night, but on an everyday basis in the years that followed.

———————

"Trading Places" has a theme similar to the Joe Paterno story. Only this time it is a single mother who faces the dilemma, and instead of being tempted to leave her job for the lure of higher pay, her struggle is whether or not to take a cut in pay and status to pursue a more meaning-filled life.

TRADING PLACES

Sarah Mahoney

The first time I felt the tug to run away from my life I was sitting on a mountaintop with my kids. It was sunny, but windy and cool. Maggie, then nine, and Evan, eight, were chasing each other around, clambering up boulders and rolling in the grass.

Miles away from e-mail and telephones, I felt peaceful in a way I hadn't for years. I felt close to the kids, safe. And I knew what they had had for breakfast, lunch, and dinner for the last eight days.

And then I heard a voice say, *Sarah, are you sure you want the life you lead, if you only get to enjoy your kids like this on holiday once a year?*

It was a thought that came out of the blue. And there were a few problems: like a job, a laptop, a PDA, a cell phone, two phones at home and two at work, a minivan, a 401(k), a college-savings plan, and a one-hour commute.

I quickly regained my senses. Walking away from my job as editor of a large women's magazine was unthinkable. I thrived on the busyness, the invigorating promise of getting a new blank canvas every month—writing headlines and cover lines, plowing through manuscripts, striving to make the same old celebrities sound fascinating.

It was a great job, and leaving it would be career suicide. The practical me said, "You'll never get another job like this one—ever." So I did what grownups are supposed to do: I told the voice, "Pipe down. People like me can't quit."

I shooed the kids down the mountain, and we headed home.

A hectic spring gave way to a busy summer that streaked by with a few trips to the beach, a handful of barbecues, camp for the kids. But it was a lovely summer, and as it stretched into September, normally kvetchy New Yorkers sang happily about the remarkable weather. Early September sparkled, one day more beautiful than the next.

As I jumped into a cab after my karate class on the morning of September 11, I remember thinking that this was the nicest day of all: cool, clear, with a brilliant sky and an easy breeze, like that day on the mountain. I closed my eyes and remembered Evan shouting "Mom!" when he spotted some mountain goats climbing nearby.

"There was an accident at the World Trade Center," the driver told me, turning up the radio. And we listened, along with the rest of the world.

The next morning, I watched my eight-year-old play in his bed, throwing one action figure on top of another into a giant heap. "Whatcha doing?" I asked, still sleepy after watching CNN late into the night and feeling the images of those burning buildings seared into my mind.

"Playing graveyard," he said. I kissed the top of his head, and cried some more. One of my friends from karate class, Capt. Patrick Brown of Ladder Company 3, had surely been called to the Towers.

The kids and I prayed: not something we usually do together. For a few weeks, we left candles burning on our front stoop all night. We talked about peace and war, vengeance and forgiveness, grief and fear.

But the days went by and hope—that some had survived the collapse and could be rescued—ebbed away. Pat, along with half the men in Ladder 3, and so many others were gone.

I, along with everyone else, limped back toward normal. But the tragedy of September 11 changed my kindly little mountaintop counselor voice into something more insistent and assertive.

"What the hell are you doing here?" I muttered to myself one day, in the middle of a magazine meeting. (I hope no one heard.)

As I commuted on the bus, or tried to fall asleep at night, two voices held a debate in my head: *Quit.* "You can't quit," a Career Path voice said. "How will you live? Who will pay for the baby-sitter, the house, the car, the food?"

The Counselor voice replied mildly, "Aren't you a writer—isn't that how come you work in magazines? You did it years ago, and loved it. And then you won't need a sitter."

"Not now," said Career Path. "This is something people do when they're easing toward retirement."

"Of course now," the Counselor answered. "You're running out of time— soon your children will be teenagers, more interested in the mall than in you."

"If not now, when?"

"New York is so expensive."

"So leave. Go to Maine."

"What about Mom, with her advancing Alzheimer's? [I had just placed my mother in an assisted-care facility in New York.] How can you leave her?"

The Counselor answered sadly, "She's leaving you—and there are assisted-care facilities in Maine."

One day in early December—just before my forty-first birthday—I told the kids we were moving. I fessed up to my boss, and called in the real estate agents.

Now I work from home as a full-time writer from a house in a little rural town, not far from Portland, Maine. Just up the road is a beautiful state park, with a small mountain that's covered with evergreens, filled with wild turkey, deer, and the occasional moose.

And any time I want, the kids, the dog and I can climb up to the top, sit on a boulder, look out at the beautiful world, and thank God for being able to hear all my voices.

Like Joe Paterno, Sarah Mahoney first determined what mattered most to her in life, and then she had the discipline to set aside all other temptations so that she would be free to pursue those greater passions.

The two previous stories illustrated discipline in making career choices. But discipline is required in all basic aspects of life, including athletic training, schooling, and even in getting up the stairs each day. And sometimes it helps to have a little help from a friend.

COACHING BRIAN

Peter Michelmore

Gusts of wind whipped across the high school football field that chill spring afternoon. But Charlie Kane buttoned his old military topcoat higher and kept his eyes fixed on the scrawny kid in red shorts running the track. His stride was too long for his size.

"Brian loves to run," the woman standing next to him said. There was just a trace of pleading in Sue Boyett's voice. Divorced for nine years, she was looking for a strong man to coach her eleven-year-old son. A friend had introduced her to Kane. The stocky man in his late fifties with sandy gray hair tied at the nape of his neck didn't look like a coach any more than Brian looked like a natural runner. In fact, he was now a proofreader at a printing plant and hadn't trained a runner in years.

After finishing his laps, Brian sauntered over to his mom, glancing at Kane out of the corner of his eye.

"Your mom says you like running. But do you really want to be coached?" Kane asked.

"Yeah, I guess," Brian said, avoiding his eyes. But Kane wasn't settling for a halfhearted commitment. He kept probing until Brian met his gaze and said, "Yes!"

"Then I'll train you," Kane said.

Charlie Kane was fifty-eight years old that spring afternoon in 1994, and he had lost a sense of purpose. His two older children were out of the house, and his youngest, also named Brian, was about to leave to join the Marines.

Kane had served a hitch himself in the late fifties. His ambition, however, was to be a high school teacher and track coach. Eventually he earned a master's, and put in thirteen years at schools in New Jersey doing what he loved best—teaching young people how to read and how to run.

But after a bitter divorce in the seventies, Kane, given custody of his kids, moved to California to make a fresh start. For two years he was a coach at a junior college. Needing a higher salary, however, he then signed on as an editor of technical manuals. Homesick for the East, Kane eventually returned to New Jersey in 1994 and took a proofreading job. It paid the bills but didn't give him any deep satisfaction. Coaching was what both he and Brian needed.

Yet, perhaps because he was the child of divorce, Brian resisted his new coach.

Soon after they started working together, Brian entered two distance races at a recreational meet in his hometown of Parsippany Hills.

"I want you to go out easy," Kane told him, "slowly pick up speed, then hammer home on the final lap."

When the gun went off in the 800 meters, Brian tore out like it was a sprint. In the last 100 meters he ran out of power and was beaten. Kane was furious. "Are you going to do it my way or yours?" he demanded. Brian didn't answer.

In his next race, the 1600 meters, Brian again charged to the front, but then, either tiring or relenting, he dropped to the rear of the pack. On the last lap, with power in reserve, he overtook the field—and won.

Panting, he trotted over to Kane and announced with a smile on his face, "Your way!"

They met at the track every day after work. Days became months, and then years.

When he was thirteen, Brian won junior cross-country events with fast, finishing kicks. "Hammering it home," is what Kane called it. "Someday," he told the boy, "you'll be a contender for the U.S. Olympic team." To show his pride, Kane presented him a running shirt with bold letters reading "The Hammer."

Brian's self-confidence grew, but Sue still worried that she wasn't doing all she should for her son and daughter, Jennifer, a year older. After her divorce, money was tight. She worked as a bookkeeper for a landscaping company, but for two months each winter the operation closed down and she had to go on unemployment.

Kane wasn't banking much either, so he talked to Sue about his moving in with them and pooling their resources. "You have a deal," said Sue. "You're part of the family anyway."

In January 1997, Kane moved into the Boyetts's basement bedroom. That same year, Brian shot up seven inches and entered high school. Now he looked like a runner—lean, long-muscled, with a smooth, disciplined stride. He was a less proficient student, however.

Freshmen had to read *The Iliad,* but Brian didn't see why. Kane did. One night he was waiting at the kitchen table with a translation of Homer's epic about the Trojan War.

"What's this all about, Coach?" Brian asked.

"It's about life!" said Kane, motioning Brian to sit down.

While Sue and Jennifer made meatloaf, Kane read the ancient verse in his best dramatic voice. Brian listened with amazement, until Kane insisted he try it.

Embarrassed, Brian finally began to read and soon got wrapped up in the story describing heroism, cowardice, loyalty, and deceit.

They kept at it night after night for weeks. Track in the early morning and afternoon, *The Iliad* after dinner. Subtly Kane was coaching Brian about something else—being a man.

The two read the passages in which the Trojan hero Hector meets the stronger Greek warrior Achilles in hand-to-hand combat. At first, knowing that powerful gods favor Achilles, Hector panics and runs. But courage, Kane told Brian, is not being impervious to fear. It's being afraid, yet confronting fear— as Hector does. He stops his flight, and though sensing he is doomed, turns to face his enemy to uphold his honor.

The daily track practice and the nightly readings went on, and gradually both exercises began to pay off. Brian's bedroom shelves started filling with books and with trophies from state and county races.

But then came the fall of 1998. Brian developed a stress fracture of his thighbone that put him out of competition. And Kane had been suffering from muscular weakness, for which he'd been hospitalized a year earlier.

Doctors were puzzled, but suspected he'd had a minor stroke. First he had to use a cane, and then a walker.

In time Brian gained strength in his legs again, but Kane did not. He had trouble walking, even standing. Brian emptied his savings account to buy him a three-wheeled scooter so Kane could still go to the track.

In March 2000, Brian entered a two-mile event at a national scholastic indoor track meet at the 168th Street Armory in New York City. The best distance runners in the country were there. Sue brought Kane in a wheelchair.

At the starting gun, Brian burst into the lead, but then strategically dropped back. Halfway through the race he moved up to the middle of the pack. There was still a big gap between him and the leader, but as he turned into the final lap, cheers, stamping feet, and the word *hammer* ringing in his brain drove him on.

From his seat near the finish line, Kane watched Brian surge to the lead with the greatest finishing kick he'd ever see him make—and win.

A month later Kane began losing his voice and choking on his food.

Finally doctors made a new diagnosis: amyotrophic lateral sclerosis (ALS), Lou Gehrig's disease. Kane, a strong man who'd molded athletes, was losing all muscle function. His spinal cord was degenerating. He would soon learn he had only months to live.

"Don't feel bad," Kane told Brian in a faltering voice. "I've had a good life, and I'll be coaching you for a while yet."

Sue took over all of his care. She drove him to the track, shaved him, cut his hair, diced his food, helped him with personal hygiene. But his big battle each day was with the stairs.

There were nine blue-carpeted steps from his basement room to the kitchen.

Every day he struggled to make it on his own. Soon he could not. Even with Sue's help they took ten painful minutes to climb, and each day it was harder.

Then Sue had to leave. In August Jennifer was heading off to Arizona State University, and Sue needed to help her settle in.

"Go ahead, Mom," Brian told her. "I can look after Charlie." On the first day after she left, Brian put in two early hours at his summer job as a recreational camp counselor, and then raced home. He found Kane, still in pajamas, sitting in a chair in his small dark room, crying.

Brian tried to get him up, telling him he had to get dressed so they could go to the track. Kane refused.

Late that afternoon Kane's son arrived from his Marine base in Virginia.

Together the two Brians urged, cajoled, prodded, and finally got him dressed and out of his room.

Now he faced the stairs. Brian could see that he was daunted. Just nine steps—stairs that this once strong man could have taken effortlessly had become a mountain for him. And Kane let out a cry of protest when they lifted him under his arms to help him climb. He pleaded to go back to bed; he wanted to quit.

"You can do it," Brian kept urging him, and finally he saw a firm resolve gather in his coach's eyes.

Leaning upon their arms—feet stumbling, legs throbbing—Charlie Kane hammered away. One step at a time—all nine. Until he stood breathless on the kitchen floor. Held up by the two sons he loved.

That evening when they returned from the track, all three men sat down together at the kitchen table where Kane and Brian had read the Greek epic aloud. And then Brian reached out and took his coach's hand. "Everything I am, Charlie, is because of you," he said.

On June 6, Brian won the 3200-meter run at the New Jersey State Meet of Champions. Kane watched from his wheelchair, stopwatch clutched loosely in his hand. The next morning he was totally paralyzed. Sue and Brian cared for him at their home until the end. Charles Kane died on June 23, 2001.

When we find purposes we truly wish to pursue, half-hearted commitments are not enough. Successful quests come only through steady, paced, every day efforts—practice after practice, night after night, step after step. And, as both Brian and Kane discovered, sometimes discipline is greatly encouraged by the sustaining help of a friend.

~&

WRAP UP

As Robert Frost noted at the beginning of this principle, "Life is tons of discipline." No matter who you are, no matter what your pursuits, living a life of meaning requires discipline. And the key is that it is much easier to say no to temptations or easier, less meaningful options when we have a deeper yes burning within. Joe Paterno and Sarah Mahoney both had a deeper yes, as well as the fortitude to say no to distractions. Brian and Kane also had deeper goals, and just as importantly they also had each other to help themselves over the hurdles. Without discipline, the noble purposes we create in our minds are no more than hollow daydreams.

REFLECTIONS

- Joe Paterno had his thoughts fixed on something that meant more than a million dollars to him. What goals and values are so important to you that you would not let them go—even if offered one million dollars?

- Sarah Mahoney asked herself, "If not now, when?" Do you ever ask yourself that question when thinking about the dreams you most want to pursue?

- Brian and Kane helped each other in achieving discipline. Are there friends you can involve to help you be more disciplined in pursuing your goals? Do you have a friend who could use a little help from a friend in being more disciplined?

FURTHER INSIGHTS ON
Discipline

~⁓

The Freedom of Discipline

Many people see discipline as the absence of freedom, when in fact it is the source of freedom.

Some people regard discipline as a chore. For me, it is a kind of order that sets me free to fly.

—Julie Andrews

Discipline is remembering what you want.

—David Campbell

No steam or gas ever drives anything until it is confined. No Niagara is ever turned into light and power until it is tunneled. No life ever grows until it is focused, dedicated, disciplined.

—Harry Emerson Fosdick

He who lives without discipline dies without honor.

—Icelandic proverb

No man is free who is not a master of himself.

—Epictetus

Self-respect is the fruit of discipline: the sense of dignity grows with the ability to say no to oneself.

—ABRAHAM JOSHUA HESCHEL

■ ■ ■

Sir Rabindranath Tagore, Nobel Prize-winning poet, once said, "I have on my table a violin string. It is free. But it is not free to do what a violin string is supposed to do—to produce music. So I take it, fix it in my violin and tighten it until it is taut. Only then is it free to be a violin string." By the same token we are free when our lives are uncommitted, but not to be what we were intended to be. Real freedom is not freedom from, but freedom for.

—ROBERT W. YOUNGS,
RENEWING YOUR FAITH DAY BY DAY

■ ■ ■

Discipline without freedom is tyranny; freedom without discipline is chaos.

—CULLEN HIGHTOWER

■ ■ ■

Freedom to be your best means nothing unless you're willing to do your best.

—COLIN POWELL

■ ■ ■

Real freedom is won through self-government, not through self-expression.

—ROY L. SMITH

STAYING FOCUSED

As Joe Paterno can attest, discipline requires concentration
until the goal line is crossed and the objective achieved.

When you let your thoughts drift to the future, you go right out of your
zone—and take your concentration with you.

Dallas Cowboys lineman Leon Lett learned that the hard way. Lett, a
defensive tackle, had not scored a touchdown since he was a ten-year-old. But
in the 1993 Super bowl, he got his chance when the Buffalo Bills'
quarterback fumbled right in front of him. Lett scooped up the ball and
headed for the goal line, 64 yards away. There was no one between him and a
sure six points. Crossing the ten-yard line, Lett threw out his arms in
jubilation, the ball in one outstretched paw. He never heard the pursuing
footsteps of Bills wide receiver Don Beebe. At the one-yard line, Beebe
reached out and knocked the ball from Lett's grasp, ending the lineman's
premature triumph.

Focusing on the future instead of the present can cripple any activity.

—EDWIN KIESTER, JR.
AND SALLY VALENTE KIESTER

■ ■ ■

As a boy I often tackled a task full of enthusiasm, only to become
discouraged quickly. One bright summer day my father showed me an
experiment with a magnifying glass and a newspaper. When he moved the
glass over the paper from one place to another, nothing happened. But when
he held it motionless in one spot for a while, focusing the sun's rays, a hole
appeared.

I was fascinated, but didn't grasp the significance of the procedure. Father
explained that the same principle applied in everything we do: That to make
a success of our lives we must learn to concentrate all our efforts on the
undertaking in hand until it is finished.

—JOHN LOUIS FELICIELLO

■ ■ ■

THE FORCE OF HABIT

Habits can work for or against you. Most successful people have achieved their goals only after arduous struggles to replace bad habits with good.

A bad habit never disappears miraculously; it's an undo-it-yourself project.

—ABIGAIL VAN BUREN

■ ■ ■

A habit cannot be tossed out the window: it must be coaxed down the stairs a step at a time.

—MARK TWAIN

■ ■ ■

The best way to break a habit is to drop it.

—LEO AIKMAN

■ ■ ■

A habit is like old-fashioned adhesive tape—easy to stick on, but the longer it stays the harder it is to get off, until finally, when it's ripped off, it takes skin and all with it.

—SYDNEY J. HARRIS

■ ■ ■

Habit is either the best of servants, or the worst of masters.

—NATHANIEL EMMONS

■ ■ ■

Moral excellence comes about as a result of habit. We become just by doing just acts, temperate by doing temperate acts, brave by doing brave acts.

—ARISTOTLE

■ ■ ■

Indeed, some habits take extra discipline to break.

While waiting to cross the street one day, I saw an old motorcycle approaching. As it stopped at the traffic light, both rider and bike slowly keeled over to one side, landing with a thud on the pavement.

The motorcyclist picked himself up. Looking distinctly embarrassed, he turned to me and said, "I've been doing this ever since I took my sidecar off."

—Contributed by P. Lewis

Tiring of the drive from the airport to his country place, a man equipped his small plane with pontoons so he could land on the lake directly in front of his cottage.

On the next trip, he made his approach down the runway as usual. Alarmed, his wife cried out, "Are you crazy? You can't land this plane here without wheels!"

The startled husband abruptly yanked up the nose of the aircraft and narrowly averted certain disaster. Continuing, he landed the plane on the lake without mishap.

As he sat there, visibly shaken, he said to his wife, "I don't know what got into me. That's the stupidest thing I've ever done!" And with that, he opened the door and stepped out, falling into the water.

—Contributed by C. Clarke-Johnson

"Hey, buddy," said the taxicab passenger, tapping the driver on the shoulder. The driver screamed and lost control of the cab, nearly hitting a bus, jumping the curb and stopping just inches from a huge plate-glass window.

For a few moments, everything was silent. Then the driver said, "Man, you scared the daylights out of me!"

"I'm sorry," said the passenger. "I didn't realize a tap on the shoulder would frighten you so much."

"It's not your fault," the driver replied. "Today is my first day driving a cab. I've been driving a hearse for the last 25 years.

—Contributed by Patricia Ridpath

THE PULL OF TEMPTATION

Along any journey to success are found many enticing distractions. Discipline is the principle that thwarts temptation.

Opportunity knocks only once, but temptation leans on the doorbell.

— *WESTERN LIVESTOCK JOURNAL*

■ ■ ■

Most people want to be delivered from temptation but would like it to keep in touch.

—ROBERT ORBEN

■ ■ ■

My seatmate on a dinner flight was a woman from Switzerland. As soon as the meal was served, I noticed that she heavily salted and peppered her dessert—a luscious-looking piece of chocolate cake. The flight attendant, somewhat taken aback, explained that it wasn't necessary to do this. "Oh, but it is," the woman replied, smiling. "It keeps me from eating it."

—CONTRIBUTED BY JACKIE TROTTA

■ ■ ■

A sudden beam of moonlight, or a thrush you have just heard, or a girl you have just kissed, or a beautiful view through your study window is seldom the source of an urge to put words on paper. Such pleasant experiences are likely to obstruct and delay a writer's work.

—OSCAR HAMMERSTEIN II

■ ■ ■

The art of living consists in knowing which impulse to obey and which must be made to obey.

—SYDNEY J. HARRIS

STARTING WITHIN

Until you make peace with who you are,
you'll never be content with what you have.
—DORIS MORTMAN

Some of life's greatest lessons suggest that before we can attain success in the world around us—our communities, workplaces, homes—we must first achieve success within ourselves. The most important element we put into any goal or relationship is not what we say or what we do or what we have, but who we are.

Principles that strengthen our capacity to start within include

- Integrity

- Humility

- Gratitude

7

INTEGRITY

Real integrity is doing the right thing, knowing that
nobody's going to know whether you did it or not.
—OPRAH WINFREY

Integrity is the common denominator that sustains every other principle of Everyday Greatness. If perceived as dishonest, for example, a person filled with courage is feared and avoided. If viewed as unethical, a person performing an act of charity is assumed to be a selfish manipulator. So without the foundation of integrity, all other principles are greatly diminished.

People with integrity are those whose words match their deeds and whose behaviors mirror their values. Their honesty and ethics can be trusted unconditionally. They honor commitments. They are dependable. They are known for doing the right things, for the right reasons, at the right times. While numerous tales of integrity take place in public settings where others can see them, often the most powerful examples occur in the quiet stillness of a private moment—when no one else is looking. Such is the case in "Catch of a Lifetime."

CATCH OF A LIFETIME

James P. Lenfesty

He was eleven years old, and went fishing every chance he got from the dock at his family's cabin on an island in the middle of a New Hampshire lake.

On the day before the bass season opened, he and his father were fishing early in the evening, catching sunfish and perch with worms. Then he tied on a small silver lure and practiced casting. The lure struck the water and caused colored ripples in the sunset, then silver ripples as the moon rose over the lake.

When his pole doubled over, he knew something huge was on the other end. His father watched with admiration as the boy skillfully worked the fish alongside the dock.

Finally he very gingerly lifted the exhausted fish from the water. It was the largest one he had ever seen, but it was a bass.

The boy and his father looked at the handsome fish, gills playing back and forth in the moonlight. The father lit a match and looked at his watch. It was 10:00 p.m.—two hours before the season opened. He looked at the fish, then at the boy.

"You'll have to put it back son," he said.

"Dad!" cried the boy.

"There will be other fish," said his father.

"Not as big as this one," cried the boy.

He looked around the lake. No other fishermen or boats were anywhere around in the moonlight. He looked again at his father.

Even though no one had seen them, nor would anyone ever know what time he caught the fish, the boy could tell by the clarity of his father's voice that the decision was not negotiable. He slowly worked the hook out of the lip of the huge bass, and lowered it into the black water.

The creature swished its powerful body and disappeared. The boy suspected that he would never again see such a great fish.

That was thirty-four years ago. Today, the boy is a successful architect in

New York City. His father's cabin is still there on the island in the middle of the lake. He takes his own son and daughters fishing from the same dock.

And he was right. He has never again caught such a magnificent fish as the one he landed that night long ago. But he does see that same fish—again and again—every time he comes up against a question of ethics.

For, as his father taught him, ethics are simple matters of right and wrong. It is only the practice of ethics that is difficult. Do we do right when no one is looking? Do we refuse to cut corners to get the design in on time? Or refuse to trade stocks based on information that we know we aren't supposed to have?

We would if we were taught to put the fish back when we were young. For we would have learned the truth.

The decision to do right lives fresh and fragrant in our memory. It is a story we will proudly tell our friends and grandchildren.

Not about how we had a chance to beat the system and took it, but about how we did the right thing and were forever strengthened.

No one would ever have known about the fish if the father-son duo had agreed to keep the catch quiet or had simply altered their watches ever so slightly. In fact, chances are that few people would even have cared about the timing of the catch had the facts been made public. So the only real pressures governing them that night were internal. It was the inner pressures they felt to be true to their values, true to their potential, and true to the trust they had with each other. They chose the higher path of integrity, which is the true source of personal security and confidence.

———————

While the father's decision to return the fish to its waters was made under quiet, private conditions, the following mother's decision to stand up for what she believed to be right was made under intense public pressure.

MOM V. STEROIDS

Lynn Rosellini

Lori Lewis never set out to be a crusader. All she wanted that day in September 2004, rummaging through her son Bryan's closet, was to locate a pair of jeans to return to the mall. Instead, she spotted an unfamiliar travel bag. Curious, Lewis opened it and found a vial of liquid and syringes. It felt like someone punched her in the stomach. She thought her son was doing heroin.

Calling a local Walgreens, Lewis was relieved to learn that the drug was an anabolic steroid. Then she got mad.

Why would Bryan be taking steroids?

"Dude, your mom's looking for you." Bryan Dyer, emerging from afternoon classes at Colleyville Heritage High School in the affluent Dallas, Texas, suburbs, looked over to where a friend was pointing. There at the curb, behind the wheel of her white Navigator, sat his mother. She looked furious.

"Get home now," she said.

Bryan, almost seventeen, a lanky six-footer who had played quarterback on the junior varsity football team the year before, was an outgoing kid who made A's and B's. Like most boys in Colleyville, he favored jeans, sneakers, T-shirts, and a ball cap pulled down over his face. His parents divorced when he was an infant, and he lived with his mother, stepfather, older brother, and younger sister. Still, his dad, a former high school football star in nearby Arlington, had remained a presence in Bryan's life as he went through T-ball, Little League, peewee football, and on into high school sports. As for his mother, she and Bryan had been close since the divorce. But at that moment, he would have chosen to face a wall of linemen rather than her rage.

When he walked into the family room of their spacious home, his mom was waiting, vial and syringes in hand.

"Why are you taking steroids?" she demanded.

Bryan stared, unable to speak. "Mom," he said finally, "the majority of the team is on them." Bryan explained that he had hoped to make varsity. His coaches and his father urged him to bulk up. Creatine and protein shakes didn't help. So using money he had earned working at Applebee's, he purchased a two hundred dollar vial of "Deca"—nandrolone decanoate—from a senior on the team. For five weeks he injected himself in the hip.

Lewis broke in. "What were you thinking?"

"Mom," he said, "coaches tell us to get bigger, stronger, faster. They don't tell us how. They just tell us to do it."

Like many parents of teenagers, Lewis was well-versed in the dangers of alcohol, inhalants, pot—even Ecstasy. All she knew about anabolic steroids was that they were illegal. Later, she went online, quickly learning that regular use can lead to liver damage, cancer, heart disease, and other physical problems, plus emotional effects like depression and road rage.

Bryan stopped the injections when his back broke out in acne, another common side effect. By the time his mother found the vial, he had been steroid-free for months. But, Lewis wondered, how many other kids out there were taking the stuff?

"I'm calling the school!" she said.

"You can't!" Bryan insisted. "I'll be screwed!"

"Don't worry," his mother assured him. "Nobody will know it's you."

To understand what happened next, it's important to appreciate the huge role played by high school football in Texas. The state's football teams are regularly among the country's best. It's not unusual for twenty thousand people to jam stadiums on Friday nights, while TV cameras roll. These arenas, rivaling some colleges', can cost twenty million dollars, heavily funded by boosters who want to see their teams win. Successful coaches can earn six-figure salaries, and competition for these coveted positions is fierce.

From hardscrabble towns like Odessa, the setting for *Friday Night Lights*, the memorable exposé of high school sports, to the affluent Dallas suburbs, teen football heroes have rock star status. The pressure is highest at schools like Colleyville, which plays in one of the state's toughest districts. Two years ago, rival Southlake Carroll finished first not only in Texas—but in the nation. Many of the team's players got scholarships to play at powerhouse colleges.

Not surprisingly, some athletes seek anything for an edge. Across America, between 1991 and 2003, steroid use in high schools more than doubled. In the 2004 Texas School Survey of Substance Abuse, more than forty-one thousand Texas seventh- through twelfth-graders said they had used the drugs. Many teens find them readily available through local dealers or online.

And since few schools test for steroids, kids don't have to worry about being discovered. "Other than pedophilia, it's the most secretive behavior I've encountered," said Charles Yesalis, a Penn State University professor who has studied steroid use for twenty-eight years. Even school officials are in denial, he said. "If I had one hundred dollars for every time a coach or principal told me, 'It's a problem, but not in our school,' I'd have a Ferrari sitting in my driveway."

The day after her discovery, Lewis telephoned Colleyville's assistant principal, Ted Beal. She related Bryan's story, and Beal said he would check into it. A few hours later, he called back. There was no problem, football coach Chris Cunningham assured him.

"That's it?" said Lewis.

Without further evidence, Beal told her, there was nothing he could do.

Lewis was livid. *They want me to go away,* she thought. This forty-year-old mother was no radical. Her political activism went no further than a stint on the board of the elementary PTA, and some campaign work for Colleyville's mayor and George W. Bush.

God knows, she thought, *I'm all for high school sports. But I'm not for kids putting themselves in danger. How could it possibly be worth it?* The next day, she called the *Colleyville Courier.*

Over the following week, reporter Scott Price and editor Charles D. Young gathered information from students, coaches, and school officials. On October 1, the paper carried the story on the front page. Without identifying Lewis, Price wrote: "It did not take long to validate this mother's concerns. *The Courier* found knowledge of steroid use at all area high schools."

Within days, the *Dallas Morning News* was calling. By now Bryan wished he'd never heard of steroids. "It's no one else's business!" he shouted. "Why do you have to go public?" But once Lori Lewis set her mind on something, she rarely backed down. "This is gonna save the life of somebody, somewhere," she told him.

In early February, the *Dallas Morning News* headlined a page-one series, "The Secret Edge: Steroids in High Schools." Reporters confirmed substantial steroid use in North Texas high schools and devoted a lengthy article to a football player named "Patrick"—a pseudonym for Bryan.

Frantic, Bryan reached his mother on her cell phone. "Mom, they're calling me 'Patrick,'" he said. His cover was blown. A local dealer was after him, he heard, and varsity football players were planning to rough him up. Someone left a threatening message: "I'm going to beat your ass!"

The school district's executive director of administration, Steve Trachier, had sent an e-mail to senior school officials in September terming Lewis's allegations "unfounded." Coach Cunningham called her a "liar." "You've got a crazy mom looking for someone to blame for her problem," he told the *Morning News*. (He later apologized publicly for his remarks.)

At night, Lewis lay in bed wondering, *What have I done?*

Lori's husband, Jack, was her biggest supporter, but he stayed in the background, shielding their eight-year-old daughter, McKenna, from publicity. Now even Jack was frustrated, calling Colleyville "Colleywood" for its backbiting ways. "People are judging you about things you did that were right," he told her. "You can't stop now!"

Nine athletes, most of them football players, eventually confessed to steroid use, proving their coach wrong. (There is no evidence that Cunningham or other coaches were aware of the drug use.) Still, Lewis had few supporters. Neighbors stopped speaking to her. Mothers of Bryan's schoolmates, whom she had known since their kids were four years old, cut her dead at the supermarket.

The final blow? She and Bryan weren't getting along. "Great, Mom, you've ruined my life!" he said. When the threats continued, they agreed he should transfer to a private school.

Thirty miles away in Plano, Texas, two people silently applauded Lewis. Don and Gwen Hooton took a special interest in the *Morning News* stories. The Hootons' seventeen-year-old son, Taylor, had committed suicide in 2003. A cheerful and gregarious boy, Taylor had taken steroids in an effort to improve his baseball game. He lapsed into depression after quitting, and his parents blamed steroids for his death.

Since then, Don Hooton has become a national spokesman in the anti-steroid effort, crisscrossing the country to warn parents, coaches, and kids. "You've done the right thing," he told Lewis. "Stick to your guns," he said, "but don't expect to make friends." In Hooton's own community, near the home of Dallas Cowboys legend Troy Aikman, critics attacked him in letters to the editor and spread false rumors that his son had been doing other drugs like meth and Ecstasy.

No more worrying what people thought. I'm not in a popularity contest, Lewis realized. I'm here to fight this epidemic. In late April, she filed a lawsuit charging Coach Cunningham with slander. A few days later, she testified before a legislative subcommittee in favor of a bill requiring drug testing of high school athletes.

In May, Lewis appeared before the Colleyville school board. And then, an extraordinary thing happened: The board unanimously approved random drug testing of students who participate in extracurricular activities. "It will not only serve as a deterrent," said a school spokesperson, "but will also reinforce that we will not tolerate drug use of any kind."

So far, no other districts in the area have followed suit. But Lewis does not intend to let the matter drop.

As for Bryan, he turned out for football at his new school—and quickly became the team's star wide receiver. He also plays cornerback on defense, and recently caught the eye of a recruiter from a college in Ohio. And he did it all without steroids.

Deep inside, this mother knew that something wrong was going on, yet if she took a stand, there might be trials and risks to herself and her family, particularly her son. But as a result of her integrity in standing up for what she believed to be right, other mothers and sons will benefit.

———————

The following young woman also felt so strongly about what she believed to be right—her responsibility to protect her siblings—that she was willing to risk her life to do it.

GIRL AGAINST A BLIZZARD

Helen Rezatto

The morning of March 15 was pleasant and sunny as William Miner, a farmer near Center, North Dakota, completed his chores. A thaw had set in, and the snow in the fields was patchy.

"Snow should be gone by night," he reported optimistically to his wife when he came in at noon. After the couple had eaten a leisurely meal, Miner glanced out the kitchen window. "Good Lord!" he exclaimed.

In the northwest a black, billowy cloud loomed over the horizon. It moved stealthily, inexorably, its dark bluish edges spreading across the sky toward the unsuspecting sun.

Blanche Miner spoke with the sure instinct of a homesteader. "A spring norther!"

They watched the advance of the formless, faceless monster. Abruptly, Miner said, "You get the stock in. I'm going to school to get the kids. I don't like the looks of it."

Miner piled on his storm clothes, saddled Kit, his best horse, and started down the slushy road to the school two and a half miles away. By now the apparition had writhed and swelled its way to overpower the sun. All nature was poised, breathless, apprehensive. Then an avalanche of blinding snow and wind slammed into the horse and rider. Miner fought through it to the school barn, tied Kit among the other stomping, nervous horses, and hurried into the schoolhouse.

The teacher and pupils had observed the approach of the blizzard, but were still pretending to concentrate on their lessons. Although many children had their own horses and sleighs in the school barn, the established blizzard rule was that no child should leave unless called for by a parent.

"Hi, Dad!" fifteen-year-old Hazel Miner exclaimed. She turned to her brother, Emmet, eleven, and her sister Myrdith, eight. "I guess somebody doesn't trust us to drive old Maude home!"

Her father smiled briefly. "Hurry! Get your wraps—here are extra scarves."

Hazel bent down to fasten her sister's overshoes and said to Emmet, "Don't forget your history book." Hazel was wonderfully dependable, Miner thought. She always far surpassed expectations.

He carried Myrdith outside to their homemade sleigh with its rounded canvas cover, settled the two children in the straw lining the bottom, covered them with two blankets and an old fur robe. Then Hazel perched on the driver's seat while her father hitched Maude to the sleigh. Above the belligerent wind he shouted to Hazel, "Stay right here! I'll get Kit and lead the way."

Maude was facing the north gate toward home. She had always been placid and easily managed, but now a thunderclap startled her, and she bolted, swerving through the south gate. Hazel, knocked off balance and hardly able to see through the swirling snow, did not realize at first that Maude was headed in the wrong direction. She shouted to the wide-eyed younger children, "Don't worry, we'll beat Dad and Kit home! Maude knows the way."

Hazel could do nothing to control the horse, for the reins trailed out of reach beneath the tugs. Finally, Maude slowed to a walk and stopped, her sides heaving.

Emmet called, "Are we home? Did we beat Dad?"

Hazel stepped down into the snow. Through the dizzying gloom she could not tell whether they were on a road or in a field. The whole world had become a white-foaming, lashing sea, threatening to swallow them all. Panting for breath, she crawled back into the driver's seat with the reins. "No, we're not home yet, but I think we're close. Now that Maude's calmed down, she'll know the way."

Maude, repentant about her escapade, plowed through the growing gloom. Once she plunged into a low place filled with water from the spring thaws and choked with ice and new snow. A tug came unhitched, and Hazel stepped down into the chilling slush, reached her bare hands into the water, fumbled for the tug, fastened it. By the time she led Maude out of the water, she was soaked to the waist and her clothes were turning into heavy armor.

Then, close by, she saw the top of a fence post sticking above the snow. She dug into the snow until she located the barbed wire. The fence would lead them to a farm and safety.

Emmet got out to see what she was doing. Together, they broke off the crystal mask that had formed over Maude's face. They grasped Maude's bridle to keep her on the fence line, but a huge drift blocked the way and they had to turn off the course. Frantically trying to get back, Emmet and Hazel pawed for the wire or another post to guide them. They could find neither. (The gate, buried in the big drift, opened to a farm only two hundred feet away.)

Almost suffocated from the onslaught of wind and snow, the two climbed back into the sleigh. Stubbornly, Maude kept on until the sleigh lurched over a concealed obstacle. It tipped over on its side, and the children were thrown against the canvas top.

Again, Hazel and Emmet got out. Blindly, they pushed, they heaved, they pulled. The sleigh, jammed into the snow, was too heavy for them to right.

In the howling darkness, Hazel realized that she must think—it was up to her, the oldest. She fumbled inside the canvas. "See," she said, "we're in a little cave. We'll fix it nice and cozy."

Since the sleigh was on its side, the narrow wooden floor formed a low wall to the east, and the canvas top, uncurtained at the ends, made a tunnel-like tent. In the dark, Hazel found the blankets and robe. Despite her now crippled hands, she placed two blankets on the canvas "floor." Following her instructions, Emmet and Myrdith lay down, curled together tightly. The wind snarled through the north opening, and Hazel tried to improvise a curtain with the fur robe. It blew down again and again. Finally she tucked the robe around her brother and sister.

The hellish wind tore and ripped at the canvas top. Hazel snatched at the flapping scraps and piled over the robe all she could salvage. There was only one way to keep them in place—to fling herself on top of them. Now there was nothing between the three children and the blizzard except some dangling strips blowing from the bare wooden framework.

The snow fell incessantly. Three human specks lay motionless, their minds and bodies stupefied, benumbed by the terrifying, pulsating forces. Hazel roused herself. "Emmet! Myrdith!" she shouted. "You mustn't close your eyes. Punch each other! I'll count to a hundred. Make your legs go up and down as though you're running. Begin—one, two, three—" She could feel the small limbs moving underneath her. She tried to move her own; her brain instructed her legs, but she wasn't sure what they did.

"I'm tired. Can't we stop?" begged Myrdith's muffled voice.

"No!" came the stern answer. "We're only at seventy-one."

Next Hazel ordered, "Open and close your fingers one hundred times inside your mittens."

Emmet stuck his head out from under the robe. "Come on, Hazel, get under here. We'll make room."

"No, I can't." Little warmth her ice-mantled clothes would provide the others. "Everything blows away. I've got to hold it down. Besides, I'm not very cold. Let's sing 'America the Beautiful' like in opening exercises this morning."

From underneath the robe came the thin, childish voices and the words they had sung only that morning—but a hundred years away. "For purple mountains majesties above the fruited plain." They sang all four verses.

"Let's pray to God to help us," suggested Myrdith. "Now I lay me down to sleep—" she began.

Hazel interrupted, "No, not that one. Let's say 'Our Father' instead." Solemnly they chanted the prayer.

On into the timeless night Hazel directed them—in exercises, stories, songs, prayers. Several times she sat up in the never-ending snow and forced her nearly paralyzed fingers to break the crusts that formed around Myrdith's and Emmet's legs; then she brushed and scraped away the creeping menace.

She said to the two children over and over, "Remember, you mustn't go to sleep—even if I do. Promise me you won't, no matter how sleepy you get. *Keep each other awake!* Promise?"

They promised.

More than once Myrdith voiced the question: "Why doesn't Daddy find us?"

When William Miner discovered his children had disappeared from the schoolyard, he urged Kit mercilessly through the fast-forming drifts, sure that Maude had gone home. His wife met him at the door. They gazed, stricken, into each other's eyes.

Immediately, he gave the alarm over the rural party lines. Nearly forty men, risking their lives, were soon moving slowly, persistently, over the fields and roads between Miner's farm and the school. They paused at farms to change teams, to treat frostbite, to gulp coffee, to devise new plans. All the other children were safe in their homes. The men found nothing.

The wind became a sixty-mile-an-hour gale, the temperature dropped to zero, the gray became utter blackness. And the maddening snow kept falling. The searchers had to give up until daylight.

The next morning one group of searchers reported tracks made by a small sleigh and a horse which went out the south schoolhouse gate—then were obliterated by the falling snow. Quickly, the search was reorganized. Men with teams and sleighs, men on horseback, men on foot fanned out for half a mile. Back and forth they forced their way across the shrouded land.

At two o'clock on Tuesday afternoon, twenty-five hours from the time the Miner children had disappeared, searchers spotted something in a pasture two miles south of the school. It was an overturned sleigh. Next to it, like a sentry, a ghostlike horse stood motionless, but still alive. They saw a bulky snow-covered mound under the arch of the naked, skeleton staves.

The rigid body of a girl lay face down with her unbuttoned coat flung wide. Her arms were outstretched over her brother and sister, sheltering and embracing them in death as she had in life.

Tenderly, the men lifted her, then slowly removed the matted robe and torn canvas pieces that she had been holding down with her body. Underneath were Myrdith and Emmet, dazed and partially frozen, but alive. They had promised never to fall into the dread sleep from which Hazel knew they could never awaken.

Today, on the courthouse grounds in the town of Center, these words are engraved on a granite monument rising, like a challenge, above the plains:

In Memory of
Hazel Miner
April 11, 1904–March 16, 1920
To the dead a tribute
To the living a memory
To posterity an inspiration
The story of her life and of her

Tragic death is recorded in the
Archives of Oliver County.
Stranger, read it

Hazel was dedicated to the protection of her younger brother and sister both in life and in death. In her mind there was never a question of what she would do under the freezing conditions. Her heroics give us all cause to wonder how far we would go in holding firm to the values we embrace.

~

WRAP UP

The word *integrity* basically means integrated around principles. It means wholeness, oneness, seamlessness. Even the word sincerity in Latin means *sin cero*—without wax—no seams or compartments, all of one piece. Therefore a person who demonstrates true integrity is not honest based on the situation or on an "every-other-day" basis. Integrity is an every day choice, an every day way of living. As you read about the fishing father, didn't you get the feeling that he was that honest and full of integrity every day and in all circumstances? As you read about the mother, didn't you get the feeling that she would fight for the good of her son, and other mothers' sons, any day of the year? As you read about Hazel, didn't you get the feeling that she nobly cared for her siblings not only in death, but every day? From their stories, it appears that the fishing duo, the mother fighting steroids, and young Hazel each demonstrated a strong capacity for every day integrity.

REFLECTIONS

- The father and son enjoyed an internal satisfaction beyond what any trophy or fillet could provide. Character, conscience, dignity, and honesty all won out that night in one solitary act. How would your integrity hold up in such a setting?

- Those who love to fish are often accused of exaggerating the size of their catches, particularly the ones that got away. What about you? Do you embellish your stories? Are you 100 percent honest with others? . . . with yourself?

- The mother battling steroids risked much and young Hazel gave her all to do what she felt was right. How far are you willing to go in doing what you feel is right?

FURTHER INSIGHTS ON
Integrity

~∂

SOLID INTEGRITY

Integrity includes consistency and an unwavering adherence to values and beliefs.

Integrity means you do what you do because it's right and not just fashionable or politically correct. A life of principle, of not succumbing to the seductive sirens of an easy morality, will always win the day.

—DENIS WAITLEY,
PRIORITIES

▪ ▪ ▪

In mathematics, an integer is a number that isn't divided into fractions. Just so, a man of integrity isn't divided against himself. He doesn't think one thing and say another—so he's not in conflict with his own principles.

—ARTHUR GORDON

▪ ▪ ▪

The way to gain a good reputation is to endeavor to be what you desire to appear.

—SOCRATES

▪ ▪ ▪

There can be no happiness if the things we believe in are different from the things we do.

—FREYA STARK

▪ ▪ ▪

Never "for the sake of peace and quiet" deny your own experience or convictions.

—Dag Hammarskjöld

■ ■ ■

The person who stands out in the crowd demonstrates that he has his own set of values and has a strong sense of self-worth. While the winds of conflicting ideas blow some people away, and the tides of various fads wash others away, he will stand firm.

—David J. Mahoney,
Confessions of a Street-Smart Manager

■ ■ ■

The time is always right to do what is right.

—Martin Luther King Jr.

■ ■ ■

Values have been carved on monuments and spelled out in illuminated manuscripts. We do not need more of that. They must be made to live in the acts of men.

—John W. Gardner,
The Recovery of Confidence

■ ■ ■

The glory of great men should always be measured by the means they have used to acquire it.

—La Rochefoucauld

CHARACTER

Nearly synonymous with integrity is character. Character is a reputation built over time, yet it can be lost in seconds.

Character is the sum total of all our everyday choices.

—MARGARET JENSEN

■ ■ ■

The reputation of a thousand years may be determined by the conduct of one hour.

—JAPANESE PROVERB

■ ■ ■

Success without honor is an unseasoned dish; it will satisfy your hunger, but it won't taste good.

—JOE PATERNO

■ ■ ■

Character is much easier kept than recovered.

—THOMAS PAINE

■ ■ ■

I've met leaders in the Army who were very competent—but they didn't have character. And for every job they did well, they sought reward in the form of promotions, in the form of awards and decorations, in the form of getting ahead at the expense of someone else, in the form of another piece of paper that awarded them another degree—a sure road to the top. You see, these were competent people, but they lacked character.

I've also met a lot of leaders who had superb character but who lacked competence. They weren't willing to pay the price of leadership, to go the extra mile because that's what it took to be a great leader.

And that's sort of what it's all about. To lead in the 21st century—to take soldiers, sailors, airmen into battle—you will be required to have both character and competence.

—GENERAL H. NORMAN SCHWARZKOPF

STANDING ON PRINCIPLE

Standing on principle involves holding firm to what you feel
to be right. How firmly are your feet planted?

In matters of principle, stand like a rock; in matters of taste, swim with the
current.

—THOMAS JEFFERSON

■ ■ ■

Be sure you put your feet in the right place, and then stand firm.

—ABRAHAM LINCOLN

■ ■ ■

The ultimate measure of a man is not where he stands in moments of
comfort and convenience, but where he stands at times of challenge and
controversy.

—MARTIN LUTHER KING, JR,
STRENGTH TO LOVE

■ ■ ■

According to the Overseas News Agency, when King Christian of Denmark
noticed a Nazi flag flying above an official Danish building during World
War II, he demanded of a German officer that the flag be removed.

The officer replied that the flag was flown according to instructions from
Berlin.

"The flag must be removed before 12 o'clock;" the monarch declared,
"otherwise I will send a soldier to do it."

At five minutes to twelve the flag was still flying, so the King announced
he was sending a soldier to take it down.

"The soldier will be shot," warned the Nazi officer.

"I am the soldier," the King replied calmly.

The Nazi flag was lowered.

It is easier to fight for one's principles than to live up to them.

—ALFRED ADLER

SILENCING INDIFFERENCE

The antithesis of integrity is indifference—when we fail to voice or stand up for what we believe.

History will have to record that the greatest tragedy of this period of social transition was not the strident clamor of the bad people, but the appalling silence of the good people.

—MARTIN LUTHER KING JR.,
STRIDE TOWARD FREEDOM

■ ■ ■

The only thing necessary for the triumph of evil is for good men to do nothing.

—EDMUND BURKE

■ ■ ■

To know what is right and not to do it is the worst cowardice.

—CONFUCIUS

■ ■ ■

More good things in life are lost by indifference than ever were lost by active hostility.

—ROBERT GORDON MENZIES

■ ■ ■

When something important is going on, silence is a lie.

—A. M. ROSENTHAL

■ ■ ■

As we must account for every idle word, so we must for every idle silence.

—BENJAMIN FRANKLIN

■ ■ ■

The hottest places in Hell are reserved for those who, in a period of moral crisis, maintain their neutrality.

—DANTE

HONESTY

Deceit breeds tension whereas honesty builds trust. Whether
in word or in deed, if we have integrity our intent cannot be
to deceive.

After listening for some time one day to a would-be client's statement,
Lincoln suddenly swung around in his chair and exclaimed: "Well, you have
got a good case in technical law, but a pretty bad one in equity and justice.
You'll have to get some other fellow to win it for you. I couldn't do it. All the
time while standing talking to the jury I'd be thinking, 'Lincoln, you're a liar,'
and I believe I should forget myself and say it out loud."

—*LINCOLN TALKS*,
EDITED BY EMANUEL HERTZ

Honesty is abandoned as much by the theft of a dime as of a dollar.

—LEONARD E. READ

One day, when I was about five, I told my grandfather a lie. It was not a very
black lie. My grandfather asked our gardener to bring a long ladder and place
it against the front of the roof. When the ladder was firmly in place he said to
the gardener: "Our boy has taken to leaping from housetops. The ladder is
for him to use when he so desires." I knew at once what this meant, for one
of the proverbs in our district was: "A lie is a leap from a house-top."

"I brooded in silence. It was awkward to have the ladder before the front
door. I began to fear that it would be there forever if I did not do something.
I found my grandfather reading a book and I went quietly up to him and
buried my face in his lap. "Grandpa," I said, "we do not need the ladder any
more." He seemed very happy. He called the gardener and said to him: "Take
the ladder away at once. Our boy does not leap from house-tops." I will
never forget that incident.

—LI YUNG KU,
AS TOLD TO MANUEL KOMROFF

PRIVATE MOMENTS

Integrity's greatest victories are won in those private moments when no one else would know.

For almost two centuries Old Ben's family had been famous dry-wall builders. As a young man I was helping him build a section of wall on a sidehill slope of a farmyard. We had dug the trench wide and deep, so that the big foundation stones would be below the frostline. Old Ben was very particular about each rock and chinking piece. To an impatient lad the idea of chinking rocks below the soil surface was particularly irksome. "Who's going to know if these are chinked or not?" I murmured. Old Ben's astonishment was genuine as he peered over his spectacles. "Why," he said, "I will—and so will you."

—HAYDN PEARSON,
IN *A TREASURY OF VERMONT LIFE*

■ ■ ■

Perfect valor is to do without witness what one would do before all the world.

—LA ROCHEFOUCAULD

■ ■ ■

At a tennis tournament in New York City's Madison Square Garden in January 1982, top-ranked pros Vitas Gerulaitis and Eliot Teltscher met in the semi-finals. They split the first two sets. In the eighth game of the deciding third set, Gerulaitis slashed his way to match point.

After one of their fiercest rallies, Gerulaitis hit a ball that struck the top of the net and dribbled over for what seemed a sure match winner. But Teltscher came tearing up to the net, dived at the ball and miraculously managed to loft it over Gerulaitis's head. Stunned, Gerulaitis moved back late, pushing his shot wide.

The crowd went nuts. Teltscher had survived match point—or so it seemed. As the cheering died, Teltscher indicated that in his lunge toward his final shot, he'd touched the net—a violation. Never mind that the umpire hadn't seen it or that a lot of money was at stake. For Teltscher, none of this changed the rules of the game or the gentleman's code that is their basis. He shook Gerulaitis's hand, nodded to the crowds and walked off the court—a winner in defeat.

—LAURENCE SHAMES,
ESQUIRE

CONSCIENCE

Exhibiting integrity often requires nothing more than showing a respect for and trust in your conscience.

Integrity means having a conscience and listening to it. "It is neither safe nor
prudent," said Martin Luther, facing his enemies in the city where his death
had been decreed, "to do aught against conscience. Here I stand; God help
me, I cannot do otherwise."

—ARTHUR GORDON

The only tyrant I accept in this world is the "still small voice"
within me.

—MAHATMA GANDHI

Martin Luther King, Jr., in his "Letter from Birmingham Jail," included a
story about a 72-year-old black woman who walked a long distance every
day during a bus boycott. She was tired and physically weak, and someone
asked her why she continued to support the non-violent protest. Her
response will always be treasured: "My feets is tired," she said, "but my soul
is at rest."

—BAYARD RUSTIN,
IN *LOS ANGELES HERALD EXAMINER*

I desire to so conduct the affairs of this administration that if, at the end,
when I come to lay down the reins of power, I have lost every other friend on
earth, I shall have at least one friend left—and that friend shall be down
inside me.

—ABRAHAM LINCOLN

There is no pillow so soft as a clear conscience.

—FRENCH PROVERB

■ ■ ■

Some years ago in our rural section of Southern California, a Mexican mother died leaving a family of eight children. The oldest girl, not yet seventeen, was a tiny thing. Upon her frail shoulders fell the burden of caring for the family. Taking up the task with courage, she kept the children clean, well fed, and in school.

One day when I complimented her on her achievement, she replied, "I can't take any credit for something I have to do."

"But, my dear, you don't have to. You could get out of it."

She paused for a moment, then replied, "Yes, that's true. But what about the have to that's inside of me?"

—VERNA RALLINGS

8

HUMILITY

Truly great men and women are never terrifying.
Their humility puts you at ease.
—ELIZABETH GOUDGE

C omedian Groucho Marx once reported that he had a
nurse who was so arrogant about her beauty that
when she took a man's pulse she always subtracted
ten points to compensate for what her looks did to his heart-
beat. Yes, humility can be elusive.

Though strong self-confidence and high self-esteem are
healthy personality traits, there is a point when they cease to
be virtues, the point at which a person feels more important
than another, or above reproach and learning. It is the point
where someone boasts in ways that can, in fact, drop another's
pulse rate. Humility, on the other hand, breeds growth and
friendship. It might be argued that one of the best learning
grounds for humility is parenthood, as illustrated by the following father in "Mike and Me and the Cake."

MIKE AND ME AND THE CAKE

Michael A. Andrews

Our nine-year-old son, Mike, came home from his Cub Scout meeting to tell us his pack would be hosting a banquet and cake sale. The cakes were to be baked by the Cub Scout and his father.

I'd never baked a cake. But, having seen my wife use instant mixes, I looked forward to the project without undue consternation.

When the day came, Mike and I selected a yellow instant cake mix. Following instructions, we mixed the ingredients and poured the batter into two round pans. Confidently we placed the pans in the oven. Taking them out after thirty minutes, in strict accordance with the instructions, I was surprised that the cakes were not the tall and fluffy ones I'd seen in ads. In fact, they only half filled the pans. Mike didn't seem to notice, and besides, I told him, some of the best cakes I'd ever eaten had been shortcakes.

We stacked one cake upon the other, and I then learned that confectioners' sugar was needed to make the frosting. We had no confectioners' sugar. We also had no time. The banquet was only an hour away.

I wasn't even sure what confectioners' sugar was. Well, sugar is sugar, I reasoned. But my wife gently persuaded me that regular granulated sugar was entirely unacceptable. I made a frantic trip to the supermarket and returned with a can of ready-made frosting.

We were already late for the banquet as we scraped and smoothed the frosting over the cake. We got it all looking frosted, even if it was a bit thin in spots. As a finishing touch I made decorative little dabs on top, inspired, I suppose, by the rough-textured paint on our kitchen ceiling. Mike and I traded grins of accomplishment. We thought it looked good.

My wife laughed. Then she said it was sweet and looked just fine. I hadn't noticed that it sloped down on one side. As we hurried to the banquet, Mike casually mentioned that the cake sale would be an auction. For a moment I wished we'd had a little more time for finishing touches.

The hall was filled with people. Dinner was in progress, so we took our cake to the auction room.

I was stunned. A long table was filled with a fantastic array of exquisitely designed masterpieces—angel-food, devil's food, spice, carrot, pound—all exotically iced and imaginatively festooned. Perhaps Mike had misunderstood and this was some kind of world cake competition. Perhaps the fathers and sons could have been assisted by mothers, professional decorators, and engineers. Perhaps we were in the wrong place.

There were cakes shaped like Indian teepees, rocket ships, Scout emblems, hats, the United States, people, and animals. There were toppings of cherries and glazes, marshmallows, and candy glitter. Cakes were displayed on ornate cake pans and porcelain serving dishes. There were cakes topped with ornaments— miniature flags, figures of Cub Scouts, *Star Wars* battle scenes, and landscapes.

Mike solemnly carried our cake forward, on the same paper plate on which we had frosted it. Seeing there was no room alongside the others, he placed it on a radiator behind the table. Carefully, almost reverently, he unwrapped the aluminum foil covering it. Frosting stuck to the foil in several spots, revealing blotches of yellow cake. I felt a flush coming to my face as I watched Mike, but he didn't seem to be ashamed of our creation.

I decided to suggest that perhaps we shouldn't participate in this auction, that perhaps . . . But those thoughts were interrupted by a deafening roar as a torrent of little blue uniforms poured into the room.

I couldn't hear the rules. A matronly den mother relayed portions of them to me as her toddler climbed my right leg. Only the Scouts could be in the auction area and bid. I hurriedly gave Mike eight dollars and, as he rushed back to where the cakes were, I shouted at him to bid low, to get the most he could for his money.

After five minutes of little boys screaming at one another to be quiet, the ordeal began. The auctioneer raised the first cake. He described its design, the intricate ornamentation, the exotic fillings, the bright colors, and the cherry topping. He suggested those attributes warranted a high opening bid. "Seventy-five cents! Eighty cents! One dollar! Going once, twice; sold for one dollar." The next cake was described and sold for fifty cents. I anticipated the audience reaction to our cake and felt a dull pain inside.

My son would probably pretend he didn't know our cake when its time came. I could almost hear the boos and groans.

I tried to make signals to him across the room. I desperately mulled the idea of somehow moving forward and accidentally bumping our cake for the purpose of destroying it, thereby sparing Mike the impending humiliation. *Son, buy a cake—any cake—and let's leave*, I thought. Then the woman beside me began watching me suspiciously. I gave up.

Was it my imagination, or was the auctioneer tactfully avoiding our cake? I began to overhear people in the audience murmuring about the one with the "yellow blotches." Some teenagers behind me called it the Leprosy Cake and laughed. My heart ached for Mike.

The moment arrived. The auctioneer raised our cake. The paper plate sagged over his hand. Crumbs fell off. The numerous holes in the frosting shone garishly beneath the bright overhead lights. He opened his mouth to speak. But before he could utter a sound, Mike was on his feet, yelling at the top of his lungs, "Eight dollars!"

There was a stunned silence. No counterbids were offered. After a couple of double takes, the auctioneer quietly said, "Well, okay . . ." Mike ran forward, wearing a wall-to-wall grin. I heard him tell friends en route: "That's my cake! My dad and I made that cake!"

He handed over the eight dollars and beamed at the cake as if it were a treasure. Smiling, he worked his way through the crowd, stopping once to sample the frosting with a deft swoop of his index finger. When he saw me, he shouted, "Dad, I got it!"

We drove home happy, Mike holding his prize on his lap. I asked why he'd opened the bidding by offering all the money he had, and he answered, "I didn't want anyone else to get our cake!"

"Our cake." It was *our* cake. But I had seen it only through my eyes—not those of that special little boy who is my son. Once we got home, we each had a piece of *our* cake before Mike went to bed. It tasted pretty good. And, by golly, it looked rather nice too.

While the father was concerned about what others would think—his ego—young Mike was proud of his work of art and his relationship with his father. Does your ego ever stand between you and the joys you might otherwise get out of life, between you and relationships important to you?

When I ask audiences to identify a great leader, no matter where I am in the world, almost inevitably Abraham Lincoln is one of the first to be mentioned. Often referred to as Honest Abe, perhaps an equally appropriate name for him might be Humble Abe.

ABE LINCOLN'S FIRST BIG FEE

Mitchell Wilson

One afternoon in 1855 a well-dressed Philadelphia lawyer arrived in the prairie town of Springfield, Illinois, and asked his way to the home of a Mr. A. Lincoln. He found it a plain frame house.

The door was opened by a gangling, shirt-sleeved man who seemed impossibly tall. His legs and arms were unusually long, his shoulders narrow and stooped, his feet and hands abnormally large. His coarse black hair looked as if it had never been combed. The only feature that impressed the visitor was the man's eyes: deep, sad, and wise.

The Philadelphian said: "My name is P. H. Watson. I am counsel for a group of manufacturers who have put up a joint fund to help a man you might know—J. H. Manny of Rockford, Illinois."

Lincoln's face came alive with interest. "The McCormick-Manny case?" he asked. Watson nodded.

The McCormick-Manny case was one of the most important legal battles of the day. Seeing Cyrus McCormick's great success, many small factories were making reapers, but none was paying McCormick royalties—all claimed that their machines differed from his. McCormick had retained the best-known lawyers in the country and was suing the competitor who seemed to have the best case—J. H. Manny & Son.

The other manufacturers realized that they all would be ruined if Manny were put out of business. Watson had advised his clients: "The case is coming up for trial before Judge Drummond in the Northern District of Illinois, probably in Springfield. It would be wise to get yourselves popular support—pick some local man out there who is a good friend of the judge."

This was why Watson was now sitting in the house in Springfield, talking to the tall, homely lawyer. He gave Lincoln his most convincing argument—an advance of five hundred dollars and the promise of the largest fee Lincoln had ever been offered. Lincoln had never handled a case that involved more than a few hundred dollars, and at that time his name was unknown outside his county.

There were, however, some facts about the case that Watson did not tell Lincoln.

When Watson left, Lincoln sat stunned. He was forty-six years old, deeply in debt, haunted by a sense of failure. Now, suddenly, here was the chance to win national fame as a lawyer. He knew nothing about patent law or the mechanics of reapers, but he laboriously set about learning what he would have to know. Still he was worried: in the courtroom he would have to match wits with polished Easterners who had experience and education which he lacked.

During this period of intense preparation Lincoln had only a few letters from Watson, but from them he got the feeling that he was being given a free hand. His confidence grew firmer. One day he was informed that the trial was being moved, by consent of both parties, from Springfield to Cincinnati, where a judge unknown to Lincoln would preside. Lincoln felt he should have been consulted in the matter but shrugged it off, telling himself that Watson was relieving him of all details.

So Lincoln went to Cincinnati to meet his clients, positive that they respected his ability and were counting on him. In his pocket was the brief on which he had worked so hard and on which his future depended.

He had dressed carefully for the occasion and carried himself with dignity. Yet this is how his Eastern colleagues saw him: He looked like an ungainly backwoodsman, with coarse, ill-fitting clothing. His trousers hardly reached his ankles and he was wearing a perspiration-stained linen duster.

Then began Lincoln's disillusionment. He discovered that another lawyer,

Edwin M. Stanton, had been chosen to fight the case—in fact, had been retained from almost the beginning.

When Manny took Lincoln up to Stanton's hotel room the door was open and Lincoln waited outside. Stanton, short and truculent, looked at him and said in a loud voice: "What's he doing here? Get rid of him. I will not be associated with such a gawky ape as that! If I can't have a man who is a gentleman in appearance associated with me in the case I will abandon it."

Lincoln remained silent. The insult was deliberate but he decided to pretend that he had heard nothing. With head high in spite of his mortification he went downstairs, when another lawyer in the case, George Harding, was introduced to him. Then the entire party went to the courthouse.

There the lawyers on both sides exchanged greetings. They had all met before. But Lincoln was not introduced, and stood alone and awkward at the defendants' table.

The custom was that only two speeches were offered by either side. From the talk on the way over, Lincoln learned that he had been retained a few days before Stanton had been brought into the case. Lincoln therefore assumed that, since he had the priority, he would make the speech summing up the legal argument on the Manny side.

McCormick's lawyer, Reverdy Johnson, rose and said suavely: "We perceive that the defendants are represented by three counsels. We are willing that they shall be fully heard and shall waive objections to there being more than two arguments on a side. We merely ask that my associate, Mr. Edward Dickerson, be permitted to speak twice if we so desire."

Lincoln saw Stanton and Harding exchange glances, as if they had some kind of understanding. Lincoln now felt himself an outsider.

Stanton said: "We seek no indulgence from our opponents. We have no intention of having more than two arguments on our side. We couldn't think of violating the usage of the court."

The argument that Stanton had been prepared to make? Lincoln frowned. *Then what had been expected of him?* Lincoln said quietly, "I have my brief prepared."

Stanton looked at him and shrugged with contempt. "Well, of course you have the right precedence," he said. Lincoln, with instinctive courtesy, replied, "Perhaps, Mr. Stanton, you would prefer to speak in my place."

Stanton snapped up Lincoln's offer as though he were accepting Lincoln's complete withdrawal from the case. Harding sat by in silence. Lincoln, realizing that there was nothing for him to do except withdraw, silently left the courtroom.

He stood alone on the steps of the courthouse: hurt, angry, shamed. Yet he had been paid to prepare a brief and was duty bound to give his clients what they had paid for, so he went back to the courtroom and sat among the spectators.

But Lincoln gave Watson his brief. "I spent a lot of time on this; maybe Harding can make some use of it," he said. Watson gave the brief to Harding, who tossed it on the table. Not once did he glance at it, and the next day it was still lying there.

During the week of the trial the lawyers on both sides often dined together, and once were entertained by the judge at his home. Only one man was not invited: the tall, homely man from Springfield.

The trial moved to its climax. McCormick's renowned lawyer, Johnson, gave an eloquent appeal for the rights of the great inventor. The man who could argue successfully against him would be famous, and this was where Lincoln was supposed to have spoken. Instead, in his place rose Stanton, the man who had pushed him aside.

Stanton did not detract from McCormick's achievement, yet he made point after point against Johnson's argument, and Lincoln forgot his hurt pride as Stanton's brilliant logic held him spellbound.

That evening Lincoln took a walk with a friend. "Stanton's argument was a revelation to me," Lincoln said. "I have never heard anything so finished and so carefully prepared." Then he burst out, "I can't hold a candle to any of them. I can't talk like them, or look like them!" But he had the determination of a man who would not stay beaten. "I'm going home to study law all over again," he said. "Those fellows from the East are coming out here more and more, and I must be ready to meet them on their own terms."

Stanton's great speech won the victory for Manny. Watson mailed Lincoln a check for two thousand dollars. The money represented a small fortune to him; but he sent the check back, saying that he did not feel that he should be paid since he had taken no part in the case.

Watson apparently now had mixed feelings about his part in thrusting Lincoln aside, and he offered the check once more. It arrived when Lincoln was in desperate straits. He accepted the money and gave half to his partner Herndon.

Lincoln could not remove the hurt—the memory of it would remain with him forever—but he could change himself so that he would never be hurt again for the same reason. His manner became more dignified, his speeches more polished, more profound.

Then he threw himself into the pursuit of his first and deepest love—politics. Ironically, the fee Lincoln had received provided him with the financial freedom to engage in the political campaign which gained him the fame he had failed to find in the McCormick-Manny case.

A short time later he became President of the United States. Among his most vitriolic critics was Stanton. But Lincoln had never forgotten the distinction between Stanton of the brutal words and Stanton of the brilliant mind—and when he selected a man for the vital post of Secretary of War he chose Edwin M. Stanton.

Only a man with Lincoln's character could have risen above Stanton's insult, and only a man with his charity could have borne no rancor.

After years of serving under Lincoln, Stanton learned who was the better man. As Lincoln lay dying Stanton stood beside him, choked with inconsolable grief. When Lincoln's eyes finally closed, the man who had once hurt him so grievously gave Lincoln the immortal tribute: "Now he belongs to the ages!"

While many would have been totally offended, Abraham Lincoln had the humility to acknowledge his weaknesses and the fortitude to work to overcome them. And when he reached the pinnacle of political life, he again demonstrated humility by promoting Stanton to a position of great prominence and authority. Humility is critical to effective leadership, yet conspicuously absent from too many executive resumes.

While some enter the legal profession with sights set on padding their pockets or representing high-profile cases, this humble lawyer's goal was simply to help people in need of help themselves.

ON THE FRONT LINES

William M. Hendryx

Walking to his office one day in Philadelphia's historic downtown, Michael Taub saw a disheveled panhandler in a wheelchair, parked under the awning of an old movie theater. The heavyset man had only one leg. He clutched a worn cardboard sign reading "Vietnam Veteran."

Rather than avoid eye contact, as so many would, Taub walked right up to him and smiled. "Thank you for having served," he said, pressing a business card into the man's hand. "Stop by my office. Maybe I can help."

Several weeks later, the vet wheeled into the headquarters of the Homeless Advocacy Project. Taub works there as a staff attorney specializing in disability benefits for homeless veterans.

"Looks like you're wearing your Sunday best," Taub said, noting the man's neatly pressed clothes. "You don't have to do that for me."

Taub escorted the man, who introduced himself as Kertis Daniels, to his cramped office, pushing aside stacks of case files—some eighteen inches thick—so that Daniels could wheel himself in.

The handouts weren't for him, Daniels explained. He was panhandling to help his daughter Robin with college. The $845 from the VA every month just didn't go far enough. Daniels lived in a second-floor apartment. Because the building had no elevator or handicap access, he was forced to go through an alley to get inside, then had to leave his wheelchair near the back door. Next he had to hop up the stairs to get to his apartment.

By the end of their meeting, Taub had added another case to his docket. In a typical year he works on about eighty benefits claims to the Department of

Veterans Affairs—all at no charge to the vets. If they qualify for additional benefits, Taub makes sure they get what's coming to them.

Today Kertis Daniels lives in a basement apartment with handicap access. He also receives an additional $250 a month in dependency benefits for Robin, who is a senior at Edinboro University of Pennsylvania, majoring in criminal justice.

Since he was in elementary school, Michael Taub has wanted to help people who couldn't help themselves. A class assignment at Villanova University Law School in 2003 cemented his resolve to fight injustice. Assigned to represent a migrant worker who'd fallen from some scaffolding, Taub fought to get the man the worker's compensation he deserved, even though his boss initially refused to pay.

"The man spoke no English and felt helpless against the system, as do many of our veterans today," explained Taub. "I knew then that my law degree would be used to improve the lives of others, though I wasn't sure how."

The "how" appeared a few months after graduation, when Taub learned of an opening at the Homeless Advocacy Project. It felt right, as if he'd found his calling. He agonized briefly over taking a huge pay cut—sixty-five thousand dollars—from the job he'd lined up with a private law firm.

But even though he owed seventy-five thousand dollars in student loans, drove an old Subaru with 114,000 miles on it, and lived in a tiny one-bedroom apartment with his fiancée, ultimately, the decision was easy.

"It's enough," Taub said of his new, smaller salary. "I use money for things that are important to me, and those aren't material things."

Taub's clients mostly come from a day shelter for homeless vets (estimated to number more than two thousand in the Philadelphia area). The facility is known as the Perimeter, a military term that suggests protection from the outside, a safe place.

Taub is young enough to be a son to most of these men. On one of his recent trips, he sat with about twenty vets, listening to their stories one by one. By the end of the day, he had six new cases.

Among Taub's most dramatic success stories is John Lavery, a fifty-six-year-old veteran who'd been turned down for disability four times, dating back to 1977. Subject to fits of violent rage due to undiagnosed bipolar disorder, Lavery had been all but banned from the Perimeter except to pick up his meds and mail.

For thirty years, he'd been sleeping in doorways, hospital emergency rooms, and abandoned cars. He ate from trash bins and smoked butts he found on the street. Plagued by depression, the decorated former Army specialist had attempted suicide eight times. In his initial meeting with Michael Taub, Lavery found hope for the first time in decades.

"When you look into Michael's eyes and hear the sincerity in his voice," said Lavery, "you know he's for real."

Taub spent months trying to sort out the troubled man's jagged life. At home in the evenings, he spent time in Vietnam Vet chat rooms, eventually tracking down men who had served with Lavery and could help verify his story.

Deemed 100 percent disabled, Lavery was awarded forty thousand dollars in back benefits, plus a monthly stipend.

He now lives with dignity in his own apartment and volunteers every day at a shelter for recovering alcoholics and addicts.

"Michael wouldn't take any credit. He said I earned it," explained Lavery, who regularly sends other veterans Taub's way. "He's very humble."

In typical modest fashion, Taub downplays his success. "We rarely win that big, and we certainly don't win every claim," he elaborated. "But these men come out ahead even when losing, because we give them something they've not experienced in a long while—fair treatment, kindness, and some closure to a difficult chapter in their lives. They leave here each feeling like a person of value."

Forgoing the glamorous, limelight cases, Michael Taub was more concerned about helping people in need—a sure sign of Everyday Greatness. And he did it humbly with no interest in publicity, while eagerly giving others the credit.

~⌒

WRAP UP

Whether in a parent, a leader, or a follower, humility is a distinguishing characteristic of Everyday Greatness. For Everyday Greatness is void of boasting or snobbery. It does not seek its own gain, or fuel a "mirror, mirror on the wall, who's the greatest of them all?" mentality. So if your motives or aspirations are centered on receiving applause or polishing your ego or on confiscating others' credit, Everyday Greatness is probably not yet a standard part of your everyday repertoire.

REFLECTIONS

- The father in the first story felt the pains of his day's behaviors. Are there people who you have offended today? Yesterday? Do you possess the humility to apologize, to change?

- Humility is the key that unlocks our minds to learning from others. Do you feel a need to have all the answers or to be the smartest in the crowd, or are you more likely to be open to others' insights?

- Lincoln is quite well known for his humility. What traits do you believe describe a leader who is humble? How well do you exemplify those traits?

- Some leaders vainly prefer to take credit for everything that goes right. How about you? Do you give credit where credit is due, or do you prefer to capture all the glory for yourself?

FURTHER INSIGHTS ON
Humility

IN ALL HUMILITY

Though humility is not a tangible commodity, we know it when we see it and feel it when we hear it.

An ego trip is something that never gets you anywhere.

—SUZAN L. WIENER

■ ■ ■

Everyone has something to be modest about.

—IRISH PROVERB

■ ■ ■

It is unhealthy to marinate in your own press clippings.

—SAM WALTON

■ ■ ■

I long to accomplish a great and noble task, but it is my chief duty to accomplish small tasks as if they were great and noble.

—HELEN KELLER

■ ■ ■

Remember that the opportunity for great deeds may never come, but the opportunity for good deeds is renewed day by day. The thing for us to long for is the goodness, not the glory.

—F. W. FABER

■ ■ ■

Humility is a strange thing. The minute you think you've got it, you've lost it.

—E. D. HULSE,
IN *BASHFORD METHODIST MESSENGER*

■ ■ ■

None are so empty as those who are full of themselves.

—BENJAMIN WHICHCOTE

■ ■ ■

Swallow your pride occasionally. It's non-fattening.

—FRANK TYGER

■ ■ ■

When hosting high-ranking friends, former U.S. President, Theodore Roosevelt, was fond of taking his guests on evening walks. Inevitably, he would point skywards and recite:

"That is the Spiral Galaxy of Andromeda. It is as large as our Milky Way. It is one of a hundred million galaxies. It is 2,500,000 light-years away. It consists of one hundred billion suns, many larger than our own sun."

Then, following a brief silence, he would grin and say, "Now, I think we are small enough. Let's go in."

— *THOUGHTS AFIELD*, BY HAROLD E. KOHN

ON EVEN GROUND

Humility disappears as soon as we think ourselves superior
or feel our needs are greater than those of another.

Do not think yourself so big that other people look small.

—CONFUCIUS

■ ■ ■

Never seem more learned than the people you are with. Wear your learning
like a pocket-watch and keep it hidden. Do not pull it out to count the
hours, but give the time when you are asked.

—LORD CHESTERFIELD

■ ■ ■

We say that people are proud of being rich, or clever, or good-looking, but
they are not. They are proud of being richer, or cleverer, or better-looking
than others. Nearly all those evils which people put down to greed or
selfishness are really far more the result of pride.

—C. S. LEWIS,
MERE CHRISTIANITY

■ ■ ■

There is perhaps not one of our natural passions so hard to subdue as pride.
Beat it down, stifle it, mortify it as much as one pleases, it is still alive. Even
if I could conceive that I had completely overcome it, I should probably be
proud of my humility.

—BENJAMIN FRANKLIN,
FROM HIS AUTOBIOGRAPHY

■ ■ ■

One day, at the first home Mother Teresa established for incurables, a man
half-consumed by cancer was brought in. A male attendant was overcome by
the stench and turned away, retching. Mother Teresa took over the task herself.

The miserable patient cursed her. "How can you stand the smell?" he
demanded.

"It's nothing," she replied, "compared to the pain you must feel."

—THE *NEW YORK TIMES*

BOASTING

It has been said that some people think they can push themselves forward by patting themselves on the back. But boasting merely amplifies the ego.

When someone sings his own praises, he always gets the tune too high.

—MARY H. WALDRIP

■ ■ ■

Heroes are people who rise to the occasion and slip quietly away.

—TOM BROKAW

■ ■ ■

Intelligence is like a river: the deeper it is, the less noise it makes.

—MILWAUKEE JOURNAL SENTINEL

■ ■ ■

Each of us is an actor trying to impress an audience, to take the center of the stage. But if you want to pay close attention to another human being, you must train your own attention-hungry ego to stop striving for the spotlight and let it fall on the other person.

—DONALD E. SMITH

■ ■ ■

When your work speaks of itself, don't interrupt.

—HENRY J. KAISER

■ ■ ■

Noise proves nothing. Often a hen who has merely laid an egg cackles as if she had laid an asteroid.

—MARK TWAIN

■ ■ ■

He who truly knows has no occasion to shout.

—LEONARDO DA VINCI

SHARING CREDIT

> Humble people who achieve success recognize that they did not get to the top all by themselves, and willingly credit others who have helped along the way.

A hundred times a day, I remind myself that my inner and outer life depends on the labors of other men, living and dead, and that I must exert myself in order to give in the same measure as I have received and am receiving.

—ALBERT EINSTEIN

■ ■ ■

In the office of *Roots* author Alex Haley hangs a picture of a turtle sitting on a fence. When Haley looks at it, he's reminded of a lesson taught to him by his friend John Gaines: "If you see a turtle on top of a fence post, you know he had some help."

Says Haley, "Any time I start thinking, 'Wow, isn't this marvelous what I've done!' I look at that picture and remember how this turtle—me—got up on that post."

—ASSOCIATED PRESS

■ ■ ■

If I have seen further, it is by standing on the shoulders of giants.

—SIR ISAAC NEWTON

9

GRATITUDE

Swift gratitude is the sweetest.
—GREEK PROVERB

Gratitude is a close companion to both integrity and humility. Gratitude without integrity is insincere flattery, while it takes humility to say, "Thanks, I could not have done it without you." So it makes sense that gratitude follows both integrity and humility in our array of principles.

Gratitude can be expressed in many ways. It can come as a small, concrete token of thanks as shown in "A Legacy from Mr. Ditto." Or it can be an every-moment, everyday experience as illustrated by "Coming to My Senses." Other times it can take the form of praise—acknowledging people for who they are or something they have done, as evidenced in "A Lesson from the Mound." But regardless of the form it takes, the ability to give and receive gratitude is a quality that attends every meaningful relationship and is a core ingredient to Everyday Greatness.

A LEGACY FROM MR. DITTO

Doris Cheney Whitehouse

I stood by Mr. Ditto's bedside at the hour of his death. He looked like a small black doll against the whiteness of the pillow, his old head almost buried in its deep folds. His pulse was barely perceptible, and I felt a strange awareness of a transformation taking place, as though by watching very closely I might be able to see his spirit soar like a newly hatched moth out of the withered husk that lay before me.

At last I heard the faint beginning of his final breath. He did not struggle, even in death, so that when it came it was gentle and easy, touched with contentment like a sigh.

The Reverend William Howard, a Negro chaplain, sat by the bed, an open Bible resting lightly in the palm of one great hand. He closed it quietly. Then he bowed his head and whispered, "Into Thy hands, O Merciful Savior, we commend the soul of Thy servant."

After a moment he touched my shoulder gently as though he understood the heaviness in my heart. "Rejoice and be exceeding glad," he said. Then he turned and left the room, closing the door softly behind him.

When he was done I did the things a nurse must do for a patient after death. I opened the drawer of the bedside table and began to gather together all Mr. Ditto's belongings—a pair of ancient spectacles, hopelessly twisted; a razor with a rusted blade; a Bible worn from years of handling. And there I found the nickel I knew that had brought him so much joy. It was the total treasure of his life, and I held it in my hand for a long time, remembering . . .

Mr. Ditto had been one of the first patients assigned to me that winter of 1947 when I took up my duties as a young nurse on the TB ward of the Veterans Administration Hospital in Louisville, Kentucky. Mr. Ditto was his real name; he was never known by any other. An American Negro born of slave parents in New Orleans at the time of the Civil War, he had been orphaned at an early age and, with the emancipation, had been cast out into the world. Except for service in the Spanish-American War, he had lived his life from day to day, doing odd jobs for anyone who would hire him, living alone in a shack provided by his former owners. Some years ago he had come to Louisville. He had been ill for a long time, and when he was admitted to the hospital he was suffering from advanced pelvic tuberculosis. A great abscess had ruptured, leaving a draining sinus.

The dreadful stench of it rose to meet me as I entered his room that first day. I wanted to turn and run away, and perhaps I might have done so had not something in Mr. Ditto's eyes reached out and held me. "Good morning, Mr. Ditto," I said. "Are you ready for the morning's activities?"

"Ah don' know what they is, ma'am," he said. "But if you think Ah need 'em, Ah's ready."

I began with a bath and the changing of the sheets. The tiny body was so emaciated that it seemed almost weightless as I gently turned him on his side. His eyes bulged with pain, but he made no sound.

I remember how my nausea rose when I removed the dressing, but a small voice saved me. "Ah don' know how you stand it, ma'am! Ah can't hardly stand it myself!" And he wrinkled up his face in such a comic grimace that I laughed out loud. When he heard my laughter, he laughed, too. We looked at each other helplessly, caught on a wave of preposterous mirth, and suddenly the air seemed fresher and the wound less offensive. The sight of it never bothered me again.

When I finally drew up the clean white sheet and folded it across his chest, his face still sparkled in reflection of our joke. "Ah sho' do thank you, ma'am," he said. "Ah's feelin' a whole heap better, and that's the truth." Then he reached out one bony hand, weak and trembling, and fumbled in the drawer of his bedside table. From it he extracted a shiny nickel and held it out to me.

"It ain't very much for all yo' goodness," he said. "But it's a powerful cold day, an' Ah just thought some good hot coffee might give you pleasure."

The drawer was open, and I could see a number of nickels, perhaps twenty, scattered among his personal effects. This was all the money he had in the world. I should have accepted his offering at once. Instead, I reacted in haste. "Oh no, Mr. Ditto," I said. "I couldn't take that! You save it for a rainy day."

I saw the light go out of his eyes and all the shining, as a dark shadow fell across his face. "Ain't never gonna rain no harder'n now," he said.

Hearing the dull despair in his voice, I knew instantly what I had done. I had reduced him to an old, old man with nothing left to give, with nothing left to accomplish except dying. Quickly I said, "You know, Mr. Ditto, I think you're right. I can't think of anything better than a cup of good hot coffee." I took the nickel out of his hand and watched the light come back into his face.

In the days that followed, Mr. Ditto grew steadily weaker. Every morning when I put him through the same exhausting routine he submitted patiently. Somehow we always managed a little conversation, a little fun and gentle laughter, so that I looked forward to the hour spent with him. And every morning before I left the room his old hand would grope for another nickel and he would say, "It ain't very much for all yo' goodness."

I watched the little pile of nickels slowly diminishing and prayed that Mr. Ditto would not outlive his treasure. His strength was now almost gone, but he never once forgot his gift to me, even when he could no longer lift his hand without my help.

One day I saw that he was reaching for the very last nickel in the drawer. I guided his hand to it, fighting back the tears that had sprung to my eyes. I searched his face for any sign of realization that there were no other nickels, but he was unaware of it. He held the coin out to me, smiling the same sweet smile, mumbling the same familiar words of gratitude. Then I knew that he was wrapped in that gentle half-awareness which enfolds the dying. He was conscious only of the joy of giving, and I knew with sudden gladness that he was past all keeping of accounts. Silently I put the nickel back in the corner of the drawer.

He lived for two weeks after that. Every day when I had finished his morning care and he was lying clean and comfortable in fresh white sheets, he would murmur over and over again, "You an angel, ma'am, you just a sure 'nough angel." Then I would know that it was time to take his hand in mine and guide it to the corner of the drawer. Every day he gave me the nickel. And every day I put it back again.

That last day I sent for Mr. Howard, the chaplain. He came and read softly as one might read to a child who was falling asleep, his voice moving smoothly over the lovely verses . . . "And seeing the multitudes, He went up into a mountain; and when He was set, His disciples came unto Him: And He opened His mouth, and taught them, saying, 'Blessed are the poor in spirit: for theirs is the kingdom of heaven. Blessed are they that mourn: for they shall be comforted. Blessed are the meek: for they shall inherit the earth.' "

I thought: *Mr. Ditto had been, indeed, the poorest and meekest of men; he had accepted fearful suffering without complaint. But now, in the final hour of his life, he could not hear again the promise of eternal joy.* Suddenly rebellion rose in my heart. Mr. Ditto. How perfectly his name described him, as though God, having made a world of men, had paused and then said "Ditto"— and there *he* was. What purpose had there been in his creation? What possible meaning to his patient, futile life?

After the chaplain had gone, I stood for a long time with the last treasured nickel in my hand. Finally I put it with the rest of Mr. Ditto's things, tied them all together into a sad little bundle and marked them with his name. Then I took them to the office and suggested that they be turned over to Mr. Howard.

Later that afternoon, just before it was time for me to go off duty, Mr. Howard appeared in the ward. He looked at me and smiled. "It seems that Mr. Ditto left a small estate," he said. "I think he would want you to have it." He took the nickel out of his pocket and pressed it into my hand.

This time I accepted it instantly. For, remembering the light in Mr. Ditto's eyes, I suddenly knew the meaning of his gift. Over and over again I had received it in grief, thinking it a mark of his poverty. Now for the first time I saw it as it really was: a shining symbol of some boundless wealth which I had never dreamed existed. In that one bright moment all sorrow was dispelled, all pity vanished. My poor little Mr. Ditto had been rich beyond belief. In his vast estate were all the patience, faith, and love a human heart can hold.

I went to the hospital canteen and bought a cup of coffee. There was a vacant table by the window, and I sat down. It was almost dark. A tiny evening star twinkled prematurely in the sky. I lifted the streaming coffee to my lips and proposed a silent toast: "To Mr. Ditto, who shall inherit the earth." Then I drank deeply of the cup.

While reading this story, you can almost hear the day-to-day silence that filled Mr. Ditto's room. With doors shut and no family or acquaintances around, the silence was broken only by those few occasions when the nurse entered. But even then, the only noise you could hear was the sound of gratitude that the nurse and Mr. Ditto expressed and received from one another. And, even those expressions were relatively quiet. For many of the deepest expressions of gratitude are softly spoken—not a lot of drums, not a lot of fanfare. Instead they are gentle but sincere "Thank you's" spoken audibly, sent by a smile, or placed in a note.

Reasons and occasions for gratitude abound, even in a harsh world. Yet, it is so easy to take the good things of life for granted. Such was certainly the case for the following woman, until the day the sky fell in on her.

COMING TO MY SENSES

Sarah Ban Breathnach

While eating out at a restaurant in the mid-1980s, I discovered that Chicken Little knew what he was talking about: The sky could fall suddenly, and it landed on my head by way of a large ceiling panel, knocking me to the table. No one else in the restaurant was hit.

I didn't lose consciousness, but I sustained a head injury that left me bedridden, confused, and disoriented for months and partially disabled for a year and a half. During the first few months of recuperation, my senses were all skewed. My eyesight was blurry and I was very sensitive to light, so the shades in my bedroom had to be drawn at all times. Even seeing the different patterns on my bed quilt jarred my equilibrium; I had to turn the quilt over to its plain muslin backing.

I couldn't listen to music because it made me dizzy. I couldn't carry on phone conversations because processing the sounds and rearranging them into meaningful patterns in my brain was impossible. And I couldn't taste my food or smell the luscious fragrance of my little girl's hair after it was washed.

There were days when the slightest touch was painful. Something as light as a sheet on my bare legs became unbearably heavy. And pulling a sweater on over my elbows caused the same kind of jolt you get when fingernails scratch across a chalkboard.

Other senses that I had taken for granted my entire life became strangers, and I sorely missed them. Like a cat who's had her whiskers trimmed, I lost my sense of balance as well as my perception of depth and distance. Just the thought of getting out of bed to fix a cup of tea was bruising because I knew I would stumble and fall. I had been writing for *The Washington Post* as a lifestyle journalist, and because of the accident I was also denied the consolation of some keen companions—the written and spoken word—not to mention my livelihood and my sense of belonging.

Having to spend my days in bed and not in the company of my family, unable to care for my daughter, Katie, who was just two years old, I also lost my sense of identity. If I wasn't a wife, mother, writer, then who was I? In one freak moment, it seemed, my sense of humor, sense of place, sense of purpose, sense of safety, but most importantly, my sense of peace, were all erased.

These unsettling side effects lasted for a few months and changed my life in ways I could scarcely have imagined. Because I was unable to speak articulately or read with comprehension, I was overcome with shame. Even when I was no longer bedridden, I felt so embarrassed by my condition that I didn't venture farther than my own backyard. Naturally this increased my already enormous sense of isolation. Instead of enjoying the companionship of family and friends, my days were now filled with a feeling of loss, my nights a terrifying dread about my future.

During my sense-less period, I went through a bitter "Why me, why this, why now?" litany. Why had God singled me out for this misery? Of course, I now know that my accident wasn't an act of God, but instead a head-on collision between circumstance, fate, karma, and human error: The ceiling panel in the restaurant hadn't been completely screwed back in place after a repair to an air-conditioning duct. I have truly come to believe that when we're struck down by adversity, God weeps with us. Then, because we're so loved, He heals us in ways we can never imagine.

My downtime was a perfect opportunity for heaven to get my complete attention. Chief among my discoveries was this: Divinity is to be found where and when you least expect it. Moses found his God in a burning bush. And I found mine in a pot of homemade spaghetti sauce. Months after my accident, the spaghetti sauce was the first thing I was able to smell distinctly.

As the aroma of a friend's kind gift simmering on the stove wafted up to my bedroom, I could scarcely believe my nose. Euphoric, I followed the strange but familiar fragrance of garlic, onions, tomatoes, peppers, and oregano down the stairs and into the kitchen. I was practically beside myself with delight. I felt like I was standing on holy ground in my own house. I had discovered the miracle of the sacred in the ordinary; from that moment my life would forever be changed.

Taking a spoon, I dipped it into the sauce and brought it to my lips. I wasn't able to taste the sauce yet, just distinguish temperature and texture. It didn't matter. I was so grateful to inhale the glorious scent of ordinary life that I was off and running. I went up to the bathroom and got out a jar of Vicks VapoRub. Yes! Eucalyptus! Then I buried my face in some freshly laundered clothes and inhaled the fragrance of a warm shirt. And so it went.

For the next few happy weeks I rediscovered life with the same sense of wonder as my little girl. Taste came next, followed by hearing, sight, and touch. Each sensory restoration was accompanied by a feeling of rapture and even sudden tears. Biting into a ripe, juicy peach. Listening to music. Seeing bright sunlight stream through a window. Being able to wear my favorite sweater. And, naturally, cradling my daughter in my arms again.

I was astonished and ashamed at my appalling lack of appreciation for what had been right under my nose. Cliché or not, we just don't know how blessed we are until misfortune strikes. No more. I swore I would never, ever forget.

And I haven't. All these years later, I strive to make each day a passionate, sensuous experience, one in which I take time to savor life's textures, tastes, sights, sounds, and aromas. Through the power and grace of gratitude, you, too, can do the same.

Fish discover water last. They are so immersed in the element that they are unaware of it. So it is with many people who become so immersed in an abundance of blessings and opportunities that they are unaware of them until they stop, pause, and reflect and allow gratitude to emerge. Sadly, too often it takes the force of circumstance rather than the force of conscience to stir up our gratitude.

Sometimes gratitude is best expressed in the form of praise. It is a way of telling a person that you are grateful for who they are, or of letting them know you appreciate something they did, as illustrated by the following all-star grandpa.

A LESSON FROM THE MOUND

Beth Mullally

My father was always the pitcher in our back-yard baseball games. He got this honor in part because my sister, brother, and I couldn't get the ball over the home plate, but also because, with one wooden leg, running after a fly ball that got hit into the cornfield out back just wasn't his strong suit. And so he'd stand under the hot sun, pitching endlessly while we took turns at bat.

He ran our games with the authority of a Yankees manager. He was boss, and he had requirements. We had to chatter in the outfield, for one. And we had to try to outrun the ball, no matter how futile it might seem.

Going up to bat against my father was not easy. None of this self-esteem stuff for him, trying to make kids feel good about hitting a ball that's standing still. He was never the least bit sorry when he struck me out, and he did it all the time. "Do you want to play ball or don't you?" he'd ask if I began whining about his fast pitches.

I wanted to. And when I'd finally connect with the ball—oh, man, I knew I deserved the hit. I'd be grinning all the way down the first-base line.

I'd turn to look at my father on the pitcher's mound. He'd take off his glove and tuck it under his arm, and then clap for me. To my ears, it sounded like a standing ovation at Yankee Stadium.

Years later, my son was to learn those same rules about baseball from my father. By then, though, Dad was pitching from a wheelchair. In some medical fluke, he had lost his other leg.

But nothing else had changed. My boy was required to chatter from the outfield. He had to try outrunning the ball, no matter how futile it might seem. And when he whined that the pitch was too fast, he got the ultimatum: "Do you want to play ball or don't you?"

He did.

My boy was nine years old the spring before his grandfather died. They played a lot of ball that season, and there was the usual litany of complaints that my father was pitching too hard.

"Just keep your eye on the ball!" Dad would holler at him.

Finally, at one at-bat, he did. He swung and connected dead-center. The ball slammed down the middle, straight at my father.

He reached for it, but missed. And in the process, his wheelchair tilted backward. In ever such slow motion, we watched him and his chair topple until he came down on his back with a thud.

My boy stood stock-still halfway to first.

"You don't ever stop running!" my father roared from the ground. "That ball's still in play! You run!"

When my boy stood safe at first base, he turned to look at my father lying on his back on the pitcher's mound. He saw him take off his glove and tuck it under his arm. And then he heard his grandfather clap for him.

Everyone deserves to have such a grandpa. There is so much negativism and criticism that we each can benefit from a little praise or an expression of gratitude from someone we respect. This tough grandfather's words of praise and expressions of applause will undoubtedly live on in the memories of his children and grandchildren well beyond his remarkable pitching career.

~

WRAP UP

In terms of the energy and know-how required, gratitude is one of the easiest of all principles to apply. Though it also generally returns rich dividends, it is vastly underutilized. Why? Perhaps because of a lack of humility—it can be hard to acknowledge the need to be helped. Or a lack of courage—a person might be too shy to tell another how much he or she means. Yet, people with Everyday Greatness are quick to exhibit everyday gratitude. They do not take life or the kindnesses of others for granted. They are eager to say thanks and among the first to express praise. Many have found the best sleeping pill comes from counting one's blessings, naming them one by one.

REFLECTIONS

- Each of Mr. Ditto's nickels represented a sincere "Thank you." What nickel deposits have you made recently?

- Mr. Ditto's nurse allowed him to feel appreciated by graciously receiving his nickels. Are there occasions when you could more graciously accept someone's "nickels"?

- It took a catastrophe for Sarah to realize she had so much for which to be thankful. What are some of the "little" things—*hidden riches*—in life that you take for granted?

- As the grandpa demonstrated, some of the most valuable forms of gratitude are packaged in the shape of praise. Is praise a regular part of your everyday vocabulary?

FURTHER INSIGHTS ON
Gratitude

~

HEARTFELT GRATITUDE

Gratitude originates from the heart and then opens our eyes to the beauties of nature and the richness of friendships most dear.

Feeling gratitude and not expressing it is like wrapping a present and not giving it.

—WILLIAM ARTHUR WARD

■ ■ ■

The hardest arithmetic to master is that which enables us to count our blessings.

—ERIC HOFFER

■ ■ ■

I wept because I had no shoes, until I saw a man who had no feet.

—ANCIENT PERSIAN SAYING

■ ■ ■

When eating fruit, think of the person who planted the tree.

—VIETNAMESE PROVERB

■ ■ ■

Health is a crown on a well man's head, but no one appreciates it like a sick man.

—EGYPTIAN PROVERB

■ ■ ■

The Pilgrims gave thanks for mighty little, for mighty little was all they expected. But now, neither government nor nature can give enough but what we think it's too little. If we can't gather in a new Buick, a new radio, a tuxedo, and some government relief, why, we feel that the world is against us.

—WILL ROGERS

PRAISE

One form of gratitude is praise. It is a way of telling another you appreciate them for who they are.

There is nothing that so kills the ambitions of a man as criticism from his superiors. So I am anxious to praise but loath to find fault. I have yet to find the man, however exalted his station, who did not do better work and put forth greater effort under a spirit of approval than under a spirit of criticism.

—CHARLES SCHWAB,
IN *HOW TO WIN FRIENDS AND INFLUENCE PEOPLE*
BY DALE CARNEGIE

■ ■ ■

A pat on the back, though only a few vertebrae removed from a kick in the pants, is miles ahead in results.

—BENNETT CERF

■ ■ ■

Catch people doing something right! Then tell everyone about it.

—KENNETH BLANCHARD

■ ■ ■

If you want your children to improve, let them overhear the nice things you say about them to others.

—HAIM GINOTT

■ ■ ■

Boy to mother: "You never mention the dirt I track out."

—*MINNEAPOLIS TRIBUNE*

■ ■ ■

I can live for two months on a good compliment.

—MARK TWAIN

■ ■ ■

Words can sometimes, in moments of grace, attain the quality of deeds.

—ELIE WIESEL

THE POWER OF A NOTE

Notes are expressions of gratitude and praise that people can treasure for years.

On my first job as sports editor for the *Montpelier* (Ohio) *Leader Enterprise*, I didn't get a lot of fan mail so I was intrigued by a letter plopped on my desk one morning. The envelope bore the logo of the closest big-city paper, the *Toledo Blade*.

When I opened it, I read, "Sweet piece of writing on the Tigers. Keep up the good work." It was signed by Don Wolfe, the sports editor. Because I was a teenager (being paid the grand total of fifteen cents a column inch), his words couldn't have been more exhilarating. I kept the letter in my desk drawer until it got rag-eared. When I doubted I had the right stuff to be a writer, I would reread Don's note and walk on air again.

Later when I got to know him, I learned that Don made a habit of jotting a quick, encouraging word to people in all walks of life. "When I make others feel good about themselves," he told me, "I feel good too."

—FRED BAUER

■ ■ ■

Dr. William L. Stidger sat down and wrote a letter of thanks to a schoolteacher for having given him so much encouragement when he had been in her class thirty years before. The following week he received an answer, written in a very shaky hand. The letter read:

"My dear Willie: I want you to know what your note meant to me. I am an old lady in my eighties, living alone in a small room, cooking my own meals, lonely, and seeming like the last leaf on the tree. You will be interested to know, Willie, that I taught school for fifty years and in all that time, yours is the first letter of appreciation I have ever received. It came on a cold, blue morning and cheered my lonely old heart as nothing has cheered me in many years."

—MARTIN BUXBAUM,
TABLE TALK FOR FAMILY FUN

TANGIBLE THANKS

On occasion gratitude is most favorably expressed in the form of tangible rewards.

In the 1994 NCAA title game, Arkansas basketball coach Nolan Richardson started Ken Biley, a benchwarming senior who hadn't played much during his career, and not at all in the semifinals.

"When I saw that kid's face after the semis," Richardson says, "I hurt so bad I couldn't sleep. So I decided that Biley would start the final game. It would mean more to him and his grandkids than whether we won or lost."

—CURRY KIRKPATRICK,
IN *NEWSWEEK*
[NOTE: BILEY STARTED, ARKANSAS BEAT DUKE 76–72]

■ ■ ■

Lawrence of Arabia kept a fortune in gold sovereigns in his camel bags, and an Arab who distinguished himself in combat could help himself to as much gold as he could scoop out with one hand.

—LOWELL THOMAS,
THE REAL LAWRENCE OF ARABIA

■ ■ ■

I wish parents would understand that if their child drops eight fly balls one day, then only drops six the next, that's reason to go to Dairy Queen. The principal thing is competing against yourself. It's about self-improvement, about being better than you were the day before.

—STEVE YOUNG,
IN *PEOPLE*

RECEIVING GRATEFULLY

As Mr. Ditto's nurse reminds us, to receive gratitude with grace is a form of gratitude by itself, and not always an easy art to master.

Giving can be so easy as to be almost automatic, whereas receiving can make demands on every nerve.

—E. V. LUCAS

■ ■ ■

Never hesitate to hold out your hand; never hesitate to accept the outstretched hand of another.

—POPE JOHN XXIII

■ ■ ■

To receive a present handsomely and in a right spirit, even when you have none to give in return, is to give one in return.

—LEIGH HUNT

■ ■ ■

To receive gratefully from others is to enhance others' sense of their worth. It puts them on a give-and-take level, the only level on which real fellowship can be sustained. It changes one of the ugliest things in the world, patronage, into one of the richest things in the world, friendship.

—HALFORD E. LUCCOCK,
LIVING WITHOUT GLOVES

CREATING
THE DREAM

When love and skill work together, expect a masterpiece.
—JOHN RUSKIN

When asked why people invent, Mark Twain replied, "To give birth to an idea—to discover a great thought—an intellectual nugget, right under the dust of a field that many a brain-plow had gone over before. To be the first—that is the idea." Indeed, one of the deepest joys in life is to be creative; to put yourself into something innovative and worthwhile, and then to see it come to fruition. But the process of creating can be a roller coaster of highs and lows—ecstasies and despairs—before you experience the rewards.

Principles that enable the art of creating include

- Vision

- Innovation

- Quality

10

VISION

Determine that the thing can and shall be done
and then we shall find the way.
—ABRAHAM LINCOLN

A ll things are created twice. All things. Vision is the first creation. For a house it's called the blueprint. For a life it's called a mission. For a day it's called a goal and a plan. For a parent it's called a belief in the unseen potential of a child. For all, it is the mental creation which always precedes the physical, or second, creation.

Vision not only helps us spot present opportunities where others might not see them, but it also points us toward the future and inspires us to ask, "Where do I want to be five years from now? Ten years from now?" To answer these questions takes time—it even takes some dreaming. A master among masters of vision and dreaming was Walt Disney. His creative genius and sense of vision helped him to spot ideas invisible to others and to look ahead to future opportunities. As you enjoy "Wish Upon a Star" and the other stories demonstrating the principle of vision, consider specifically your vision of the accomplishments and plans you most want to achieve over the next year to five years and how you might best accomplish them.

WISH UPON A STAR

Richard Collier

It was a brilliant October day in 1965, and the setting, sixteen miles southwest of Orlando, Florida, was an undeveloped wilderness, twice the size of Manhattan, which Walt Disney Productions had just purchased. But where the ordinary observer saw only swamps and cypress groves, already Disney could see the beckoning future—an unparalleled vacation kingdom called Walt Disney World. And this was to be only the beginning. For now Disney revealed a dream which would surpass even these achievements. "Wouldn't it be something," he asked, "if we could build a city here, an experimental community of tomorrow, where people could live without traffic or smog or slums?"

"But, Walt," objected Joe Potter, a Disney vice president, "that would cost hundreds of millions of dollars!"

Disney's brown eyes sparkled. "Joe," he asked, "can't you keep your mind on the subject and away from inessentials?"

It was a typical remark. All his life Walter Elias Disney had dreamed such dreams. He was a whole industry in himself.

THE FIRST KINGDOM

When Walt was four years old, his father, Elias Disney, made a decision that was to be pivotal in shaping the boy's future. A carpenter by trade, Elias Disney was a dignified and devout man, and a strict observer of the Sabbath. When three saloons opened near his house, he was outraged. "The city is no place to raise children," he told his wife, Flora, and soon afterward he bought property known as Crane Farm, one hundred miles northeast of Kansas City.

Besides Walt and his parents, there were four other Disneys: Herbert seventeen, Raymond fifteen, Roy twelve, and Ruth two. The disparity in ages meant that Walt had no companions on the farm. So he took to slipping off to seek the company of the farm animals. He evolved games, played according to rules, and it was as if his companions responded and understood. Skinny, the piglet, squealed deliriously through games of hide-and-seek; Pete, the family terrier, proved adept at tug-of-war. And old Charley, the buggy horse, contrived a game of his own—heading for the five-acre orchard in a cavalry charge whenever Walt climbed on his back. The animals were the toys and friends that Walt Disney never had, and the farm itself was the first of his magic kingdoms.

Like most farmers, Elias saved rainwater in tarred barrels. One day Walt noticed that the tar in one of them was melting under the sun. A few feet away in the pigpen, the old sow whom he had often ridden into the hog pond was snorting contentedly. She seemed a perfect subject for a portrait and, seizing a brush, Walt dipped it in the tar and set to work, using the side of the house as his canvas.

Hauled off by his father to the barn, Walt learned that his family didn't appreciate his genius. But one relative saw genuine talent in the picture: Aunt Margaret. She bought Walt a five-cent tablet and a box of crayons, and soon the boy was sketching everything in sight in the barnyard.

"I'm Going to Be an Artist"

Always Walt was drawing. The margins of his schoolbooks were a veritable frieze of animals: squirrels, goats, pigs, his friends from Crane Farm, endowed with uncannily human qualities. Once a teacher set the class a routine still-life exercise: a bowl of spring flowers. To her amusement, Walt's flowers took on a life of their own: tulips pouted prettily, with petal lips and expressive eyelashes. Daffodils talked in cartoon balloons, and stems and leaves became arms and legs.

In 1917 Elias moved again, this time back to Chicago. Walt attended McKinley High School. Just one thing mattered now: to draw, and three nights a week he studied under professional cartoonists at the Chicago Academy of Fine Arts. He then spent nearly a year in France driving a Red Cross ambulance. He returned with $600 in savings and a new determination: "I'm going to be an artist."

On his first job at a small advertising agency, where he was paid $50 a month, he met another young artist, Ub Iwerks. Soon the two became partners and began doing ads on their own. The first month they netted $135; the next, they nearly starved.

Both then landed jobs at the Kansas City Slide Company, which made one-minute commercials to be shown in local movie theaters. It was Disney's first step into the world of cartoon animation, an art which at this time was primitive, the animation jerky and unrealistic.

Walt began to experiment. By degrees he hit on a method that was both costly and time consuming, but which came closer to the illusion of motion he was seeking. To depict a boy kicking a ball he made an unprecedented twenty drawings, each advancing the action slightly.

With Ub, Walt completed a series that he styled Laugh-O-Grams for a local chain of theaters. These were one-minute fillers designed to promote local products, and the theater manager was favorably impressed. "But are they expensive?" he asked.

"I can make them for thirty cents a foot," Walt assured him. The manager agreed to buy all he made.

Then, en route to his office to hand in his resignation, Walt stopped dead on the sidewalk, as the realization swept over him: thirty cents a foot was his cost of production. He had forgotten to include his profit. "But it will pay for more experimentation," he exulted to Ub. For all his life, this was often the sole criterion of any new venture.

In time, Laugh-O-Grams went into bankruptcy. Disney, banished from his rooming house, had to sleep at his office on cushions from the chairs.

Months earlier the Disney office had been visited by a plague of mice, attracted by the remnants of lunches left in wastebaskets. Soon erasers and pencils became the victims of their needle-sharp teeth, and some of the artists proposed setting a mousetrap. But Walt sternly forbade it. He devised a harmless trap, caught ten of the little rodents, then constructed a roomy cage from a wire wastebasket. In the midnight hours when he worked alone, one mouse, whom Walt christened Mortimer, became so tame that Walt allowed it to frisk along the top of his drawing board, where it boldly cleaned its whiskers.

In his struggle to keep going, Walt decided that the one place where a man of destiny might see his dreams come true was Hollywood. He scraped up enough for a train ticket and began to pack. The night before he left, he decided that the time had come to part with his family of mice. Carefully he carried their cage to a vacant lot. Nine mice skittered off into the weeds, but the tenth stayed put. It was Mortimer, watching him with bright eyes.

THE PERFECTIONIST

Before leaving Kansas City, Disney had begun work on a new series called *Alice in Cartoonland.* The idea was to film a young girl against a white background and then surround her with cartoon animals whose movements were synchronized to hers. He had sent the film to the Winkler Corporation, a cartoon distributor in New York. Several weeks later, unemployed in Hollywood, he received word that Winkler wanted twelve of the films.

Successful at first, the *Alice* series turned out badly. Disney would order scene after scene redrawn and reshot—swallowing up every cent of his profit. All told, Walt produced fifty-seven of these adventures, but the sixteenth was the last to make money.

His skilled animators could command $120 a week, but Walt himself drew a maximum of $50, and when times were tough, he slashed that to $15. One staffer drew less than any: Lillian Bounds, a petite brunette. It was Roy who one day discovered that for two weeks in succession Lilly had not cashed her checks. He noted, too, that Walt was unusually solicitous in driving Miss Bounds home from work.

Immersed in his creation of a world of fantasy, Walt had never found girls interesting, but somehow this one was different. One evening, he suddenly leaned across the desk and kissed her. His formal proposal was not long in coming.

By early 1928 the possibilities of *Alice in Cartoonland* had been exhausted, and Walt and his staff had started work on a series of cartoons called *Oswald the Lucky Rabbit.* Though *Oswald* was popular with audiences, Walt's perfectionism was driving the studio out of business. To Walt, the solution was simple: more credit and more cash. But the Winkler Corporation proved alternatively evasive or uncooperative. Determined on a face-to-face showdown, Walt set out for New York with Lilly.

The meetings did not go Walt's way, and ended with the relationship being terminated. Angrily, Walt stormed back to his hotel, where Lilly awaited him. "I'm out of work and I'm glad!" he flung at her defiantly. "I'll never work for anyone else again as long as I live." Then, with the incorrigible optimism that was so much a part of him, he telegraphed Roy: "Everything o.k. coming home." Somehow, he was convinced that he would find a character to replace Oswald.

"WE'VE GOT IT!"

On March 16, 1928, Walt and Lilly boarded a train for the return trip. As soon as they reached their section, he began scribbling furiously—tearing off sheet after sheet, crumpling it, scribbling afresh. Sometimes he stared into space. He was dreaming of a mouse—a mouse named Mortimer.

A sleepless night followed. Then the next day, westward bound from Chicago, Walt's star was born: a mischievous and undaunted mouse, wearing red-velvet pants with pearl buttons. A mouse, moreover, who ruffled his hair like Charles Lindbergh and was spurred by the great aviator's example to build his own backyard plane. That was it! *Plane Crazy*, starring Mortimer Mouse.

Irrepressibly, he gabbled out details of his scenario to Lilly, but she immediately objected.

"Mortimer is a *horrible* name for a mouse!" she said.

"Well, then," Walt replied, "how about Mickey? Mickey Mouse has a good friendly sound."

Daily, Mickey came to life. His head was a circle, which was easy to draw, and no matter which way he turned, his ears were circles, too. The body was pear-shaped, with a tapering tail and pipestem legs set in oversized shoes. And since four gloved fingers were easier and cheaper to draw than five, Mickey was to live out all his life minus one finger on each hand.

Meanwhile, Walt sped back to New York with sample reels. He ran full tilt into a stone wall of apathy. His star was rejected. "It was one of the low points in Walt's life," Ub recalled. "He'd gambled everything, but after a whole month in New York he could interest no one."

Walt had a last desperate inspiration. A year earlier, in October 1927, movies had talked for the first time. Since then more than one thousand theaters had been wired for sound, and audiences had soared to ninety-five million a week. "We'll make over Mickey Mouse with sound," Disney decided.

It had never been done before. A method for recording sound on film worked well when live actors spoke the words, but how could a cartoonist's creation be synchronized with sounds made long after the drawings were completed? Roy and Walt set up a test with thirty-five feet of film, which ran for just thirty seconds. They assembled noisemakers, cowbells, slide whistles, even a washboard. Walt himself, fingers clamped on his nose, spoke for Mickey in a boyish falsetto (a role he was to undertake for eighteen years).

Laughing excitedly, they ran through the test again and again until late at night, striving for better synchronization. "This is it," Walt kept repeating. "We've got it!"

A SPRING OF CREATIVITY

Overnight Mickey Mouse became a world-wide sensation. Mickey's success tapped a spring of creativity, and a host of new characters poured from the Disney studios. Pluto, Goofy, Horace Horsecollar, and Clarabelle Cow, all of them modeled on Walt's barnyard friends.

Donald Duck was born after Walt and some of his animators had listened to an imitator named Clarence Nash. "It's a duck blowing its top!" Walt said, and soon Nash was added to the payroll. "Make this duck kind of cocky," Walt suggested to animator Fred Spencer. "And since he's a duck and likes water, how about giving him a little middy blouse and a sailor hat?"

Unsophisticated and uncomplicated, Disney's films all pointed to a gentle but inescapable moral. Courage and virtue vanquished wickedness and fear; industry triumphed over sloth; false ambition produced only defeat. In Walt's own words, they appealed to "the Mickey in us—that precious, ageless something in every human being which makes us laugh at silly things and sing in the bathtub and dream."

When Disney's children were young, Saturday was always "Daddy's Day," and Walt often spent the afternoon with them visiting a neighborhood amusement park. "Those were some of the happiest days of my life," Walt later reminisced. "They would ride the merry-go-round, and I would sit on a bench eating peanuts. And sitting there alone, I felt there should be something built, some kind of a family park where parents and children could have fun together." He envisioned his own park, based on Disney stories and characters. It would be a sort of Disneyland.

His plan was to have a single entrance, from which would extend four separate areas: Adventureland, Frontierland, Fantasyland, Tomorrowland—the dream worlds of childhood. Always in these worlds, it would be spring or summer, and you would enter them by way of Main Street, U.S.A. Ahead would lie Sleeping Beauty's Castle, while girdling the park would be a railroad, its steam engine blowing its ghostly whistle. Mickey Mouse would be the first to welcome you to his creator's world.

He began buying up a 244-acre orange grove twenty-five miles south of Los Angeles. A reporter asked Walt when the project might be completed. Walt's reply was simple, "Never, not as long as there is imagination left in the world!"

THE CITY OF DISNEY

For years Lilly had been asking Walt to retire and take it easy. Indeed, there was no compelling financial reason to work any longer. But Walt always resisted Lilly's pleas. "I'd die," he said, "if I couldn't go out and conquer new worlds."

He put his staff to work assembling a 27,500-acre tract of land near Orlando, Florida, and one morning he arrived at the offices of his design organization with his plan for a new city sketched out on a napkin. He called it EPCOT—short for Experimental Prototype Community of Tomorrow.

All of these plans, however, were still in the drawing-board stage in the fall of 1966 when Walt, in constant pain, reluctantly took time out for an X-ray. Surgeons found that Disney was stricken by a malignant tumor. On November 7, the doctors removed his left lung; and within two weeks, chafing at the unaccustomed idleness, he attempted to resume his old routine. But some vital spark had been snuffed out. On November 30, mortally ill, he was readmitted to the hospital. About nine fifteen the morning of December 15, his restless heart stopped beating.

That evening, at five o'clock, there came a moment which none who witnessed it would ever forget. At Disneyland, into the square by City Hall marched the sixteen-strong Disneyland band. Drums stuttered, a bugle shrilled, and Old Glory slipped down the flagstaff. Then, tears streaking his face, the bandmaster, seventy-three-year-old Colonel Vesey Walker, once more raised his baton. And onto the winter's evening drifted the notes of a melody from *Pinocchio* that seemed to symbolize Walt Disney's life:

> *When you wish upon a star,*
> *Makes no difference who you are,*
> *Anything your heart desires,*
> *Will come to you . . .*

Walt Disney was a dreamer—a visionary. He saw entire worlds in plants, animals, playgrounds, and technology that others could not even begin to imagine. He kept his sights constantly on the future. As his brother Roy remarked, "I visited him in the hospital the night before he died. Although desperately ill, he was as full of plans for the future as he had been all his life." And even today, years after his death, his vision continues to expand within the legacy he created.

Walt Disney had visions of making people happier by building theme parks and cities of the future. Don Schoendorfer, who lived in the Orange County shadows of Disneyland, also had his sights set on making people happier. But he did it by building something of an entirely different and affordable kind.

FREE WHEELS

Janet Kinosian

Barely awake, Don Schoendorfer stepped onto the cold cement floor of his garage at 4:00 a.m. Determined to create the world's cheapest wheelchair, the Orange County, California, mechanical engineer squeezed in three hours every day before work, tinkering at a worktable he'd set up in his overstuffed garage.

First he tried a chair with a conventional canvaslike seat, but scrapped it as too expensive. He knew he needed something cheap and durable to the point of indestructible. The chair had to traverse mountains, swamps and deserts, and endure heat and frost with minor upkeep. Many of the world's poor, Schoendorfer knew, live on less than two dollars a day and could never dream of buying a Western-type wheelchair for hundreds or even thousands of dollars.

Finally, he hit on it: the ubiquitous white plastic lawn chair. Perfect. Schoendorfer scouted out sales, buying chairs by the dozen for three dollars apiece. Then he wandered the aisles of the Home Depot and Wal-Mart in search of the most inexpensive bike tires, even the most cost-effective screws.

During all the aisle-wandering, he flashed back to a road in Morocco almost thirty years ago. In 1977, he and his wife, Laurie, had stopped in Tétouan and, in the suffocating afternoon heat, saw a disabled woman dragging herself across the road, almost like a snake, using her fingernails to pull herself along. Schoendorfer remembers the disdain of the street beggars: the handicapped were considered even lower on the food chain than they were. On that dusty road, Schoendorfer decided to help.

Now, as he screwed two Toys "R" Us bike tires on to the chair, and welded on black metal casters and bearings, the MIT grad felt things come together. As he pirouetted the simple chair one last time, he thought, *This may just be it.*

"You've got a winner, Don," Schoendorfer's pastor declared when he saw the little white chair. In nine months Schoendorfer had made one hundred wheelchairs, and his garage looked like a prosthetics rehabilitation center.

The pastor suggested they bring the whole lot of them on an upcoming church medical mission to India. But when Schoendorfer arrived at the first planning meeting, the missionaries in the group were less than impressed. "How much do you think shipping these chairs will cost?" one asked.

Deflated and discouraged, Schoendorfer kept showing up to meetings. "I think they figured if they humored me—this odd man with the weird idea—I might just disappear," he recalled with a smile.

Finally, they agreed to let him bring four chairs to India. In an overcrowded medical ward outside Chennai, Schoendorfer saw a father carrying his disabled eleven-year-old son. *Here's the moment,* he thought. Schoendorfer ran outside and wheeled in the chair.

From the moment the boy, Emmanuel, first sat down, Schoendorfer knew his invention had some power to heal. Emmanuel looked alternately stunned and overjoyed. His mother said in translation: "Bless you for this chariot."

When Schoendorfer got back home, the company he worked for suddenly went bankrupt. He decided to stop working as an engineer and make the chairs his life's work. His family lived off years of savings, and when that started to run out, Laurie went to work for the Social Security Administration.

Since that first donation, Schoendorfer's nonprofit organization, Free Wheelchair Mission, has delivered more than sixty-three thousand of the lightweight contraptions at no charge to people desperate for mobility. One hundred thousand more are on the way.

Today, the chairs are made in two Chinese factories and can be delivered anywhere in the world for just $41.17. They've been shipped to forty-five countries—Angola, Zimbabwe, Mongolia, China, India, Peru, Fiji, as well as Iraq, where U.S. Marines passed them out to hundreds of civilians in 2004. With more than one hundred million disabled poor in developing countries, Schoendorfer knows his work is far from done.

"I have a small goal," he says quietly from beneath his chunky mustache. "Twenty million chairs given away free by 2010."

On every trip to deliver more, the inventor sees firsthand the effect his invention has on people's lives. Indra, from Chennai, never went to school, yet is now studying to become an architect. A young Angolan mother had her legs blown off by a land mine while working in the fields; today she cares for her infant children. An Indian man from Cochin, nicknamed "Fifty-two," told volunteers how he prayed daily for fifty-two years that someone would be kind to him, and this chair was the first time anyone had done anything for him, ever.

Volunteers photograph recipients as they first maneuver their newfound wheels. "It's like their wedding or graduation day," explained Schoendorfer. "Without question, it's the most important day of their lives. It's the day they get their dignity back."

Don Schoendorfer will likely never be famous like Walt Disney. But like Walt, he wanted to light up people's eyes and bring them joy. He held his vision firm in his mind for more than thirty years and when the opportunity finally arose for him to pursue it, he seized the moment. Starting in his garage and eventually moving into factories in China, he quietly set out to create his affordable wheelchairs and bring them to those in need. His visionary eyes now are set on a goal of twenty million chairs delivered around the globe. I think he will make it.

Walt Disney and Bill Schoendorfer both set high expectations in pursuing their visions. But their visions were not accomplished overnight, rather they developed over time and one step at a time. In the following woman's case, her vision unfolded day by day, blossom by blossom.

WHERE THE SUN SPILLED GOLD

Jaroldeen Edwards

It was a bleak, rainy day, and I had no desire to drive up the winding mountain road to my daughter Carolyn's house. But she had insisted that I come see something at the top of the mountain.

So here I was, reluctantly making the two-hour journey through fog that hung like veils. By the time I saw how thick it was near the summit, I'd gone too far to turn back. *Nothing could be worth this*, I thought as I inched along the perilous highway.

"I'll stay for lunch, but I'm heading back down as soon as the fog lifts," I announced when I arrived.

"But I need you to drive me to the garage to pick up my car," Carolyn said. "Could we at least do that?"

"How far is it?" I asked.

"About three minutes," she said. "I'll drive—I'm used to it."

After ten minutes on the mountain road, I looked at her anxiously, "I thought you said three minutes."

She grinned. "This is a detour."

Turning down a narrow track, we parked the car and got out. We walked along the path that was thick with old pine needles. Huge black-green evergreens towered over us. Gradually the peace and silence of the place began to fill my mind.

Then we turned a corner—and I stopped and gasped in amazement. From the top of the mountain, sloping for several acres across folds and valleys, were rivers of daffodils in radiant bloom. A profusion of color—from the palest ivory to the deepest lemon to the most vivid salmon—blazed like a carpet before us. It looked as though the sun had tipped over and spilled gold down the mountainside.

At the center cascaded a waterfall of purple hyacinths. Here and there were coral-colored tulips. And as if this bonanza were not enough, western bluebirds frolicked over the heads of the daffodils, their magenta breasts and sapphire wings like a flutter of jewels.

A riot of questions filled my mind. *Who created such beauty? Why? How?*

As we approached the home that stood in the center of the property, we saw a sign: "Answers to the questions I know you are asking."

The first answer was: "One woman—two hands, two feet, and very little brain." The second one was: "One at a time." The third: "Started in 1958."

As we drove home, I was so moved by what we had seen I could scarcely speak. "She changed the world," I finally said, "one bulb at a time. She started almost forty years ago, probably just the beginning of an idea, but she kept at it."

The wonder of it would not let me go. "Imagine," I said, "if I'd had a vision and worked at it, just a little bit every day, what might I have accomplished?"

Carolyn looked at me sideways, smiling. "Start tomorrow," she said. "Better yet, start today."

Disney's vision came to life frame by frame. Don Schoendorfer's was produced chair by chair. This woman's vision arose blossom by blossom. People with vision not only can see the end results, they see the everyday small steps that will take them to where they want to go . . . to be who they want to become.

~~

WRAP UP

Vision takes a purpose and starts to turn it into specifics—what specifically you will do, when you will do it, and how you will accomplish it. Walt Disney and Don Schoendorfer, for example, both had the same purpose—to make others happy. But their visions of what to do and how to go about it were vastly different. And in both cases, once they had their visions (their first creations) fixed in their minds, they then set out confidently—step-by-step, blossom-by-blossom—to bring their second creations to life.

Of course, one of the most important visions you will ever possess is the vision you create in your mind's eye of yourself. Your self-vision demonstrably connects your subconscious and conscious minds and eventually forms your habits. So always believe in yourself and set realistic, yet challenging expectations for yourself—even if it takes a bit of "wishing upon a star."

REFLECTIONS

- Disney was always dreaming of the future. What future dreams do you hold? Where do you see yourself five years from now? Do you ever take time out of your busy schedule to dream a little?

- Disney's visions tended to shoot for the stars, yet were based on reality. Are your expectations set high enough? Too high?

- Don Schoendorfer had a long-term vision that was broken into meaningful short-term goals. First one hundred chairs, then one hundred thousand chairs, then twenty million. Do you break your goals down into meaningful milestones—points of celebration?

- Everyday Greatness happens one day, one blossom at a time. What specifically can you do today that will help propel you toward achieving your vision of tomorrow?

FURTHER INSIGHTS ON
Vision

~~

LOOKING FORWARD

Vision helps us see the possibilities of tomorrow within the realities of today, and motivates us to do what needs to be done.

Dreams are extremely important. You can't do it unless you can imagine it.

—GEORGE LUCAS

■ ■ ■

Superstar Wayne Gretzky holds more hockey records than anyone in the history of the sport. When asked about his success, season after season, Gretzky said, "I skate to where the puck is going, not to where it's been."

—QUOTED BY JAMES R. PAUL,
IN *VITAL SPEECHES OF THE DAY*

■ ■ ■

Peak performers want more than merely to win the next game. They see all the way to the championship. They have a long-range goal that inspires commitment and action.

—CHARLES A. GARFIELD,
PEAK PERFORMER

■ ■ ■

The trouble with not having a goal is that you can spend your life running up and down the field and never scoring.

—BILL COPELAND

■ ■ ■

When a man does not know what harbor he is making for, no wind is the right wind.

—SENECA

HIGH EXPECTATIONS

Walt Disney was always shooting for the stars. We too should set goals that challenge us to stretch beyond our current capacity.

Achievement is largely the product of steadily raising one's levels of aspiration and expectation.

—JACK NICKLAUS,
MY STORY

■ ■ ■

Celebrate what you've accomplished, but raise the bar a little higher each time you succeed.

—MIA HAMM

■ ■ ■

In the long run men hit only what they aim at.

—HENRY DAVID THOREAU

■ ■ ■

So many of our dreams seem impossible, then improbable, then inevitable.

—CHRISTOPHER REEVE

■ ■ ■

In order to be a realist you must believe in miracles.

—DAVID BEN-GURION

■ ■ ■

A man must have his dreams—memory dreams of the past and eager dreams of the future. I never want to stop reaching for new goals.

—MAURICE CHEVALIER

■ ■ ■

Lord, grant that I may always desire more than I accomplish.

—MICHELANGELO

SMALL STEPS

At times the ladder of success appears insurmountable. But remember, the field of flowers was created seed by seed, blossom by blossom, step by step.

The man who removes a mountain begins by carrying away small stones.

—CHINESE PROVERB

■ ■ ■

Nothing is particularly hard if you divide it into small jobs.

—HENRY FORD

■ ■ ■

The world is moved not only by the mighty shoves of the heroes but also by the aggregate of the tiny pushes of each honest worker.

—HELEN KELLER

■ ■ ■

Robert J. Kriegel learned the value of taking life in little steps as a ski instructor, when taking novices to the edge of a difficult slope:

"They would look all the way down to the bottom. Invariably the hill would seem too steep and too difficult, so they'd back away. I would tell them not to think of skiing the whole hill. Instead, just try making the first turn. This changed their focus. After a few turns they would become more confident and, without any prodding, take off down the slope."

—ROBERT J. KRIEGEL WITH LOUIS PATLER,
IF IT AIN'T BROKE, BREAK IT

■ ■ ■

If you can't feed a hundred people, then feed just one.

—MOTHER TERESA

PREPARATION

To bring dreams to pass, we must prepare the steps and details that will get us where we want to go.

Before everything else, getting ready is the secret of success.

—HENRY FORD

■ ■ ■

Dig a well before you are thirsty.

—CHINESE PROVERB

■ ■ ■

People don't plan to fail—they just fail to plan.

—SHERATON-PARK HOTEL NEWS

■ ■ ■

The beginning is the most important part of the work.

—PLATO

■ ■ ■

The will to win is not nearly as important as the will to prepare to win.

—BOBBY KNIGHT

■ ■ ■

Well begun is half done.

—GREEK PROVERB

■ ■ ■

After Michelle Kwan won her first national championship in 1996, she stunned her more seasoned rivals by winning the world title.

"I know I'm supposed to be surprised by what I've accomplished," says Kwan. "But why should I be? Everyone says it happened so fast, but it didn't seem fast to me. I was out there every day, all the time, working and skating well. Winning isn't about miracles on ice, it's about training."

—MARK STARR,
IN *NEWSWEEK*

■ ■ ■

Workaholics are addicted to activity; superachievers are committed
to results. They work toward goals that contribute to their mission.
In their mind's eye they see the end they want and the actions leading to it.

—CHARLES A. GARFIELD,
PEAK PERFORMER

■ ■ ■

Apathy can only be overcome by enthusiasm, and enthusiasm can only be
aroused by two things: first, an ideal that takes the imagination by storm;
second, a definite, intelligible plan for carrying that ideal into practice.

—ARNOLD TOYNBEE

11

INNOVATION

The mind celebrates a little triumph
every time it formulates a thought.
—RALPH WALDO EMERSON

I t is said that Greek mathematician Archimedes solved a
particularly vexing problem one day while taking a bath. His
joy was so immense that he ran naked through the streets
of ancient Syracuse exclaiming, "Eureka!"—I have found it!

The act of innovating can generate many emotions. It can
bring agony, sweat, tears, and exhaustion. But, yes, it can also
bring great thrills, satisfaction, and joy—though we hope it will
not cause everyone to run naked through their community or
workplace. But innovation does not come without a price.
Many of the emotions and arduous effort associated with it
are demonstrated in each of the following three stories, beginning with Charles Dickens and "The Second Greatest Christmas
Story Ever Told."

THE SECOND GREATEST CHRISTMAS STORY EVER TOLD

Thomas J. Burns

On an early October evening in 1843, Charles Dickens stepped from the brick-and-stone portico of his home near Regent's Park in London. The cool air of dusk was a relief from the day's unseasonal humidity, as the author began his nightly walk through what he called "the black streets" of the city.

A handsome man with flowing brown hair and normally sparkling eyes, Dickens was deeply troubled. The thirty-one-year-old father of four had thought he was at the peak of his career. *The Pickwick Papers, Oliver Twist,* and *Nicholas Nickleby* had all been popular; and *Martin Chuzzlewit,* which he considered his finest novel yet, was being published in monthly installments. But now, the celebrated writer was facing serious financial problems.

Some months earlier, his publisher had revealed that sales of the new novel were not what had been expected, and it might be necessary to sharply reduce Dickens's monthly advances against future sales.

The news had stunned the author. It seemed his talent was being questioned. Memories of his childhood poverty resurfaced. Dickens was supporting a large, extended family, and his expenses were already nearly more than he could handle. His father and brothers were pleading for loans. His wife, Kate, was expecting their fifth child.

All summer long, Dickens worried about his mounting bills, especially the large mortgage that he owed on his house. He spent time at a seaside resort, where he had trouble sleeping and walked the cliffs for hours. He knew that he needed an idea that would earn him a large sum of money, and he needed the idea quickly. But in his depression, Dickens was finding it difficult to write. After returning to London, he hoped that resuming his nightly walks would help spark his imagination.

The yellow glow from the flickering gas lamps lit his way through London's better neighborhoods. Then gradually, as he neared the Thames River, only the dull light from tenement windows illuminated the streets, now litter-strewn and lined with open sewers. The elegant ladies and well-dressed gentlemen of

Dickens's neighborhood were replaced by bawdy streetwalkers, pickpockets, footpads, and beggars.

The dismal scene reminded him of the nightmare that often troubled his sleep: *A twelve-year-old boy sits at a worktable piled high with pots of black boot paste. For twelve hours a day, six days a week, he attaches labels on the endless stream of pots to earn the six shillings that will keep him alive.*

The boy in the dream looks through the rotting warehouse floor into the cellar, where swarms of rats scurry about. Then he raises his eyes to the dirt-streaked window, dripping with condensation from London's wintry weather. The light is fading now, along with the boy's young hopes. His father is in debtors' prison, and the youngster is receiving only an hour of school lessons during his dinner break at the warehouse. He feels helpless, abandoned. There may never be celebration, joy, or hope again . . .

This was no scene from the author's imagination. It was a period from his early life. Fortunately, Dickens's father had inherited some money, enabling him to pay off his debts and get out of prison—and his young son escaped a dreary fate.

Now the fear of being unable to pay his own debts haunted Dickens. Wearily, he started home from his long walk, no closer to an idea for the "cheerful, glowing" tale he wanted to tell than he'd been when he started out.

However, as he neared home, he felt a sudden flash of inspiration. What about a Christmas story! He would write one for the very people he passed on the black streets of London. People who lived and struggled with the same fears and longings he had known, people who hungered for a bit of cheer and hope.

But Christmas was less than three months away! How could he manage so great a task in so brief a time? The book would have to be short, certainly not a full novel. It would have to be finished by the end of November to be printed and distributed in time for Christmas sales. For speed, he struck on the idea of adapting a Christmas-goblin story from a chapter in *The Pickwick Papers.*

He would fill the story with the scenes and characters his readers loved. There would be a small, sickly child, his honest but ineffectual father, and, at the center of the piece, a selfish villain, an old man with a pointed nose and shriveled cheeks. As the mild days of October gave way to a cool November, the manuscript grew, page by page, and the story took life. The basic plot was

simple enough for children to understand, but evoked themes that would conjure up warm memories and emotions in an adult's heart.

> *After retiring alone to his cold, barren apartment on Christmas Eve,
> Ebenezer Scrooge, a miserly London businessman, is visited by the spirit of
> his dead partner, Jacob Marley. Doomed by his greed and insensitivity to
> his fellow man when alive, Marley's ghost wanders the world in chains
> forged of his own indifference. He warns Scrooge that he must change, or
> suffer the same fate. The ghosts of Christmas Past, Christmas Present, and
> Christmas Yet to Come appear and show Scrooge poignant scenes from his
> life and what will occur if he doesn't mend his ways. Filled with remorse,
> Scrooge renounces his former selfishness and becomes a kind, generous, lov-
> ing person who has learned the true spirit of Christmas.*

Gradually, in the course of his writing, something surprising happened to
Dickens. What had begun as a desperate, calculated plan to rescue himself from
debt—"a little scheme," as he described it—soon began to work a change in the
author. As he wrote about the kind of Christmas he loved—joyous family parties with clusters of mistletoe hanging from the ceiling, cheerful carols, games,
dances, and gifts; delicious feasts of roast goose, plum pudding, fresh breads, all
enjoyed in front of a blazing yule log—the joy of the season he cherished began
to alleviate his depression.

A Christmas Carol captured his heart and soul. It became a labor of love.
Every time he dipped his quill pen into his ink, the characters seemed magi-
cally to take life: Tiny Tim with his crutches, Scrooge cowering in fear before
the ghosts, Bob Cratchit drinking Christmas cheer in the face of poverty.

Each morning, Dickens grew excited and impatient to begin the day's work.
"I was very much affected by the little book," he later wrote a newspaperman,
and was "reluctant to lay it aside for a moment." A friend and Dickens's future
biographer, John Forster, took note of the "strong mastery" the story held over
the author. Dickens told a professor in America how, when writing, he "wept,
and laughed, and wept again." Dickens even took charge of the design of the
book, deciding on a gold-stamped cover, a red-and-green title page with colored endpapers, and four hand-colored etchings and four engraved woodcuts.

To make the book affordable to the widest audience possible, he priced it at only five shillings.

At last, on December 2, he was finished, and the manuscript went to the printers. On December 17, the author's copies were delivered, and Dickens was delighted. He had never doubted that *A Christmas Carol* would be popular. But neither he nor his publisher was ready for the overwhelming response that came. The first edition of six thousand copies sold out by Christmas Eve, and as the little book's heartwarming message spread, Dickens later recalled, he received "by every post, all manner of strangers writing all manner of letters about their homes and hearths, and how the *Carol* is read aloud there, and kept on a very little shelf by itself." Novelist William Makepeace Thackeray said of the *Carol:* "It seems to me a national benefit, and to every man or woman who reads it a personal kindness."

Despite the book's public acclaim, it did not turn into the immediate financial success that Dickens had hoped for, because of the quality production he demanded and the low price he placed on the book. Nevertheless, he made enough money from it to scrape by, and *A Christmas Carol*'s enormous popularity revived his audience for subsequent novels, while giving a fresh, new direction to his life and career.

Although Dickens would write many other well-received and financially profitable books—*David Copperfield, A Tale of Two Cities, Great Expectations*—nothing would ever quite equal the soul-satisfying joy he derived from his universally loved little novel. In time, some would call him the Apostle of Christmas. And, at his death in 1870, a poor child in London was heard to ask: "Dickens dead? Then will Father Christmas die too?"

In a very real sense, Dickens popularized many aspects of the Christmas we celebrate today, including great family gatherings, seasonal drinks and dishes and gift giving. Even our language has been enriched by the tale. Who has not known a "Scrooge," or uttered "Bah! Humbug!" when feeling irritated or disbelieving. And the phrase "Merry Christmas!" gained wider usage after the story appeared.

In the midst of self-doubt and confusion, a man sometimes does his best work. From the storm of tribulation comes a gift. For Charles Dickens, a little Christmas novel brought new-found faith in himself and in the redemptive joy of the season.

Fearing his career may have peaked and facing financial problems, Dickens's every step was accompanied by inner darkness as he walked the blackened, cobblestone streets in hopes of uncovering a spark of imagination. And it was there in the city that he got in touch with his readers. The sights and smells brought back memories of his own childhood emotions. Soon vistas of creativity were opened. He found himself laughing, crying, "excited and impatient to begin the day's work." Dickens's experience reminds us how difficult the process of innovation can be. It also sends a clear signal that a good starting point from which to launch your creative powers is being out and about, exploring your environment with ever observant eyes and ears.

It is not uncommon to come across a great little invention and think, I wish I had thought of that. But bringing even simple ideas to full fruition involves a process, one that is not always as easy as it may appear.

How the Wiffle Won

Stephen Madden

It was the summer of 1952, and David A. Mullany, twelve, of Fairfield, Connecticut, had a single care in the whole world: finding a way to play even more baseball. "We played from first light until after dark, seven days a week," Mullany said. "There was always a game. And it was usually in my backyard. We were just a bunch of kids, and we were happier than hell."

For young Dave and all his baseball-crazy friends—John Belus, Bill Hackman, Dave Osbourne, and the others—the Mullanys' backyard was the ball field of last resort. Older kids had kicked them off the diamond at Fairfield's Gould Manor Park, and the police had chased them away from the field at the local elementary school when their home run blasts broke too many windows. Dave Osbourne's mother let them play in her backyard, but only if they used a tennis ball instead of a hard ball.

"If you know what a tennis ball does to a garage door, which we used as the backstop, you know that she was still very forgiving," Mullany said. The gang's run at the Osbourne Field ended the day left-handed Mullany pulled a line drive by the clothesline, where Mrs. Osbourne was hanging laundry. "I missed her nose by a fraction of an inch," he said with a small smile, "and the ball smashed the porch light."

So they ended up at the Mullanys' much smaller yard.

But the tennis ball, driven with frequency and ardor into the side of the Mullanys' house, was loosening shingles at an alarming rate. "I looked in the garage for something that would do less damage," Mullany said. "I found these perforated plastic golf balls in my dad's golf bag. We played with those and a broom handle."

The guys called the game "whiff ball" since, with a bat and ball so small, batters struck out a lot. They devised a unique set of ground rules that allowed them to play with as few as two players (a pitcher and a batter) or as many as eighteen. There was no base running; rather, if a batter hit a grounder past the pitcher, he had hit a single and thus had an imaginary runner on first. If he hit it past the pitcher in the air, he had a double. "Off the house was a triple, and over the house was a home run," said Mullany.

Dave's father, David N. Mullany, took in all this every night, even though he was down on his luck. With the optimism he inherited from his Irish immigrant parents, Mr. Mullany had left a good job as a purchasing agent at a small pharmaceutical maker to start his own metal-polish business. The business prospered for a while, but problems with cash flow and the tax man undid its bottom line until it went bankrupt.

Not that his wife, Ivy, or Dave knew that. Each morning, Dave's dad, upbeat as ever, would put on a sharp suit and head to "the office." In truth, he was out looking for work or performing odd jobs. Each evening he'd come home with a newspaper under his arm and a smile on his face. On Fridays he'd give Ivy a pay envelope filled with money, the proceeds from a life insurance policy he'd cashed in. "And every night he'd come home and find his yard full of kids," Mullany said.

Dave's dad had pitched, southpaw, for the University of Connecticut and had won his pharmaceuticals job in the depths of the Depression because the company's baseball team was looking for someone with good stuff. He knew a thing or two about the game.

"Dad noticed I was trying to throw curves with this little ball and he could see the damage I was probably doing to my elbow," Mullany said. "One night he asked me if the game would be even better if I could throw a curve."

The answer was an enthusiastic yes. They then set out to create a ball that even the smallest player could make curve. Dave's dad called around to some of his contacts from his days as a purchasing agent, looking for things from which to fashion such a ball. He found a packaging salesman with leftover half-orbs from the Coty cosmetics company.

So after Mr. Mullany spent the day looking for a job, he and his son would sit around the kitchen table, carving holes in the white plastic with razor blades, looking for the pattern that guaranteed a curve. They glued in washers to make a ball that wobbled. They cut big holes and they cut small holes. In the morning, when the glue was dry, Dave and the gang tested the creations.

After three nights and nearly two dozen designs, one pattern stood out. It had eight oblong holes in one hemisphere; the other half was solid. "It worked like a charm," Dave said. "I could throw curve balls, sliders, fast-balls, and knuckle balls."

It was an instant hit with the twelve-year-olds, who quickly wore out the homemade balls. Dave's dad, who by then was thinking that he may have invented a better mousetrap, asked the manufacturer of those little plastic golf balls to make an order of his balls out of polyethylene. By the spring of 1953, the Mullanys were almost ready to put their invention on the market.

All they needed was a name. "I said we should call it the Whiff Ball, because that was the game we played," Dave said. "Dad said it should have two syllables, like Whiffle. I agreed, but said we should leave off the 'h' because if we ever started a company, it would mean one less letter to buy for the sign."

The Mullanys sold their first dozen Wiffle Balls on consignment to the owner of a diner off Connecticut's Merritt Parkway. "He put them by the cash register and sold them for forty-nine cents each," Dave said. Throwing instructions came inside the box. "The following Saturday he said 'Give me another box. The last one sold out.' When we got out to the car, Dad said, 'We might have something here.'"

After a little research, Mr. Mullany found an enterprising New York City toy salesman named Saul Mondschein, who agreed that they did. "Saul said we might get a couple of good years out of the ball, but it was probably a fad," Dave remembered. "He also said we needed to sell it with a bat." The Mullanys started making a tapered bat from ash—Dave's job was to wrap electrical tape on the handle—and soon Woolworth's was carrying Wiffles.

It's been fifty years since the Mullanys took their funny little ball to that diner. The wooden bat was discontinued in 1972, but other than that not much has changed. The Wiffle Ball Inc. still operates from the same unpretentious brick factory in Shelton, Connecticut, where millions and millions of balls have rolled off the line.

Dave's dad died in 1990, well after repaying the friends who loaned him money to start his business, and well after confessing to Ivy the family's financial straits before the invention of the Wiffle. Today, Dave and his two sons run the place.

And how do the Mullanys unwind once they've finished a week at the factory? After a recent Sunday dinner with his sons and grandchildren, Dave was sore—from pitching. "It's a great game," he said. "Always has been."

The story of the Wiffle Ball demonstrates the innovation process that is behind so many of the products sold today. From identifying a need to taking a financial risk to market testing to delivery to refinement, all these steps and more were involved in the creation of the Wiffle Ball. But I believe that the real key to innovation highlighted by this story—a cornerstone that is often overlooked—is the principle of synergy. While the father may have incubated and sustained the idea from start to finish, it should be noticed that his young son helped with the ball's design and name, while several others provided financial, technical, production, and marketing expertise. It was a synergistic team effort.

———————

Certain people seem to have a knack for being creative. But if you observe them for any length of time, it becomes quickly evident that their innovative powers do not appear by magic or luck. Indeed, it is no coincidence that innovative people also tend to be constant learners with broad interests.

THE MOST GIFTED MAN WHO EVER LIVED

Leo Rosten

He could draw a leaf or a hand, a fern or a rock, in ways miraculous to behold. No one ever matched his renditions of light and shade, or his genius for investing a flat surface with a scene of haunting mystery. Yet, for Leonardo da Vinci—creator of the *Mona Lisa* and *The Last Supper*—artistic greatness was but one of his incredible endowments.

Leonardo da Vinci was bewitched by everything: a baby's smile, birds in flight, the pageant of the planets. He loved the human face and form, and sketched an absorbing gallery of warriors, crones, old men—and bodies with the skin peeled off to reveal the architecture of ligaments and muscles.

But Leonardo was far, far more than an artist. He was an engineer, a musician, an architect, a cartographer, a mathematician. He was an astronomer, a botanist, a zoologist, a geologist, a physiologist. He was the first man to make wax impressions of the brain's interior, to consider using glass or ceramic models so that the workings of the heart and eye could be understood. He was the first to draw an accurate representation of an opened womb (with an embryo inside) and the first to investigate why leaves are arranged the way they are around a stem.

In one of his many notebooks he drew a male figure in a square inside a circle, the legs together, then set apart, the arms horizontal, then at a forty-five-degree angle. "The span of a man's outstretched arms is equal to his height," he revealed. "The center of the circle formed by the extremities of the outstretched limbs will be the navel. The space between the legs . . . will form an equilateral triangle."

He was the first modern thinker and scientist, for he sought to discover the causes of things by direct observation and experiment—not, as did most fifteenth-century seers, in the words of Holy Writ, Aristotle, or Thomas Aquinas. Science, he contended, is "the knowledge of all things that are possible," and he was obsessed by what he called *saper veder* ("knowing how to see").

One of the most remarkable things about Leonardo is that he assumed he was able to understand anything. The entire universe, from the wing of a dragonfly to the birth of the earth itself, was the playground for his deft intelligence.

Before Copernicus, he noted that the sun does not move around the earth and that the earth is "a star, like the moon." Before Galileo, he said falling objects accelerate their speed with distance, and suggested that "a large magnifying lens" should be used to study the surface of the moon. He was a pioneer in optics, in hydraulics, in the physics of sound and the nature of light. Sound moves in waves, he noted—which is why two church bells, one farther away than the other, struck simultaneously, are heard separately. And, noting a lag between a flash of lightning and a thunderclap, he concluded that light must travel faster than sound. In his investigations into the circulation of blood, he was able to describe arteriosclerosis, which he attributed to lack of exercise!

Nor is that all. Long before the Industrial Revolution, in a world that did not even have screwdrivers, he created a monkey wrench, ratchets, jacks, winches, a lathe, and a crane that could lift an entire church. He designed a piston that moved by steam pressure and a sprocket chain with a round-toothed gear that would not slip. He invented a differential transmission that permitted a cart to take a curve with the inside wheel moving more slowly than the outside wheel.

He drew innumerable varieties of pulleys, springs, portable bridges, double-deck streets; a device to measure changes in the weather; an automatic "feed" for printing. He invented roller bearings and a scissors that opened and closed with one hand movement; also, air-inflated skis—for walking on water.

He was the first man to recommend that air be harnessed as a source of power. He described an internal-combustion engine, an air-conditioning device, a pedometer, an odometer, a hygrometer. He even enumerated the cost benefits of mass production.

This supreme artist, who called war "a bestial madness," served as military engineer for Cesare Borgia. He invented a machine gun, the tank, the submarine.

He created a frogman's diving suit, the snorkel, a warship with a double-hull. (It could stay afloat after the outside hull was hit.)

He was forever fascinated by water: in ocean tides and waterfalls, breaking against rocks, in a quiet pool, a stream, a river. He described things no one else had observed before: that the surface of a pond is moved by wind, yet the bottom remains still; that rivers run faster near the surface than they do near the bottom; that water never moves of its own volition except when it descends. He designed and supervised the building of canals all around the city of Milan, a feat still praised by engineers.

In no field was Leonardo more bold and original than in aerodynamics: "A bird works according to mathematical law, which it is within the power of man to reproduce." He set caged birds free to study their takeoff, lift, wing-spread. His eyesight was phenomenal, for he saw and drew things that were simply not visible to most men—until high-speed photography "froze" motion.

In the fifteenth century, he invented the glider. And the parachute. And the helicopter. He described the value of retractable landing gears and wheels . . .

Leonardo was born in Vinci, near Florence, in 1452, the illegitimate son of a notary and a peasant girl. He was raised by his father and paternal grandfather. At an early age he showed extraordinary curiosity and exceptional skill in music, geometry, and drawing. At fifteen, he was apprenticed to the famous painter Verrocchio, whom he astounded with his masterful draftsmanship and the luminous beauty of his painting.

"He was tall, graceful, very strong," raved contemporary artist Giorgio Vasari. He was also a fine fencer and a superb horseman. He improvised poetry, which he sang in a melodious voice to the accompaniment of a lute he had fashioned. By the time he was twenty-eight, Leonardo was acknowledged to be the greatest painter of his time—a period that included Michelangelo, Raphael, Botticelli.

But there was a dark, secretive side to Leonardo. He was restless and moody and feared crowds. He was never satisfied with his work, forever blaming himself for not undertaking enough, yet breaking off commission after commission to begin some new, glittering project—which in turn remained uncompleted. "I wish to work miracles," he had written in his youth; later he often lamented having "wasted" so many days of his life.

Leonardo's famous notebooks were a potpourri of pages of various sizes, left unstitched, or bound in small batches. His spelling was as wayward as his grammar—and he taught himself to write backward in what appeared to be a special code. Some six thousand pages have been discovered in collections all over Europe. They are surely the most remarkable record of creativity ever produced by one human being.

Leonardo died near Amboise, France, while at the court of Francis I. He was sixty-seven, a ripe old age in that distant day.

No one can explain him. "Genius" does scant justice to the phenomenal range and originality of his work. There is no name, from all history, to place alongside his. Put most simply, Leonardo da Vinci remains the most gifted human being who ever lived.

Leonardo da Vinci was one of the most learned and well-rounded persons ever to live. The entire universe—from the wing of a dragonfly to the birth of the earth—was the playground of his curious intelligence. But did Leonardo have some mystical or innate gift of insight and invention, or was his brilliance learned and earned? Certainly he had an unusual mind and an uncanny ability to see what others did not. But the six thousand pages of detailed notes and drawings present clear evidence of a diligent, curious student—a perpetual learner in laborious pursuit of wisdom who was constantly exploring, questioning, and testing. Expanding your mind is vital to being creative. Therefore, investing regularly in learning opportunities is one of the greatest gifts you can give yourself.

~

WRAP UP

The Wiffle Ball was hardly what many would consider a high-tech innovation. Sure, there was advanced technology applied in coming up with the right materials and perhaps even a bit of science in finding the right hole sizes and formations. But it was not rocket science. Yet, what we learned from the Wiffle Ball and from Dickens's writing of *A Christmas Carol* was that innovation follows a process. It begins with identifying a need and is followed by careful research, experimentation, and the involvement of the right people to pursue the idea from birth to maturity. Sometimes the process spreads over years and requires loads of patience. Occasionally a little luck or serendipity speeds it along. But in most cases, the key to innovation is the people behind it — people like Leonardo who are curious, persistent, and knowledgeable, who can see things from multiple perspectives.

REFLECTIONS

- Charles Dickens's innovation was stimulated by wandering around his community, tapping into his readers' needs and hearts. In your attempts to be innovative, do you make time for exploration?

- The Wiffle Ball involved input from the kids, from the dad, from plastics experts, from savvy marketers. Do you involve the right people in your efforts to be innovative?

- Leonardo's knowledge ranged from art to music to geometry to science and beyond. How broad are your interests and studies? Do you invest enough resources to learn what you must know to accomplish your dreams and goals?

- Leonardo was impatient with himself and critical of his own work. In your efforts to learn and create, are you patient with yourself?

FURTHER INSIGHTS ON
Innovation

THE GIFT OF IMAGINATION

The gift of imagination is at the core of your ability to innovate.

Imagination is more important than knowledge.

—ALBERT EINSTEIN

■ ■ ■

The opportunities of man are limited only by his imagination. But so few have imagination that there are ten thousand fiddlers to one composer.

—CHARLES F. KETTERING

■ ■ ■

Creativity is more than just being different. Anybody can play weird; that's easy. What's hard is to be as simple as Bach. Making the simple complicated is commonplace; making the complicated simple, awesomely simple—that's creativity.

—CHARLES MINGUS,
JAZZ MUSICIAN, IN *SPORTS ILLUSTRATED*

■ ■ ■

One of the virtues of being young is that you don't let the facts get in the way of your imagination.

—SAM LEVENSON

■ ■ ■

Discovery consists of seeing what everybody has seen and thinking what nobody has thought.

—ALBERT SZENT-GYORGYI

IN PURSUIT OF KNOWLEDGE

Creative people make the pursuit of knowledge a priority. They study the important questions of life, and compile a reservoir of knowledge for instant access.

Perhaps imagination is only intelligence having fun.

—GEORGE SCIALABBA

■ ■ ■

Learning is not attained by chance. It must be sought for with ardor and attended to with diligence.

—ABIGAIL ADAMS

■ ■ ■

If you're not learning while you're earning, you're cheating yourself out of the better portion of your compensation.

—NAPOLEON HILL

■ ■ ■

In a time of drastic change, it is the learners who inherit the future. The unlearned usually find themselves equipped to live in a world that no longer exists.

—ERIC HOFFER

■ ■ ■

Most people are willing to pay more to be amused than to be educated.

—ROBERT C. SAVAGE

■ ■ ■

He who is afraid to ask is ashamed of learning.

—DANISH PROVERB

■ ■ ■

The person who knows how will always have a job. But the person who knows why will be his boss.

—CARL C. WOOD

■ ■ ■

To acquire knowledge, one must study; but to acquire wisdom, one must observe.

—MARILYN VOS SAVANT

■ ■ ■

Reading is to the mind what exercise is to the body.

—JOSEPH ADDISON

■ ■ ■

Curiosity is the wick in the candle of learning.

—WILLIAM A. WARD

■ ■ ■

I think, at a child's birth, if a mother could ask a fairy godmother to endow it with the most useful gift, that gift would be curiosity.

—ELEANOR ROOSEVELT

WELL ROUNDED MINDS

Some of the most interesting people are those like Leonardo with widespread interests and talents.

When five hundred learned societies from around the world held in 1956 an international celebration of the 250th anniversary of Benjamin Franklin's birth, the occasion had to be broken down into ten different sections: 1. science, invention, and engineering; 2. statesmanship; 3. education and the study of nature; 4. finance, insurance, commerce, and industry; 5. mass communication; 6. printing, advertising, and the graphic arts; 7. religion, fraternal organizations, and the humanities; 8. medicine and public health; 9. agriculture; 10. music and recreation.

Yet we have reduced his achievements in pure science, which were so deep as to make him the Newton of the 18th century, to the dimensions of the lightning-and-kite-string experiment, because it is easy to grasp.

—BRUCE BLIVEN

■ ■ ■

I try to make time for reading each night. In addition to the usual newspapers and magazines, I make it a priority to read at least one newsweekly from cover to cover. If I were to read only what intrigues me— say, the science and business sections—then I would finish the magazine the same person I was when I started. So I read it all.

—BILL GATES,
IN *THE GUARDIAN*

■ ■ ■

A human being should be able to change a diaper, plan an invasion, butcher a hog, conn a ship, design a building, write a sonnet, balance accounts, build a wall, set a bone, comfort the dying, take orders, give orders, cooperate, act alone, pitch manure, solve equations, analyze a new problem, program a computer, cook a tasty meal, fight efficiently, die gallantly. Specialization is for insects.

—ROBERT A. HEINLEIN,
THE NOTEBOOKS OF LAZARUS LONG

SERENDIPITY

Exploration is at the root of innovation. Serendipity is the unintended consequences, the happy surprises, or the synergistic blossoms that occasionally arise from exploration.

Serendipity is looking in a haystack for a needle and discovering the farmer's daughter.

—QUOTED BY JULIUS H. COMROE, JR.

■ ■ ■

Don't keep forever on the public road, going only where others have gone. Leave the beaten track occasionally and dive into the woods. You will be certain to find something you have never seen before. It will be a little thing, but do not ignore it. Follow it up, explore all around it; one discovery will lead to another, and before you know it you will have something worth thinking about.

—ALEXANDER GRAHAM BELL

■ ■ ■

It's extremely important not to have one's life all blocked out, not to have the days and weeks totally organized. It's essential to leave gaps and interludes for spontaneous action, for it is often in spontaneity and surprises that we open ourselves to the unlimited opportunities and new areas brought into our lives by chance.

—JEAN HERSEY,
THE TOUCH OF THE EARTH

■ ■ ■

All that is gold does not glitter; not all those that wander are lost.

—J. R. R. TOLKIEN

■ ■ ■

Originality is unexplored territory. You get there by carrying a canoe—you can't take a taxi.

—ALAN ALDA

■ ■ ■

Examples of serendipity are scattered throughout our day-to-day lives, even beneath our feet, before our very eyes, or at the tip of our tongues.

A French scientist named Benedictus accidentally dislodged a bottle from his laboratory shelf. It fell to the floor with a crash and shattered. But to Benedictus' astonishment it retained its shape. None of the particles was scattered. He recalled using collodion solution in the bottle. By chance the solvent had evaporated, leaving a thin, invisible skin on the walls of the bottle. Shortly thereafter, he read of an auto accident in which a young woman had been seriously cut by flying glass. The two events connected in Benedictus' mind, and laminated safety glass was the outcome.

—BYRON C. FOY,
SCIENTIFIC AMERICAN

■ ■ ■

A certain young man worked in a factory where heavy machinery rattled the entire building. Not very robust, he did not like the constant jarring. So one day he brought a rubber mat to the factory, and stood on it. As hoped, the vibrations no longer annoyed him when he stood on the mat.

After several days, however, somebody stole his mat. He responded by getting two pieces of rubber and nailing them to his heels. This gave him two little rubber mats that nobody could steal.

The name of the young man was O'Sullivan. And, yes, he became the original inventor of rubber heels.

—HERBERT N. CASSON,
WILL POWER IN BUSINESS

■ ■ ■

A Damascus-born pastry vendor named Hamwi obtained a concession permit to sell zalabia (a wafer-thin Persian waffle, served with sugar or other sweets) at the World's Fair in 1904. A nearby stand offered ice cream in small dishes. One warm day, the ice cream vendor ran out of dishes, so Hamwi took his hot zalabia, formed it into a cone, let it cool and plopped a scoop of ice cream on top. The "World's Fair Cornucopia," known today as the ice cream cone, was an immediate hit.

—BRUCE FELTON AND MARK FOWLER,
*FENTON & FOWLER'S FAMOUS
AMERICANS YOU NEVER KNEW EXISTED*

12

QUALITY

In the race for quality, there is no finish line.
—DAVID T. KEARNS

Who does not like the feel of quality? Whether it comes in the form of a well-made car, a fine-woven piece of clothing, a stable building, a delectable meal, an intricate technological device, a precise musical performance, a finely tuned work team, or a solid piece of furniture, quality has an appealing feel.

But quality also has its price, as demonstrated by the following three individuals, starting with Johnny Carson who for thirty years tickled the delights of enormous television audiences. His smile and laughter were absolutely contagious, as nightly he relieved listeners of their day's stresses. But while he made it all appear so effortless, in "Here's Johnny," we learn just how hard Johnny worked to maintain his high standard of quality. Where Johnny got some of his appetite for quality is revealed in Jack Benny's "Working on the Hard Parts," which is followed by a glimpse of the man whose name has become synonymous with quality, César Ritz.

HERE'S JOHNNY!

Ed McMahon

Almost five thousand times over the course of thirty years, Johnny Carson walked through the curtains of *The Tonight Show* after I had taken a considerable amount of time to say two words: "Heeeeeere's Johnny!" Almost five thousand times he walked out to the sound of a song he'd helped write, in a unique style that defined debonair and with a grin that brought to mind the cutest kid in detention, showing millions of Americans the happiest way to end the day.

My first audition with Johnny lasted all of six minutes. It was for the daytime game show *Who Do You Trust?* that he was hosting in 1958. On a street east of Times Square, I walked into Johnny's dressing room. "Glad you could come up, Ed," he said, warmly shaking my hand.

Two of the windows in Johnny's dressing room overlooked 44th Street and had a view of the Shubert Theatre. Its entire marquee was being changed for a hit show called *Bells Are Ringing* that starred Judy Holliday. As Johnny and I watched four cranes lift the big billboard, he asked me, "Where'd you go to school, Ed?"

"Catholic University," I said.

"Has a fine drama school, doesn't it?"

"Yes, excellent."

"What are you doing now?"

"I've got a couple of shows in Philadelphia—variety shows that I host."

"You came up on the train from Philadelphia?"

"Yes, I did."

And then, shaking my hand again, he said, "Well, thanks very much for coming up, Ed. It was good meeting you."

Translating his words, I heard, "Don't call us, we'll call you. But not in this lifetime."

A little later on, his producer called me. "Hi, Ed, this is Art Stark. When you show up, we want you to wear a suit. Johnny wants to wear sports clothes and we'd like to emphasize your size when you're next to him."

"But . . . What are you talking about?" I said.

"Oh, didn't they call you? You got the job. You start next Monday."

"I've Hitched My Wagon to a Star"

Johnny always seemed to come up with the right line, or the right gesture, or both. *He's got it,* I thought. *I've hitched my wagon to a star.*

While growing up in Norfolk, Nebraska, he'd honed his skills by studying the timing of his idol, Jack Benny. "I used to lie on the rug with my face in my hands and listen to him," Johnny told me once. "That's when I knew what I wanted to do: grow up and get laughs just the way Benny did."

By mid-1962, NBC began looking for a replacement for Jack Paar, the star of *The Tonight Show* since 1957. When the network offered the show to Johnny, he didn't jump at the offer. He was self-confident, but he was nervous.

"I don't think I can cut it, Ed," he told me.

"Of course you can," I said, amazed he had such reservations.

"I can handle a half-hour daytime quiz," he said, "but the jump to an hour and forty-five minutes at night . . . Well, it feels like a jump from a bridge."

In thirty years together, Johnny never gave me a single piece of direction. For just a few minutes before I went out to warm up the audience, he and I talked in his dressing room—about the news of the day, the stock market, our kids, baseball. We never talked about the show. Early on, Johnny told me privately, "Ed, I know we've got all these writers, but let's never do anything that sounds like it's had lots of planning."

"Don't worry," I said. "This show feels as planned as a food fight."

"Let's keep it that way," he said. "I don't want to come out with something that smacks of a month's preparation. I couldn't keep that up every night. I'm just going to be my natural self and see what happens."

What happened was the high-water mark of American TV.

I once heard a fan ask him, "What made you a star?"

And Johnny replied, "I started out in a gaseous state and then I cooled."

The Work Behind the Wit

Every morning over coffee, Johnny would go through the newspapers, looking for grist for his monologue. *The Tonight Show* both shaped and reflected American opinion, because Johnny began every day making circles with a pencil. And he wasn't picking horses.

He was the greatest perfectionist I have ever known. While he always wanted the show to look unrehearsed, most people didn't see all the work behind the wit. Near the end of any show that he felt hadn't been excellent, he would tell me, "Well, there's always tomorrow." Or he'd say, "How much longer do you think we can get away with this?"

He expected other people to do their jobs as he did his: like a pro. On and off the air, two things made him angry: rudeness and lack of professionalism. "My bugging point is low," he once said. His standards were so high that Doc Severinsen, his bandleader, told me he began to sweat every time Johnny came through the curtain. Doc was afraid he might screw up and have to face the steely-eyed wrath of a perfectionist who often sat alone for hours polishing his monologue.

AN EYE FOR NEW TALENT

No matter what coast we were on, Johnny launched the careers of more big stars than anyone else in show business. I was there at the launching pad, for example, when a thin, nervous young woman from New York stood on the stage and said, "We lived in Westchester and my mother was so worried that I wouldn't get married that she put a sign outside our house: Last Girl Before Thruway."

After delivering several other lines just as good as this one, the young woman was invited over to the couch—the cushioned rocket to stardom. And Johnny told Joan Rivers, "You're funny. You're going to be a star."

He made the same point when a short, skinny comic came out onstage and said, "I don't believe in the afterlife, but I'm still taking a change of underwear." And Woody Allen's career was launched.

I always knew when Johnny liked a comedian's performance. He would lean on his left elbow with his wrist under his chin. When the comedian finished, that same hand waved him over to the couch and a career was sent into orbit.

Many other stars owe either the launching or the speeding-up of their careers to Johnny. Ironically two of them were Jay Leno and David Letterman. I admired Johnny for having no jealousy of other comics, an attitude as rare as a bar mitzvah on the West Bank.

As host of the show, Johnny had another quality. He was fearless—of man or beast. Jim Fowler, the naturalist and wildlife expert, once brought a tarantula along and placed it on Johnny's hand. With a sick smile, Johnny asked, "He's poisonous, right?"

"Not that poisonous," Fowler replied.

"So I won't be that dead," said Johnny.

"Just don't anger him."

"How am I going to make a tarantula angry?" Johnny asked. "By saying 'You're ugly'?"

"By blowing on him."

"I never blow on a tarantula," said Johnny. "That's one of the things my mother taught me."

You Can't Fake That on TV

Though he was always aware of his place on the public scene, Johnny also acted less like a star than any other star I've ever known. Devoid of visible ego, he drove himself to the Burbank studio each day, carrying his lunch with him in a paper bag.

By 1991, so many people watched *The Tonight Show* that Johnny was making sixty million dollars for NBC, 30 percent of its operating profit. That year he made twenty million dollars. But he didn't use it for three hundred suits. He once told me, "I don't need eight houses or eighty-eight cars or three hundred suits. How many houses can you live in?"

Johnny gave millions to the University of Nebraska and to public schools in his hometown. He made large donations to organizations most people have never heard of, and he made all his contributions secretly because he wanted no fuss. "I have an ego like anyone else," he told me. "But I don't need it to be stroked."

On his farewell show in 1992, I was deeply moved when Johnny told America, "This show would have been impossible to do without Ed. Some of the best things we've done have just been . . . Well, he starts something, I start something. A lot of people who work together on television don't like each other, but Ed and I have been good friends. You can't fake that on TV."

No, you can't.

Here Johnny Carson's longtime sidekick, Ed McMahon, revealed what was not seen on TV—hours upon hours of behind the scenes effort invested by Johnny in polishing lines and perfecting facial gestures.

Where did Johnny get his work ethic and focus on quality? One clue is found in Jack Benny—the man Johnny called his idol. As a kid, "I used to lie on the rug with my face in my hands and listen to him," Johnny recalled. He studied Jack's every glare and penny-pinching smirk, and couldn't help but notice how he seldom appeared on stage without his trademark violin. What it would take Johnny a career to fully appreciate, however, was that there was a story and a work ethic—along with a message—behind the violin.

THE BEST ADVICE I EVER HAD

Jack Benny

I didn't really understand my father until almost the day he died. I loved him and respected him, but he seemed to me a singularly unimaginative man. Meyer Kubelsky ran a small haberdashery in Waukegan, Illinois, and his life seemed circumscribed by his store, our apartment over a butcher shop, and the walk between.

On my sixth birthday something happened that should have made me realize there were hidden depths in Father. That evening he handed me a large package. Excitedly, I unwrapped it. It was a violin.

"Benny, you should become a violinist," he said. "I'll hire the best teacher and maybe one day you'll be a great musician."

"Yes, Pap," I said. "Thank you very much." I was pleased with the present, but I would have preferred a bicycle or a baseball mitt. I didn't know then what this instrument represented to him.

I began my lessons and soon discovered that my fingers were strong and flexible, and that I had a good sense of rhythm and pitch. I had one major shortcoming, however: I was lazy.

Each night when Father came home he would say to me, "How is Benny Kubelsky, the violinist?"

"Fine, Pap," I'd answer.

"You practice?"

"Sure."

"That's a good boy."

There came a night, however, when my glib answer did not suffice. When he asked, "You practice?" and I said, "Sure," he said, "Show me."

I gestured toward the music stand. "That one."

He looked at the music sheet carefully. Then he snorted, "That's an easy piece," he said. "You learned that one a month ago."

"I practiced," I said stubbornly.

With a sigh he sat down in his chair. "I talked to your teacher, Benny. You have talent, he says, but you cheat on the lessons. All the time you play the easy pieces. You could be a great musician, but you must practice the hard parts." He thought a moment and then said, "Not only in music but in any business, some things are easy and some are hard. To be a success in anything, you must practice the hard parts. You should remember that."

"Yes, Papa," I said.

When I was sixteen years old I got a job playing in the pit orchestra at Waukegan's Barrison Theater, accompanying the vaudeville acts. After the first show Father came backstage, his face puzzled. "That is all?" He asked. "Just that jig-jig music for those tummlers up on the stage?"

"That's all."

He shook he head. "I had hoped, maybe a little Schumann."

"I'm sorry, Papa, but after all it is an orchestra and I'm learning all the time."

His face cleared a bit. "That is right," he acknowledged. "You keep studying. Keep practicing the hard parts."

It was a short step from the pit orchestra into a vaudeville act of my own. I started with a lady pianist named Cora Salisbury, then took the stage name of Jack Benny Woods for a piano-and-violin musical act. One day, on the spur of the moment, I took the violin from under my chin and told a joke. The audience laughed. The sound intoxicated me. That laughter ended my days as a musician, for I never again put the violin back where it belonged, except as a gag.

Music was hard work for me, even though I hadn't really been applying Father's advice. Now, I reasoned, if I could entertain an audience by just breezing out on the stage and telling a few jokes—that was for me! I became a single, a comedian.

Ah, but I soon discovered that telling jokes was not a breeze after all. Sometimes you could throw a punch line away, other times you had to ride it hard. A pause could set up a joke—or bury it. Timing was the key. In short, there were skills to be mastered in comedy, just as there had been in music. And there were just as many hard parts to practice. The difference was that I had found a field where I really wanted to dig in.

During the next few years I wrote my family frequently, but I never quite had the courage to tell them I wasn't playing Schumann in concert halls. Then, inevitably, I was booked into Waukegan. I went to Father's haberdashery and thrust two passes at him. "For you and Mom. Tickets to the show."

"Oh . . . the show," he mumbled, not looking at me. "Your cousin Cliff saw it in Chicago last week. He said you carry the violin out on the stage, but you don't play."

"Well, no. You see, Pap, my act has changed. I tell jokes."

He thought for a moment. "Then why do you carry the violin?"

"It's a prop. It gets a laugh."

"The violin . . . is funny?" He stared at me incredulously. Then he smiled apologetically. "I'm sorry, Benny, but I couldn't laugh."

In the years that followed I began to have success in show business. Always, though, the memory of Father's disappointment dulled it. Always there was the sound of his voice saying, "I couldn't laugh." I drove myself, determined to become a star. For every show I rehearsed and rehearsed, revised and rewrote, often to the annoyance of directors and casts who called me a perfectionist. I labored over entrances, exits, music cues, even the commercials.

Just before World War II, I made a picture with Dorothy Lamour titled *Man About Town,* and I asked the studio to hold the premiere in Waukegan. Father had refused to come to the vaudeville theater, but he couldn't very well ignore a big parade in which I wanted Meyer Kubelsky to sit in the lead car between Dorothy Lamour and me.

Father was eighty then, and a widower. His frame had become lean and shrunken, but he had a blaze of white hair, and his eyes were bird quick. He settled down in the seat and off we drove, along streets lined with cheering neighbors. Then came a civic reception, followed by a dinner at which people said nice things about me. Finally, it was my turn to say something. I had worked hard over the "impromptu" talk, and it got some good laughs. From time-to-time I'd sneak a look at Father, but his eyes were never on me. He was watching the audience attentively.

When I delivered him home, he still made no comment. I said goodnight and was about to leave when he took my arm.

"There is going to be a war," he announced in his thin, old voice.

"Yes," I said.

"America will crush Hitler."

He fell silent, but his hand on my arm held me close. When he spoke again, his eyes were far off, on the past. "There have always been problems in Europe. That's why your mother and I came to the United States, so our children would never know them. It always seemed to me we owed a debt to America, and I wanted very hard to pay some of it back. Yet I was only a small haberdasher, a nothing. But when I gave my son a violin, I thought if he could be a great musician, he could make beautiful music."

He sighed and gave a slight shrug of his bony old shoulders. "That was why I was so sad when you stopped playing, Benny. But now I understand. You found you were better at making people laugh, and it is good for people to laugh in these times."

"You think so?" I asked eagerly.

He nodded. "In the old country we never laughed at bad times, and during the good times we didn't laugh much either because we were thinking about the bad times. It is good to laugh, and I'm glad it's Benny Kubelsky who makes it possible.

He paused, then smiled. "And I've heard how you practice the hard parts. Is that true, Benny?"

"Yes, Papa."

"That's a good boy," he said.

Jack Benny echoed a message we have all heard many times before—if not from a parent, then perhaps from a school-teacher, coach, or friend: hard work—both physical and mental—is what paves the road to achievement. Of course, as Jack and his father discovered together, hard work is much more satisfying when you enjoy the work that you do, and most particularly when it also brings joy to others. For the combination of work and joy can bring a person the greatest satisfaction—even when working on the hard parts.

———————

The name "Ritz" has become synonymous with "quality." When we hear phrases such as "puttin' on the ritz" or "this is a ritzy place," our minds automatically conjure up images of fine quality and high-class living. This connection originates, of course, from the impeccable attention to detail of none other than César Ritz.

THE WORD FOR ELEGANCE

George Kent

When you put on the ritz, or describe something as ritzy, you are paying tribute to a Swiss peasant whose education never took him beyond simple arithmetic. His name has become a synonym for luxury. The story of César Ritz is the story of a genius who did much to transform hotel living into an art. You will find his mark on every continent today, wherever a hotel puts an accent on grace, comfort, and imaginative good taste.

Ritz lived at the turn of the century, when women were beginning to demand equality. He encouraged them, helped bring them out of their Victorian cloisters. When he arrived in London in the late nineties, for example, no woman of good family would dare be seen dining in public. Ritz persuaded a few great ladies—like the Duchess of Devonshire and Lady Dudley—to come to his hotel dining rooms. Others followed, and soon dining at the Savoy Carlton became a social must.

Ritz introduced soft lighting to flatter women's complexions and show their gowns to best advantage. He planned his dining rooms so that women, mounting a short flight of stairs, could make an "entrance." He conspired with his famous chef, Auguste Escoffier, to create scores of dishes that would appeal especially to women. And he presented dinner music—for the first time in London. Always the perfectionist, he chose the orchestra of Johann Strauss to play for his guests.

César Ritz was born in the Swiss mountain village of Niederwald, and went to work at sixteen in a hotel dining room in the nearby town of Brieg. A few months later he was discharged. "In the hotel business," commented his employer, "you need an aptitude—a flair. You haven't a trace of it."

Ritz got another job as a waiter—and again was booted out. He went to Paris, where he got—and lost—two more jobs. His career really began with the fifth job, in a chic little restaurant near the Madeleine where he climbed from bus boy to waiter and finally to manager. He was still only nineteen when his employer invited him to become his partner. To any other young fellow this might have been a wonderful opportunity. But Ritz knew now what he wanted: the world of great names, of epicurean feasts.

Rolling up his aprons, he walked down the street to the number one restaurant of the day, Voisin's, and went to work as an assistant waiter, once more at the bottom. He watched and learned—how to press a duck and carve a roast; how to decant a Burgundy; how to serve food in a way that pleased the eye as well as the palate.

In 1871 Ritz left Paris and for three years worked in fashionable resort restaurants in Germany and Switzerland. He was by then restaurant manager of the Rigi-Kulm, an Alpine hotel noted for its view and its cuisine. One day the heating plant broke down. Almost at the same moment a message arrived— forty wealthy Americans were on their way for lunch!

The temperature of the dining room was down around freezing. Ritz, wrapped in an overcoat, ordered the lunch table set up in the drawing room— it had red curtains and *looked* warmer. Into four huge copper pots, employed until then for holding palm trees, he poured alcohol and set it ablaze. Bricks were put into the ovens.

When the guests arrived the room was tolerably warm, and under the feet of each diner went a hot brick wrapped in flannel. The meal was a cold-weather masterpiece, starting with a peppery hot consommé and ending with flaming crepes suzette.

This small miracle of quick thinking was gossiped about wherever hotel-men gathered. Finally it reached the ears of the owner of a large hotel in Lucerne that was steadily losing money. He asked Ritz to become general manager. In two years the twenty-seven-year-old peasant put the hotel on a paying basis.

For Ritz no detail was too picayune, no enterprise too large if it meant the happiness of a guest. "People like to be served," Ritz used to say, "but *invisibly.*" The rules he formulated are the four commandments of a good hotel-keeper today: to see all without looking; to hear all without listening; to be attentive without being servile; to anticipate without being presumptuous.

If a guest complained of the size of a bill he smiled genially, took it away and forgot to bring it back. If the diner did not like the meat or the wine it was whisked from the table. Ritz had a prodigious memory. He remembered who liked a certain brand of Turkish cigarettes, who had a passion for chutney—and when they arrived these things were waiting for them.

He also catered to his more permanent guests. The tall man found an eight-foot bed in his room. Mrs. Smith, who could not bear flowers, was never annoyed with them but Mrs. Jones, who loved gardenias, always found a bowl of them on her breakfast tray.

In 1892 Ritz went to London to take over the financially tottering Hotel Savoy. The public responded and the hotel was out of the red in an astonishingly short time. Roving from room to room, Ritz remade beds to be sure they were right; once, inspecting the dining room, he smelled soap on a glass and sent several hundred glasses back to be rewashed.

He was redoing the decorations of a bridal suite one day, and the bronze chandelier protruding from the ceiling offended him. As he looked for a way to light the room less obtrusively, the projecting cornices gave him an idea. He put the lights in back of them—and indirect lighting was introduced.

Arranging a party for Alfred Beit, the South African diamond king, Ritz flooded the Savoy ballroom—transformed it into a miniature Venice. Guests were served as they reclined in gondolas.

Ritz's golden era at the Savoy ended with a quarrel between him and the directors. He returned to his beloved Paris and realized a dream he had cherished for years: he established, in the Place VendÛme, the grandest of all Ritz hotels. To discourage idlers he planned a small lobby. To encourage conversation over tea or coffee he designed a garden. Wanting cleanliness, he painted the walls instead of papering them because paint could be washed. For the design of his furniture he went to Versailles and Fontainebleau. The color scheme he borrowed from a painting by Van Dyck.

An innovation was the number of rooms equipped with private baths. On the day of the opening people streamed through the corridors as through a museum, largely to inspect the bathrooms.

The success of the Ritz of Paris was never in doubt. On one dinner menu preserved by an old Ritz employee were the autographs of four kings, seven princes, and assorted nobility. On all Ritz lavished his extraordinary attention, sensitive to every mood and price.

Here Ritz fixed the traditional waiter's costume: white tie for the waiter, black tie for the maitre d'hotel. He also gave the bellhop his brass buttons.

At the turn of the century Ritz built and opened the Carlton Hotel in London, and a few years later came the hotel in Piccadilly, which bears his name. The latter was the first building in England to use steel-frame construction, which Ritz, enamored of the Eiffel Tower, had insisted on. A group of financiers joined with Ritz to create the Ritz Hotel Development Corporation, which produced most of the Ritz hotels scattered through the world.

As he lay dying, in October 1918, he murmured, thinking his wife was at his side, "Take care of our daughter." They had two sons, but no girl. Between them, "daughter" was the way they referred to the Ritz Hotel in Paris.

Even today, years after his death, the hotels and services attached to César Ritz's name set the standard for quality. Quality was his every day mind-set. Meal by meal, hotel after hotel, he paid the price to produce high quality, and people were willing to pay a price to enjoy it. But like other success stories in this collection, his reputation did not come overnight. Rather it evolved gradually as he attended to the lighting, music, staging, temperature, cleanliness, and aroma—thereby creating an ambiance that attracted guests with high standards. To this day, people the world over continue to expect nothing but quality when they hear the name Ritz.

~

WRAP UP

Over the past few decades, the word quality has predominantly been relegated to a business term. And businesses do need to pay attention to quality as a matter of survival, just as Johnny Carson, Jack Benny, and César Ritz all made it an integral part of their professional reputations. But quality is a way of living and a key factor in Everyday Greatness whether in the business arena or in your personal life. Quality affects how you speak, dress, work, entertain, and eat. It impacts how you walk, teach, listen, exercise, learn, and play. It is one of those principles that weaves itself throughout the entire tapestry of life, both directly and indirectly touching everything you are and everything you do. And, no, quality does not require a lot of expense, but it does require a careful attention to detail.

REFLECTIONS

- Both Jack Benny and Johnny Carson found success through working on the hard parts. When it comes to the hard parts, do you persist or procrastinate?

- Jack Benny found laughter and joy to be an "intoxicating" part of his work. Do you find joy and laughter in your work?

- Jack Benny's father was concerned that Jack do something that brought other people joy. In what ways can you make the hard work you do more enjoyable, both for yourself and for others?

- Johnny Carson, Jack Benny, and César Ritz all built their reputations for quality one day at a time. Are you easily satisfied with mediocrity, or is your name and reputation also synonymous with quality?

FURTHER INSIGHTS ON
Quality

~

ONLY THE BEST

Quality means striving to do your best. It is a highly sought after attitude and reputation.

Doing your best at this moment puts you in the best place for the next moment.

—OPRAH WINFREY

■ ■ ■

Whether you are flying the Atlantic, selling sausages, building a skyscraper, driving a truck, or painting a picture, your greatest power comes from the fact that you want tremendously to do that very thing well. And a thing well done usually works out to the benefit of others as well as yourself. This applies to sport, business, friendship.

—AMELIA EARHART,
IN *AMERICAN MAGAZINE*

■ ■ ■

A professional is someone who can do his best work when he doesn't feel like it.

—ALISTAIR COOKE

■ ■ ■

The quality of a man's life is in direct proportion to his commitment to excellence, regardless of his chosen field of endeavor.

—VINCE LOMBARDI

■ ■ ■

The work praises the man.

—IRISH PROVERB

MATTERS OF DETAIL

Some "experts" suggest that leaders should not bother with details. While certainly some details should be left to others, attention to important details is the sure mark of a leader.

Following an exhausting day-long training march, Colin Powell was preparing troops to parachute from a helicopter. Twice already he had hollered for everyone to double-check their static lines—the lines that when hooked to a floor cable would open their chutes. Then:

"Like an old fussbudget, I started pushing through the crowded bodies, checking each line myself. To my alarm, one hook was loose. I shoved the dangling line in the man's face. He gasped. This guy would have stepped out of the helicopter and dropped like a rock.

Moments of stress, confusion and fatigue are exactly when mistakes happen. When everyone else is distracted, the leader must be doubly vigilant. 'Always check the small things' became one of my rules."

—COLIN POWELL
WITH JOSEPH E. PERSICO,
IN *MY AMERICAN JOURNEY*

■ ■ ■

Beware of the man who won't be bothered with details.

—WILLIAM FEATHER, SR.

■ ■ ■

Power often lies in the details, and the tenacious pursuit of such hidden levers can pay off enormously. While you don't want to get a reputation as a prissy worrywart, worrying about details in private is important. You may think you're the world's greatest speaker, but if the auditorium's sound system is singing static—well, forget it.

—TOM PETERS,
THE PURSUIT OF WOW!

■ ■ ■

This typxwritxr is xxcxllxnt xxcxpt for onx kxy. The 25 othxr lxttxrs work finx; but just onx goof-off lousxs up thx wholx job.

—WILLIAM D. XLLIS

WORK

Work puts dreams into action. True success requires the sweat of the brow.

If you want a place in the sun, you've got to put up with a few blisters.

—ABIGAIL VAN BUREN

■ ■ ■

Nothing great and durable has ever been produced with ease. Labor is the parent of all the lasting monuments of the world, whether in verse or in stone, in poetry or in pyramids.

—THOMAS MOORE

■ ■ ■

The body of every organization is structured from four kinds of bones. There are the wishbones, who spend all their time wishing someone would do the work. Then there are the jawbones, who do all the talking, but little else. The knucklebones knock everything anybody else tries to do. Fortunately, in every organization there are also the backbones, who get under the load and do most of the work.

—LEO AIKMAN,
ATLANTA CONSTITUTION

■ ■ ■

Marriage is not just spiritual communion and passionate embraces; marriage is also three meals a day, sharing the workload and remembering to carry out the trash.

—JOYCE BROTHERS
IN *GOOD HOUSEKEEPING*

■ ■ ■

When asked why he kept working at the same pace as ever as he grew older, Colonel [Harland Sanders] snorted. "Work never hurt anyone," he said. "More people rust out than wear out. But not me. I'll be damned if I'll rust out."

—JAMES STEWART-GORDON
IN *LOUISVILLE MAGAZINE*

■ ■ ■

The heights by great men reached and kept
Were not attained by sudden flight,
But they, while their companions slept,
Were toiling upward in the night.

—Henry Wadsworth Longfellow

■ ■ ■

I am only an average man, but, by George, I work harder at it than the average man.

—Theodore Roosevelt

■ ■ ■

The dictionary is the only place where success comes before work.

—Arthur Brisbane

■ ■ ■

Consider the lengths the following artists went to in order to put quality into their works.

Famed artist Norman Rockwell put passion into capturing details. How did he pose a chicken?

You pick up the chicken and rock him back and forth a few times. When you set him down, he will stand just as you've placed him for four or five minutes. Of course, you have to run behind the easel quickly to do much painting before the chicken moves.

If you want to paint the chicken full face, the procedure is even more complicated because the eyes of a chicken are on the sides of his head and when he looks at you he turns his head. I finally got a long stick, and after I'd set the chicken down and gone behind my easel, I'd rap the wall at one side of the chicken and he'd turn his head toward me to look at the wall. It's very strenuous painting a chicken.

—Norman Rockwell,
My Adventures as an Illustrator

How did Louis L'Amour capture the intrigue of millions with his Western novels?

L'Amour combed libraries and bookstores for genealogical histories, old diaries, and family journals. Once, he found an abandoned cabin whose occupants seventy years earlier had used newspaper to insulate the structure against frigid winds. He spent days removing the insulation, took it home and gleaned facts for two stories.

By the time L'Amour started a novel, he was armed with copies of every topographical map, relief map, and mine chart that existed on the area covered in his story. "My descriptions must be right," he insists. "When I tell my reader about a well in the desert, he knows it's there, and that the water is good to drink."

Once, for $3 a day, he agreed to help an 80-year-old trapper, hired to skin all the dead cattle on a rancher's spread. "There were 925 of them, and some had been dead for a while," he remembered. "Nobody else would come near the place. But the old man had a story to tell: he had been kidnapped by Apaches when he was seven years old and had been brought up as one of them. He had ridden with the great chiefs Nana and Geronimo. I had him all to myself for three months and got a lot of material for books I wrote later: *Hondo, Shalako,* and *The Skyliners.*"

—JOHN G. HUBBELL

THE JOY OF WORK

The easiest way to work hard is to find work that is both meaningful and enjoyable. The more we find joy in our work, the more drive we will possess.

Look at a day when you are supremely satisfied at the end. It's not a day when you lounge around doing nothing. It's when you've had everything to do, and you've done it.

—MARGARET THATCHER

Pleasure in the job puts perfection in the work.

—ARISTOTLE

I enjoyed the writing of books and magazine matter; it was merely billiards to me.

—MARK TWAIN, AT AGE 72

The Presidency is an all-day and nearly an all-night job. Just between you and me and the gatepost, I like it.

—HARRY S TRUMAN

I took violin lessons from age six to fourteen, but had no luck with my teachers, for whom music did not transcend mechanical practicing. I really began to learn only after I had fallen in love with Mozart's sonatas. The attempt to reproduce their singular grace compelled me to improve my technique. I believe, on the whole, that love is a better teacher than sense of duty.

—ALBERT EINSTEIN,
CREATOR AND REBEL
BY HELEN DUKAS AND BANESH HOFFMAN

Aviation combined all the elements I loved. There was science in each curve of an airfoil, in the gap of a spark plug or the color of the exhaust flame. A pilot was surrounded by beauty of earth and sky. He brushed treetops with the birds, leapt valleys and rivers, explored the cloud canyons he had gazed at as a child. Adventure lay in each puff of wind.

—CHARLES A. LINDBERGH,
THE SPIRIT OF ST. LOUIS

■ ■ ■

Happiness walks on busy feet.

—KITTE TURMELL

■ ■ ■

Action may not always be happiness, but there is no happiness without action.

—BENJAMIN DISRAELI

■ ■ ■

A man who works with his hands is a laborer; a man who works with his hands and his brain is a craftsman; a man who works with his hands and his brain and his heart is an artist.

—LOUIS NIZER,
BETWEEN YOU AND ME

LAZINESS SUFFOCATES DREAMS

All pathways to success are dotted with enticing rest areas where laziness can cause even the best of dreams to sputter and stall.

If hard work is the key to success, most people would rather pick the lock.

—CLAUDE McDONALD

■ ■ ■

Just as iron rusts from disuse, even so does inaction spoil the intellect.

—LEONARDO DA VINCI

■ ■ ■

An employment office, checking references of a job applicant, asked one ex-employer: "Was he a steady worker?"

"Steady?" came the indignant reply. "He was motionless."

—TERRY TURNER,
IN *AKRON BEACON-JOURNAL*

■ ■ ■

Laziness travels so slowly that poverty soon overtakes it.

—BENJAMIN FRANKLIN

■ ■ ■

The world is full of willing people; some willing to work, the rest willing to let them.

—ROBERT FROST

■ ■ ■

Memo posted at the Pappas Refrigeration Co, in Houston: TO ALL EMPLOYEES. Due to increased competition and a desire to stay in business, we find it necessary to institute a new policy. We are asking that somewhere between starting and quitting time, and without infringing too much on the time usually devoted to Lunch Periods, Coffee Breaks, Rest Periods, Story Telling, Ticket Selling, Vacation Planning and the re-hashing of yesterday's TV programs, each employee endeavor to find some time that can be set aside and known as the "Work Break."

—GEORGE FUERMANN,
HOUSTON POST

TEAMING WITH OTHERS

Snowflakes are one of nature's most fragile things,
but just look at what they can do when they stick together.
—VESTA M. KELLY

We live in an interdependent world. Though some of us are more social and gregarious than others, none of us is an island unto ourselves. Therefore, we must learn how to live, work, and team with others. This is not always easy as people come in all shapes, sizes, colors, ages, genders, and social varieties. But the people who seem to get the most out of life—the people with Everyday Greatness—do not just tolerate the diverse natures of people; they value, celebrate, and capitalize on the wide range of differences.

Principles that enhance one's ability to team with others include

- Respect

- Empathy

- Unity

13

RESPECT

If we cannot now end our differences,
at least we can help make the world safe for diversity.
—JOHN F. KENNEDY

German philosopher Johann Goethe taught, "Treat a man as he is and he will remain as he is. Treat a man as he can and should be and he will become as he can and should be." In fact, most people respond to being treated with respect by elevating their thoughts and actions to the same level of respect they are given—or beyond.

I always enjoy accounts of seemingly "average" individuals whose lives sparkle and blossom as a result of someone taking an interest in them and treating them with respect. "Johnny Lingo's Eight-Cow Wife" and "A Little Help from a Friend" are two such stories. Both send a powerful message that parents, spouses, or anyone who leads or works with others should take to heart. "Change of Heart" broadens the principle of respect to include relationships or interactions involving people whose cultures and values may be different from ours.

JOHNNY LINGO'S EIGHT-COW WIFE

Patricia McGerr

When I sailed to Kiniwata, an island in the Pacific, I took along a notebook. After I got back it was filled with descriptions of flora and fauna, native customs and costumes. But the note that still interests me is the one that says "John Lingo gave eight cows to Sarita's father." And I don't need to have it in writing. I'm reminded of it every time I see a woman belittling her husband or a wife withering under her husband's scorn. I want to say to them "You should know why Johnny Lingo paid eight cows for his wife."

Johnny Lingo wasn't exactly his name. But that's what Shenkin, the manager of the guest house on Kiniwata called him. Shenkin was from Chicago and had a habit of Americanizing the names of the islanders. But Johnny was mentioned by many people in many connections. If I wanted to spend a few days on the neighboring island of Nurabandi, Johnny Lingo could put me up. If I wanted to fish, he could show me where the biting was best. If it was pearls I sought, he would bring me the best buys. The people of Kiniwata all spoke highly of Johnny Lingo. Yet when they spoke they smiled, and the smiles were slightly mocking.

"Get Johnny Lingo to help you find what you want and let him do the bargaining," advised Shenkin. "Johnny knows how to make a deal."

"Johnny Lingo!" A boy seated rocked with laughter.

"What goes on?" I demanded. "Everybody tells me to get in touch with Johnny Lingo and then breaks up. Let me in on the joke."

"Oh the people like to laugh," Shenkin said, shrugging. "Johnny's the brightest, the strongest young man in the islands and for his age, the richest."

"But if he's all you say, what is there to laugh about?"

"Only one thing. Five months ago, at fall festival, Johnny came to Kiniwata and found himself a wife. He paid her father eight cows!"

I knew enough about island customs to be impressed. Two or three cows would buy a fair-to-middling wife, four or five a highly satisfactory one.

"Good Lord!" I said. "Eight cows! She must have beauty that takes your breath away."

"She's not ugly," he conceded, and smiled a little. "But the kindest could only call Sarita plain. Sam Karoo, her father, was afraid she'd be left on his hands."

"But then he got eight cows for her? Isn't that extraordinary?"

"Never been paid before."

"Yet you call Johnny's wife plain?"

"I said it would be kindness to call her plain. She was skinny. She walked with her shoulders hunched and her head ducked. She was scared of her own shadow."

"Well," I said, "I guess there's just no accounting for love."

"True enough," agreed the man. "And that's why the villagers grin when they talk about Johnny. They get special satisfaction from the fact that the sharpest trader in the islands was bested by dull old Sam Karoo."

"But how?"

"No one knows and everyone wonders. All the cousins were urging Sam to ask for three cows and hold out for two until he was sure Johnny'd pay only one. Then Johnny came to Sam Karoo and said, 'Father of Sarita, I offer eight cows for your daughter.' "

"Eight cows," I murmured. "I'd like to meet this Johnny Lingo."

I wanted fish. I wanted pearls. So the next afternoon I beached my boat at Nurabandi. And I noticed as I asked directions to Johnny's house that his name brought no sly smile to the lips of his fellow Nurabandians. And when I met the slim, serious young man, when he welcomed me with grace to his home, I was glad that from his own people he had respect unmingled with mockery. We sat in his house and talked. Then he asked "You come here from Kiniwata?"

"Yes."

"They speak of me on that island?"

"They say there's nothing I might want that you can't help me get."

He smiled gently. "My wife is from Kiniwata."

"Yes, I know."

"They speak of her?"

"A little."

"What do they say?"

"Why, just—" the question caught me off balance. "They told me you were married at festival time."

"Nothing more?" The curve of his eyebrows told me he knew there had to be more.

"They also say the marriage settlement was eight cows." I paused. "They wonder why."

"They ask that?" His eyes lighted with pleasure. "Everyone in Kiniwata knows about the eight cows?"

I nodded.

"And in Nurabandi everyone knows it too." His chest expanded with satisfaction. "Always and forever, when they speak of marriage settlements, it will be remembered that Johnny Lingo paid eight cows for Sarita."

So that's the answer, I thought—vanity.

And then I saw her. I watched her enter the room to place flowers on the table. She stood still a moment to smile at the young man beside me. Then she went swiftly out again. She was the most beautiful woman I have ever seen. The lift of her shoulders, the tilt of her chin, the sparkle in her eyes all spelled a pride to which no one could deny her the right.

I turned to Johnny Lingo and found him looking at me.

"You admire her?" he murmured.

"She . . . she's glorious." I said.

"There's only one Sarita. Perhaps she does not look the way they say she looked in Kiniwata."

"She doesn't. I heard she was homely. They all make fun of you because you let yourself be cheated by Sam Karoo."

"You think eight cows were too many?" a smile slid over his lips.

"No, but how can she be so different?"

"Do you ever think," he asked, "what it must mean to a woman to know that her husband has settled on the lowest price for which she can be bought? And then later, when the women talk, they boast of what their husbands paid for them. One says four cows, another maybe six. How does she feel, the woman who was sold for one or two? This could not happen to my Sarita."

"Then you did this just to make your wife happy?"

"I wanted Sarita to be happy, yes. But I wanted more than that. You say she is different. This is true. Many things can change a woman. Things that happen inside, things that happen outside. But the thing that matters most is what she thinks about herself. In Kiniwata, Sarita believed she was worth nothing. Now she knows she is worth more than any other woman in the islands."

"Then you wanted—"

"I wanted to marry Sarita. I loved her and no other woman."

"But—" I was close to understanding.

"But," he finished softly, "I wanted an eight-cow wife."

Every human being from cradle to coffin responds to respect, responds to people who see and draw out their hidden potential. You see it in their countenance; you hear it in their voice. No, they may not all turn into physical beauties like Sarita, but their inner beauty will shine in ways that I believe will significantly influence their physical presence and bring new light to their eyes.

———————

Some people are born into environments where there is no respect, and often their behavior and personality reflect the void. But sometimes it only takes one person giving them respect to change everything.

A LITTLE HELP FROM A FRIEND

Dudley A. Henrique

The weather was beautiful on the November morning. The city of Fredericksburg, Virginia, passed beneath the left wing of the rebuilt P51 Mustang fighter as I rolled out on a heading of 330 degrees. Ahead was the place I was looking for, the town of Culpeper.

My altitude was fifteen thousand feet. Pushing the stick forward, I started the Mustang down in a hurry. I found the spot I was looking for, then rolled the fighter into a dive. The airspeed indicator showed over 400 m.p.h. when I eased out of the dive. I was at treetop level and headed up the correct country road. I counted three seconds and performed the finest climbing roll of my life.

I realized that I had violated a number of federal flying regulations, including unauthorized low buzzing, flying in illicit proximity to buildings, and performing aerobatics under fifteen hundred feet. And this by an official of the Combat Pilots Association and a play-it-by-the-book flying instructor! But I had no regrets about my single outburst of lawlessness. Right or wrong, that moment was mine forever.

I was six when my father divorced my mother and left us in New York City to fend for ourselves. It was 1943 and times were tough.

Mother was working in a defense plant when she married a man who became known to me as Jack. He was a man prone to fits of rage. Life with Jack was a series of loud arguments in the night, sometimes followed by sounds of hitting. I remember Mother crying a lot.

One night Jack told me that he and my mother were going out and that I was to go to bed and stay there. Then he turned off my light and left.

I had a habit of sneaking out of bed and watching from the window as they drove away. As I was walking across the room in the dark, the light snapped on. Jack was standing at the door, holding a belt and a piece of clothesline. He cursed at me, shouting that I had disobeyed him. He threw me on the bed and tied my hands and feet to the frame. Then he beat me until I was bleeding.

I lived under those conditions for the next two years. Then one night my father's mother came up from Wilmington, Delaware. After a violent argument with my mother, Grandmother whisked me out to a waiting car and drove away. That was the last time I saw my mother.

For the next eight years I lived in Wilmington. My grandmother was a good woman but very strict; she almost never used the word *love* in conversation. Meanwhile, my father had remarried and was living in Texas with his second wife. He came to visit from time to time, but I hardly knew him. I remember him as a man who brought me presents.

Grandmother was a business manager for a large company and had little time for me. I would see her before I left for school, and not again until after

6:00 p.m. when she came home. At school I constantly got into fights with the other kids, and my attitude was surly and aggressive.

When I was fifteen, I was expelled. Grandmother enrolled me at a military academy in Bryn Mawr, Pennsylvania, which had a reputation for handling problem children. In a way, this was the first taste of education, along with fair and firm discipline. But I couldn't make it there, either, and I was expelled at the age of sixteen.

Back again at a Wilmington public school, I had weekends to myself and little to do. One Saturday I took a bus to the New Castle Air Base, which was located outside the city. There at the Delaware Air National Guard hangar I got my first close-up look at an airplane. It was a World War II P51 Mustang fighter. I was hypnotized! I walked around the P51 touching the wings and propeller; then I jumped up on the wing and slid into the cockpit. In an instant a man wearing three stripes on his green sleeve appeared and shouted, "Hey, kid, get out of there!"

I was scared stiff and started to climb out. Then a hand touched my shoulder and pushed me back into the cockpit. Turning, I came face-to-face with an officer in a flight suit. He was standing on the wing; his hair was red, his eyes were smiling.

The pilot's name was James Shotwell, and he was a captain. Before I left the field that day he had become "Jim." Thereafter, I visited New Castle each weekend. Jim had been a fighter pilot in the Pacific during the war. After coming home he graduated from college with a degree in electrical engineering, and went to work for an engineering firm in Georgetown, Delaware.

The weeks came and went and I found myself drawn closer and closer to Jim Shotwell. I told him about the rotten time I had had so far. He responded with warmth and friendship. I had found my first real friend—and as a result my life was to be forever changed.

Jim and I would sit under the wing of his Mustang and talk about airplanes and subjects like math, history, and physics. It was wonderful! Perhaps most important, Jim introduced me to the other pilots. For the first time in my life I experienced the feeling of belonging to a group.

One day I told Jim I wanted to quit school and find a job. Suddenly he got quite serious. "Dud," he said, "you remind me of a blind sparrow. He knows how to fly but he can't, because he can't see. Even if he got off the ground he would bump into things that would stop him cold. He wanders through life accomplishing nothing. He has no sense of direction. You have *all* the tools, Dud. For God's sake, use them! No matter what you do in this life, you need to develop one thing: a sense of direction! Think about it."

Away from Jim and the air base though, my life was still unchanged. I continued to get into trouble and my grades were bad. Finally my grandmother decided I should go to California to live with my aunt. I told Jim about this. Several nights later, he came and talked to my grandmother for hours. But it changed nothing, and at the end of August 1953, I was on a plane bound for Los Angeles.

My aunt was very kind to me and tried to help in every way she could. I missed New Castle and Jim, but I did my best to adjust to my new surroundings. Letters from Jim brightened my days.

Then one night in March 1955, the telephone rang. My aunt answered. As she spoke I could tell that something was wrong. She replaced the receiver and gently told me that Jim Shotwell had been killed. He had lost an engine while returning to New Castle from a practice mission. He could have ejected, but chose to stay with the plane, steering it away from the populated area—until it was too late to bail out.

Emotions I had never felt welled up inside me. I tried to hold back the tears but could not. Everything seemed fragmented and confused.

Gradually I stopped crying and started to think of Jim and the many things he had said to me. His analogy of the blind sparrow kept coming back. I had always known that what Jim had told me about myself was true. But until that night I hadn't been able to piece together the puzzle my life had become. Finally, I fell asleep, waking at dawn in a cold sweat. My mind was strangely clear. Instinctively, I was aware that something had changed. Now I knew where I was going in my life and what I would have to do to get there.

That year I enlisted in the air force and became an air-traffic controller. The air force finished the job Jim had started. By the time I was discharged in 1959, my negative attitude had been reversed and my faith in God and man restored. I wanted to go places!

I hurled myself into an intense year of hard work and study, and obtained my FAS pilot ratings. Employment as a flight instructor soon followed. It

turned out I had some talent in aerobatic flying, and through teaching and flying air shows every weekend, I developed a reputation of sorts.

By 1971, I had accumulated thousands of flying hours, flown more than a
hundred air shows, and lectured all over the country to flight instructors learning the trade. During those years I flew just about everything, including some
experimental and military aircraft.

In the fall of that year, a New York doctor contracted me to ferry a P51
Mustang from Newark, New Jersey, to Manassas, Virginia. I carefully plotted a
course that would take me somewhat south of Manassas. With 180 gallons of
fuel in the wings, I calculated I could include an extra thirty minutes of flying
time before arrival at my final destination.

On November 21 at 7:30 a.m., I climbed into the Mustang on the ramp
at Newark and angled south across Cape May, New Jersey. There I picked up a
heading for Cambridge, Maryland. Reaching Cambridge on time, I swung to
starboard and headed toward Culpeper.

The place where I violated the federal flying regulations that morning was
the Mount Carmel Baptist Cemetery. There beneath a tombstone were the
remains of my friend Captain James R. Shotwell, Jr. It had taken me 16 years
to find the right opportunity to pay my respects to the man who changed my
life. And I did it flying the same type of airplane I had been sitting in the day
I met him at New Castle. That climbing roll was my cry of triumph and gratitude, the salute of the fighter pilot.

Today my wife still kids me about my flight over Jim Shotwell's grave. "The
Day Baron von Leftover Led the Great Culpeper City Raid," she calls it. But
she knows how much that moment means to me. It keeps alive in my mind two
potent lessons: One man *can* make a difference in the lives of others—as Jim
Shotwell proved. And you can accomplish almost anything with hard work,
perseverance . . . and a little help from a friend.

The respect Jim Shotwell showed to Dudley literally changed
his life. What higher result of Everyday Greatness can there be?

But notice how Jim did not help Dudley by doing everything for him. No, he did not pull him along and tell him what to do every step of the way. Instead, he helped Dudley by showing him respect—by pointing him toward loftier heights, by speaking of more worthy purposes, and by expressing confidence. He showed respect by listening and by not overjudging. And, even well after Jim's death, the respect Dudley had received was still blooming in his innermost thoughts. Everyday Greatness never underestimates the power of respect.

Jim Shotwell showed respect to a young man and it changed the young man's life. There are also times when showing others respect can end up changing our own lives.

CHANGE OF HEART

Mary A. Fischer

In 1992, like many people in Los Angeles, I watched TV news reports of Rodney King speaking to the press after four officers accused of beating him in 1991 were acquitted, leading to riots in the city. As King spoke to reporters, he plaintively asked, "Can we all get along?"

"No! We can't," I shouted back at the TV, though no one else was in the room to hear me. Mine was not an idle, uninformed response. I knew what I was talking about. In late 1989, I had bought a house in an affordable eastside neighborhood of Los Angeles called Highland Park, which was being transformed by waves of new immigrants, and I was convinced racial harmony was impossible. Statistics said that each year, tens of thousands of new immigrants, mostly from Latin America and Asia, were pouring into Southern California, yet for most whites, these trends remained in the abstract realm of statistics.

When I moved to Highland Park, however, the statistics became my daily reality and brought my prejudices to the surface. Many of my neighbors were from Mexico, El Salvador, the Philippines and Vietnam, and for the first time, I was in the minority and didn't like it.

Convinced that we had nothing in common, I fortressed myself in my lovely pink Spanish house on the hill. I rarely spoke to my neighbors, waving occasionally when we took out our trash cans or passed by in our cars. I fit their stereotype—the unfriendly white "gringa" who owned the nicest house on the block—just as they fit my preconceived notions of immigrants who stubbornly refused to assimilate.

I was annoyed when Hispanic salespeople in Radio Shack didn't understand when I asked for lithium batteries or extension cords. It irritated me that the local supermarkets didn't carry things like blue cheese or soy milk, and that some billboard ads for movies and cars were written in Spanish.

For years, I complained to various officials when my neighbors behaved in ways I didn't agree with. One woman from El Salvador kept a rooster in her backyard that woke me up at five every morning. When I reported her to the Animal Regulation Department, she responded to the complaint by cutting off the bird's head. I felt guilty about being the impetus for the rooster's brutal demise, but rationalized it as being necessary to restore peace and quiet to the neighborhood.

When my neighbors from Mexico played their music too loud, I called the police, who put a stop to it. Surmising that I had reported them, my neighbors stopped speaking to me. It was a punishment I could live with, since I reasoned that I was bringing the neighborhood into compliance with my values.

Then, two years ago, something happened that changed me and how I live in my neighborhood. In a matter of two days, I lost the things that mattered most to me. My six-figure job as a senior writer for a national magazine came to an end, and a relationship with a man I loved ended badly. Suddenly, all my anchors were gone and, sunk deep in grief, I wondered how—or if—I would be able to pull myself out.

The losses I experienced humbled me and made me vulnerable, but as a consequence I began to connect more fully with my neighbors and the world around me. I discovered how extraordinary they were. They were nothing like my biases had made them out to be. They were hard-working, honorable people who, like me, were just looking to live well and experience some measure of happiness.

I learned that the woman from El Salvador had fled her country with two young daughters after death squads murdered her husband. She cleaned houses to make ends meet and send her daughters to college.

I learned that when my neighbors from Mexico came to Los Angeles fifteen years ago, they did not speak English and the father cleaned offices for eight dollars an hour. Later, he drove delivery trucks. Today he owns three apartment buildings and has made more money than I probably ever will in my lifetime.

Now, many of my neighbors are my friends. At Christmas, I give them red wine and cakes and they give me potted flowers and platters of burritos. When my car wouldn't start a few months ago, and it looked like it would have to be towed, another neighbor from Guatemala, a sweet man named Angel who's a gardener, quickly brought out his jumper cables and got the car started.

Today, I would answer Rodney King's question differently. I'd say that it is possible for us to get along if people from different cultures don't make the mistake I did. When I first moved to my neighborhood, I neglected to view my neighbors as individuals and I saw them as different and apart from me. I see now how their lives and mine include experiences universal to us all: loss, disappointment, hope, and love.

Last month, I heard a rooster crow early in the morning. It seems my neighbor from El Salvador got another one, but I no longer mind.

I like watching the rooster as it wanders the neighborhood. Somehow, he makes me feel like I'm home.

One of the most thrilling and inspiring experiences I have as I travel throughout the world is to experience cultures that not only respect differences, but actually celebrate them, where every religious tradition is observed by almost every person. Celebration is more than tolerance—the current buzzword of diversity circles. You know, tolerance for people's opinions, tolerance for people's cultures, tolerance for people's belief systems, and tolerance for people's styles. We hear the word every day. But what Mary did involved more than tolerance, more than respect, and even more than valuing differences. What Mary did was to celebrate her neighbors' differences.

~

WRAP UP

The principle of respect always sobers and humbles me, perhaps as much as any other principle. It contains a spirit of reverence for people. It brings a feeling of awe for the human spirit and for whom each person has the potential to become as a unique, progressing individual. I would love to see what would happen if everyone reading this book would do as Johnny Lingo did in showing Sarita respect, or as Jim Shotwell did in working with young Dudley, by identifying someone in need of respect and opening their eyes to the good that is within them. I would love to see what would happen if everyone gained a respect for their neighbors' differences, as Mary did. One definition I have used for leadership over the years that I believe well represents the principle of respect is this: Leadership is communicating people's worth and potential so clearly that they are inspired to see it in themselves.

REFLECTIONS

- Have you ever had someone believe in you in ways that you did not even believe in yourself? How did it make you feel? Did you behave differently as a result of their respect?

- Are there people you know who would benefit from added respect? What can you do to enhance their self-esteem and release their potential? What "cows" can you offer them as a symbol of your respect?

- Like Johnny Lingo, most everyone has been the victim of undue gossip—a clear violation of the principle of respect. When you hear gossip in social circles, do you pass it on or smother it at its roots?

- For the first time at sixteen, Dudley felt part of a group. Are there people you know who would benefit from being part of your circle?

- When was the last time you celebrated a neighbor's differences?

FURTHER INSIGHTS ON

Respect

~~

Unleashing Potential

When we treat people with respect, we help them gain confidence and reveal inner potential that otherwise might go untapped.

Few things help an individual more than to place responsibility upon him and to let him know that you trust him.

—Booker T. Washington

■ ■ ■

The greatest good you can do for another is not just to share your riches but to reveal to him his own.

—Benjamin Disraeli

■ ■ ■

I remember it like it was yesterday. Tenth grade, Frederick Douglass High School in Atlanta. Tall and gangly, I was pushing my way through the crowded hallway. All of a sudden a big, booming voice pealed like a thunderclap behind me: "Hey, son!"

It was Coach William Lester. He was a big, barrel-chested man, six feet, four inches. Besides being the junior varsity basketball coach, he also had a reputation as the school disciplinarian, so the first thing I thought was, uh-oh, somebody's in trouble. He fixed me with his piercing eyes and bellowed, "Yeah, you, son!"

Weak-kneed, I started walking toward him. Oh my, what had I done? I stopped in front of him, all six feet, five inches of me trembling in my shoes. "Son!" he said, looking me up and down. "You're too big to be walking these halls and not playing basketball. I'll see you in the gym at 3:30 today."

"But Coach!" I sputtered. "I've never played basketball. I don't have any basketball clothes or shoes."

"Son! Did you hear what I said? I'll see you at 3:30!" And he walked away.

So I went.

And from that day until now, there's no question in my mind that everything that has happened to me since, becoming a basketball player, then a coach, raising my three kids, writing a book, is a result of that day when Coach called me out and said "Hey, son! Yes you!"

Up until that point, I hadn't been a troublemaker, but I was drifting. I had no idea what my goals were or where I was heading.

Coach Lester helped me see something bigger out there. I remember when he told me "You can get a college scholarship."

When I said, "But I don't know how. I don't have it," he said "Yes, you do. I'm going to show you. I'm going to work with you. You can do it."

And he was right. I knew it the day I set foot on a college campus, scholarship in hand. He believed in me.

Many times since the day I heard that big voice bellow, "Hey, son!" I've thought, if only every kid had a Coach William Lester to believe in him, what a difference it would make.

—RICKY BYRDSONG,
FORMER BASKETBALL COACH AT NORTHWESTERN UNIVERSITY,
IN *COACHING YOUR KIDS IN THE GAME OF LIFE*

■ ■ ■

A severely impaired person never knows his hidden strength until he is treated like a normal human being and encouraged to try to shape his own life. Annie Sullivan regarded the blind as human beings endowed with rights to education, recreation, and employment, and she strove to arrange my life accordingly. Teacher believed in me, and I resolved not to betray her faith.

—HELEN KELLER,
TEACHER

WHAT FRIENDS ARE FOR

One of the greatest forms of respect we can extend to another is friendship. Friendship accepts people for who they are and stands by them in difficult moments.

A friend hears the song in my heart and sings it with me when my memory fails.

—PIONEER GIRLS LEADERS' HANDBOOK

■ ■ ■

A friend is someone who can see through you and still enjoys the show.

—FARMER'S ALMANAC

■ ■ ■

What makes friendship such a wonderful gift is that it blesses you just for being who you are.

—CONSTANCE BUXER,
in WOMAN'S DAY

■ ■ ■

On her frequent trips on foot to Temuco, an old Araucanian Indian woman used always to bring my mother a few partridge eggs or a handful of berries. My mother spoke no Araucanian beyond the greeting "Mai-mai," and the old woman knew no Spanish, but she drank tea and ate cake with many an appreciative giggle. We girls stared fascinated at her layers of colorful hand-woven clothing, her copper bracelets and coin necklaces, and we vied with each other in trying to memorize the singsong phrase she always spoke on rising to leave.

At last we learned the words by heart and repeated them to the missionary, who translated them for us. They have stayed in my mind as the nicest compliment ever uttered:

"I shall come again, for I like myself when I'm near you."

—ELIZABETH MAUSKE

RESPECTING DIFFERENCES

It is easy and even ego-boosting to respect people similar to us. But it is valuing people different from us that unveils the most noble forms of respect.

All men are born free and equal—free at least in their right to be different. Some people want to homogenize society everywhere. I'm against the homogenizers in art, in politics, in every walk of life. I want the cream to rise.

—ROBERT FROST

■ ■ ■

Some people march to a different drummer—and some people polka.

— LOS ANGELES TIMES SYNDICATE

■ ■ ■

Much of the vitality in a friendship lies in the honoring of differences, not simply in the enjoyment of similarities.

—JAMES L. FREDERICKS

■ ■ ■

It's the things in common that make relationships enjoyable, but it's the little differences that make them interesting.

—TODD RUTHMAN

■ ■ ■

Tolerance is the first principle of community; it is the spirit which conserves the best that all men think. No loss by flood and lightning, no destruction of cities and temples by the hostile forces of nature has deprived man of so many noble lives and impulses as those which his intolerance has destroyed.

—HELEN KELLER,
THE OPEN DOOR

GOSSIP

Johnny Lingo was the target of gossip. But one of the true signs of respect is when people are loyal to the absent by not speaking behind their backs.

Gossip needn't be false to be evil—there's a lot of truth that shouldn't be passed around.

—FRANK A. CLARK

■ ■ ■

A peasant circulated slander about a friend, only to find out later that it was not true. He came to a wise old monk for advice.

"To make peace with your conscience," said the monk, "you must fill a bag with chicken down, go to each house in the village, and place one feather at the threshold."

The peasant did as he was told and returned announcing he had completed his penance. "Not yet!" said the monk. "Take up your bag and gather each feather that you have dropped!"

"But the wind must have blown them all away."

"Yes," replied the monk. "And so it is with gossip. Words are easily spread, but no matter how hard you try, you can never get them all back again."

—MERLE CROWELL,
THE AMERICAN MAGAZINE

■ ■ ■

Who gossips to you will gossip of you.

—TURKISH PROVERB

■ ■ ■

A rumor without a leg to stand on will get around some other way.

—JOHN TUDOR

JUDGING OTHERS

We fail to treat people with respect when we are constantly judging or misjudging their every word and deed.

Oh, Great Spirit, help me never to judge another until I have walked two weeks in his moccasins.

— SIOUX INDIAN PRAYER

■ ■ ■

A friend of mine, returning to South Africa from a long stay in Europe, found herself with some time to spare at London's Heathrow Airport. Buying a cup of coffee and a small package of cookies, she staggered, laden with luggage, to an unoccupied table. She was reading the morning paper when she became aware of someone rustling at her table. From behind her paper, she was flabbergasted to see a neatly dressed young man helping himself to her cookies. She did not want to make a scene, so she leaned across and took a cookie herself. A minute or so passed. More rustling. He was helping himself to another cookie.

By the time they were down to the last cookie in the package, she was very angry but could still not bring herself to say anything. Then the young man broke the remaining cookie in two, pushed half across to her, ate the other half and left.

Some time later, when the public-address system called for her to present her ticket, she was still fuming. Imagine her embarrassment when she opened her handbag, and was confronted by her package of cookies. She had been eating his.

—DAN P. GREYLING

■ ■ ■

When nobody around you seems to measure up, it's time to check your yardstick.

—BILL LEMLEY

■ ■ ■

As we read the school reports on our children, we realize with a sense of relief that can rise to delight that—thank Heaven—nobody is reporting in this fashion on us.

—J. B. PRIESTLEY,
DELIGHT

■ ■ ■

Prejudice is a disease characterized by hardening of the categories.

—WILLIAM ARTHUR

■ ■ ■

See everything, overlook a great deal, correct a little.

—POPE JOHN XXIII

14

EMPATHY

Empathy involves understanding another's heart, mind, and spirit—including their motives, backgrounds, and feelings. The more empathy we have for others, the more we come to appreciate and reverence who they are. For to touch the inner feelings and soul of another human being is to walk on holy ground.

To gain empathy for another, we must listen to them with our eyes and hearts, as well as our ears. But most people do not listen with the intent to understand, rather they listen with the intent to reply. They are busy filtering everything through their own perspectives rather than trying to understand another's frame of reference. The effects of such nonempathic behaviors are expressed in "Lend an Ear." Listen as Roberta describes her failures and successes in both experiencing and practicing empathy. Then observe as two doctors are taught the importance of taking time to listen, and what an impact that can have on a meaningful relationship.

LEND AN EAR

Roberta Israeloff

My in-laws had just returned from a harrowing drive back to New York City after wintering in Florida. "The first time the car broke down we were somewhere in North Carolina," my mother-in-law told me over the phone. "We had it fixed and then it stalled again in Delaware. But the worst was on the Verrazano Bridge during rush hour. It seemed as if we'd never get home."

"That sounds horrible," I said, ready to launch in to my own horror story—a car that conked out at 9:30 p.m. in a deserted mall parking lot.

But someone knocked at her door so she had to say good-bye. "Thank you for listening," she added, "but thank you most of all for not telling me your worst car story."

My cheeks burning, I hung up. In the days ahead I found myself thinking about the wisdom of her parting words.

I can't count the number of times I've begun to complain about a fight with my son, a professional disappointment, or even car problems, only to have my friend cut me off with "the same thing just happened to me."

Suddenly we're talking about *her* ungrateful kid, *her* lousy boss, *her* leaky fuel line. And I'm left nodding my head in all the right places, wondering if we haven't all come down with a bad case of emotional attention deficit disorder.

It's easy to see how this version of empathy "I know just how you feel and I can prove it" gets confused with the real thing. Nothing's more natural than trying to soothe an overwrought friend with assurances that she's not alone.

But calamities resemble one another only from afar. Up close they're as unique as fingerprints. Your friend's husband may have been downsized out of a job, just like your own, but no two families have identical bank accounts, severance packages, or backup plans.

Saying "I feel your pain" also can be a prelude to offering advice— "Here's what I did and here's what you should do." But when a car trip takes three times as long as it should, or your child runs a high fever in the middle of the night, do you really want to hear how your friend coped with a similar situation?

What we all hope for when we're feeling low or agitated or wildly happy is to find a friend who sounds as if she has all the time in the world to listen. This ability to be with someone in her pain or happiness is the cornerstone of genuine empathy.

Fortunately, empathy is eminently easy to learn. Ever since the conversation with my mother-in-law, for example, I've squelched my impulse to interrupt a friend when she confides in me. I'm learning to follow the other person's lead, paying attention to body language, facial expressions, tone of voice, and what's left unsaid.

I'm also more likely to recognize and appreciate empathy when I'm the beneficiary. The other day I called a friend to complain that I was feeling nervous and couldn't concentrate.

"Want to tell me about it?" she offered. So I rambled on for a while.

Finally, I thanked her for listening and asked how *she* was feeling, "We can talk about me tomorrow," she said. Now that's empathy.

We don't always want answers or advice. Sometimes we just want company.

As Roberta concluded, "Sometimes we just want company." True. But what we really prefer is company who understands us, or who will at least do their best to understand us. Such understanding begins with empathy. And as Roberta suggested, empathic people learn to see things through others' eyes rather than filtered through their own autobiographies or philosophies. They know how to hold their tongue by not forcing their own stories, advice, judgment, or opinions on others.

———————

In the final analysis, isn't one of the biggest barriers to empathic listening a matter of time—taking time to listen?

IT'S ABOUT TIME

Noah Gilson, MD

The wheelchair-bound young man, a patient of mine, was pushed to the lectern at the high school to deliver his commencement address. His face still partially paralyzed, he spoke in a soft voice. But Mark Orsini delivered a powerful speech and received a standing ovation from his fellow students, who had wondered if he'd live to graduate.

The eighteen-year-old had developed Guillain-Barré syndrome, an autoimmune reaction that can cause paralysis. Soon he was almost completely paralyzed.

His parents insisted that he was a fighter; he'd get through this and go on to attend Dartmouth. But meanwhile, immobile and on a ventilator, how was he going to ask questions or be involved in his care?

The solution was remarkable: The Orsinis would sit at Mark's side and recite the alphabet. When they got to a letter Mark needed to spell a word, he'd nod "yes." They'd write it down, then start over and wait for him to nod again. They never lost patience, and Mark was involved with every decision.

Standard therapy hadn't helped, so I proposed a risky procedure to filter his blood. After the treatment he showed improvement, and soon he could move his toes, his legs, and his arms.

Mark has graduated from Dartmouth. I saw him in my office some time ago, and he was feeling great. But there was a lot left unsaid. I wanted to say I was in awe of him, and that his parents were some of the most amazing people I'd ever met, sitting by his bed for hours, patiently listening to their child speak, letter by letter. I wanted to tell him of my shame when my children tried to talk to me, and I brushed them off because I didn't have time to listen. I wanted to say I'd never forget him or his parents. But words failed me.

At the pace the world is moving, time is at a premium and efficiency seems to be everyone's objective. But empathy takes time, and efficiency is for things, not people. These parents were more than willing to take the time for their son, and the results were priceless.

In this next story, another doctor learns the value of taking time to listen and the cost of trying to be efficient with people. He learns that the most important part of his job takes place outside the operating room, and it involves listening.

CRASH COURSE
Michael J. Collins, MD

As an orthopedic surgeon, I'm not always the most perceptive of men or the best spoken. I can fix things with my hands, but words sometimes fail me.

Maybe it was because there was no training for the emotional aspects of my work. The focus was on action. During my four-year residency at the Mayo Clinic in Rochester, Minnesota, the scalpel was a symbol of operating rooms and surgery, of "hot lights and cold steel," as the older guys called it. We rebuilt knees, realigned bones, made patients whole again. My wife, Patti, knew I'd chosen surgery because I wanted to help people. But sometimes my cases ended up teaching me things I didn't expect.

One night on call during my third year of training, the ER paged me. A five-year-old kid had fallen out of his bunk bed and fractured his wrist. I groaned. Not another one! It seemed Rochester was having a special on kids with wrist fractures that year. From the ortho floor I trudged down to the ER, picked up the chart and went to see my patient.

He was sitting in his father's lap, sniffling. The boy was wearing Donald Duck pajamas and holding a worn stuffed animal that looked like Goofy. His left wrist was bent back about forty-five degrees. I introduced myself to the father and asked the boy what happened. He wouldn't answer me or even look at me. He just shrank deeper into his father's arms.

I was impatient. I knew what needed to be done, how long it would take. I had work to do. So I gave up talking to the boy and quickly called X-ray.

Five minutes later the technician appeared. She squatted down next to the boy. "Oh, Danny," she said. "Did you hurt your arm, sweetheart?"

As the kid looked at her, his eyes filled with tears. "I fell out of my bed."

"Oh, you poor thing." She put her hand on his cheek. "Well, I'm going to take a picture of your arm, and then this nice doctor is going to fix it. Would you like me to take a picture of Goofy too?" Danny nodded his head.

I stood in the corner, wondering why the child would talk to the X-ray tech and not his doctor. As the tech kept jabbering away, I thought, *We're wasting time here!* Finally she set up the machine and took the films. Then she placed Goofy on a cassette and took a film of him too.

While I waited for the X-rays, I arranged to take the boy to the OR and called Bonnie, the anesthesia resident. Then I called the cast tech, John "Ski" Kowalski, and asked him to meet me in the cast room.

The X-rays showed a badly displaced fracture. But the kid wasn't interested. He was staring at the faint gray silhouette of Goofy outlined against the black film. I told the boy's parents that the bones would have to be reduced. The least painful way to do this was under a general anesthetic.

"I don't think I'll have to make an incision," I said. "I can usually manipulate the bones back in position, then put on a cast."

We got Danny up to the cast room and had to wait fifteen minutes for anesthesia to show up. Ski, quiet and competent as usual, wheeled the cast cart over and started selecting the plaster rolls we'd need. When Bonnie finally appeared and got the kid asleep, she nodded and said I could go ahead.

"Okay, Ski," I said. "You know the drill."

I bent the elbow to ninety degrees. While Ski held the arm, I applied traction to the hand, stretching the fracture. Then I increased the deformity just enough for me to wedge my left thumb under the edge of it. I levered the top edge of the fracture over the bottom edge, and pushed the whole thing together. I heard a crunch as the bones slipped back into place.

The reduction was perfect. I had become good at this, proficient. That's why I was here, right? Now I needed to put Junior's cast on and finish up.

"YOU'RE ALL FIXED, KIDDO"

Ski held the arm as I began wrapping cast padding around it. Suddenly I noticed a blue tattoo under the edge of Ski's scrub shirt. "Hey, Ski," I said, pointing to the tattoo, "what does 28 mean?"

"That was my regiment," he answered quietly. "The Twenty-eighth Infantry. I was a corpsman in Nam." Ski had never mentioned this before.

As I continued applying the roll of plaster and then another, Ski told me about his time in Vietnam. "It was a hellhole, Doc. I saw a lot of guys burned up and blown apart, or shot to pieces. I spent every day bandaging and splinting. After a while, it became mechanical. I didn't want to think about it. I just wanted to get it done and go home."

"Yes," I murmured, "I know what you mean."

"But I was wrong, Doc," Ski added quickly. "I'd forgotten about the poor grunts who were getting shot up for no reason. I finally realized that what those guys needed from me wasn't just my work, but knowing that I cared about them. It wasn't just about bandaging wounds, any more than what we're doing here tonight is about realigning bones."

As my hands ran over the surface of the kid's cast, smoothing the finish, my mind was twisting, turning. *Of course it's about realigning bones. Isn't that what the father brought his kid to the ER for? Isn't that my job?* Then I got it.

You are a fool, I told myself. *You have been missing the boat.* Ski must have wondered what had become of Captain Efficiency, who just stood there rubbing a dry cast instead of rushing the tech to get the films done. I watched dumbly as Ski positioned the boy's arm for another X-ray, checking that the fracture hadn't slipped.

I had let my work become automatic, forgetting the essence of what a doctor is called to do. I'd let pragmatism take me too far. Even the X-ray tech knew how to show an injured little child that someone cared. All I could do was hurry the boy up and get on to the next order of business.

The films were back in five minutes. Ski snapped them up on the view box, and we took a look. "Very nice reduction, Doc—as usual," Ski said. Why hadn't I noticed the irony in his voice before?

"You can wake him up, Bonnie," I said quietly to the anesthesiologist. When Danny started to awaken, we wheeled him to recovery. I took Goofy and wrapped a small bit of plaster around his arm. I fashioned a little sling out of some tissues and tied it around his neck.

"Don't be afraid, Danny," I said as his eyelids fluttered open and he looked around in panic. "We're all done. Your arm is all fixed. And look, we fixed Goofy too."

He reached out with his good arm. He took Goofy from me. "I want my mommy," he said, his lip quivering.

"You're all fixed, kiddo," I repeated. "We're going to let you and Goofy go home in just a little while."

I picked up the chart and looked at his name. Oestmann, Daniel, from Byron, Minnesota. I hadn't even known his full name. I wiped the dried plaster from my arm, picked up the X-rays and went to see the parents.

"Hi, Mr. and Mrs. Oestmann," I said. "Danny's fine. Everything went well. His fracture is back in place. He should be able to go home tonight."

"Did you have to open it?" the father asked.

"No, sir. I was able to push it back into place without opening it."

The parents beamed. When had I stopped noticing things like this? When had I become so impatient to deliver my news and be off? "Please," I said, gesturing at the couch behind them, "sit down." I sat with the Oestmanns for fifteen minutes. They told me they had two other children, ages ten and twelve. "So Danny's your baby, huh?" I asked Mrs. Oestmann.

"You got that right, Doc," said Mr. Oestmann before his wife could answer. "Nancy thinks the earth revolves around him." She offered a shy smile.

I told them what to watch for, gave instructions about getting a follow-up X-ray and asked them to call with any concerns. I said I would check if the nurses would let them see Danny. They got to their feet and shook my hand. "Thanks, Doc," Mr. Oestmann said. "Thank you so much."

I said good-bye. I had learned a valuable lesson that night. When I finished talking to the nurses, I headed for the cast room. There was someone I needed to thank.

Initially, the surgeon was so caught up in being efficient and in center-staging his technical competence that he did not even notice the effect he was having on his patients. Efficiency with people is usually ineffective. Have you ever tried to be efficient with your spouse or a close friend on a tough issue? How did it go? Have you ever tried to be efficient with a son or daughter on an emotional issue? How did that go? You can be efficient with things, but not with people. It is only when you are on the same page about what is important that efficiency with people can become effective.

~

WRAP UP

The key to these three stories is caring. All the best listening "techniques" in the world pale in comparison to the impact that truly caring about a person can have on a listening exchange. Added to that is a measure of integrity and of inward personal security, because empathy involves being vulnerable and at risk, and if our security is not deep down within us, we cannot afford that much risk, that much vulnerability. So while listening skills might represent the tip of an iceberg, a character base of caring, integrity, and inner security would form the much larger, unseen portion of the iceberg that lies beneath the water.

REFLECTIONS

- When was the last time you set aside time solely for the purpose of listening to someone important to you? Did you listen in an empathic way?

- If in a leadership role, how frequently do you get out and listen to people—employees, customers, suppliers, field experts? Do you more naturally remain behind a desk, or are you more known for mixing with people?

- Do you actively seek feedback from others as a way of listening, or do you more often wait for feedback to find its way to you? Are you best described as defensive or open to criticism?

FURTHER INSIGHTS ON
Empathy

∽

LISTENING TO UNDERSTAND

Listening with the intent to understand goes a long way toward allowing others to feel comfortable in expressing their thoughts and innermost feelings.

The most called-upon prerequisite of a friend is an accessible ear.

—MAYA ANGELOU,
THE HEART OF A WOMAN

■ ■ ■

There is a way of listening that surpasses all compliments.

—JOSEPH VON LIGNÉ

■ ■ ■

Listening is a rare happening among human beings. You cannot listen to the word another is speaking if you are preoccupied with your appearance or with impressing the other, or are trying to decide what you are going to say when the other stops talking, or are debating about whether what is being said is true or relevant or agreeable. Such matters have their place, but only after listening to the word as the word is being uttered.

—WILLIAM STRINGFELLOW,
FRIENDS JOURNAL

■ ■ ■

Everyone you meet has some interest you don't have. The judicious use of ears will suffice to acquire it.

—W. SOMERSET MAUGHAM

■ ■ ■

No one appreciates the very special genius of your conversation as a dog does. If you chat with him a while, gradually building up the argument and the intonation, he relishes it so that he will roll all around the floor, lie on his back kicking and groaning with joyous worship. Very few wives are so affected.

—CHRISTOPHER MORLEY

Real communication happens when we feel safe.

—KEN BLANCHARD,
THE HEART OF A LEADER

One girl to another: "I can only stand him for an hour. He gets tired of listening after that."

—SALO

A class in music appreciation was asked the difference Between listening and hearing. At first there was no response. Finally, a hand went up and a youngster offered this sage solution: Listening is wanting to hear.

—CONTRIBUTED BY M. C. HESS

The golden rule of friendship is to listen to others as you would have them listen to you.

—DAVID AUGSBURGER, MAN,
AM I UPTIGHT

There is no greater loan than a sympathetic ear.

—FRANK TYGER

GOLDEN SILENCE

Sometimes the most challenging requirement of empathy is holding your tongue when tempted to reply, to give counsel, or to share your own stories.

The word "listen" contains the same letters as the word "silent."

—ALFRED BRENDEL

■ ■ ■

At a party once, I found myself talking with a botanist. I sat fascinated while he told me astonishing facts about the humble potato. After I said good-night, the botanist turned to our host, paid me several compliments and ended by saying I was a "most interesting conversationalist." An interesting conversationalist? I had said hardly anything. But I had listened intently, and he felt it.

—DALE CARNEGIE,
HOW TO WIN FRIENDS AND INFLUENCE PEOPLE

■ ■ ■

His thoughts were slow,
His words were few, and never formed to glisten.
But he was a joy to all his friends—
You should have heard him listen.

—ANONYMOUS,
QUOTED BY WAYNE MACKEY
IN *OKLAHOMA CITY TIMES*

■ ■ ■

Give every man thy ear but few thy voice.

—WILLIAM SHAKESPEARE

WHAT ISN'T SAID

Truly empathic listeners can even hear what is being said in the silence.

The most important thing in communication is to hear what isn't being said.

—PETER F. DRUCKER

■ ■ ■

Sometimes the news is in the noise, and sometimes the news is in the silence.

—THOMAS L. FRIEDMAN
IN THE *NEW YORK TIMES*

■ ■ ■

It's amazing how much you can hear when no one is saying anything.

—ELAINE ST. JAMES,
INNER SIMPLICITY

■ ■ ■

The eyes shout what the lips fear to say.

—WILL HENRY

Seeing Through Another's Eyes

We never fully understand another until we take our glasses
off and see the world through his or her eyes.

If there is any one secret of success, it lies in the ability to get the other
person's point of view and see things from his angle as well as your own.

—Henry Ford

■ ■ ■

Don't confuse being "soft" with seeing the other guy's point of view.

—George H.W. Bush,
All the Best, George Bush

■ ■ ■

We have not really budged a step from home until we take up residence in
someone else's point of view.

—John Erskine

■ ■ ■

Approach each new person you meet in a spirit of adventure. Try to discover
what he is thinking and feeling; to understand as far as you can the
background from which he comes, the soil in which his roots have grown, the
customs and beliefs and ideas which have shaped his thinking. If you care
enough to make the effort, you can establish an understanding relationship
with people who are entirely outside your own orbit.

—Eleanor Roosevelt,
You Learn by Living

■ ■ ■

He best can pity who has felt the woe.

—John Gay

■ ■ ■

Isn't it funny, when the other fellow takes a long time to do something, he's slow. When I take a long time to do something, I'm thorough. When the other fellow doesn't do it, he's lazy. When I don't do it, I'm busy. When the other fellow does it without being told, he's overstepping his bounds. When I go ahead and do it without being told, that's initiative. When the other fellow states his opinion strongly, he's bullheaded. When I state my opinion strongly, I'm firm. When the other fellow overlooks a few rules of etiquette, he's rude.

—TOM KNIGHT,
QUOTED BY CHARLES McHARRY,
NEW YORK DAILY NEWS

■ ■ ■

When we put ourselves in the other person's place, we're less likely to want to put him in his place.

—*FARMER'S DIGEST*

■ ■ ■

Preconceived notions are the locks on the door to wisdom.

—MERRY BROWNE IN NATIONAL ENQUIRER

■ ■ ■

A new idea is delicate. It can be killed by a sneer or a yawn; it can be stabbed to death by a quip, and worried to death by a frown on the right man's brow.

—CHARLIE BROWER

RECEIVING FEEDBACK

Successful people know the importance of feedback as it helps them assess progress toward their vision and aids them in course correcting as needed.

Your most unhappy customers are your greatest source of learning.

—BILL GATES

■ ■ ■

Nobody wants constructive criticism. It's all we can do to put up with constructive praise.

—MIGNON MCLAUGHLIN

■ ■ ■

Pay attention to your enemies, for they are the first to discover your mistakes.

—ANTISTHENES

■ ■ ■

If one man calleth thee a donkey, pay him no mind. If two men calleth thee a donkey, get thee a saddle.

—YIDDISH PROVERB

■ ■ ■

Most of us would rather be ruined by praise than saved by criticism.

—NORMAN VINCENT PEALE

But there is a point when one can listen to feedback too much . . .

A statesman who keeps his ear permanently to the ground will have neither elegance of posture nor flexibility of movement.

—ABBA EBAN

■ ■ ■

A man who trims himself to suit everybody will soon whittle himself away.

—CHARLES SCHWAB

OPENNESS

Empathy requires openness. Openness declares our acceptance that others may have thoughts or abilities superior to
our own.

Bring ideas in and entertain them royally, for one of them may be
the king.

—MARK VAN DOREN

■ ■ ■

Minds are like parachutes—they only function when open.

—LORD THOMAS DEWAR

■ ■ ■

An age is called Dark, not because the light fails to shine, but because people
refuse to see it.

—JAMES A. MICHENER, SPACE

15

UNITY

We're all only fragile threads, but what a tapestry we make.
— JERRY ELLIS

Mahatma Gandhi suggested that one of the greatest challenges of our day is finding unity amongst diversity. Unity implies oneness. But oneness does not necessarily imply sameness. In other words, we may all be different, unique individuals but through unity of purpose we can team together synergistically to accomplish great tasks— tasks where the whole is greater than the sum of its parts.

Unity is sought on sports teams, in work units, in community projects, and essentially in all group-based endeavors. Perhaps nowhere is unity exhibited more strongly than in close families where harmony prevails. This is particularly so on occasions when the family needs to bond their talents to overcome an obstacle or a special need. The strength of such unity is vividly portrayed in "The Family That Couldn't Be Broken."

THE FAMILY THAT
COULDN'T BE BROKEN

John Pekkanen

Soon after the birth of his son, Steven, Lindy Kunishima gathered his daughters, Trudi, thirteen, and Jennifer, nine, in the living room of their Honolulu home.

"I want to tell you a story," the American-born descendant of Japanese samurai said. "One day a samurai warrior sat down with his three sons and took out an arrow. He asked each son to break it. All of them broke it easily. Then he took three arrows, all bound together, and placed them before his sons. 'Now break these three arrows,' he said. None of them could do it."

As he neared the end of this story, Lindy gazed steadily into his daughters' eyes. "Then the samurai turned to his sons and said, 'That is your lesson. If you three stick together, you will never be defeated.'"

As the only boy in Lindy and Geri Kunishima's close-knit family, Steven occupied an honored place. His two sisters doted on him from the day he was born in September 1982.

When Steven reached six months, however, his mother grew concerned. Schoolteacher Geri Kunishima couldn't understand why her son still woke up crying several times every night to be fed. His daytime behavior was also puzzling. Steven would stay wherever Geri put him, seldom moving or making a noise. "He's not like the girls were at this age," Geri told her pediatrician.

"You're overanxious," he said. "Steven is doing just fine. Little girls tend to develop faster."

At eighteen months, Steven still could not walk or talk, and early in 1984 Geri took her son to a neurologist. A CT scan revealed that the vermis, an area of the brain that transmits messages to and from the body's muscles, had not developed.

This condition—called bypoplasia of the vermis—explained why Steven's muscles remained soft and flaccid. It also explained why he woke up so often at night—his tongue muscles were too weak for him to swallow enough milk to satisfy his hunger.

"Mrs. Kunishima," the neurologist said, "I'm afraid your son will never walk or talk, or do much of anything else that requires muscle control."

Struggling to get a grip on herself, Geri asked how this would affect Steven's intelligence. "He will be profoundly retarded," the doctor replied, "uneducable for all but the simplest task. At some future time, you might consider putting him into an institution."

Shattered by the diagnosis, she couldn't eat or sleep for days. Late at night, Trudi and Jennifer could hear their mother's muffled sobbing and the gentle words of their father, trying to console her.

Jennifer, now eleven, was also struggling with her emotions. She was a top student and a natural athlete with a wide circle of friends. Although she loved Steven deeply, she couldn't cope with her friends' knowing she had a brother who was not perfect. So, around them, she avoided any mention of Steven.

Trudi was also a top student and an achiever. However, at fifteen she had the wisdom of someone older than her years. She was more able to accept Steven's handicap—and yet she wondered how disabled he really was. One day, trying to ease her mother's sadness, Trudi challenged the doctor's prognosis. "Mom," she announced, "I just don't believe what he said about Steven. Jen and I see a spark in his eyes. You can't give up on him. He won't have a chance if you do."

Trudi's words forced Geri to summon her fighting spirit. She called a family council around the kitchen table.

"I've thought about what Trudi said to me today," Geri began. "When the two of you were little, your father and I read to you a lot. We felt it would stimulate your minds and help teach you language. I think we should do the same for Steven."

"Yes!" Trudi agreed excitedly.

"We won't miss a night," Jennifer promised.

The four joined hands across the table and bowed their heads. "From this moment," Geri said, "we pledge to do everything in our power to help Steven."

The next evening, as Geri prepared dinner, Trudi unfolded a small futon on the white-tiled kitchen floor and propped her brother upright on cushions.

She cradled his head in her arms because he couldn't hold it up for long and, snuggling next to him, began to read from a children's book.

Another reading followed the next night—and the next, until it became a half-hour ritual every dinnertime. Along with reading, Jennifer and Trudi asked questions and pointed out animals or people illustrated in the books. But week after week Steven only kept staring blankly into space, seemingly lost in a dark, empty world. *He's not even looking at the pictures*, Geri thought. *Will we ever unlock what's in this child?*

Gradually, Geri felt despair winning again. One morning in the predawn stillness of their bedroom, she poured out her feelings to Lindy. "The girls are trying everything," she said, "but nothing registers with Steven. I don't even know whether the reading is helping or hurting."

"We may never be sure," Lindy conceded. "But in my heart, I know doing something is better then doing nothing."

"Time for reading, Steven," Trudi announced, nestling with her brother on the kitchen floor. After three months, he had still shown no response. He seldom even moved. That evening, however, he suddenly wriggled away from the cushions.

"Look at Steven!" Trudi called to her mother. In stunned surprise, they watched as he dragged himself across the floor. Inching to the children's books along the wall, he pawed at one.

"What's he doing?" Trudi asked.

Unable to turn the pages with his fingers, Steven whacked through the book with his hands. When he came to a page filled with pictures of animals, he gazed at it for a long time. Then, just as quickly as it opened, Steven's world shut down again.

The following night, the scene was repeated. As Jennifer prepared to read, her brother crawled to the same book and pawed it open to the same page. Speechless, the two sisters gave him a hug, laughing and crying at the same time.

"Steven's got a memory!" Geri marveled.

By now, Geri was on leave of absence from her job so she could devote more time to her son. As the months passed, Steven showed more and more response to the nightly reading. From her study of the subject, Geri learned that other parts of the brain can often compensate when one area is damaged. *Maybe that's happening with Steven,* she thought.

Both Trudi and Jennifer played the piano, and now they propped Steven under the grand piano while they played. One day after practicing, Jennifer lifted Steven from his place under the piano. This time, he was uttering a new sound. "He's humming the music he just heard!" Jennifer shouted to her parents. "Steven," she said, "you understand music, don't you?" The boy broke into a smile.

At the same time, the family also worked to build up his muscles. Lindy attended a massage school and learned how to knead his son's arms and legs. Geri, Trudi, and Jennifer dabbed peanut butter on the boy's lips. By licking it off, he exercised his tongue and jaw. They also gave him gum to chew and feathers to blow. Slowly, flaccid muscles in Steven's face began to strengthen.

When Steven was four and a half years old, he still couldn't speak words, but he could make "aaah" and "waaah" sounds. Also, with a walker, he could now stand and take slow, shuffling steps. Moreover, he displayed a surprising visual memory. After studying the picture on a three-hundred-piece jigsaw puzzle, he could assemble the pieces in one sitting.

Still, Steven was rejected by every preschool his mother applied to. Finally she took him to Louise Bogart, then director of the L. Robert Allen Montessori School at Honolulu's Chaminade University.

Bogart watched as Steven crawled on her office floor. He lifted his head, trying to speak to his mother. "Aaaah . . . aaaaah," he repeated again and again, gesturing insistently. Bogart saw the pain and frustration in his face. But she also saw something else: Steven was determined to make himself understood.

"Mrs. Kunishima," Bogart said, "we would be happy to have Steven in our school."

In the months that followed, the boy continued making slow progress. One morning, in his second year at Montessori, he was playing idly with blocks on a mat. Bogart stood off to the side, watching the teacher work with another child on numbers.

"What number comes next?" the teacher asked.

The child drew a blank.

"Twenty!" Steven blurted.

Bogart's head swiveled. Steven had not only spoken clearly, but also given the correct answer.

Bogart approached the teacher. "Did Steven ever work on this?" she asked.

"No," the teacher answered. "We worked with him a lot on numbers one through ten, but we didn't know he had learned any beyond ten."

When Geri picked Steven up after school, Bogart told her what had happened. "This is just the beginning of what he's capable of," Bogart said.

Jennifer felt a knot in her stomach as her father drove her to her first high-school basketball game one night in February 1990. Steven, now seven, sat silently in the back seat, watching the passing traffic.

Jennifer's love for her brother was as strong as ever, but she still tried to keep his disability a secret. And that was becoming more difficult. Two years before, Steven had learned to speak, and his speech revealed his problem. "Please Dad," Jennifer whispered before heading to the locker room, "try to keep Steven from yelling during the game."

When the game started, Steven became caught up in the excitement. "Come on Jennifer!" He shouted in his slow and halting speech. Jennifer cringed in embarrassment and refused to look at her brother. She knew she was letting him down; she was not being the strong third arrow.

At home, however, Jennifer lavished affection and attention on her brother. His motor skills remained poor, so Jennifer, Geri, and Trudi worked hard at making his written scrawl legible. "I can do it," Steven assured Jennifer one day. "Just give me time."

For Steven, the biggest challenge of all was simply getting around. One typical morning, Geri heard a thud from the kitchen. "He's fallen again," Geri said, rushing to her son's side.

By now, Steven had fallen so many times that his knees were crisscrossed with scars. Yet Steven never cried when he fell. He even developed a sense of humor about it. Once, wearing slippers when he tumbled, he turned to his parents, eyes dancing. "Now I know why they call these slippers," he said.

"I really need to go to this camp," Jennifer told her high-school principal one day in March 1991. "It's very important to me."

Camp Paumalu, located twenty-five miles north of Honolulu, was held twice a year for four days to help students meet challenges, develop leadership skills, and confront their fears and problems. Jennifer had begun to realize that a major obstacle was the torment she felt about mentioning Steven to her friends.

At camp one afternoon, as she walked on the grounds talking with a boy from her high school, Jennifer felt her problem boiling to the surface, and words poured forth. "I have a brother," she told the boy. "I was never mean to him, but in a sense I was. I never wanted to face the fact that he has a disability. I always wanted to pretend it would go away." When Jennifer finally finished, she sensed the burden lifting.

On the last day of camp, each student wrote the fear or problem to be overcome on a pine board. Then the camper ceremonially broke the board with a chop of the hand or foot, symbolically breaking through the obstacle. On her board, Jennifer printed out her problem in large letters. Then she slammed her hand downward, but not until her fifth try was there a resounding crack as the wood splintered in two.

The next day, arriving home, Jennifer threw both arms around her mother, "I'm free, Mom," she said. "I'm really free."

Jennifer's acceptance of Steven was now total. That fall, at her first basketball game of the season, she again heard Steven's loud voice cheering her on. Turning toward her brother, she waved to him eagerly, *Now*, her father thought, *the three arrows are truly bound together*.

For three years, beginning in 1990, Steven attended Holy Trinity School, a mainstream Catholic school. Learning still came hard, but Steven's speech and writing had improved to normal, and his physical movement was close to normal. By age eleven, he was working at grade level for his age. He could run and jump, and—like Jennifer—started playing basketball.

In 1992, Steven came to the attention of Lynne Waihee, wife of Hawaiian Governor John Waihee. Hawaii's first lady had chaired a "Read to Me" program that encouraged people to read to children. Impressed by how much reading had helped Steven, she arranged for the Governor's Council for Literacy to honor the Kunishimas.

In a reception at the governor's mansion, Geri introduced Steven, who told more than two hundred area leaders of his struggles over the years. He received a standing ovation.

In March 1993, the Hawaiian chapter of the American Red Cross presented Lynne Waihee its 1993 Humanitarian Award. She asked Steven to write a dedication for her awards banquet program. For hours, Steven pondered what to say. Finally, he summed up what reading meant to him, and in so doing he spelled out the triumph of the Kunishima family. "My family reads to me and now I can read to myself."

> This was an entire family effort. The mother, father, and all three arrows, including Steven, worked together. Each contributed in his or her own way—the father's advice; the mother's research, persistence, and sacrifice; the girls' reading, playing the piano, and showering attention (even though at times it was difficult to do). All demonstrated the remarkable and healing power that family unity can bestow.

Another strong bond is evidenced in national ties, occasions when people willingly give their all to protect their freedoms and come to the aid of fellow citizens.

A QUESTION OF HONOR
Allan Sherman

On May 26, 1940, as Hitler's armies overran France, British and French troops retreated by the tens of thousands into the little French port of

Dunkirk. From Dunkirk there was no place left to go but into the English Channel.

The mighty British navy had few ships small enough or agile enough to go in and evacuate the men. Thus the Free World could do nothing but sit by the radio in frustration and anguish, waiting for news that these vast armies of brave men had been wiped out.

Then, in the early hours of May 27, a miracle began to unfold. From everywhere in the British Isles they came—poor fishermen with creaky, beat-up fishing boats, noblemen with yachts, sportsmen with racing yawls and motor launches. The first of this motley fleet, captained by men with neither guns nor uniforms, set sail by moonlight from Sheerness, putt-putting across U-boat- and mine-infested water. As the morning sun lighted the beaches of Dunkirk, the first of the hundreds of small boats pulled onto the shore. The cheers of the trapped soldiers were drowned out by the roar of the Luftwaffe overhead, strafing and bombing the beach, and by the crackle of British Spitfires trying to fight them off.

Under that hell in the sky, the miracle of Dunkirk continued for nine days and nights. All together, 338,226 British and French lives were saved.

On June 18, Winston Churchill said, "Let us therefore brace ourselves to our duties and so bear ourselves that, if the British Empire and its Commonwealth last for a thousand years, men will still say, 'This was their finest hour.'"

I have a deep fondness and respect for the people of the British Isles that has come as I have both lived and worked among them. Though greatly diverse in their thinking and unafraid to speak their differences or disagree on opinions, when someone is in need they are also some of the first and the stoutest of nations in working together for the good of the common cause.

When people are unified in purpose, differences are not only respected, but they can be truly valued for their synergistic value.

DIFFERENT STROKES

Jeanne Marie Laskas

We're excited, the whole gang of us, talking about how much fun this will be. A painting party! We'll get a bunch of rollers, some drop cloths, cans of primer and a few cheerful pastels, and we'll all hang out and have those rooms painted in no time.

"It will be like an Amish barn raising!" Sue says. "A whole community coming together to create something awesome."

"Great!" I say, feeling as excited as anyone, being that it's my house we're talking about painting. Apparently, I made a mistake when I told the contractor who did the renovation not to bother with paint; you forget how tedious it can be to cover four rooms with multiple coats of latex.

"We'll all pitch in and do it together," Jack says. "It'll be a blast."

That's when Beth chimes in. She looks sullen. "Well, I don't paint," she announces.

Ohforgodssake. That's the look that goes around the room.

"Listen," she says. "There's a reason I pay a guy twenty bucks an hour to paint at my house. I don't paint."

"This isn't about painting," says Bill, her boyfriend. "This is about helping, this is about all of us accomplishing something together."

"Right," Beth says. "So how about I donate food or something instead?"

Fine. That's what everyone says. Fine. But Beth is unceremoniously disqualified from the Group Consciousness that forms as the week goes by and the painting party plans come together.

Seventeen people agree to show up, and one by one and two by two they arrive bearing gifts. Leslie has poles to help with the ceilings, Nancy and Jack have rollers and pans, Vince and Chris have assorted contraptions to make corners and edges easier, Sue and Heidi have plastic sheeting to cover furniture. We divide into teams. A group upstairs in the bathroom, another in the office, two people in the stairwell, and a rowdy group in the nursery.

Beth stays in the kitchen. "I don't paint," she says to those who haven't already heard. And you can feel the resentment rise like paint fumes swirling around the house.

Team Spirit inevitably splinters Group Consciousness as we work in our separate rooms. Yellow (bathroom) vs. Blue (nursery) vs. Eggshell A (office) and Eggshell B (stairwell). Soon Blue is hollering out to Yellow about having the most perfect ceiling, while Egg A challenges Egg B to a baseboard race.

"We are taking a break!" Yellow (my team) announces, because we are determined not to care about competition. (And also because we hate to lose). Besides, our backs hurt.

We go into the kitchen to find Beth standing over a buffet of sandwiches with little pickles arranged just so and a mix of fresh veggies and dip. Hmmm, good timing. Because come to think of it, Hunger is here. We grab all the good sandwiches before Blue and the Eggs discover that lunch awaits them. We stand there chewing and discussing masking-tape techniques, and then resume work.

On our next break, we head into the kitchen to find Beth standing over the sink, washing lettuce. Come to think of it, it's nice having her always right here where we left her. She points to a buffet of cookies, brownies, and some kind of amazing coconut squares, only two of which are left, thanks to the Blue team, which cut in line and who we think is made up of a bunch of buffaloes anyway.

I watch Beth standing at that sink and I think of my mother, my friend's mother, everybody's mother. The mother is the one who is always just there, right where you left her.

By nine o'clock Team Spirit descends into Get This Darned Thing Done. All of us are now in the nursery, which is taking forever, what with the way the woodwork keeps drinking primer, and a few people are getting a little testy, asking whose dumb idea was this anyway?

"Come on, guys," Beth says as she walks in. "Someone is going to get hurt." We look at her. We scorned her for not being a part of us, and now we love her for the same reason. And we love her for what she says next: "Come on down and have some dinner, and you can clean up afterward."

We return to the kitchen to find two types of lasagna, crusty bread, and a salad with Gorgonzola cheese and toasted pecans. We fill our plates and sink like exhausted construction workers into chairs or down onto the kitchen floor, dinners balanced on our laps.

"We are so glad you don't paint," Vince says to Beth, who seems, like any mom, to have been expecting at least a small amount of thanks.

I like Beth's attitude. Yet in the beginning it was her attitude that appeared to come into immediate conflict with the group. "What do you mean you don't paint? None of us paint!" they fumed. But as the day wore on, stroke by stroke the group learned a lesson about synergy and particularly the valuing of differences. And they certainly gained a greater appreciation for Beth's attitude. For most people who "don't paint" simply would have stayed home and avoided the rude glares. But Beth showed up with what she had to offer, and the end result was a greater experience for the group than they would have enjoyed in her absence. A complementary team, family, or work unit is one where strengths are made productive and weaknesses are made irrelevant— a point that is becoming more and more relevant as the world becomes increasingly interdependent.

WRAP UP

Again, unity does not mean sameness. In fact, unity is strengthened by diversity—as long as there is unity of purpose. People with Everyday Greatness know how to be team players. They know how to work together in groups, not just being compatible with others, but truly synergistic. They are not worried about setting aside their own interests for the good of the whole. This, of course, does not mean that they abandon who they are just to blend in with the group, but that they magnify their strengths toward causes that are win-win. They not only find joy in other's successes, but also strive to make those successes a reality. They know that they are stronger when "all arrows" stick together, and search out others' strengths to paint a better life for everyone involved.

Reflections

- The Kunishima family united their time, love, and talents on behalf of Steven. What purposes are your family or work team or other groups united around? Is everyone clear regarding what those purposes are?

- Steven's sister struggled in public with her commitment to him. How committed are you to team efforts?

- Think of those you love the most. Do you more often dwell on their weaknesses, or celebrate and optimize their strengths?

- Beth's strength was cooking. As you think of someone you interact with frequently, what strengths do you see in that person that are different from your own? What strengths do you have that other team members do not possess? In what ways can your differing strengths be combined in synergistic ways?

FURTHER INSIGHTS ON
Unity

WORKING TOGETHER

Finding unity among diversity is one of civilization's greatest challenges, yet working together is essential to the well-being of the whole.

Coming together is a beginning; keeping together is progress; working together is success.

—HENRY FORD

■ ■ ■

There are parts of a ship which, taken by themselves, would sink. The engine would sink. The propeller would sink. But when the parts of a ship are built together, they float.

—RALPH W. SOCKMAN
IN *THE TREASURE CHEST*
EDITED BY CHARLES L. WALLIS

■ ■ ■

I know that I would be a liar or a fool if I said that I have the best of the three Apollo 11 seats, but I can say with truth and equanimity that I am perfectly satisfied with the one I have. This venture has been structured for three men, and I consider my third to be as necessary as either of the other two.

—ASTRONAUT MICHAEL COLLINS
(APOLLO 11, FIRST EXPEDITION TO MOON, HE WAS PILOT
WHILE ARMSTRONG AND ALDRIN LANDED ON MOON),
CARRYING THE FIRE: AN ASTRONAUT'S JOURNEY

BUILDING A TEAM

Our chances for Everyday Greatness increase when we surround ourselves with a team and network of other strong individuals.

One day a small boy tried to lift a heavy stone, but couldn't budge it. His father, watching, finally said, "Are you sure you're using all your strength?"

"Yes, I am!" the boy cried.

"No, you're not," said the father. "You haven't asked me to help you."

— *BITS & PIECES*

■ ■ ■

Don't be afraid of those who might have a better idea or who might even be smarter than you are.

David Ogilvy, founder of the advertising firm Ogilvy & Mather, made this point clear to his newly appointed office heads by sending each a Russian nesting doll with five progressively smaller figures inside.

His message was contained in the smallest doll: "If each of us hires people who are smaller than we are, we shall become a company of dwarfs. But if each of us hires people who are bigger than we are, Ogilvy & Mather will become a company of giants."

—DENIS WAITLEY,
PRIORITIES

■ ■ ■

First-rate men hire first-rate men; second-rate men hire third-rate men.

—LEO ROSTEN

MIXING TALENT

Diversity of talent and thought adds flavor to life and opens the way for teamwork and synergy.

You don't get harmony when everybody sings the same note.

—DOUG FLOYD

■ ■ ■

The goal in marriage is not to think alike, but to think together.

—ROBERT C. DODDS

■ ■ ■

Husbands and wives complete themselves through each other, and the whole of the union becomes stronger and more wonderful than the sum of the two parts.

—WILLIAM J. BENNETT

■ ■ ■

Many ideas grow better when transplanted into another mind than in the one where they sprang up.

—OLIVER WENDELL HOLMES

■ ■ ■

An idea can turn to dust or magic, depending on the talent that rubs against it.

—WILLIAM BERNBACK

■ ■ ■

Where opinions, morals and politics are concerned, there is no such thing as objectivity. The best we can hope for is that freedom will enable subjective points of view to meet and complement each other.

—JEAN D'ORMESSON

WIN-WIN

Most of life is interdependent in nature. Thus, when we hold another down, we hold ourselves down. But when we lift another, we also lift ourselves.

Help thy brother's boat across and lo! thine own has reached the shore.

—HINDU PROVERB

■ ■ ■

One man cannot hold another man down in the ditch without remaining down in the ditch with him.

—BOOKER T. WASHINGTON

■ ■ ■

There is no happiness for people at the expense of other people.

—ANWAR EL-SADAT

■ ■ ■

Cooperation is the thorough conviction that nobody can get there unless everybody gets there.

—VIRGINIA BURDEN,
THE PROCESS OF INTUITION

■ ■ ■

As long as you keep a person down, some part of you has to be down there to hold him down, so it means you cannot soar as you otherwise might.

—MARIAN ANDERSON

■ ■ ■

There are victories of the soul and spirit. Sometimes, even if you lose, you win.

—ELIE WIESEL

■ ■ ■

Consider the following Olympic-sized portions of win-win thinking . . .

BERLIN—Jesse Owens seemed sure to win the long jump at the 1936 games. The year before he had jumped 26 feet, 8¼ inches—a record that would stand for 25 years. As he walked to the long-jump pit, however, Owens saw a tall, blue-eyed, blond German taking practice jumps in the 26-foot range. Owens felt nervous. He was acutely aware of the Nazis' desire to prove "Aryan superiority," especially over blacks.

On his first jump Owens inadvertently leaped from several inches beyond the takeoff board. Rattled, he fouled on his second attempt too. He was one foul away from being eliminated.

At this point, the tall German introduced himself as Luz Long. "You should be able to qualify with your eyes closed!" he said to Owens, referring to his two jumps.

For the next few moments the black son of a sharecropper and the white model of Nazi manhood chatted. Then Long made a suggestion. Since the qualifying distance was only 23 feet, 5½ inches, why not make a mark several inches before the takeoff board and jump from there, just to play it safe? Owens did and qualified easily.

In the finals Owens set an Olympic record and earned the second of four golds. The first person to congratulate him was Luz Long—in full view of Adolf Hitler.

Owens never again saw Long, who was killed in World War II. "You could melt down all the medals and cups I have," Owens later wrote, "and they wouldn't be a plating on the 24-carat friendship I felt for Luz Long."

—DAVID WALLECHINSKY,
THE COMPLETE BOOK OF THE OLYMPICS

■ ■ ■

INNSBRUCK—In 1964, Italy's Eugenio Monti and Sergio Siorpaes were heavily favored in the two-man bobsled event. But as they awaited their second run, the lightly regarded British team of Tony Nash and Robin Dixon was in a state of despair. After a sensational first run, their sled had broken an axle bolt, and it seemed certain they would have to drop out.

Monti, his second run already completed, acted swiftly. He stripped the bolt from his own sled and offered it to Nash. In one of the greatest upsets in the history of the Olympics, the British team went on to win the gold medal, while the sportsmanlike Monti finished third.

Four years later, Monti drove both his two- and four-man sleds to Olympic victory.

—BUD GREENSPAN,
PARADE

OVERCOMING ADVERSITY

If you are kicking up a storm, don't expect clear sailing.
—P. P. SULLIVAN

Whether working independently or teaming with others, we can expect opposition. So how we choose to respond to adversity can make or break our ability to accomplish the purposes we choose to pursue. Fortunately, much of the opposition we face in life ultimately works in our favor. It challenges us. It teaches us. It causes us to reach a little higher and dig a little deeper.

Principles that aid in overcoming life's obstacles include

- Adaptability

- Magnanimity

- Perseverance

16

ADABTABILITY

As soon as there is life there is danger.
—RALPH WALDO EMERSON

Though some individuals allow adversity to bend or break their spirits, others quickly adapt to their surroundings and surmount the opposition. The ability to adapt and make the best of difficult situations is a sure test of Everyday Greatness.

Over the years, *Reader's Digest* has published hundreds of touching and dramatic stories of individuals who have overcome all types of opposition imaginable—from physical attacks, to losses of loved ones, to economic despair, to natural disasters, and more. Think back, for example, on earlier stories in this collection—including John Baker, Betty Ford, Walt Disney, Maya Angelou, and Luba Gercak. Every one is a tale of overcoming adversity. While each trial is as unique as the individual who faced it, there are some common threads in how successful people adapt and conquer, several of which are demonstrated in "Message of the Maples" and the other two stories of adaptability that follow.

MESSAGE OF THE MAPLES

Edward Ziegler

I know him to be a wise man, living in seclusion with his wife, but willing, he said, to receive me if I were ever in his part of New England.

I had heard him speak years before and recently had read several of his books. Now I was seeking him out, because I had hopes his wisdom might relieve the gnawing melancholy that darkened my days. Financial losses and an old disability had combined to take much of the savor from life.

On a clear, late-winter day, I found him on his farm near Corinth, Vermont, surrounded by fields and woodlands shrouded in snow. After years of writing and lecturing and helping others, as a minister and "physician to the soul," Edgar N. Jackson was now applying his own wisdom to himself. He had been struck down by a severe stroke. It left him paralyzed on his right side and unable to speak.

The early prognosis had been grave. They told Estelle, his wife of fifty-three years, that recovery of speech was unlikely. Yet within a few weeks he had regained his ability to talk and he was determined to recover still more of his faculties.

He rose to greet me. He was a distinguished-looking man of middle height, moving slowly, aided by a cane, with an unmistakable sparkle in his gaze. He led me into his study. It was lined with books, new and old, all surrounding a desk on which sat a word processor and reams of papers and magazines.

He said he was glad to hear that his books had helped me. They had, indeed, I said, but still, a series of setbacks had added up to a sorrow I wasn't sure I could master.

"Then, in a sense, you're grief-stricken," he said.

But I hadn't lost anyone close to me, I protested.

"Nevertheless, what you're going through is related to grief. What's essential is to mourn your losses fully and find solace by learning to live with them." People who don't, he added, wind up bitter and disillusioned by sorrow. They're unable to find solace. But others who creatively use the act of mourning can gain new sensitivity and a richer faith. "That's why you so often hear that we have to talk out our feelings, express our emotions. That is part of the mourning process. Only then can healing follow.

"Let me show you something," he offered, pointing through the window to a stand of bare sugar maples, stolidly facing the sharp winds that plucked at their barren branches and sent a dusting of yesterday's snowfall shimmering downward. A former owner had planted the maples around the perimeter of a three-acre pasture.

We walked out a side door and moved slowly on the crunching snow to the pasture. It was a rocky expanse rife with grass and wild flowers in summer, but now brown and wizened by frost-kill. Strung between each large tree, I noticed, were strands of old barbed wire.

"Sixty years ago the man who planted these trees used them to fence in this pasture, and saved a lot of work digging post holes. It was a trauma for the young trees to have barbed wire hammered into their tender bark. Some fought it. Others adapted. So you can see here, the barbed wire has been accepted and incorporated into the life of this tree—but not of that one over there."

He pointed to an old tree severely disfigured by the wire. "Why did that tree injure itself by fighting against the barbed wire, while this one here became master of the wire instead of its victim?"

The nearby tree showed no marks at all. Instead of the long, anguished scars, all that appeared was the wire entering one side and emerging on the other—almost as if it had been inserted by a drill bit.

"I've thought a lot about this grove of trees," he said as we turned to go back to the house. "What internal forces make it possible to overcome an injury like barbed wire, rather than allowing it to distort the rest of life? How can one person transform grief into new growth instead of allowing it to become a life-destroying intrusion?"

Edgar could not explain what happened to the maples, he admitted. "But with people," he continued, "things are much clearer. There are ways to confront adversity and work your way through that mourning period. First, you try to keep a youthful outlook. Then you don't bear grudges. And perhaps most important, you make every effort to be kind to yourself. That is the tough one. You have to spend a lot of time with yourself, and most of us tend to be far too critical. Sign a peace treaty with yourself, I say. Forgive yourself for the dumb mistakes you've made."

After another pensive glance at the maple grove, he led the way back into the house. "If we are wise in the way we handle grief, if we can mourn promptly and fully, the barbed wire doesn't win. We can overcome any sorrow, and life can be lived triumphantly."

Estelle appeared with a piece of applesauce cake and a cup of coffee. "I try to keep a growing edge on my life, seeking new knowledge, new friendships, new experience," Edgar continued, glancing over to the new computer and a half-dozen new books on his desk. He had been waging his own battle. He was still frustrated by his partially paralyzed right side, but he wasn't conceding defeat.

"We can use our painful experiences as excuses for retreat. Or we can accept the promises of resurrection and rebirth." His gaze turned toward the snow-mantled pasture across the road. "You have your problems. I have my own struggles. I'll work on mine," he offered, "if you work on yours."

"Thanks, I will," I promised, and we shook hands. We had a deal. I felt I had won some new understanding—and now had a strategy for handling my sorrows.

As I drove down the valley, I could glimpse his farm across the meadows. The wind toyed with the lofty tops of those living fence posts, which, though still mysterious, had so much to say to all of us.

Many of life's adversities are short-term and quickly come to a halt as we find a new job, or mend an argument, or recover from a cold. But other forms of adversity are long-term: the loss of a loved one, a permanent physical ailment, a disheartening family relationship, or a tragic accident are not temporary and are not so easily removed from beneath your bark. In such cases, Edgar Jackson's maples provide hope and guidance. They teach us the power of confronting adversity, adapting, and moving on.

Sometimes adapting means "you've got to do what you've got to do." The following young man knows how to do that well.

THE CONTENDER

Derek Burnett

Kyle Maynard was trying hard not to lose it with the Six Flags guy. Over the years, he'd developed a repertoire of persuasive tactics, from turning on the charm to performing feats of strength, like whipping off a couple dozen push-ups. But the ride operator wouldn't budge. There was no way he was letting Kyle on the roller coaster, because when he looked at Kyle, he didn't see a star athlete or a well-adjusted, competent kid. He saw a lawsuit and, in the list of defendants, just beneath the name of the amusement park, he saw his own name in twelve-point type. Not a chance, pal.

Thus embarrassed in front of his friends, Kyle gave up on charm and humor. Before an audience of two hundred onlookers, he offered up this challenge: "You go and find the biggest guy who works here, and if he can stop me from getting on this ride, I won't ride it."

To a complete stranger, the challenge might have been laughable. A complete stranger might have even seen things the Six Flags guy's way.

After all, Kyle Maynard, standing next to his wheelchair, is a mere three feet tall. His arms end in stumps at the elbows; his legs are further stunted. Would someone built like that be able to stay in the chair's shoulder harness?

If you're Kyle Maynard or one of his friends, nothing could be more ridiculous than the notion that he couldn't ride a roller coaster. You'd hope for the sake of Six Flags's biggest employee that the challenge wasn't taken up. Because once you've stepped into Kyle Maynard's universe, you learn that disabled doesn't mean not able.

When Anita Maynard was pregnant with her first child, the doctors told her and her husband, Scott, that they couldn't find the baby's legs on the ultrasound. Upon second inspection, however, they reassured the Maynards that the child was indeed possessed of lower limbs. Then Kyle was born.

What the doctors had mistaken for legs turned out to be a pair of misshapen feet protruding just beneath the baby's hips. He had no hands.

His arms were only half there. In sum, Anita recalled, "he was gorgeous. His face was just glowing. Blond hair, blue eyes, peachy skin."

The young couple didn't know what to expect. They'd never seen anyone built like Kyle, so they decided to take things a day at a time. And very quickly, they forgot to think of Kyle as handicapped. "He did everything like any baby would," said Scott. "Crawled. Played with toys. Cried. Laughed."

Reassured that Kyle's condition was not genetic—and highly unlikely to appear in their future offspring—Scott and Anita went on to have three more children, all daughters. And if Kyle didn't seem handicapped to his parents, he was even less a novelty to his sisters. He played with them like any other big brother, joining them for hide-and-seek or water fights with the neighborhood kids.

Before he started school, he was outfitted with prosthetics. Normally agile, Kyle was now restricted by the false limbs. The legs prevented his rising from a seated position on the floor. The arms involved latex sockets up to his armpits and harnesses crossing his back. He was never comfortable. At story time in kindergarten, Kyle and his classmates would sit on the rug, and when it was time to return to their seats, he would stay behind until an adult could help him up.

"Mom," Kyle said with a sigh one day, "I don't want to wear these things anymore. I want to be able to get down and play with the kids."

That was the last time he wore prosthetics. "We're just going to get rid of them," Anita announced. "And he can jump down and do a cartwheel and a flip and sit down for story time, and then run over to his chair."

Kyle thrived without the limbs. When his classmates learned to color in the lines, so did he, grasping the crayon between the ends of his arms.

When they learned handwriting, he developed perfect penmanship right alongside them. For long distances, and to stay up out of the grime, Kyle got an electric wheelchair—but he put it aside when he was at home, or any other place where it was practical to use the body God gave him.

Kyle learned to feed himself by grasping a spoon between the ends of his arms (one atop the other), scooping up the cereal or what have you, then swiveling the whole affair around and placing the food neatly into his mouth. There is nothing to it; the maneuver requires about as much concentration as it would take for you to do the same thing. Yet Kyle has performed the operation for television cameras. Imagine a world in which people come to your home to film you eating with a spoon. Now you're getting an idea of life in Kyle Maynard's universe.

Early on, the entire Maynard family learned to use humor to deal with strangers and their reactions. More than once, Scott and Anita have given the kids their speech about how people should be forgiven for their natural curiosity, and yet they have their limits. "We give people maybe five minutes to stare," Anita grinned. "Then they get a tiger-attack story."

Once, at the beach, Kyle and some buddies took their humor perhaps a bit too far. They slathered his limbs with tomato sauce, then rushed him out of the water screaming about a shark. People were not amused.

Kyle took up football at age eleven. Scott thought it a great idea, but Anita took some convincing. The men of the household prevailed, and the middle school squad had a new, and very small, tackle.

Watching video of Kyle's games, you wonder how Anita could have stood it, seeing her son slogging around in the mud next to all those swinging knees. You're struck by how fearless and relentless the kid is. He's never owned a pair of shoes in his life because of the shape of his feet; on the football field he wore socks with elbow pads over them—feeble protection against the rain of stamping cleats.

This was when Kyle first began getting attention from people calling him inspirational and brave. It was surreal to Kyle and his family. He wasn't trying to inspire people or make a name for himself; he just wanted to play football. Nevertheless, he took it all graciously. Handsome and precocious, he fielded questions from the media. He did the spoon trick for them.

Kyle began strength training, powering up his arms and torso impressively. He decided that the sport for him was wrestling. Now it was Scott, himself a former high school wrestler, who took convincing. This was different from being on a football team where if you lose it's no one's fault in particular. If Kyle lost a wrestling match, it would be because his opponent had outperformed him. Could he handle that?

The answer turned out to be yes. For two seasons, Kyle lost every match.

Wrestling tournaments tend to be long, all-day affairs, and sometimes Kyle would get up at 5:00 a.m. for a match, lose, then have to sit around idly waiting to wrestle again in the late afternoon, then lose again. It was demoralizing. Yet he refused to quit.

Fortunately, Kyle's coach, Cliff Ramos, had taken an open-minded and creative approach to working with Kyle. "At first, I didn't know what to make of Kyle," Ramos admitted. "His body was so different. But then we began trying to use his shape as an advantage, and we invented some locks and holds using his chin and arms."

And Kyle began winning. With his massively strong torso and his smart strategies, he became a respected contender in his 103-pound weight class.

Opponents who felt squeamish or sorry for him soon found themselves mercilessly bested. Some parents and coaches even complained that since most 103-pounders were stringy-limbed kids, Kyle had an unfair advantage over them.

Which seems ridiculous, until you consider that Kyle once earned a Strongest Teen title by performing twenty-three butterfly repetitions with 240 pounds chained to padded cuffs on his arms. Once he did a single rep with 420 pounds. He's gradually working up to 500 pounds. But, he said, "I need to get some thicker chains."

On a summer afternoon, Kyle drove to wrestling practice in his mother's minivan, outfitted with extensions allowing him to manipulate the pedals with his arms. At school, Kyle discovered he'd forgotten his key to the elevator that gives him wheelchair access to the second-floor wrestling room. "Oh, well," he said, zipping over to the stairs and jumping from the wheelchair, ditching it in the hallway. He scrambled up the filthy stairwell, which looked like it had been recently visited by the cross-country team just in from practice.

Later, back home, he mentioned this to Anita, a confessed germ freak, who visibly flinched. "Why didn't you get a janitor to bring you the elevator key?" she asked. "I didn't want to wait," Kyle replied. "Besides, sometimes you've got to do what you've got to do."

That particular cliché is one that rolls easily off Kyle's tongue. He'll also drop this one on you: "I know what I can do, and I'm going to do it."

His earnestness is what inspires people, because it so clearly comes from a rock-solid self-image completely devoid of self-pity.

The spotlight found Kyle again toward the end of his high school career when he became a standout on the varsity wrestling team. With football, it had been a gesture of kindness that he was allowed to play with the "able-bodied" kids. But with wrestling, he was dominating them.

At one tournament, a middle-aged guy approached Scott. He'd seen Kyle on TV and wanted to meet him, since, he said, Kyle had saved his life.

Overweight, diabetic, unhealthy and depressed, the man had been overwhelmed by Kyle's positive attitude and had completely turned his life around. "Your son is a human antidepressant," he told Scott.

As his final season waned, Kyle hung in there with some of the top wrestlers in the Southeast. He placed second at regionals. For the month leading up to the state tournament, he stayed for two or more hours after practice each night, working long after his teammates had gone home. His goal every evening, he said, "was to not be able to make it to my wheelchair because of fatigue." At state, he suffered two heartbreaking losses. But, because of his record, he was granted a waiver allowing him to wrestle in the national Senior Wrestling Championship, where he finished in the top twelve.

Kyle confessed genuine bewilderment at the attention bestowed on him for being, as he put it, "an average high school athlete." As he explained two months after graduation, standing as keynote speaker at a forum for the disabled, there are no excuses. "Anyone," he told the crowd, "can overcome their boundaries and achieve their dreams."

In August 2004, Kyle began studies at the University of Georgia. (He finished high school with a 3.6 average, and types fifty words per minute, using the subtle variations on the ends of his arms.) Because the university has no league team, he joined club wrestling. He wants to continue public speaking, study sports psychology, maybe even become a coach or run a fitness center.

A judge once sentenced a troubled kid to spend a day with Kyle to learn something about adversity. A child of divorce, the kid was expelled from school for fighting, and was on the wrong track. Yet it was Kyle who learned about hardship.

"People think I have a bad life,"

Kyle explained. "Look at my life compared to this kid's. I have a beautiful family who loves me. Everybody has struggles. My struggles are just more apparent."

And, once you get it, that's the part that makes you a member of Kyle Maynard's universe. The magic of Kyle Maynard is that he can make you believe that were you in his skin, you would do exactly what he's done.

You begin to see that Kyle's specialness isn't diminished because he turned out to be a normal guy; he's special exactly because he's just a normal guy. And when he convinces you of that, you begin to see yourself and the people around you as potentially irrepressible, unstoppable forces of nature. We all just need to be reminded every once in a while.

Everyone has challenges; no one is exempt. But what Kyle teaches us is that it does no good to sit around complaining. Instead, he acknowledged his "boundaries," accepted them, and looked for ways to overcome them. Then he went out and did what he "had to do."

———————

When life comes at us hard, sometimes a portion of properly placed humor can help us to adapt.

THE LAUGHTER CURE

Robert Schimmel

I remember the first time I walked into the Mayo Clinic in Scottsdale, Arizona, after being told I had cancer. It reminded me of that poster "The Evolution of Man." Except what I was looking at was a row of balding, skinny, chalky-skinned chemotherapy patients with IV tubes in their arms. *So much for evolution,* I joked to myself. That was the beginning of my road to recovery.

I've been fascinated by the power of laughter since I was a boy. My parents, who were Holocaust survivors, had terrific senses of humor and introduced me to some of the greatest comedians of our time. I grew up watching Jackie Gleason, Ernie Kovacs, Sid Caesar, Jonathan Winters, the Three Stooges, and the Marx Brothers. As a kid, I learned that if you could make people laugh, everyone liked you. And the feeling I got from making people laugh was addictive. I had no way of knowing then that the power of laughter would save my life.

In March 1999, I performed at the U.S. Comedy Arts Festival in Aspen, Colorado, a gathering of a lot of top comics and the Hollywood executives who (might) hire them. For some reason, I was lucky. I was the talk of the festival. A few days later I was offered my own HBO special. Next came a contract for my third comedy CD. Networks were soon offering me my own sitcom, and Fox chose my show, *Schimmel,* for its fall 2000 lineup.

On June 2, 2000, I arrived in Las Vegas for my first appearance at the Monte Carlo Resort & Casino. At the airport, I saw a huge sign with my picture on it. Outside the hotel, there was another sign, "Robert Schimmel: June 2 & 3." I was on my way to stardom, headed there on a rocket.

Two days later, I felt run-down and feverish, so I went to my doctor. I thought I had the flu. He found a small lump under my left arm and asked how long it had been there. I didn't know. I hadn't noticed it. He ordered a CT scan and a biopsy.

When I woke up in the recovery room, there was a large bandage over my right armpit. My doctor came in and said he'd found a larger lump, about the size of an apricot, under my right arm. The next thing I remember is being in the doctor's office with my mom, dad, and wife. The doctor walked in with my films. He told me the lump was malignant. Cancer. Non-Hodgkin's lymphoma. Just my luck, I said. I got the one not named after the guy.

The hardest thing was telling my kids. This wasn't our first experience with cancer. In 1992, I lost my son Derek to brain cancer. He was eleven. Now my other kids were going to watch me go through the same treatment he went through. I knew I had to do whatever I could to stay positive—to try to eliminate their fear of losing me too.

Since my cancer had metastasized, radiation therapy wasn't an option. I would get chemotherapy instead. I had six months if the chemo didn't work. If it did, I had a 49 percent chance of going two years without a recurrence. One more thing: there was a risk I'd become sterile, and be unable to have kids again.

"If I die," I said to my wife, "I'm sorry for all the bad things I ever did to you." She replied, "What if you don't die? Then are you still sorry?"

My first day at the Mayo Clinic, I found a seat next to this guy Bill, who was also getting chemo. He was in his fifties. He was thin and his hair was falling out. I asked him how he was doing. "How does it look like I'm doing?" he said. "I've got cancer."

I tried to start a conversation. "My name's Robert. I've got cancer too!"

"Well, this must be your first treatment, Robert. Let's talk after you've had two or three more. Then we'll see how 'up' you are."

My nurse suggested that I should change seats. She said Bill had a negative attitude and people like him dragged everybody down with them.

One of my doctors later told me there are two kinds of people when it comes to cancer: transmitters and transformers. Transmitters take the negative experience and transmit the negativity to everyone around them. Transformers turn the negativity into something positive. Though I didn't know these terms when I met Bill, I decided right then to be a transformer.

I asked Bill if he'd been to any support groups. He said no; he didn't like listening to a bunch of sob stories. I said I'd gone to one the night before, to prepare for what I was facing. A woman there was upset because she thought her husband wouldn't find her sexy once she started losing her hair.

I told Bill that I looked at her and thought, *Sexy? Lady, if you think you're sexy-looking now, maybe you need to get your eyes examined too.*

He began to laugh. The nurses asked me what I'd said; they'd never seen him smile. And when I arrived for my next chemo session, Bill was there, saving me a seat. We told each other jokes all day while we got our treatment.

I started bringing comedy CDs with me to the clinic and listening to them while getting chemo. Before I knew it, my session would be over. I loaned my CDs to other patients. Pretty soon, they were laughing too.

When I was in the hospital, I promised myself that if I got out of there, I'd never forget the ones still fighting the disease. I also made a promise to my doctor: I'd use comedy to raise cancer awareness—and I wouldn't stop making people laugh until he was unemployed.

When you're diagnosed with cancer, you start to bargain with God: "Let me get through this, and I'll take better care of myself. I'll get my priorities in order. I'll learn to live every day to the fullest." Once, while I was getting chemo, I thought, *Isn't it sad that you have to get sick before giving yourself permission to live life to the fullest?*

On June 5, 2000, I believed I'd never see the light at the end of the tunnel. In a weird way, though, it's like the cancer was the first glimmer of light. For me, getting sick was a gift. Before it happened, I spent my life in the dark, like a horse wearing blinders. When I was diagnosed, the blinders came off. Now I'm basking in the light.

One more thing: On June 5, 2003, my son Sam was born—three years to the day I was told I had cancer.

Robert Schimmel was determined to be a transformer. A transformer is the same thing as a transition person, which I referred to in the Introduction—one who takes the negative events of life and turns them into something positive. Robert chose to do it the way he knew best—through laughter. Laughter not only has healing effects, it is also contagious. And though it will not solve all problems, it will lighten the load and smooth the path.

~~

WRAP UP

Adversity always insists that we respond to a series of questions: Will we adapt, do what we've got to do, and move forward, or will we allow the opposition to win out? Will we be transmitters or transformers? Will we find opportunity and silver amongst the clouds, or will we find storms in every sunset? When I think of possible answers to these questions, I am reminded of my sister who, during the last months of her life and her battle with cancer, grasped the opportunity to use her illness as a training ground to teach her children how to cope and how to smile in the face of opposition. She used her cancer to teach them how to act upon life right to the end. In death, she left a legacy of Everyday Greatness that will always be embedded not only in the minds and hearts of her children, but in all of us who were fortunate to know her. Opposition is the stage upon which so many acts of Everyday Greatness are performed.

REFLECTIONS

- Do you know someone who is a model of dealing with adversity? What characteristics does he or she exhibit when faced with opposition?

- Faced with opposition, is your tendency to adapt and, like Kyle, do what you've got to do to move forward, or do you let opposition stifle and deter you? What examples from your past best represent your ability to overcome adversity?

- When faced with adversity, are you more of a transmitter or a transformer?

- Robert Schimmel used humor not only to help him adapt, but to help others through their difficulties as well. Have you shared any good jokes lately?

FURTHER INSIGHTS ON
Adaptability

~

RISING ABOVE

When encountering opposition, successful people find ways
to rise above and make the best of circumstances.

Although the world is full of suffering, it is also full of the overcoming of it.

—HELEN KELLER

■ ■ ■

Adversity causes some men to break, others to break records.

—WILLIAM ARTHUR WARD,
IN *QUOTE*

■ ■ ■

Most people think the Holocaust camps were like snake pits—that people
stepped on each other for survival. It wasn't like that at all. There was
kindness, support, understanding.

A childhood friend of mine, Ilse, once found a raspberry in the camp and
carried it in her pocket all day to present to me that night on a leaf. Those
are the moments I want to remember. People behaved nobly under
unspeakable circumstances.

—GERDA WEISSMANN KLEIN,
IN *THE CHRISTIAN SCIENCE MONITOR*

■ ■ ■

In many instances we can't control what happens to us, but we can control
our reactions to what happens to us. We can stay down for the count and be
carried out of the ring, or we can pull ourselves back to our feet.

—ANN LANDERS,
THE ANN LANDERS ENCYCLOPEDIA A TO Z

Silver Linings

Adversity often brings out the true spirit and character within people and leads them to make the noblest of choices.

Adversity is the trial of principle. Without it, a man hardly knows whether he is honest or not.

—Henry Fielding

■ ■ ■

At 83 Thomas Edison was still as intensely active as ever, and when it was proposed to relieve him of deafness, he declined, saying that his infirmity helped him to think, and, "I want to do a lot more thinking before I die."

—Gamaliel Bradform,
Nations Business

■ ■ ■

Golf without bunkers and hazards would be tame and monotonous. So would life.

—B. C. Forbes
in Forbes Epigrams

■ ■ ■

Everybody at some point is going to have adversity. I think if we don't learn from that, then it was just a penalty. But if you use it, then it becomes tuition.

—Dr. Phil McGraw

■ ■ ■

The gem cannot be polished without friction.

—Chinese proverb

■ ■ ■

One early spring day I met an old farmer. It had been a rainy spring, and I commented about how good it must be for the crops to have so much rain early in the season. He replied, "No, if the weather is too easy on the crops now, the plants may only grow roots on the surface. If that happens, then a storm could easily destroy the crops. However, if things are not so easy in the beginning, then the plants will have to grow the strong and deep roots they need to get at the water and nourishment down below. If a storm or drought comes, they are more likely to survive." Now I look at rough times as an opportunity to put down some roots to help me weather future storms that may come my way.

—JERRY STEMKOSKI

■ ■ ■

May there be enough clouds in your life to make a beautiful sunset.

—REBECCA GREGORY

■ ■ ■

Birds sing after a storm. Why shouldn't we?

—ROSE KENNEDY

■ ■ ■

Wherever we look upon this earth, the opportunities take shape within the problems.

—NELSON A. ROCKEFELLER

PROBLEM SOLVING

*When problems arise, we do well if we act quickly to drain
their momentum and move forward ourselves.*

I never varied from the managerial rule that the worst possible thing we could
do would be to lie dead in the water with any problem. Doing nothing is a
comfortable alternative because it is without immediate risk, but it is an
absolutely fatal way to manage a business.

—THOMAS J. WATSON, JR.,
IN *FORTUNE*

■ ■ ■

There is a time in the life of every problem when it is big enough to see, yet
small enough to solve.

—MIKE LEAVITT

■ ■ ■

One day in Grand Central Station, I watched the man behind the
information desk. People crowded around him, clamoring, demanding, but
he never became flustered. He would pick out one person, look directly at
him and answer his question slowly and deliberately. He never shifted his
eyes, never paid the slightest attention to anyone else until he was finished
and had singled out his next questioner. When my turn came, I
complimented him on his poise and concentration. He smiled. "I've learned,"
he said, "to focus on one person at a time and to stick with his problem until
it's settled. Otherwise, I'd go mad."

—NORMAN VINCENT PEALE

■ ■ ■

A problem well stated is a problem half solved.

—CHARLES F. KETTERING

■ ■ ■

There are a thousand hacking at the branches of evil to one who is striking at
the root.

—HENRY DAVID THOREAU

Bring It Down to Size

One way to find relief from stress is to bring challenges down to size by taking them one at a time.

Sir Henry Morton Stanley, when asked if he had been frightened by the jungle that had daunted previous explorers:

I did not see the whole. I only saw this rock ahead of me; I only saw this poisonous snake which I had to kill in order to take the next step. I only saw the problem directly in front of me. If I had seen the whole thing I would have been too overwhelmed to have attempted this.

—JOHN MACK CARTER AND JOAN FEENY,
STARTING AT THE TOP

■ ■ ■

Never bear more than one kind of trouble at a time. Some people bear three— all they have had, all they have now, and all they expect to have.

—EDWARD EVERETT HALE

■ ■ ■

Army doctor to a GI faced with combat fatigue:

Think of your life as an hourglass. The thousands of grains of sand in the top of the hourglass all pass slowly and evenly through the narrow neck on the middle, one grain of sand at a time. You and I and everyone else are like this hourglass. When we start in the morning, there are hundreds of tasks which we feel we must accomplish that day, but if we do not take them one at a time and let them pass through the day slowly and evenly, we are bound to break our own physical or mental structure.

—DALE CARNEGIE,
HOW TO STOP WORRYING AND START LIVING

■ ■ ■

The real key to relieving stress is gaining control over irritants you have the power to change and accepting those you don't. There's a lot of truth to the Serenity Prayer recited at Alcoholics Anonymous meetings: "God grant me the courage to change what I can, the strength to accept what I can't, and the wisdom to know the difference."

—DR. PAUL J. ROSCH

WORKING FROM THE INSIDE-OUT

People who encounter opposition often look externally for causes or blame. But the best way to initiate change and to make progress is to first look inside—to start with yourself.

Often we change jobs, friends, and spouses instead of ourselves.

—AKBARALI H. HETHA

■ ■ ■

A Chinese general put it this way: "If the world is to be brought to order, my nation must first be changed. If my nation is to be changed, my hometown must be made over. If my hometown is to be reordered, my family must first be set right. If my family is to be regenerated, I myself must first be."

—A. PURNELL BAILEY

■ ■ ■

Everybody thinks of changing humanity and nobody thinks of changing himself.

—LEO TOLSTOY

■ ■ ■

He who cannot change the very fabric of his thought will never be able to change reality.

—ANWAR EL-SADAT,
IN SEARCH OF IDENTITY

■ ■ ■

Let everyone sweep in front of his own door, and the whole world will be clean.

—GOETHE

■ ■ ■

When one is out of touch with oneself, one cannot touch others.

—ANNE MORROW LINDBERGH,
GIFT OF THE SEA

HUMOR

Sometimes when we are down the best solution is to laugh and move on, for some aspects of life just cannot be taken too seriously.

Laughter is the sun that drives winter from the human face.

—VICTOR HUGO

■ ■ ■

So many tangles in life are ultimately hopeless that we have no appropriate sword other than laughter.

—GORDON W. ALLPORT, PhD.

■ ■ ■

If you're going to be able to look back on something and laugh about it, you might as well laugh about it now.

—MARIE OSMOND

■ ■ ■

Laughter gives us distance. It allows us to step back from an event, deal with it and then move on.

—BOB NEWHART

■ ■ ■

On why she started making comedy out of minor adversities at an early age:
Comedy is tragedy revisited. For example, I baked a custard pie,
set it to cool, and it developed a puddle of water on top. I took it over
to the sink and tilted it very slightly to get the water off. But the whole
inside went down the drain. Two hour's work was shot.

—PHYLLIS DILLER,
ON NATIONAL PUBLIC RADIO'S
MORNING EDITION

■ ■ ■

A man without mirth is like a wagon without springs. He is jolted disagreeably by every pebble in the road.

—HENRY WARD BEECHER

17

MAGNANIMITY

*I will permit no man to narrow and degrade
my soul by making me hate him.*
—BOOKER T. WASHINGTON

The ability to control your emotions and actions in response to indignities done by others is becoming increasingly rare in today's litigious society. Yet such control is at the very core of the principle of magnanimity. For a magnanimous person is one who rejects revenge and rises above anger while in pursuit of more worthy ends.

One who knew well the meaning of magnanimity was Mahatma Gandhi. Throughout his life there were many occasions when he could easily have allowed anger to govern his thoughts and actions. But instead, he chose magnanimity over revenge as his guide for making decisions. In the process, he greatly influenced those near to him. One such person was Vijaya Lakshmi Pandit, former High Commissioner for India in the United Kingdom. She learned firsthand from Gandhi about the depth and healing power of magnanimity, and then followed what she called "The Best Advice I Ever Had."

The Best Advice I Ever Had

Vijaya Lakshmi Pandit

The best advice I ever had came from one of the greatest souls the world has ever known—Mahatma Gandhi—on a sunny afternoon.

Most people pass through a period of anguish when their belief in humanity is at a low ebb. I was in such a period. My husband had recently died. My deep sorrow over his loss was followed by the humiliating realization that in the eyes of Indian law I had no individual existence. Along with other Indian women I had participated for years with men in the national struggle for freedom, working and suffering side by side with them until it had finally been achieved—yet in law we women were still recognized only through our relationship to men. Now as a widow without a son, I was not entitled to any share of the family property, nor were my two daughters. I resented this galling position. I was bitter toward those members of my family who supported this antiquated law.

At this time I went to pay my respects to Gandhi and say good-bye before leaving for America to take part in the Pacific Relations Conference. After our talk he asked, "Have you made your peace with your relatives?"

I was amazed that he would take sides against me. "I have not quarreled with anyone," I replied, "but I refuse to have anything to do with those who take advantage of an outworn law to create a difficult and humiliating situation for me."

Gandhi looked out of the window for a moment. Then he turned to me and smiled and said, "You will go and say good-by because courtesy and decency demand this. In India, we still attach importance to these things."

"No," I declared, "not even to please you will I go to those who wish to harm me."

"No one can harm you except yourself," he said, still smiling. "I see enough bitterness in your heart to cause you injury unless you check it."

I remained silent, and he continued: "You are going to a new country because you are unhappy and want to escape. Can you escape from yourself? Will you find happiness outside when there is bitterness in your heart? Think it over. Be a little humble. You have lost a loved one—that is sorrow enough. Must you inflict further injury on yourself because you lack courage to cleanse your own heart?"

His words would not leave me. They gave me no peace. After some days of severe struggle with myself, I finally telephoned my brother-in-law. I would like to see him and the family, I said, before leaving.

I hadn't been with them five minutes before I sensed that my visit had brought a feeling of relief to everyone. I told my plans and asked their good wishes before starting on this new stage of my life. The effect on me was miraculous. I felt as if a great burden had been lifted and I was free to be myself.

This small gesture was the beginning of a significant change in me. A year and a half later I was in New York, leader of the Indian Delegation to the United Nations. Important to us was India's complaint regarding the treatment of people of Indian origin in the Union of South Africa. Harsh things were said by both sides. I resented the manner in which my opponents made personal attacks harmful to India's prestige and to mine. I struck back with the same sharp weapons.

Then, after a distressing duel of words, I suddenly thought of Gandhi. Would he approve? To him, means were as important as the end—in the long run, perhaps more important. What if we succeeded in getting our resolution passed by questionable tactics that injured our self-respect?

Before going to bed that night I resolved that, come what might, no word of mine would be lightly used in the U.N. From then on, I lifted the debate back to where it belonged, refusing to retaliate to personal attack or to score a cheap point. Our opponents met us on the new level and from then on we argued the case on its merits.

Before leaving the committee room on the last day, I went up and spoke to the leader of the opposing delegation. "I have come to ask you to forgive me if I have hurt you by any word or action in this debate."

He shook my hand warmly and said, "I have no complaint."

It was good to feel right with him, but even better to feel right with myself. Once more, Gandhi's advice had saved me from myself.

His words have helped me retain perspective even in small matters. Many women, I imagine, share with me a recurring nightmare: someone important to you is coming to dine; the guests have arrived, it is time to eat—but there is no dinner. You wake, perspiring, relieved to find it is only a dream.

But recently it really happened to me. My guests of honor, the prime minister of Great Britain and Lady Eden, could hardly have been more important to me, high commissioner for my country in the United Kingdom. I had planned everything meticulously, from the menu to the color scheme of the flowers and the candles. When the guests had arrived and drinks had been passed twice, I signaled the butler to announce dinner. But still we waited. When for the third time drinks came round I excused myself and ran downstairs to the kitchen.

It presented a shocking sight. In one corner stood a frightened little kitchen maid, in another the housekeeper. At the table sat my cook, waving a ladle and singing, beating time with his foot. His eyes were glazed and he was far away in some other sphere. The table was littered with pieces of chicken.

My knees felt too weak to support me, but I asked in as normal a voice as I could command: "Why isn't the dinner ready?"

"But it *is* ready, Madame," my cook chanted. "All ready. Everybody sit down, sit down. . . ."

I was furious. It was on the tip of my tongue to say, "Get out. You're dismissed!" when I thought of the counsel that had calmed me so many times. If I lost control, I would only hurt myself.

I pulled myself together. "Let's get something on the table," I said.

Everyone pitched in. The food served wasn't quite what the menu described, but when I told my guests what had happened there was a chorus of surprise. "If this is what your cook gives you when he's drunk," someone exclaimed, "what *must* he provide sober!"

The relief in my laughter must have sounded a little hysterical. My perspective restored, I realized that a dinner party, however important, is not the pivot of existence.

To retain a sense of proportion is as important as being able to keep one's heart free from hatred. For all of us, no matter what our work, the advice Gandhi gave me is meaningful: "No one can harm you but yourself."

Gandhi's message to Vijaya was not that it is wrong to experience negative emotions or feelings of anger. Nor was his message that she should go through life allowing people to take unfair advantage of her. Rather, what Gandhi taught and demonstrated for Vijaya and the rest of us is that we must not let the actions or words of others determine our responses. Magnanimous people make the choice to respond to the indignities of others based upon their own principles and their own value system rather than their moods or anger.

———————

Cowboy humorist Will Rogers was known for his quick wit and edgy satire. But there was another more serious and magnanimous side of him that also added to his being so well liked and respected.

A LITTLE HUMAN HAPPINESS
Albert P. Hout

"I never met a man I didn't like," said Will Rogers and probably the reason the great American cowboy humorist could make that statement was that few, if any, were the men who did not like Will Rogers. An incident that happened when Rogers was a young cowboy in Oklahoma helps explain it.

In the winter of 1898, Rogers fell heir to a ranch near Claremore. One day a farmer who lived nearby killed one of Will's steers that had broken down a fence and eaten his young corn. According to range custom, the farmer should have informed Will what he had done and why. He did not do so, and when Rogers found out about it, he was fit to be tied. Flaming with wrath, he called a hired hand to accompany him and rode forth to have it out with the farmer.

During the ride, a blue norther struck, coating the cowboys and their horses with ice. When they arrived at the farmer's cabin, he wasn't home. But the farmer's wife insisted that the frozen men come in and wait by the fire for his return. While warming himself, Rogers noticed how thin and work-worn the woman was. He also noticed five scrawny children peeking at him from behind various pieces of furniture.

When the farmer returned, his wife told him how Rogers and his companion had ridden out of the storm. Will started to light into the man, then suddenly closed his mouth and offered his hand instead. The farmer, unaware of the reason for Will's visit, accepted the proffered hand and invited them to stay for supper. "You'll have to eat beans," he apologized, "for the storm has interrupted the butchering of my steer." The two visitors accepted the invitation.

All during the meal, Rogers's companion kept waiting for Will to say something about the slaughtered steer, but Rogers just continued to laugh and joke with the family, and watch as the children's eyes lighted up every time they mentioned the beef they would eat on the morrow and during the weeks to come.

The norther was still blowing when supper was finished, so the farmer and his wife insisted that the two men stay the night. They did.

The next morning they were sent on their way with a bellyful of black coffee and hot beans and biscuits. Still, Rogers had not mentioned the reason for his visit. As they rode away, Will's companion began to chide him. "I thought you were going to lay that sodbuster low about our steer," he said.

Will remained silent for a few moments, then replied, "I intended to, but then I got to thinking. You know, I really didn't lose that steer. I just traded it for a little human happiness. There are millions of steers in the world, but human happiness is kind of scarce."

Will arrived at the family's doorstep with venom on his tongue and a strong man at his side. But seeing the family's circumstances and the hungry eyes of the children caused him to pause and recognize that sometimes in life there are battles that are better left unfought—certain steers that are better left alone.

———————

In this next story we travel to the far reaches of magnanimity to be reminded of the principle of forgiveness.

FROM DARKNESS TO LIGHT

Christopher Carrier

After so many years, and so much pain, could he find the strength to forgive?

The day David McAllister died brought both great sorrow and relief to me. It rained in Miami that September morning in 1996. There was no funeral procession for the old man, no flowers, no tearful eulogies. But it wasn't because of the weather that no one else showed up to pay last respects. In death, McAllister was reaping the bitterness he had sowed all his life. He was a thief, a con man and worse, driven by a malignant energy fueled by anger and hate. Yet today I realize that few things have affected me as powerfully as did the death of that old man.

The story really began twenty-two years earlier, on a sunny afternoon in December 1974.

A ten-year-old boy had just climbed off the school bus on Aledo Avenue near his house in the tree-laden Miami suburb of Coral Gables. Hugh was the lanky kid's middle name, and that's what his father, a corporate attorney, often called him. He had brown hair, trusting eyes, and a ready smile.

That afternoon Hugh's mind was on Christmas, only five days away. He wasn't aware of the man walking toward him until he spoke.

"Hi, I'm a friend of your father's," the stranger said, smiling. In those days no one in Coral Gables worried much about strangers, especially one as well dressed and polite as the graying, middle-aged man standing before him. Hugh smiled back.

"We're throwing a party for your dad," the man continued. "But I have some questions about what gifts to get him. Could you help me pick them out? We'll come right back."

Hugh agreed, eager to do something for his father. They walked to a motor home, which was parked two blocks away, and got in. The man drove north and said little as city streets gave way to open fields. On a remote stretch, he pulled over. "I think I got off on the wrong street," he said, handing Hugh a map.

"See if you can find the main highway." While Hugh studied the map, the man got up and walked back through the motor home.

A moment later Hugh felt a sharp pain, like a bee sting, in his back. He felt another sting, then twisted in his seat and recoiled in horror. The man, his eyes cold and intense, stood over him, holding an ice pick in his raised hand.

Hugh tried to protect himself, but the man pulled him to the floor. The ice pick plunged again and again. Yet even in his fear, Hugh sensed it was not penetrating deeply. The man held the pick over Hugh's chest for a moment, his hand shaking, then put the weapon down. Without saying a word, he let the terrified boy go back to his seat, then continued driving, farther away from the city.

"Your father cost me a lot of money and made things hard on me," the man said in a flat voice. Hugh shrank back into his seat, too frightened to speak. His wounds were not serious, but he ached with fear. The man turned onto Interstate 75—known as Alligator Alley where it crosses the Everglades, home to many thousands of alligators and hundreds of crocodiles.

After a moment he said, "I'm going to drop you off a few miles from here. I'll call your dad to come and get you." They drove for some time, then they turned onto a dirt road and pulled into a secluded clearing. "Let's get out of here," the man told Hugh.

Relieved to be out of the motor home, Hugh walked a short distance and sat facing a thicket. He did not see his assailant coming toward him with a small-caliber pistol. Nor did he feel the bullet as it tore through his left temple.

For six days Hugh's mother and father did not know if the boy was alive or dead. Hope faded with every passing day. No one had witnessed the abduction, and police had no leads. It was as if their youngest son had vanished off the face of the earth.

The day after Christmas, they got a call from the Coral Gables Police Department (CGPD). Hugh had been found sitting on a rock next to a road in the Everglades.

The story of Hugh's abduction and survival made headlines in Miami.

After lying unconscious in the Everglades for almost a week, the boy had awakened and staggered to the road, where a passing motorist picked him up. The bullet, which exited Hugh's right temple, had severed the left optic nerve, leaving him permanently blind in his left eye. But everyone agreed it was a miracle he had survived.

In the ensuing days and weeks, detectives worked closely with Hugh in trying to identify his attacker. He described the anger the assailant expressed toward his father and gave a detailed description of the man to the police artist, including the faded tattoo on his arm. Detectives developed a list of potential suspects. Among them was a male nurse hired by Hugh's father to care for an elderly uncle. Recently Hugh's father had fired the nurse for drinking on the job. To detectives, the firing provided the perfect motive—revenge.

The suspect owned a motor home just like the one Hugh described, and he had a police record that included armed robbery, auto theft, forgery, and a jail escape. His name was David McAllister.

For weeks Hugh studied hundreds of photos, but perhaps because he was still traumatized by the kidnapping, he was unable to identify McAllister as his attacker. Without a positive ID, detectives felt they did not have enough evidence for an arrest.

As the months, then years, went by, McAllister continued to walk the streets a free man.

Few people were more deeply affected by the case than Major Chuck Scherer of the CGPD. Scherer, who as a sergeant had helped in the investigation, had two children about Hugh's age. He was horrified by the crime and, like the other investigators, felt strongly that McAllister was responsible.

When police had gone to question him, McAllister opened his door with a smirk.

"Well," he said, "what kept you? I've been waiting two weeks." Then he denied any involvement with the assault.

McAllister's cocky attitude quickly got under Scherer's skin. For the next several years, Scherer kept tabs on him, hoping he'd slip up. From talking to the man's acquaintances, Scherer was able to piece together a picture of a mean, spiteful, functioning alcoholic. McAllister had no friends, and his family wouldn't have anything to do with him.

Scherer took some comfort in the fact that life had sentenced Hugh's kidnapper to a lonely and unhappy existence. Still, he was determined one day to make McAllister face up to his crime.

For Hugh, life continued on a downward spiral. He no longer felt safe and rarely ventured outside alone. Nearly every night for the next three years he slept on the floor at the foot of his parents' bed, fearful of every sound.

As he grew older, he became more self-conscious about his injured eye, which drooped half shut, and he found few reasons to smile. He sensed that people stared at him and was convinced he could never lead a normal life. Eventually his fear turned to resentment that his innocence had been stolen. Despite the support and encouragement of his parents and friends, he continued to live in the grip of insecurity.

When he was thirteen, Hugh realized there was one place outside his home that offered a measure of security: his neighborhood church. He was struck deeply by the Christian message of hope and forgiveness, which seemed to speak to him directly. Ever since the attack he had been looking for a way to cope with his fear and anger. Here, at last, he found it.

One evening, at the urging of several friends he met at church, he told them his story. He spoke haltingly, not knowing how they would react.

When he finished, to his surprise, they were very supportive and full of encouragement. With tears in his eyes he realized for the first time that his miraculous survival could be a source not of fear and hatred, but of inspiration.

As his faith deepened, his fears diminished, and he began to smile again. He grew to realize that sharing his faith was what he wanted to do with his life.

Hugh graduated from high school and attended Mercer University in Macon, Georgia, where he studied Christianity and psychology. He went on to the Southwestern Baptist Theological Seminary in Fort Worth, Texas, where he was awarded a master's degree in Divinity.

In 1991 Hugh met Leslie Ritchie, an attractive redhead who shared his faith and desire to work with young people. A year later they were married, and in 1994 Leslie gave birth to Amanda, the first of their three children.

"I knew God must have had a reason for keeping me alive in the Everglades," he told Leslie, holding little Amanda in his arms. "Now I know what it is."

After moving back to Miami in 1995, Hugh took a job as a director of youth ministries at his local church in Coral Gables. His students often asked about his eye, and telling the story was a great icebreaker. Once they learned all he'd been through, the youngsters readily opened up to him with their problems.

In 1996 Hugh was thirty-two years old and deeply satisfied with his life. He had, for the most part, come to grips with the horror in his past, yet one question haunted him still: What would he do if he ever came face to face with the man who tried to kill him? The question inevitably came up whenever he told his story, and he would always reply, "I hope I would have the strength to forgive him. Otherwise, I'd end up living in a world of anger and revenge, just like him."

In his heart, though, he knew he couldn't be certain of the answer.

In early 1996 Hugh was surprised to get a phone call from Chuck Scherer, now an internal-affairs commander with the CGPD. Scherer explained that a colleague, knowing Scherer's interest in Hugh's case, had recently visited a nursing home in north Miami. David McAllister was one of the patients there. Scherer had driven to the home and spoken to McAllister. "He was cagey at first," Scherer told Hugh. He hesitated, then said, "But McAllister admitted to kidnapping you that day." Hugh was silent. Scherer added, "Would you like to confront the man who tried to kill you?"

A confusion of thoughts and emotions raced through Hugh's mind. But he heard himself answer, "Yes . . . I want to meet him." The next day Hugh arrived at the nursing home. He felt his stomach tighten as he walked down the long hallway toward McAllister's room.

He had never been so nervous. Could he even shake the hand of the man who shot him and left him for dead? If not, was everything he had taught his students about forgiveness a lie?

As he approached the room, Hugh feared that seeing McAllister might open a floodgate of emotions. He stood outside the door and took a deep breath. It took all his strength and courage to enter.

He was not prepared for what he saw. Lying on the bed was not the monster of his nightmares, but a withered seventy-seven-year-old man weighing less than seventy pounds. His face was a skintight mask. His eyes, rendered sightless by glaucoma, stared blankly at the ceiling.

Hugh introduced himself, and as he spoke, the old man showed flickers of his old cockiness. "I don't know what you're talking about!" he said when reminded of his confession to Scherer.

After several minutes something seemed to give way inside the old man. He was quiet for a long moment, and his face softened. He began to tremble, and then to cry. He reached out a frail hand, and Hugh took it in his own. "I'm sorry," McAllister finally said. "I'm so sorry."

Hugh gazed at him, feeling tenderness and pity. "I just want you to know that I have been blessed," he said. "What you did was not the end of meaning in my life. It was a beginning."

McAllister squeezed Hugh's hand. "I'm very glad," he whispered.

For the next three weeks, Hugh visited McAllister nearly every day. The old man visibly brightened when he heard Hugh's voice.

Although he was almost too weak to speak, McAllister told Hugh bits about his life. Growing up without a father, he spent much of his childhood in juvenile halls and was drinking heavily by the time he was a teenager. He was rejected by his family and had no friends. It was clear to Hugh that he regretted having lived a life full of anger and shame.

McAllister explained he'd always considered God to be something only "suckers believed in." But with Hugh's help, he began to pray.

One autumn afternoon at the nursing home, Hugh spoke of his own faith and his hopes that McAllister's budding belief would grow. "I'm planning on going to heaven," Hugh said to him, "and I want you there too. I want our friendship to continue." That night McAllister died in his sleep.

Even today it's difficult for me to walk down Aledo Avenue without thinking of that afternoon so long ago when David McAllister stepped out of the shadows.

There's a part of me that is relieved he's finally gone, a part that finds, in his death, the assurance that the monster will never return.

But it was a different man who emerged, as if from the shadows, in the final days of McAllister's life. That man experienced far more pain than most of us could ever imagine. Perhaps, in a sense, he paid for the suffering he caused.

Strange as it seems, that old man did more for me than he ever could have known. In his darkness I found a light that guides me still. Forgiving David McAllister gave me a strength I will have forever.

You see, Hugh is my middle name. I was that boy.

When we don't forgive, we give our futures away. We empower other people's weaknesses, past or present, to take away our power. Today and tomorrow are held hostage by yesterday.

~

WRAP UP

Magnanimity is not a common term. Many people do not recognize it when they hear it. But they know it immediately when it is explained, and most know it as one of the areas they can personally improve upon. For too many of us are quick to seek revenge, swift to criticize, fast to find fault, and speedy to get even. Yes, too many of us are slow to hold our tongues, slow to forgive, and even slower to forget. One of the leading reasons for a lack of magnanimity is what I call a scarcity mentality. People with a scarcity mentality think there is only so much in the world to go around. It's as if they see life as a pie. When another person gets a big piece, then they get less. Such people are always trying to get even, trying to pull others down to their level so they can get an equal or even bigger piece of the pie. But it is an abundance mentality and a feeling of inner security that truly are at the root of magnanimity. And though magnanimity may not be an everyday term, it will always be one of the most distinguishing characteristics of Everyday Greatness.

REFLECTIONS

- How would you rate your ability to control your emotions, to pause before acting or reacting? How would your friends, children, or work colleagues rate your emotional control, especially under heated conditions?

- Has someone deeply offended you recently? How did you respond? Were you magnanimous? How would you respond differently if again given the same circumstances?

- One of the highest forms of magnanimity is forgiveness. Is forgiveness a consistent part of who you are as a person?

FURTHER INSIGHTS ON
Magnanimity

~

CONTROLLING EMOTIONS

While all people have emotions, secure people remain in control of them and know how to temper their tempers.

Anyone can become angry. That is easy. But to be angry with the right person, to the right degree, at the right time, for the right purpose and in the right way—that is not easy.

—ARISTOTLE

■ ■ ■

Hot heads and cold hearts never solved anything.

—THE REV. BILLY GRAHAM

■ ■ ■

Nothing gives one person so much advantage over another as to remain always cool and unruffled under all circumstances.

—THOMAS JEFFERSON

■ ■ ■

When I feel the fires of frustration begin to heat up my mind, I think back to something Winston Churchill said during World War II. "Sir," growled the Prime Minister to an explosive, impatient general, "you do not possess your emotions. They possess you!"

—NORMAN VINCENT PEALE

■ ■ ■

After an unusually difficult traffic impasse caused by a thoughtless motorist, I complimented a Chicago cab driver on his even temperament. "Aw," he replied, "you can't let nothin' aggravate you or you'd be fightin' yourself all day."

—E. G. Swanson

Men are like steel. When they lose their temper, they lose their worth.

—Chuck Norris

The way to change others' minds is with affection, and not anger.

—The Dalai Lama

Anger is a bad counselor.

—French Proverb

I will permit no man to narrow and degrade my soul by making me hate him.

—Booker T. Washington

HOLDING YOUR TONGUE

When circumstances turn heated, often the wisest thing to say is nothing.

Once on a railway journey my father unintentionally perpetrated some slight infraction and was unmercifully bawled out by a minor train employee. I was young then and hotly told my father afterward that he should have given the man a piece of his mind.

My father smiled. "Oh," he said, "if a man like that can stand himself all his life, surely I can stand him for five minutes."

—ANONYMOUS,
CATHOLIC QUOTE

■ ■ ■

The greatest remedy for anger is delay.

—SENECA

■ ■ ■

When angry, count to ten before you speak; if very angry, a hundred.

—THOMAS JEFFERSON

■ ■ ■

In the midst of great joy, do not promise anyone anything. In the midst of great anger, do not answer anyone's letter.

—CHINESE PROVERB

■ ■ ■

Never insult an alligator until after you have crossed the river.

—CORDELL HULL

■ ■ ■

I argue very well. Ask any of my remaining friends. I can win an argument on any topic. People know this and steer clear of me at parties. Often, as a sign of their great respect, they don't even invite me.

—DAVE BARRY,
MIAMI HERALD

FROM FOE TO FRIEND

One of magnanimity's finest rewards occurs when enemies are made into friends.

> He drew a circle that shut me out—
> Heretic, rebel, a thing to flout.
> But Love and I had the wit to win:
> We drew a circle that took him in.

— EDWIN MARKHAM

■ ■ ■

Booker T. Washington struggled against deep-seated white prejudice to establish his Tuskegee Institute in Alabama. One day, as he passed the mansion of a wealthy woman to whom he was just another black, he heard her call out, "Come here, boy, I need some wood chopped."

Without a word, Washington peeled off his jacket, picked up the ax and went to work, not only cutting a pile of wood but carrying it into the house.

He had scarcely left when a servant said, "That was Professor Washington, Ma'am." Abashed, the woman went to the Institute to apologize. Replied the educator: "There's no need for apology, madam. I'm delighted to do favors for my friends." The woman became one of Tuskegee's warmest and most generous supporters. Washington refused to be disturbed by insult or persecution.

— CLARENCE W. HALL

■ ■ ■

Our family of eight had a nice plot with a vegetable garden bordered by lilac bushes. A tenement in back of us was populated by folks who used to throw their trash—old shoes and socks, an assortment of things—into our garden. My older brothers and I thought that these people—they weren't called polluters then—should be told off.

Mother, who had never got beyond grammar school in the Old Country, and who had never heard of "psychology," told us to go out and pick lilacs. Then, she directed us to give each of the dozen families in back a bouquet, and say our mother thought they might enjoy them.

Somehow, a miracle happened. No more pollution.

— AS TOLD TO LEO AIKMAN,
ATLANTA CONSTITUTION

RESPONDING TO CRITICISM

Critics are found around every corner. But we don't have to take insults personally, nor let them govern our thoughts or actions.

Theodor Leschetizky, the great piano teacher, remarked, "We learn much from the disagreeable things people say, for they make us think; whereas the good things only make us glad."

Ask yourself honestly if there is any truth in the criticism. Beware of self-excuses or rationalizations; if you give in to these, you may just compound the original error. If you are forced to the conclusion that what your critic is saying is true, the best thing to do is admit it.

—NORMAN VINCENT PEALE

■ ■ ■

If I tried to read, much less answer, all the criticisms made of me and all the attacks leveled against me, this office would have to be closed for all other business. I do the best I know how, the very best I can. I mean to keep on doing this, down to the very end. If the end brings me out all wrong, then ten angels swearing I had been right would make no difference. If the end brings me out all right, then what is said against me now will not amount to anything.

—ABRAHAM LINCOLN

But if you cannot resist the urge to respond to someone's criticism, you might as well place some humor and cleverness in your repartee.

The captain of a ship once wrote in his log, "Mate was drunk today." When the mate became normal, he was terribly chagrined and angry; he pleaded with the captain to strike out the record; he declared that he had never been drunk before, that he would never drink again. But the captain said, "In this log we write the exact truth." The next week the mate kept the log, and in it he wrote, "Captain was sober today."

—WILLIAM LYON PHELPS,
ADVENTURES AND CONFESSIONS

GETTING EVEN

Trying to get revenge is a practice that seldom, if ever, pays dividends.

You can't get ahead while you are getting even.

—DICK ARMEY

■ ■ ■

There is no passion of the human heart that promises so much and pays so little as that of revenge.

—H. B. SHAW

■ ■ ■

People who fight fire with fire usually end up with ashes.

—ABIGAIL VAN BUREN

■ ■ ■

A man who studieth revenge keeps his own wounds green.

—FRANCIS BACON

■ ■ ■

I've had a few arguments with people, but I never carry a grudge. You know why? While you're carrying a grudge, they're out dancing.

—BUDDY HACKETT

■ ■ ■

Hating people is like burning down your own house to get rid of a rat.

—HARRY EMERSON FOSDICK,
THE GOLDEN BOOK

■ ■ ■

Resentment is like taking poison and waiting for the other person to die.

—MALACHY MCCOURT

FORGIVING

Surely one of the highest forms of magnanimity is forgiveness.

Never does the human soul appear so strong and noble as when it forgoes revenge and dares to forgive an injury.

—E. H. CHAPIN

One of the most lasting pleasures you can experience is the feeling that comes over you when you genuinely forgive an enemy—whether he knows it or not.

—O. A. BATTISTA

One of the secrets of a long and fruitful life is to forgive everybody everything every night before you go to bed.

—ANN LANDERS

Every man should keep a fair-sized cemetery in which to bury the faults of his friends.

—HENRY WARD BEECHER

After burying the hatchet, don't mark the spot.

— THE ENGLISH DIGEST

Write injuries in the sand, kindnesses in marble.

—FRENCH PROVERB

Raised in an abusive home, a young woman felt bitterness toward her parents. But when diagnosed with breast cancer, she determined to love them in spite of the past.

Each morning as she left for work she'd tell her mother she loved her. Her mother never answered.

Then one day, after about three months, the daughter was late for work and rushed out of the house. Her mother hurried to the door. "You forgot something," she yelled. "What?" the young woman asked. "You forgot to say I love you." They embraced. They cried. They healed.

—BERNIE S. SIEGEL,
PRESCRIPTIONS FOR LIVING

18

PERSEVERANCE

In three words I can sum up everything
I've learned about life: It goes on.
—ROBERT FROST

Two of the greatest obstacles for people to overcome in life are failure and fatigue. They get a good idea, put together some plans, and all goes well until they meet their first failure. Or they jump into their work, enjoy a few successes, and then realize that there is so much more work to do than they ever expected, and their energy fizzles.

Perseverance trumps both failure and fatigue. It gets people through both hardship and drudgery. The first of the following three accounts of perseverance, "The Man Who Wrote Messiah," will likely bring back memories of the earlier story about Charles Dickens and his writing of A Christmas Carol as it is the account of another gifted writer—only this time it involves a composer. Discover how George Frederick Handel used perseverance to ride the up and down waves of success and failure. The remaining two accounts then point out how perseverance requires a forward-looking perspective—focusing ahead, not behind—as well as the ability to ignore the naysayers.

THE MAN WHO WROTE MESSIAH

David Berreby

Barren masts swayed in the wind alongside the mist-covered wharves of Chester, a port in western England. At the steamy, leaded window of the Exchange Coffee House, a large, heavyset man stood anxiously watching idle sailors stomping their feet in the cold. The wind was still unfavorable, and once again no packet boats would be setting out. Yet he had to get to Ireland, and soon.

Once, he had been the toast of Europe, its single most celebrated composer. But by this unpromising day in November 1741, George Frederick Handel was on the verge of financial, and perhaps even artistic, bankruptcy. He was barely one step ahead of his creditors, and his public had abandoned him.

He left the window, settled uneasily on a hard oak chair, and puffed his pipe. It was a day made for glum reflection.

Music had been Handel's passport to the world ever since the day his father, a surgeon in the German town of Halle, had taken him as a youth to the court of Duke Johann Adolf at Weissenfels. His father wanted the boy to be a lawyer.

While the elder Handel attended to business at the court, George Frederick, bored, wandered into the palace chapel and began improvising on the organ. The sound of footsteps made him turn. Standing there, watching, was Duke Johann Adolf.

"Who," the Duke asked, "is this remarkable child?" Handel's father was summoned, and he was told that it would be a crime to make such a prodigy into a lawyer.

George Frederick was a quick study. While in his teens he left Halle, first for Hamburg, then for Italy, where he mastered the art of composing operas. By his midtwenties, he had set his sights on London, with its lively musical life and money to spare for grand shows.

In 1711, *Rinaldo*, Handel's first opera in Italian for English audiences, played for a remarkable fifteen nights to packed houses at the new Haymarket Theatre. It was a success such as the London musical scene had never known, and it launched Handel into society. Dukes and duchesses quit their country estates to hear the opera, and on the city's crowded streets those who had been lucky enough to get tickets whistled its tunes.

After Handel's "Te Deum" was performed at St. Paul's Cathedral to celebrate a peace treaty in 1713, Queen Anne granted Handel an annual stipend of two hundred pounds. With that and his opera receipts, Handel was now probably the best paid composer in the world.

For good measure, Queen Anne's successor, King George I, added two hundred pounds to the stipend. And the king also joined the company of many fashionable Londoners by investing thousands in Handel's opera company, the Royal Academy of Music.

The academy was the culmination of Handel's dream. Most musicians depended on handouts from aristocratic patrons. But Handel had learned to be both artist and entrepreneur. Even as he composed, he recruited investors, engaged singers, and performed various administrative duties. As long as his operas pleased the people, they would buy tickets, and the academy would turn a handsome profit.

Investing in Handel seemed a safe bet. At performances of *Amadigi* in 1715, the public kept clamoring to hear arias repeated until finally the theater management banned repetitions so the show could end before dawn. At the opening of *Radamisto* in 1720, unruly crowds fought to get at seats.

Those were the glory days, when all London buzzed with stories of how Handel had refused to be intimidated by patrons or celebrated singers. One tenor had threatened to jump headfirst into a harpsichord if Handel did not alter a tune. "That," the composer replied, "would be vastly more entertaining than your singing."

But by the mid-1720s, Handel's fortunes began fading. Audiences dwindled, and in 1728 the academy had to declare bankruptcy. Also that year, poet John Gay offered *The Beggar's Opera,* a parody of Italian opera, sung in English. It was a huge hit, and spawned a fad for shows with catchy music and English lyrics. The new craze was another nail in the coffin of Handel's Italian repertory.

But he kept on composing and doggedly producing his operas. In 1737 stress and overwork brought on an attack of the palsy, which took away the use of four fingers of his right hand. Letters expressing concern about his decline flew across England and to the Continent. The future Frederick the Great of

Prussia wrote his royal cousins in England, "Handel's great days are over, his inspiration is exhausted and his taste behind the fashion."

It was a desperate Handel who left England that summer for a cure at the famous hot springs of Aachen in Germany. There, he sat each day in the bubbling water. Little trays floated by bearing simple meals and snacks. It was a pleasant place, and it cheered him.

He had not been there long when one afternoon he left the baths and dressed quickly. Several hours later, he had not returned for his next treatment. The nuns who tended the spa grew concerned. Then, from the abbey church, came a burst of glorious music. Habits flying, the nuns ran to investigate. There was Handel, his health unaccountably restored, happily improvising on the organ.

But the return of Handel's health was not accompanied by a return of his operas to public favor. He was deep in debt, and his savings were exhausted by past operatic ventures.

For several years, he barely kept his head above water by giving concerts, as opera after opera failed. By the summer of 1741 Handel, age fifty-six, must have wondered if the time had come to give up the stage altogether.

One morning a servant brought a thick bundle of papers, wrapped in parchment. It was a text assembled by one of Handel's wealthy admirers, a part-time poet named Charles Jennens.

Jennens had been trying for years to interest Handel in setting his words to music. He had already sent Handel a dramatization of the Biblical story of Saul and David. Handel wrote an oratorio, a sort of stripped-down opera performed by singers in ordinary clothes without scenery, but it was not a success. How could it be? No special effects, no grand costumes.

Handel surveyed this new script. Like Jennens's earlier effort, its plot was taken from the Bible. But this was different. The text actually was the Bible. Jennens had skillfully assembled Old and New Testament quotations into a stirring narrative of Christ's birth, sacrifice, and resurrection. He had called the piece *Messiah*.

It began with a prophecy from Isaiah, promising deliverance: "Comfort ye, my people." Here were words of solace so simple and familiar that they seemed to draw melody from Handel as easily as he breathed. He was deeply inspired.

The Lord Lieutenant of Ireland had invited Handel to Dublin, to present a work for charity. Here was an occasion that would at least benefit those in greater need. Handel set to work.

He composed confidently. He began the *Messiah* on August 22, and twenty-three days later he was done. This music had given him something more precious than box-office appeal—it had given him hope.

Handel roused himself, paid his bill, and left the Chester coffeehouse. He wandered back to the Golden Falcon Inn. It was a far cry from the palaces and spas to which he had been accustomed. As he entered his small room, he was again fighting despair. After so monumental an effort, was his music to be stopped by the exigencies of wind and tide? He went to bed with a troubled mind, trying to rekindle the hope that the miraculous composition had engendered in him.

The next morning the wind had changed!

Dublin's music-lovers were expecting something extraordinary. Handel had been rehearsing his new work for months, and now the leading newspaper was requesting that at the opening performance ladies not wear hoops in their skirts and "gentlemen come without their swords," to permit an extra one hundred people to fit into the theater on Fishamble Street.

It was a hot, noisy crowd that Handel saw as he sat down at the harpsichord on April 13, 1742. He looked at his small force of instrumentalists and nodded. Without further ceremony, on the serene tones of its opening sinfonia, the *Messiah* entered the world.

Before it was over, the music had moved Dubliners to tears. Reviewers were ecstatic.

The next performance was so enthusiastically attended that panes of glass were removed to keep the hall from overheating. Best of all, the work proved a windfall for charity. Four hundred pounds went to hospitals and infirmaries, and 142 prisoners were freed from prison after the *Messiah* paid their debts.

But the London premiere of the *Messiah* on March 23, 1743, was a different story. Sermons were preached against it. Was the Bible's text to be sung by actors for mere entertainment? And the audience that did seek entertainment was disappointed by the lack of action and showy arias. Later, these opera zealots hired thugs to beat people who went to see Handel's works.

No matter, thought Handel. His renewed inspiration extended to other pieces. *Samson, Judas Maccabaeus* and the *Music for the Royal Fireworks* were all successes. He also had failures. But with renewed faith, he went about writing the best music he could. When friends commiserated about the empty seats at a performance of *Theodora,* Handel shrugged and replied, "The music will sound the better."

Through thick and thin, Handel stubbornly clung to his beloved *Messiah,* offering it every year for charity during the last decade of his life. London audiences began to flock to the performances. When King George II heard the oratorio for the first time, the story goes, he could not contain his enthusiasm. As trumpets rang out in the great "Hallelujah" chorus, he rose to his feet. A stir went through the audience and, in a rustle of silks and clanking of swords, everyone else stood up. To this day, when the joyous strains of this chorus are heard, audiences in the English-speaking world stand.

The mysteriously powerful inspiration that gave birth to the *Messiah* restored Handel's wavering confidence and helped save him from ruin and obscurity. Though late in life he went blind, he still composed and played the organ. It was after the blind composer had conducted a performance of the *Messiah* that he fainted and had to be carried home. He lingered through the night of Good Friday, April 13, 1759—seventeen years to the day after the *Messiah's* Dublin premiere. In the early-morning hours, George Frederick Handel died.

But to the delight of listeners of all faiths throughout the world, his *Messiah* lives.

Anyone who has ever stood in a great cathedral and listened to Handel's work resounding through massive organ pipes knows of the tremendous gift he had. Yet despite his great triumphs, Handel encountered occasions when he could have easily chosen to give up on his talents and dreams, particularly as his friends, health, and fame began to abandon him. But instead he found ways to forge on and persevere.

———————

Part of persevering and moving forward is leaving behind distracting baggage from the past.

TWO WORDS TO AVOID, TWO TO REMEMBER

Arthur Gordon

Nothing in life is more exciting and rewarding than the sudden flash of insight that leaves you a changed person—not only changed, but changed for the better. Such moments are rare, certainly, but they come to all of us. Sometimes from a book, a sermon, a line of poetry. Sometimes from a friend . . .

That wintry afternoon in Manhattan, waiting in the little French restaurant, I was feeling frustrated and depressed. Because of several miscalculations on my part, a project of considerable importance in my life had fallen through. Even the prospect of seeing a dear friend (the Old Man, as I privately and affectionately thought of him) failed to cheer me as it usually did. I sat there frowning at the checkered tablecloth, chewing the bitter cud of hindsight.

He came across the street, finally, muffled in his ancient overcoat, shapeless felt hat pulled down over his bald head, looking more like an energetic gnome than an eminent psychiatrist. His office was nearby; I knew he had just left his last patient of the day. He was close to eighty, but he still carried a full case load, still acted as director of a large foundation, still loved to escape to the golf course whenever he could.

By the time he came over and sat beside me, the waiter had brought his invariable bottle of ale. I had not seen him for several months, but he seemed as indestructible as ever. "Well, young man," he said without preliminary, "what's troubling you?"

I had long since ceased to be surprised at his perceptiveness. So I proceeded to tell him, at some length, just what was bothering me. With a kind of melancholy pride, I tried to be very honest, I blamed no one else for my disappointment, only myself. I analyzed the whole thing, all the bad judgments, the false moves. I went on for perhaps fifteen minutes, while the Old Man sipped his ale in silence.

When I finished, he put down his glass. "Come on," he said. "Let's go back to my office."

"Your office? Did you forget something?"

"No," he said mildly. "I want your reaction to something. That's all."

A chill rain was beginning to fall outside, but his office was warm and comfortable and familiar: book-lined walls, long leather couch, signed photograph of Sigmund Freud, tape recorder by the window. His secretary had gone home. We were alone.

The Old Man took a tape from a flat cardboard box and fitted it onto the machine. "On this tape," he said, "are three short recordings made by three persons who came to me for help. They are not identified, of course. I want you to listen to the recordings and see if you can pick out the two-word phrase that is the common denominator in all three cases." He smiled. "Don't look so puzzled. I have my reasons."

What the owners of the voices on the tape had in common, it seemed to me, was unhappiness. The man who spoke first evidently had suffered some kind of business loss or failure; he berated himself for not having worked harder, for not having looked ahead. The woman who spoke next had never married because of a sense of obligation to her widowed mother; she recalled bitterly all the marital chances she had let go by. The third voice belonged to a mother whose teenage son was in trouble with the police; she blamed herself endlessly.

The Old Man switched off the machine and leaned back in his chair. "Six times in those recordings a phrase is used that's full of a subtle poison. Did you spot it? No? Well, perhaps that's because you used it three times yourself down in the restaurant a little while ago." He picked up the box that had held the tape and tossed it over to me. "There they are, right on the label. The two saddest words in any language."

I looked down. Printed neatly in red ink were the words: *If only.*

"You'd be amazed," said the Old Man, "if you knew how many thousands of times I've sat in this chair and listened to the woeful sentences beginning with those two words. 'If only,' they say to me, 'I had done it differently—or not done it at all. If only I hadn't lost my temper, said that cruel thing, made that dishonest move, told that foolish lie. If only I had been wiser, or more unselfish, or more self-controlled.' They go on and on until I stop them.

Sometimes I make them listen to the recordings you just heard. 'If only,' I say to them, 'you'd stop saying *if only*, we might begin to get somewhere!' "

The Old Man stretched out his legs. "The trouble with 'if only,' " he said, "is that it doesn't change anything. It keeps the person facing the wrong way—backward instead of forward. It wastes time. In the end, if you let it become a habit, it can become a real roadblock, an excuse for not trying anymore.

"Now take your own case: your plans didn't work out. Why? Because you made certain mistakes. Well, that's all right: everyone makes mistakes. Mistakes are what we learn from. But when you were telling me about them, lamenting this, regretting that, you weren't really learning from them."

"How do you know?" I said, a bit defensively.

"Because," said the Old Man, "you never got out of the past tense. Not once did you mention the future. And in a way—be honest, now!—you were enjoying it. There's a perverse streak in all of us that makes us like to hash over old mistakes. After all, when you relate the story of the chief character, you're still in the center of the stage."

I shook my head ruefully. "Well, what's the remedy?"

"Shift the focus," said the Old Man promptly. "Change the key words and substitute a phrase that supplies lift instead of creating drag."

"Do you have such a phrase to recommend?"

"Certainly. Strike out the words 'if only'; substitute the phrase 'next time.'"

"Next time?"

"That's right. I've seen it work minor miracles right here in this room. As long as a patient keeps saying 'if only' to me, he's in trouble. But when he looks me in the eye and says 'next time,' I know he's on his way to overcoming his problem. It means he has decided to apply the lessons he has learned from his experience, however grim or painful it may have been. It means he's going to push aside the roadblock of regret, move forward, take action, resume living. Try it yourself. You'll see."

My old friend stopped speaking. Outside, I could hear the rain whispering against the windowpane. I tried sliding one phrase out of my mind and replacing it with the other. It was fanciful, of course, but I could hear the new words lock into place with an audible click.

"One last thing," the Old Man said. "Apply this little trick to things that can still be remedied." From the bookcase behind him he pulled out something that looked like a diary. "Here's a journal kept a generation ago by a woman who was a teacher in my hometown. Her husband was a kind of amiable ne'er-do-well, charming, but totally inadequate as a provider. This woman had to raise the children, pay the bills, keep the family together. Her diary is full of angry references to Jonathan's inadequacies.

"Then Jonathan died, and all the entries ceased except for one—years later. Here it is: 'Today I was made superintendent of schools, and I suppose I should be very proud. But if I knew that Jonathan was out there somewhere beyond the stars, and if I knew how to manage it, I would go to him tonight.' "

The Old Man closed the book gently. "You see? What she's saying is, 'if only; if only, I had accepted him, faults and all; if only I had loved him while I could.' " He put the book back on the shelf. "That's when those sad words are the saddest of all: when it's too late to retrieve anything."

He stood up a bit stiffly. "Well, class dismissed. It has been good to see you, young man. Always is. Now, if you will help me find a taxi, I probably should be getting on home."

We came out of the building into the rainy night. I spotted a cruising cab and ran toward it, but another pedestrian was quicker.

"My, my," said the Old Man slyly. "If only we had come down ten seconds sooner, we'd have caught that cab, wouldn't we?"

I laughed and picked up the cue. "Next time I'll run faster."

"That's it," cried the Old Man, pulling his absurd hat down around his ears. "That's it exactly!"

Another taxi slowed. I opened the door for him. He smiled and waved as it moved away. I never saw him again. A month later, he died of a sudden heart attack, in full stride, so to speak.

Much time has passed since that rainy afternoon in Manhattan. But to this day, whenever I find myself thinking "if only," I change it to "next time." Then I wait for the almost-perceptible mental click. And when I hear it, I think of the Old Man.

A small fragment of immortality, to be sure. But it's the kind he would have wanted.

The land of "If only—" is wide open territory. Though lacking anything of lasting value, it is a tempting place to visit when times get tough or things do not go your way. On the other hand the road to "Next time—" opens entire vistas of opportunity and is far more likely to lead you to the rewards of perseverance. So again, a significant part of persevering and moving forward is leaving behind the baggage of the past.

Some of perseverance's greatest foes are naysayers—those people who hollowly insist that something cannot be done. Captured in "Yes, I Can" are four short, inspiring stories of people who proved the naysayers wrong.

"YES, I CAN"

YOU'RE STUDYING DIRT
—Fran Lostys

Dr. Judah Folkman keeps a reproduction of a 1903 *New York Times* article in his archives. In it two physics professors explain why airplanes could not possibly fly. The article appeared just three months before the Wright brothers split the air at Kitty Hawk.

In the early 1970s, Folkman proposed an idea in cancer research that did not fit what scientists "knew" to be true: that tumors did not generate new blood vessels to feed themselves and grow. He was convinced that they did. But colleagues kept telling him, "You're studying dirt," meaning his project was futile science.

Folkman disregarded the catcalls of the research community. For two decades, he met with disinterest or hostility as he pursued his work in angiogenesis, the study of the growth of new blood vessels. At one research convention, half the audience walked out. "He's only a surgeon," he heard someone say.

But he always believed that his work might help stop the growth of tumors, and might help find ways to grow blood vessels where they were needed—like around clogged arteries in the heart.

Folkman and his colleagues discovered the first angiogenesis inhibitors in the 1980s. Today more than one hundred thousand cancer patients are benefiting from the research he pioneered. His work is now recognized as being on the forefront in the fight to cure cancer.

"There is a fine line between persistence and obstinacy," Folkman says. "I have come to realize the key is to choose a problem that is worth persistent effort."

THE MANAGER WHO COULDN'T WRITE
—Gary Sledge

What launched Amy Tan's career was not a big break, but a kick in the butt.

Before the million-copy sales of *The Joy Luck Club, The Kitchen God's Wife,* and *The Hundred Secret Senses,* Amy Tan was a writer. A business writer. She and a partner ran a technical-writing business with lawyerlike "billable hours."

Her role with clients was largely that of account management—but this daughter of immigrants wanted to do something more creative with words, English words.

So she made her pitch to her partner: "I want to do more writing." He declared her strength was doing estimates, going after contractors, and collecting bills. "It was horrible stuff." The very stuff Tan hated and knew she wasn't really good at. But her partner insisted that writing was her weakest skill.

"I thought, I can believe him and just keep doing this or make my demands." So she argued and stood up for her rights.

He would not give in.

Shocked, Tan said, "I quit."

And he said: "You can't quit. You're fired!" And added, "You'll never make a dime writing."

Tan set out to prove him wrong, taking on as many assignments as she could. Sometimes she worked ninety hours a week as a freelance technical writer. Being on her own was tough. But not letting others limit her or define her talents made it worthwhile. And on her own, she felt free to try fiction. And so *The Joy Luck Club*, featuring the bright, lonely daughter of Chinese immigrants, was born. And the manager who couldn't write became one of America's best-selling, best-loved authors.

FAILING HIS WAY TO SUCCESS
—*Janice Leary*

Working in the control room of the salvage vessel *Seaprobe* at two o'clock one morning in 1977, Robert Ballard was jolted by a massive piece of equipment that crashed onto the deck just three feet above him. The ship shook with the force of an explosion. A drill pipe and its attached pod full of sonar and video gear had snapped and plunged into the Atlantic, abruptly ending the explorer's test run to find the RMS *Titanic*.

"I lost a lot of credibility with sponsors, who had loaned the six hundred thousand dollars worth of stuff [for the 1977 expedition]. It took me eight years to recover from that." But recover he did, despite skepticism from other scientists, failed fund-raising efforts and other setbacks.

After the *Seaprobe* debacle, Ballard said, "I was back to square one. I had to come up with another way to search for the *Titanic*."

He returned to active duty as a U.S. Navy officer assigned to intelligence work. At a time when the Cold War was still being waged, the marine geologist cut a deal with navy officials. He would offer his expertise if they funded the development and testing of Argo, a camera-equipped underwater robot critical to the *Titanic* mission, and allowed him to use it for exploration.

The navy sent Ballard and Argo on classified missions to survey *Thresher* and *Scorpion*, two nuclear submarines that sank during the 1960s. Those vessels lay in waters not far from the *Titanic*. After surveying the *Scorpion* in 1985, Ballard began looking for the doomed luxury liner. And two miles down, in the dark sea at 49° 56' W, 41° 43' N, he found it.

The oceanographer, who later found the German battleship *Bismarck*, the liner *Lusitania,* and other historic wrecks, has a simple philosophy. "Failure and success are bedfellows, so I'm ready to fail."

Ballard's current port is the University of Rhode Island's Graduate School of Oceanography, where he has launched an archeological program.

THE UNDERSTUDY
—Joseph K. Vetter

"Angie, I know you like to sing," her father, a practical autoworker, told Angela Brown, "but you gotta have something to fall back on."

Brown took her father's advice. She got a degree in secretarial science before enrolling in Oakwood College, in Huntsville, Alabama. Her aim was to become a singing evangelist. But then the opera bug bit.

So after graduation she headed to Indiana University to study with legendary soprano Virginia Zeani.

Once, when Brown was plagued by self-doubt, Zeani challenged her: "If you want to be the next Aretha Franklin, go, you need no more lessons," Brown remembers her saying. "But if you want to be the best Verdian soprano this world has ever seen, you must work."

Work she did. Three times she competed in the Metropolitan Opera National Council auditions. Three times she failed to make the final round in New York. Then, in 1997 at age thirty-three, the age limit for sopranos to audition, she gave it one more try. She signed up at the last minute and didn't even practice, figuring: "All they could do was tell me no, and that didn't hurt my feelings anymore." She had the strength she needed to fall back on if she failed.

She won. But making it to New York was just the beginning. Singers don't spring into starring roles. It took her three more years to become a Met understudy. But waiting in the wings was fine with her. Finally, her time came. When the featured singer fell ill, Brown earned the chance to sing the lead role in *Aida.* And the *New York Times* proclaimed her debut a triumph. Angela Brown, soprano, who had prepared for twenty years, was an "overnight" sensation at age forty.

Each of these individuals heard loud and clear the "No" of the crowd, but inside they each had a deeper "Yes, I can." The key, as Dr. Folkman observed, was to find something worthy of persistent effort, combined with the strength to overcome a few failures along the way.

~~~

WRAP UP

The late leadership guru Peter Drucker once noted that the problem with all innovative ideas is that they quickly degenerate into hard work. Unfortunately, it is the lack of a capacity for hard work that causes many people to quit well short of the finish line, even when pursuing goals important to them. Other times it may be the fear of failure or an unhealthy dependence on outside support that causes people to give up and fall short of expectations. But what the people in these stories demonstrate is that perseverance is not something a person does one day, but not the next. It is an everyday trait supported by everyday actions that make perseverance an important part of Everyday Greatness.

REFLECTIONS

- Handel could easily have succumbed to despair. When life does not go as you desire, do you get hampered by the negatives or do you persevere and let the positives carry you forward?

- As the "Old Man" pointed out, some people cannot persevere today because they are stuck in their past. Do you catch yourself saying "if only" very often? What will you say instead, "next time"?

- If you were to rate your persistence on a scale of one to ten with ten being high, would you rate in double digits? If not, what commonly keeps you from being at a ten?

- How easy it is to dwell on personal weaknesses or use them as sticks to beat down our self-esteem. Do you dwell more on your weaknesses or your strengths, your failures or your successes?

FURTHER INSIGHTS ON
Perserverance

~~

PERSISTING

Whether we are up or down, life goes on. Therefore, we too must go on and persist if we want to achieve the dreams that matter most.

Perseverance is not a long race; it is many short races one after another.

—WALTER ELLIOTT

■ ■ ■

Perseverance is the hard work you do after you get tired of doing the hard work you already did.

—NEWT GINGRICH

■ ■ ■

Quiet minds cannot be perplexed or frightened, but go on in fortune or misfortune at their own private pace, like a clock during a thunderstorm.

—ROBERT LOUIS STEVENSON

■ ■ ■

Dr. Jean-Louis Etienne, the man who walked alone to the North Pole, explains what these forays into the world of ice and snow bring him: There are two great times of happiness—when you are haunted by a dream and when you realize it. Between the two there's a strong urge to let it all drop. But you have to follow your dreams to the end. . . . I almost gave up a thousand times before reaching those moments of happiness when I forgot that I was cold.

—L'EXPRESS, PARIS

BOUNCING BACK

Some people let one-time failures thwart their dreams. But successful people use failures as stepping stones toward their next success.

Fall seven times, stand up eight.

—JAPANESE PROVERB

■ ■ ■

If you have made mistakes, even serious ones, there is always another chance for you. What we call failure is not the falling down, but the staying down.

—MARY PICKFORD

■ ■ ■

He struck out 1330 times. But that isn't what we remember about Babe Ruth. His 714 home runs completely obliterated the strike-outs. Pitcher Cy Young accumulated 511 victories, a mark that never has been threatened. But what is generally forgotten is that Young lost almost as many games as he won.

—HAROLD HELFER
KIWANIS MAGAZINE

■ ■ ■

Life is pretty simple: You do some stuff. Most fails. Some works. You do more of what works. If it works big, others quickly copy it. Then you do something else.

—TOM PETERS

■ ■ ■

You may have to fight a battle more than once to win it.

—MARGARET THATCHER

■ ■ ■

Character consists of what you do on the third and fourth tries.

—JAMES MICHENER,
CHESAPEAKE

SEEING SUCCESS

> Sometimes the reason people don't persevere is because the lenses through which they view life are focused on failing, not succeeding.

Recalling the pep talk he gave the Dallas Cowboys before their victory in the 1993 Super Bowl game: "I told them that if I laid a two-by-four across the room everybody there could walk across it and not fall, because our focus would be that we were going to walk that two-by-four. But if I put that same two-by-four ten stories high between two buildings, only a few would make it, because the focus would be on falling."

—JIMMY JOHNSON

■ ■ ■

A man would do nothing if he waited until he could do it so well that no one could find fault.

—JOHN HENRY CARDINAL NEWMAN

■ ■ ■

Bad times have a scientific value. These are occasions a good learner would not miss.

—RALPH WALDO EMERSON

■ ■ ■

We're brought up, unfortunately, to think that nobody should make mistakes. Most children get de-geniused by the love and fear of their parents—that they might make a mistake. But all my advances were made by mistakes. You uncover what is when you get rid of what isn't.

—BUCKMINSTER FULLER,
IN THE *WASHINGTON POST*

■ ■ ■

I try to regret just enough to learn, so I don't do something again.

—JOHN TRAVOLTA

FACING FORWARDS

Some people get caught up or lost in their yesterdays. But
the past is to be understood within the context of the future.

You can clutch the past so tightly to your chest that it leaves your arms too
full to embrace the present.

—JAN GLIDEWELL

■ ■ ■

Those who gaze too much upon the past, who think too much about what
might have been, are running something of the same risk as the driver who
keeps his eyes too much upon his rear-view mirror and is inattentive to the
road ahead. Experience is a great teacher; it is the road we have been over.
But the wrecks in the rear aren't the ones we are now trying to avoid. It's the
curves ahead that count now.

—RICHARD L. EVANS,
TONIC FOR OUR TIMES

■ ■ ■

Life can only be understood backward, but it must be lived forward.

—SÖREN KIERKEGAARD

■ ■ ■

Memories are the key not to the past, but to the future.

—CORRIE TEN BOOM,
THE HIDING PLACE

■ ■ ■

Past experience should be a guide post, not a hitching post.

—D. W. WILLIAMS

■ ■ ■

I can tell you about a sawmill man with whom I sat one night while every
dollar he owned was going up in smoke before our eyes. He was very quiet. I
tried to be sympathetic. "I'm imagining how the new mill will look," he said.

—CLARENCE BUDINGTON KELLAND
IN THE *AMERICAN MAGAZINE*

PATIENCE

Patience is often equated with passivity, but patience is a proactive choice and a vital form of perseverance.

Patience is the companion of wisdom.

—St. Augustine

■ ■ ■

Patience is a necessary ingredient of genius.

—Benjamin Disraeli

■ ■ ■

In my grandmother's garden a rosebud seemed such a long time unfolding that I grew impatient, wanting to see its color and beauty. I thought we should do something about it, and appealed to Grandmother. When she told me to unfold the petals, I was thrilled. But after the petals were unfolded there was no beautiful full-blown rose such as I had visioned. I had destroyed its beauty, and the rose quickly withered and died. Grandmother then explained that it was thus with all things—we must let them unfold in their own way and in their own time.

—Dorothy E. Minck

■ ■ ■

I had no special sagacity—only the power of patient thought.

—Sir Isaac Newton

■ ■ ■

Be patient with everyone, but above all with yourself.

—St. Francis De Sales

BLENDING
THE PIECES

The art of living is more like wrestling than dancing.
—MARCUS AURELIUS

Everyday terms such as burnout, red-eye flights, stress, power lunches, workaholism, and overtime often cram together to spell the phrase, "I need a life." One of the greatest challenges we face in pursuing Everyday Greatness is that of dealing with all the competing demands that are placed upon us. There seem to be so many choices and so little time. To get the most out of life, we must find ways to simplify by focusing only on that which matters most and by taking the opportunity to refresh our minds and bodies.

Principles that help us properly blend the various demands of life include

- Balance

- Simplicity

- Renewal

19

BALANCE

*Tonight my wife and I had dinner alone
for the first time in twenty years.*
—GEORGE WASHINGTON'S DIARY

Whether you are single or married, retired or employed, old or young, demands on your time seem endless. There are never enough hours in a day to spend with those who matter most to us or to do that which brings us the most joy. We always seem to be looking for a better balance.

In fact, we so often rush through life that we fail to take time out to enjoy it. We are so busy getting ready for the next project or responding to urgent demands that we forget to stop and enjoy our todays. This message is somewhat somberly illustrated in each of the following three stories. Fortunately, each one, as well as the accompanying quotes and anecdotes, also offers insightful suggestions about how we can find greater joy in our todays while bringing more balance to our lives.

A LESSON FROM AN ESKIMO

Gontran de Poncins

We had been thirty days on the trail—I and the Eskimo family I traveled with. What with the wind, the cold—it was fifty below—and the Eskimo mentality, it was the toughest trip I had ever experienced.

I felt as if fate were working maliciously to delay us. One day the blizzard would keep us squatting in an igloo. Another, some queer fancy would take my native companions and, though the day was good, they would stop to build a new igloo instead of pushing ahead.

Several times I had asked the old man of the family: "How many more days is it to King William Land?" He had never answered directly. Eskimos do not like questions. They think them rude. Only a white man would ask a thing like that. Besides, Eskimos don't like to commit themselves. "What will the weather be tomorrow?" you ask. The Eskimo knows well enough, but he will answer politely: *"mauna"* ("I don't know")—and pretend to be busy with the dogs, as if to say, "Why should I answer? If my answer is right I shall be no better for it; if wrong I shall look a fool!"

All the morning, all the afternoon we pushed across the frozen sea, stopping only to untangle the dogs' traces or to light a pipe. We sighted land. Perhaps we would reach it. Then when hope was in sight the wind rose, the land was obscured by whirling snow, lost in what, for me, was the gray despair of nothingness.

We stopped again. Slowly, without haste, with that perfect urbanity in which the Eskimo accepts life and fate, Ohudlerk, the old man, talked with his wife and his little girl. At home in France a peasant in a rainstorm would stop with the same coolness to inspect his plow.

Hardly able to bear my distress, I again asked the old man my questions. "When do you think, now, that we shall get to King William Land?" Whether this time his patience was at an end, or whether he was really concerned, I shall never know. He turned back to his wife and they had some silent understanding together.

Then he came to me and looked up. He spoke in that light, almost careless way the natives have when they are prudent and afraid at the same time:

"Don't the dogs go as well as you would like?"

There was silence. The dogs had turned their heads as they do when they pull up, and were looking at me. The woman and the child pretended to be busy but I knew that I was the focus on their attention too. In the instant everything seemed to come to a standstill. Eskimos give you that feeling in their tense moments. They have a way of giving weight to silence. Would they leave it at that? No, it had gone too far. Finally the old man, as if he could not rid himself of his doubts, said: "Isn't that sled a good sled? Aren't you glad that the snow over the sea is lasting through our journey?"

He kept looking at me with deeply troubled eyes. The stone age with its simplicity, the Orient with its wisdom were looking at me, trying to understand—or, rather, trying to make themselves understood. Then suddenly I saw what the old eyes were saying.

"Why hurry?" they said. "And where is it that you are always wanting to be going? Why concern yourself with the future when the present is so magnificent?"

The old man, that day, taught me a lesson, which I have not forgotten. In my feverish thinking of tomorrow I had failed to appreciate today. In the old man's presence I remembered what someone had said to me: "To think of the past is to regret it; to think of the future is to fear it." But the present! Is not that the only understandable reality?

The world is what your mind makes of it. To me the Arctic had been heartbreaking; to the Eskimos it had been a great empire of which they were the kings. To me the snow had been loathsome; to them it was a blessing and a sacred gift. From the thousand facets of life we are free to choose between sorrow and hope.

We rush along the highways of life, ignoring the landscape. Who was it who said, "Luxury consists in having time to spare"—time to stop and think? The Eskimos stop when they please, though tomorrow holds for them, as for us, the eternal possibility of starvation and death. So death when it comes finds them still happy in the present, and they go without regret.

I have learned, since Ohudlerk spoke to me with his eyes, what poverty of soul I had suffered in the Arctic. I have learned to make each day as rich as if there were to be no tomorrow. Nothing the future may do to me can change what I now possess.

In Vancouver, when the long trek was over, I caught myself rushing to the hotel as if there were no time to lose. Suddenly I stopped in the middle of the traffic. Horns sounded from all directions but I didn't hear them. It was as if Ohudlerk stood in the street before me, watching me with those wise, ancient, questioning, and troubled eyes, asking me if the dogs were not good dogs and was not the snow indeed a gift from heaven.

And I found myself laughing. *What fools we are!* I thought. I still do.

No matter the latitude or longitude of where we live, today's world is revolving at such a pace that both our days and nights appear to be getting shorter and shorter. Before we can pause to enjoy the romance of a full moon, the sun is up again and off we go chasing the next set of appointments and to-do lists. It is easy to dash by life so fast that we fail to enjoy our todays. People with Everyday Greatness may live in a rush, rush world, but they determine the weather of their minds and survive the storms of life by learning to live in and enjoy the present.

———————

It is difficult to take time to smell the roses and to enjoy. Here columnist and advice giver extraordinaire, Erma Bombeck, looks back at her life and describes a few things she wishes she had done differently.

IF I HAD MY LIFE TO LIVE OVER

Erma Bombeck

Someone asked me the other day, if I had my life to live over, would I change anything?

No, I answered, but then I began to think . . .

If I had my life to live over, I would have talked less and listened more.

I would have invited friends over to dinner, even if the carpet was stained and the sofa faded.

I would have eaten popcorn in the "good" living room and worried much less about the dirt when someone wanted to light a fire in the fireplace.

I would have taken the time to listen to my grandfather ramble about his youth.

I would never have insisted the car windows be rolled up on a summer day because my hair had just been teased and sprayed.

I would have burned the pink candle sculpted like a rose before it melted in storage.

I would have sat on the lawn with my children and not worried about grass stains.

I would have cried and laughed less while watching television—and more while watching life.

I would have shared more of the responsibility carried by my husband.

I would have gone to bed when I was sick instead of pretending the earth would go into a holding pattern if I weren't there for the day.

I would never have bought anything just because it was practical, wouldn't show soil, or was guaranteed to last a lifetime.

Instead of wishing away nine months of pregnancy, I'd have cherished every moment and realized that the wonderment growing inside me was my only chance in life to assist God in a miracle.

When my child kissed me impetuously, I would never have said, "Later. Now go get washed up for dinner."

There would have been more I love yous, more I'm sorrys, but mostly, given another shot at life, I would seize every minute, look at it and really see it, live it, and never give it back.

What I hear Erma Bombeck and so many other people I know saying is that they wish they had stopped to enjoy life a little more. That they wish they had placed relationships ahead of things, their missions ahead of their clocks. Living life solely on the basis of efficiency and cost effectiveness does not come without a price.

———————

Perhaps nowhere more frequently or more forcefully do people feel the pains or hear the cries of imbalance than in the ongoing struggle between career and family demands.

BRICK BY BRICK

Bill Shore

For years I worked in politics, a career choice that required long hours and a lot of traveling. When Senator Bob Kerrey ran for president in 1992, for example, I helped on his campaign and spent a great deal of time away from my wife, Bonnie, and our two young children, Zach and Mollie.

After the campaign, I came home to learn an important lesson about balancing career and family, about what kids really need from a dad—and about the building and dismantling of walls.

Shortly before Mollie's third birthday, I had just returned from a series of long trips with the Senator, some of which had lasted six or seven days, with only a quick stop at home to change laundry.

Mollie and I were driving through our Silver Spring, Maryland, neighborhood on the way back from the grocery store, when from her car seat in the back, she said, "Dad, what street is your house on?"

"What?" I thought I hadn't heard correctly.

"What street is your house on?"

It was a telling moment. Although she knew I was her dad and she knew her mom and I were married, she did not know I lived in the same house that she did.

SECRET HIDE-OUT

Though I was able to convince her that we resided at the same address, her uncertainty about my place in her life continued and manifested itself in many ways. A skinned knee sent her toppling toward Mom, not me. A question raised by something overheard at school would be saved for hours until Mom was around to ask.

I realized that not only did I have to spend more time with Mollie, I also had to spend it differently. The more I sensed her distance from me, the more goal-oriented things I tried to do with her—like going to the swimming pool or to the movies.

If Mollie and I didn't have some specifically scheduled activity, I would typically go off and work on chores. For maximizing time and being productive, it made perfect sense.

When it was time to read a bedtime story, Bonnie would call me after the rest of the pre-sleep routine had been completed, and I would walk into Mollie's room like a dentist who waited until the patient was prepped so he wouldn't have to waste a minute's time. It was the way I felt and I'm sure now it was the way it made Mollie feel too.

A turning point came one summer evening. Mollie was growing increasingly frustrated trying to build a secret hideout in the backyard. The sun was setting and Mollie should have been winding down for bed, except that the thin slate tiles she tried to prop against one another kept falling over. She'd been at it for days, sometimes with a neighboring friend, sometimes on her own. When the walls fell for the last time, cracking as they did, she burst into tears.

"You know what you need to make this work, Molls?" I said.

"What?"

"You need about sixty bricks."

"Yeah, but we don't have sixty bricks."

"But we could get them."

"Where?"

"The hardware store. Get your shoes on and hop in the car."

We drove the three or four miles to the hardware store and found the bricks. I started to load them, a few at a time, onto a big, flat cart. They were rough and heavy, and I realized that I had my work cut out for me. After being loaded onto the cart, they would need to be unloaded into the Jeep, and then unloaded yet again at the house.

"Oh, please, let me do that, Dad. Please!" Mollie begged.

If I let her, we'd be there forever. She would have to use two hands just to pick up one of them. I glanced at my watch and tried to keep my impatience in check.

"But sweetie, they're very heavy."

"Please Dad, I really want to," she begged again, moving quickly to the pile of bricks and hoisting one with both hands. She lugged it over to the cart and laid it next to the handful I had placed there.

This was going to take all night.

Mollie waked back to the pile and carefully selected another brick. She took her time making her choice.

Then I realized she wanted it to take all night.

It was rare for the two of us to have time like this alone together. This was the kind of thing her older brother Zach, would usually get to do—impulsive, past bedtime, just the two of us. Only with Zach, in maybe typical male fashion, I would see this as a task to finish quickly so that we could go build the wall. Mollie wanted this moment to last.

MOLLIE'S MOMENT

I leaned back against one of the wood pallets and took a deep breath. Mollie, working steadily at the bricks, relaxed and became chatty, talking to me about what she'd build, and about school and her girlfriends and her upcoming horseback-riding lesson. And it dawned on me, here we were buying bricks to make a wall, but in truth we were actually dismantling a wall, brick by brick. The wall that had threatened to divide me from my daughter.

Since then I've learned what her mother already knew. How to watch a TV show with Mollie, even if it isn't a show I wanted to see, how to be with her without also reading a newspaper or magazine—to be fully present. Mollie doesn't want me for what I can give her, for where I can take her, or even for what we can do together. She wants me for me.

Our days travel at such dizzying speeds that it is challenging to find a balance between careers, friends, hobbies, and families—particularly families. But as the father in this story learned, balance does not just happen. It is earned brick by brick, or in this case, conversation by conversation.

~

WRAP UP

We are not animals. We are self-aware human beings, and between all that has happened to us and our responses to it is a space, and in that space lies our power and our freedom to choose our responses, and in those choices lie our growth and our happiness. I learned that from an unknown book, many years ago while wandering through the stacks of a library in Hawaii. It profoundly affected the rest of my life, all my work and my writing included. It lies at the base of this entire book as well. We can stop and pause and reflect. We can decide what is most important and separate out that which is urgent but not truly important. Though we may have seasons of imbalance for various, even wise reasons, our lives can ultimately reflect a deep inner balance. This may require us to reinvent ourselves, something animals cannot do. I have found that the best way to do this is to schedule priorities first, letting less important activities fill in any open gaps—should there be any. There is a significant difference between prioritizing your schedule and scheduling your priorities.

REFLECTIONS

- Do you find joy in your todays, or do you mostly find yourself waiting for joy in some future event? What can you do this very day that will bring you a greater measure of joy?

- The term balance does not imply that we spend equal time with family, equal time with work, equal time with friends, and so forth. Rather it means that we find in our schedules a proper proportion or blend for each. With that in mind, how well balanced or well proportioned is your life? Are you overweighted in some areas?

- Are there idle habits or hobbies in your life—such as too much television or too much sleep—that distract you from being more balanced? Are there limits you need to place on them?

FURTHER INSIGHTS ON
Balance

~

BUSY SIGNALS

Life travels at a pace so fast that too many people end up bypassing that which matters most.

True enough, we all have obligations and duties toward our fellow men. But it does seem curious enough that in modern, neurotic society, men's energies are consumed in making a living, and rarely in living itself. It takes a lot of courage for a man to declare, with clarity and simplicity, that the purpose of life is to enjoy it.

—LIN YUTANG,
THE PLEASURE OF A NONCONFORMIST

■ ■ ■

Plenty of people miss their share of happiness, not because they never found it, but because they didn't stop to enjoy it.

—WILLIAM FEATHER

■ ■ ■

We're time warriors who keep huge appointment calendars on the kitchen wall and message pads by every phone to balance our hectic schedules. We buy gadgets that promise to save us time, give up such activities as reading as luxuries from the past, try to do everything just a bit faster and wonder why none of the above seems to ease time's crushing pressure.

—RALPH KEYES,
TIMELOCK

■ ■ ■

There is more to life than increasing its speed.

—MOHANDAS K. GANDHI

LIVING EACH MOMENT

To make the best use of time, we need to live each moment
as if it is vitally important.

How we spend our days is, of course, how we spend our lives.

—ANNIE DILLARD

■ ■ ■

Most people don't think in terms of minutes. They waste all the minutes. Nor
do they think in terms of their whole life. They operate in the mid-range of
hours or days. So they start over again every week, and spend another chunk
unrelated to their lifetime goals. They are doing a random walk through life,
moving without getting anywhere.

—ALAN LAKEIN,
QUOTED IN *NEW YORK MAGAZINE*

■ ■ ■

Lose an hour in the morning and you will be looking for it the rest
of the day.

—LORD CHESTERFIELD

■ ■ ■

Ultimately, time is all you have and the idea isn't to save it but to
savor it.

—ELLEN GOODMAN,
WASHINGTON POST

■ ■ ■

What I do today is important because I am exchanging a day of my life
for it.

—HUGH MULLIGAN,
ASSOCIATED PRESS

■ ■ ■

Millions long for immortality who don't know what to do with themselves on a rainy Sunday afternoon.

—Susan Ertz

■ ■ ■

Time flies, but, remember, you're the navigator.

—St. Louis Bugle

■ ■ ■

Decide what your priorities are and how much time you'll spend on them. If you don't, someone else will.

—Harvey Mackay

■ ■ ■

You don't get to chose how you're going to die. Or when. You can only decide how you're going to live. Now.

—Joan Baez

■ ■ ■

Most time is wasted in minutes, not hours. The average person diddles away enough minutes in ten years to have earned a college degree.

—Dale Turner,
Seattle Times

BLENDING WORK AND FAMILY

When asked what is most important to them, most people say family. Yet, oddly enough it is often family that is first to be pushed aside from busy schedules.

Recently I read an article about the "Thank God It's Monday" syndrome, the tendency of many people to be excited by their work and bored by their unstimulating weekends at home. Indeed, our society seems to believe that making money is more valuable than shaping people's souls, that dealing with adults is more valuable than dealing with children.

—RABBI HAROLD S. KUSHNER,
REDBOOK

■ ■ ■

A few years ago I had a problem—I couldn't wait to get to the office in the morning and only left it at night reluctantly. Being a member of the President's Cabinet was so much better than any job I'd had that I couldn't get enough of it.

Not surprisingly, the rest of my life shriveled into a dried raisin. I lost contact with old friends. I saw little of my wife, and even less of our two sons, Adam, then 15, and Sam, 12.

One evening, for the sixth time in a row, I phoned home to tell the boys that once again I'd miss their bedtime. That's okay, said Sam. But could I wake him up when I did get home? That would be real late, I said. He would have gone to sleep long before. It was probably better if I saw him the next morning.

Sam listened, but insisted. I asked him why. He said he just wanted to know I was there.

To this day I can't explain precisely what happened at that moment, but I suddenly knew, with utter finality, that I had to leave my job.

—ROBERT REICH,
FORMER U.S. SECRETARY OF LABOR

■ ■ ■

The most important work you and I will ever do will be within the walls of our own homes.

—HAROLD B. LEE

■ ■ ■

In the Yiddish song "Mayn Yingele" ("My Little One"), a father sings to his sleeping child:

> I have a son, a little son,
> A boy completely fine.
> Whenever I see him, it seems to me
> That all the world is mine.
> But seldom, seldom do I see
> My child awake and bright.
> I only see him when he sleeps;
> I'm only home at night.
> It's early when I leave for work;
> When I return, it's late.
> Unknown to me is my own flesh,
> Unknown is my child's face.
> When I come home so wearily
> In the darkness after day,
> My pale wife exclaims to me:
> "You should have seen our child play."
> I stand beside his little bed;
> I look and try to hear.
> In his dream he moves his lips:
> "Why isn't Papa here?"

That song was written in 1887. Today, Papa and Mama are no longer in the sweatshops, but the anguish of the parent who has impaled himself on the sword of ambition has not changed. It has merely changed addresses.

—JEFFREY K. SALKIN,
BEING GOD'S PARTNER

ENJOYING THE LULLS

Part of achieving happiness is learning to enjoy even the less
invigorating parts of the journey.

A certain power of enduring boredom is essential to a happy life. The lives of
most great men have not been exciting except at a few great moments. A
generation that cannot endure boredom will be a generation of little men.

—BERTRAND RUSSELL

■ ■ ■

The people who fail to meet the stresses and strains of life are often those
who have never learned to cherish what the French call *le petit bonheur*—the
little happiness—when it comes along. It is too bad; for most lives hold little
that is dramatic and overwhelming. But every day has its quota of *le petit
bonheur.*

—ARDIS WHITMAN,
WOMAN'S DAY

■ ■ ■

Norman Lear on the joys of success: Success is how you collect your minutes.
You spend millions of minutes to reach one triumph, one moment, then you
spend maybe a thousand minutes enjoying it. If you were unhappy through
those millions of minutes, what good are the thousands of minutes of
triumph? It doesn't equate.

Life is made of small pleasures. Good eye contact over the breakfast table
with your wife. A moment of touching with a friend. Happiness is made of
those tiny successes.

—*PARADE*

LIVING FOR TODAY

While we reap benefit from the past and dream for the future, to enjoy the greatest satisfaction we must live and find happiness in our todays.

One of the most tragic things I know about human nature is that all of us tend to put off living. We are all dreaming of some magical rose garden over the horizon—instead of enjoying the roses that are blooming outside our windows today.

—DALE CARNEGIE,
HOW TO STOP WORRYING

■ ■ ■

How strange it is, our little procession of life! The child says, "When I am a big boy." The big boy says, "When I grow up." And, grown-up, he says, "When I get married." Then, when retirement comes, he looks back over the landscape traversed; a cold wind seems to sweep over it; somehow he has missed it all, and it is gone. Life, we learn too late, is in the living, in the tissue of every day and hour.

—STEPHEN LEACOCK

■ ■ ■

Now and then it's good to pause in our pursuit of happiness and just be happy.

—THE COCKLE BUR

■ ■ ■

The future is purchased by the present.

—SAMUEL JOHNSON

■ ■ ■

Happiness is not a station you arrive at, but a manner of traveling.

—MARGARET LEE RUNBECK

■ ■ ■

Look to this day
For yesterday is but a dream,
And tomorrow is only a vision,
But today, well lived,
Makes every yesterday a dream of happiness
And every tomorrow a vision of hope.
Look well, therefore, to this day.

—SANSKRIT PROVERB

■ ■ ■

Each day is a new life. Seize it. Live it. For in today already walks tomorrow.

—DAVID GUY POWERS,
LIVE A NEW LIFE

20

SIMPLICITY

I can do only one thing at a time,
but I can avoid doing many things simultaneously.
—ASHLEIGH BRILLIANT

When asked why he did not smoke, Sir Isaac Newton replied, "Because I do not want to acquire any new necessities." Newton and other successful people know the value of keeping their lives uncluttered and simple. But simplicity is often a hard-to-find destination.

When thinking of simplicity, Henry David Thoreau's literary classic, *Walden*, comes to mind. Written more than a century and a half ago, it gives us pause today. Thoreau recorded how he decided to leave behind a complicated society for a time and live in the woods. His aim? To see what he could learn from the simple life. "Simplify! Simplify!" is a version of Thoreau's seminal work. As you read, reflect on how well you would fare if living under the conditions described by Thoreau. Consider how Thoreau's insights might translate into your own day-to-day choices. Then search "Riding the Bus with Beth" and "Lighten Your Load" for helpful hints on how you might simplify your everyday life amidst today's reality.

SIMPLIFY! SIMPLIFY!

Henry David Thoreau

When I wrote the following pages, or rather the bulk of them, I lived alone, in the woods, a mile from any neighbor, in a house which I had built myself, on the shore of Walden Pond, in Concord, Massachusetts, and earned my living by the labor of my hands only. I lived there two years and two months (July 4, 1845, to September 6, 1847).

I went to the woods because I wished to live deliberately, to front only the essential facts of life, and see if I could not learn what it had to teach, and not, when I came to die, discover that I had not lived. I did not wish to live what was not life, living is so dear; nor did I wish to practice resignation, unless it was quite necessary. I wanted to live deep and suck out all the marrow of life, to drive life into a corner, and reduce it to its lowest terms, and, if it proved to be sublime, to know it by experience, and be able to give a true account of it.

The mass of men lead lives of quiet desperation. What is called resignation is confirmed desperation. But it is a characteristic of wisdom not to do desperate things.

We live meanly, like ants. Our life is frittered away by detail. An honest man has hardly need to count more than his ten fingers, or in extreme cases he may add his ten toes, and lump the rest. Simplicity, simplicity, simplicity! I say, let your affairs be as two or three, and not a hundred or a thousand; instead of a million, count half a dozen, and keep your accounts on your thumbnail.

Simplify, simplify. Instead of three meals a day, if it be necessary eat but one; instead of a hundred dishes, five; and reduce other things in proportion. The nation itself, with all its so-called internal improvements, which, by the way, are all external and superficial, is just such an unwieldy and overgrown establishment, tripped up by its own traps, ruined by luxury and heedless expense, by want of calculation and a worthy aim, as the million households in the land; and the only cure for it, as for them, is in a rigid economy, a stern and more than Spartan simplicity of life and elevation of purpose.

Why should we live with such hurry and waste of life?

Let us spend one day as deliberately as Nature, and not be thrown off the track by every nutshell and mosquito's wing that falls on the rails. Let us rise early and fast, gently and without perturbation. Why should we knock under and go with the stream? If the bell rings, why should we run?

The gross necessaries of life for man in this climate may, accurately enough, be distributed under the several heads of Food, Shelter, Clothing, and Fuel; for not till we have secured these are we prepared to entertain the trustworthy problems of life with freedom and a prospect of success. But most of the luxuries, and many of the so-called comforts of life, are not only not indispensable, but positive hindrances to the elevation of mankind. The ancient philosophers were a class than which none has been poorer in outward riches, none so rich in inward.

No man ever stood the lower in my estimation for having a patch in his clothes, yet I am sure that there is greater anxiety, commonly, to have fashionable clothes than to have a sound conscience. If my jacket and trousers, my hat and shoes, are fit to worship God in, they will do, will they not? I say, beware of all enterprises that require new clothes, and not rather a new wearer of clothes.

As for shelter, I will not deny that this is now a necessary of life. But when I consider my neighbors, the farmers of Concord, I find that for the most part they have been toiling twenty, thirty, or forty years, that they may become the real owners of their farms—and we may regard one third of that toil as the cost of their houses.

With consummate skill, the farmer has set his trap with a hair spring to catch comfort and independence, and then, as he turned away, got his own leg into it. And when the farmer has got his house, he may not be the richer but the poorer for it, and it be the house that has got him.

Most men appear never to have considered what a house is, and are actually though needlessly poor all their lives because they think that they must have such a one as their neighbors have. It is possible to invent a house still more convenient and luxurious than we have, which yet all would admit that man could not afford to pay for. Shall we always study to obtain more of these things, and not sometimes to be content with less? Our houses are cluttered and defiled with furniture. I would rather sit in the open air, for no dust gathers on the grass.

But to make haste to my own experiment in the woods by Walden Pond. I have built a tight shingled and plastered house, ten feet wide by fifteen feet long, and eight-feet posts, with a garret and a closet, a large window on each side, one door at the end, and a brick fireplace opposite. Before I finished my house, wishing to earn ten or twelve dollars to meet my unusual expenses, I planted about two acres and a half of light and sandy soil chiefly with beans, but also a small part with potatoes, corn, peas, and turnips.

I learned that if one would live simply and eat only the crop which he raised, and raise no more than he ate, he could do all his farm work as it were with his left hand, and thus he would not be tied to an ox, or horse, or coworker. I was more independent than any farmer in Concord, for I was not anchored to a house or farm, but could follow the bent of my genius, which is a very crooked one, every moment.

I have maintained myself solely by the labor of my hands, and I found that, by working about six weeks a year, I could meet all the expenses of living. The whole of my winters, as well as most of my summers, I had free and clear for study.

In short, I am convinced both by faith and experience, that to maintain one's self on this earth is not a hardship but a pastime, if we will live simply and wisely.

Why should we be in such desperate haste to succeed and in such desperate enterprises? If a man does not keep pace with his companions, perhaps it is because he hears a different drummer. Let him step to the music he hears, however measured or far away.

Again, Thoreau wrote that classic piece more than a century and a half ago. Though I doubt it has many of us scrambling to build shacks or grow gardens beside a pond in the woods, the underlying ideas stimulate our thinking and bring into question, "What is it I value most?" and "What things can I do without?"

What we learn from Thoreau is that if we want to keep life simple, we must determine what we need to let go of in our lives, and learn to say no to distracting sideshows. But Rachel Simon was so caught up in life that she never saw the need to simplify, until she spent a day on a bus.

RIDING THE BUS WITH BETH

Rachel Simon

(Some names have been changed to protect privacy.)

"Wake up," says Beth. "Or we won't make the first bus." It's 6:00 a.m. and my sister is dressed already, in a purple T-shirt and pistachio shorts. I struggle awake and into my writer-and-teacher-off-for-a-day clothes: black sweater, leggings.

Beth and I, both in our late thirties, are just eleven months apart. But unlike me, my short and stout younger sister owns a wardrobe of blazingly bright colors and can leap out of bed before dawn. Something else is different about her: She is a woman with mental retardation. For six years she's lived on her own in a subsidized apartment in a medium-sized Pennsylvania city. Laid off from a fast-food job, she has a lot of time. And since she receives government assistance for her disability, she has enough money to live on.

She's also ingenious, something not normally ascribed to people on the periphery of society's vision. So she rides buses. Not to get from one place to another, but to ride them her way. Looping through the city from dawn to dusk, she befriends drivers and passengers. She gets to know birthdays, anniversaries, where people shop and what they eat for breakfast. She helps with destinations and carries bags of groceries. And people return her friendship.

Completely on her own, my sister has found a traveling community. Now I'm about to find it too. At her invitation, I'm hopping aboard her life. For the next year I'm making regular visits to Beth and riding the buses with her—spending meaningful time with my sister for the first time in our adult lives.

We hurry down Main Street and into a McDonald's, where Beth buys a cup of coffee, which stays unopened. We make a beeline for the bus shelter, and when our bus draws up, Claude, the driver, throws open his door as if welcoming us to his house. Beth clomps aboard and thrusts the coffee at him. He takes it and thumbs some quarters into her hand.

"Our agreement," he says to me.

Beth then spins toward "her" seat—the premier spot on the front sideways bench, catty-cornered from Claude, close to him. I sit beside her, and as the bus pulls out, Beth announces that Claude is forty-two years old and has a birthday soon. He laughs as she names the exact date. "She remembers everything," he says. Claude laughs a lot with my sister.

All day long, in fact, as we ride Jacob's, Estella's, and Rodolpho's buses, driver after driver greets Beth heartily. She reminds them where to turn on runs they haven't driven in a while; keeps them posted on schedule changes; teaches them Top Ten songs.

When she was younger, Beth would have crumpled if people looked askance at her, which they often did. Now she doesn't trouble herself with such worries. She seems to relish zipping about to her own inner beat. I think, *This is my sister!* She's so confident and exuberant. So unlike me, so wrapped up in my work I've been cutting myself off from life.

While Beth was riding her buses, I was being whisked around by cars, trains, and jets. And I was going places, I thought. I was writing for the Philadelphia *Inquirer* and had published a few books. I was teaching writing classes and hosting events at a bookstore. But I worked seven days a week, from the minute I threw off the covers at 7:00 a.m. until I disintegrated back inside them at 1:00 a.m. I had become hyperbusy, hypercritical, hyperventilating.

Because my life was so consumed by work, I lost friends. But perhaps the greatest forfeit was love. When my longtime boyfriend, Sam, asked me to marry him a few years earlier, I couldn't bring myself to make the commitment. So the relationship reluctantly, tearfully ended. Ever since then I'd been working so hard I'd practically forgotten I was lonely.

Visiting Beth, I felt myself starting to thaw a bit toward other people. I'd never even imagined my sister had friends who were bus drivers, never imagined they could be as kind as they were. Then came the problems with Beth's eyes—and a new round of lessons for this older sis.

An ophthalmologist is on the phone to me with a diagnosis: interstitial keratitis. Beth's corneas have become scratched and numb. "And she has a secondary eye condition," the doctor says. "Her eyelashes are growing into her eyes." She needs surgery. "It's her decision, of course. I hope you'll be able to help." Though Beth has invited me to ride her buses, I have no idea if she's accepted me in her heart. She's just so proud. Would she let me help her?

I talk to Beth about the problems. Without surgery, I explain, her eyes may worsen. Reluctantly, she agrees to it. But she won't stay home while the stitches heal, she says. Once the anesthesia wears off, she wants to get right back to riding the buses.

"I have a wish," I say suddenly. "I wish I had a *Help Anyone Anytime* book." What I want is a guide to being a good sister, to doing well by Beth. It would tell how to adjust my tendency to micromanage her, to steer her self-reliant nature—and how to find the difference between caring and controlling. Instead, I say to her, "I'd like a book that would help me find you a new pair of eyes."

"That'd be nice," she says. Then: "Can you make them purple?"

"I'm scared," she says on the day of her outpatient operation. I'm surprised and impressed: Beth is revealing herself, something she's never done with me until now. It's going to be okay, I tell her. I'll be with you the whole time. So, it turns out, will Jacob, Beth's bus driver friend. When he arrives to chauffeur us to the hospital, she seems truly reassured. Jacob cranks up the Beatles song "She Loves You" on his radio. From the backseat of his car, Beth belts out, "Yeah, yeah, yeah!"

In the hospital's waiting room, we review the paperwork together. Beth says she's nervous. "I'll be with you," I tell her again. "Don't worry."

"Hey, you've got your whole entourage," Jacob adds cheerfully.

Her body relaxes. She asks me to join her in the room where she answers medical questions, gets her blood pressure checked, and is handed a hospital gown. She asks if I'll stay at her side as she undresses. I help Beth change into gown and slippers. Then we pad over to the surgery unit, where Jacob is waiting for us beside her gurney. "These clothes feel funny," Beth says. "I'm not used to these weird shoes."

Finally it's time for her to get onto the gurney. I say gently, "You have to lie down, to get operated on."

She says, "I will," but doesn't move.

"You need to do it now," I say.

"I'll get around to it," she replies.

I climb onto the gurney beside her and lie down. "Do it like me," I say. With more coaxing from both Jacob and me, she finally lies down.

A nurse comes over with the dreaded knockout shot. "Beth," I say, "you have to turn over now."

"I don't want to," she says.

Jacob and I seem to agree without speaking. Together we turn Beth onto her side. She's laughing now, enjoying the attention. The nurse jams the shot in, and we roll Beth back. Then her fight is over.

It stays over as the nurses put up the side rails of the gurney and wheel her toward surgery. It stays over as I sit on a stool beside her in the holding area, where the drug begins to take effect, and where I caress my sister's arm while we wait.

I look into Beth's eyes. They're stripped of her usual defiance and mischief. I notice something else. My sister is looking at me with a fullness of trust I've seldom ever seen.

Jacob stays with us into the night. Afterward he drives us back to Beth's apartment, gets dinner, and keeps us company while Beth rests. The next day another bus driver, Rodolpho, visits. Then another, Rick, arrives with a chocolate milk shake. And Betty, a dispatcher, sends flowers on behalf of the drivers. For two days Beth does what the doctor has asked: Lies calmly beneath the ice packs. Accepts ointment in her eyes.

Then, amazingly, Jacob invites Beth to his house. Since I need to return home for a while, Jacob and his wife, Carol, have offered to continue caring for Beth until her eyes heal. I think, *So this is my sister's life.*

"These drivers," I muse to her one day. "They seem too good to be true. How did you find so many nice, wise people all in one place?"

"It just happened," Beth answers. "I rode, and I guess they were just there." I look at her, brimming with life. And realize that nothing "just happens." Beth has sought out friends where others might not look. She's taken the time to weed out drivers who are decent and kind from those who are indifferent or hostile. Beth's invitation to ride her buses didn't "just happen" either, I realize. Beth may have wanted me to meet her drivers because I needed them too.

Near the end of my rides with Beth, I came to want a different life for myself than the one I'd had. And a few months after that, I phoned Sam. We talked for a long time, and I was no longer scared. From there we began a surprising and wonderful courtship that resulted in our wedding in May 2001. When I told Beth I was getting married, she sent me a card. It was a colorful burst of stars and exclamation points:

> Dear Rachel,
> Hi. I am so happy for you.
> Signed, Cool Beth

The card—written in purple ink—was also signed by some of Beth's bus drivers: Len, Jack, Melanie, Henry, Lisa, Jerry and, last but not least, Jacob. The man who had helped take care of my sister wrote: "May many happy and prosperous adventures be with you. Love, Jacob."

Rachel's life was packed full of career ambitions and promotions. Her sister Beth's life was simple, focused on relationships. As Rachel experienced Beth's simplicities and felt the impact of the relationships she had developed on the bus routes, Rachel realized that there was an important part of life that she was missing. She knew that if she wanted to enjoy those same simplicities, there would be some things she would need to let go of and to say no to in her future. To her credit, she did.

As Thoreau noted, sometimes it is a preoccupation with "things" that in very subtle ways gobbles up our time and prevents us from enjoying the pleasures that go with a simple life.

LIGHTEN YOUR LOAD

Edward Sussman

Three years ago, Ann Richards, the feisty, charismatic former governor of Texas, shepherded her mother through a final illness. During that time, Richards saw a dramatic change in her ailing parent. After a lifetime obsessed with collecting cut glass, silver services, lace tablecloths, china, and costume jewelry, her mother suddenly lost interest in her prized possessions.

"All that really mattered was who was coming to see her, her family and friends," said Richards. "It was a complete shift."

After her mother's death, Richards rid herself of the antiques that sometimes kept her mother more interested in things than people. She held a garage sale. "We couldn't compete with Jackie O in quality," Richards said wryly. "But in quantity we were competitive."

In a day, except for one or two keepsakes, it was all gone. "I learned that if I'm going to enjoy the here and now, I need to relieve myself of the things that slow me down. Now I can pick up and do anything at the drop of a hat."

In the economy of life, it returns huge dividends—both financially and emotionally—to let some things go. In Ann Richards's case, the return benefit was freedom—she was free to pick up and do anything she wanted at the drop of a hat. Are there "things" in your life that you would be more "free" without?

～

WRAP UP

Years ago my family made a trip through Europe, hauling our baggage from country to country, hotel to hotel. Along the way we picked up small mementos and interesting literature to remind us of the beautiful places and historical sights. At one point, one member of the family had to return home, so we decided to send along some boxes filled with items of clothing and keepsakes that had burdened us throughout the trip. Once relieved of our non-necessities, we felt ourselves free — free to move from location to location without burden, free to enjoy the sights without extra baggage sapping our energy. And so it is with many aspects of life.

It is not until you have a burning yes inside of you about what is truly important, that you can pleasantly, smilingly, cheerfully, say no to all of that which is urgent, but not truly important. Our deepest guilt comes from doing the opposite, implicitly saying no to the truly important and yes, yes, yes to the urgent that is not important. The more we are free from non-necessities, the more we are free to do the more meaningful actions of our lives.

REFLECTIONS

- If you were to create a mental wastebasket, what activities from last week would you place in it? Are there activities that you do on a regular basis that need to be reduced or tossed out?

- When was the last time you said no to an unimportant request? What fears, if any, prevent you from saying no more often? What activities will you say no to this week?

- Look around. Are there frivolous "things" or "clutter" that steal away valuable time? Do you spend hours cleaning, repairing, or paying for things that in your overall scheme of life are not that important? What things can you let go of?

FURTHER INSIGHTS ON
Simplicity

~

KEEPING LIFE SIMPLE

To get the most out of our life we may need to get some things out of our life.

A simple life is its own reward.

—GEORGE SANTAYANA

■ ■ ■

Slow down, simplify and be kind.

—NAOMI JUDD

■ ■ ■

Everything should be made as simple as possible, but not simpler.

—ALBERT EINSTEIN

■ ■ ■

The motto that should be engraved over the entrance to every university and institution of higher learning is the one proposed by philosopher Alfred North Whitehead for scientists: "Seek simplicity, and distrust it."

—SYDNEY J. HARRIS

■ ■ ■

All of us are generally cumbered up with the thousand and one hindrances and duties which wind us about with their spider threads and fetter the movement of our wings. In order to simplify his duties, his business and his life, a man must know how to disengage what is essential from the detail in which it is enwrapped, for everything cannot be equally considered. It is lack of order which makes us slaves; the confusion of today discounts the freedom of tomorrow.

—HENRI-FRÉDÉRIC AMIEL,
AMIEL'S JOURNAL IN TIME

LETTING GO

Keeping life simple requires letting go of old baggage and things that are of no lasting value.

I must strip my vines of all useless foliage and concentrate on what is truth, justice, and charity.

—POPE JOHN XXIII

■ ■ ■

The most pleasant and useful persons are those who leave some of the problems of the universe for God to worry about.

—DON MARQUIS

■ ■ ■

To comprehend a man's life, it is necessary to know not merely what he does but also what he purposely leaves undone. There is a limit to the work that can be got out of a human body or a human brain, and he is a wise man who wastes no energy on pursuits for which he is not fitted; and he is still wiser who, from among the things that he can do well, chooses and resolutely follows the best.

—WILLIAM E. GLADSTONE

■ ■ ■

Besides the noble art of getting things done, there is the noble art of leaving things undone. The wisdom of life consists in the elimination of non-essentials.

—LIN YUTANG

■ ■ ■

The art of being wise is the art of knowing what to overlook.

—WILLIAM JAMES

■ ■ ■

Some people think it's holding on that makes one strong. Sometimes it's letting go.

—SYLVIA ROBINSON,
IN *THE CHRISTIAN SCIENCE MONITOR*

SAYING NO

A companion to letting go is the noble art of saying *No*. Decide your highest priorities then have the courage—pleasantly and firmly—to say *No* to distractions.

Learn to say no. It will be of more use to you than to be able to read Latin.

—CHARLES HADDON SPURGEON

■ ■ ■

A survey of executives in two hundred large American companies conducted by Accountemps, a worldwide personnel service, finds that people waste about two months a year attending "unnecessary" meetings. Another month is spent reading and writing unimportant memos. The survey also finds that big companies tend to lose more time than smaller firms, which are more willing to "just say no" to procedures that serve no useful purpose.

—RANDALL POE,
ACROSS THE BOARD

■ ■ ■

All the mistakes I ever made in my life were when I wanted to say No, and said Yes.

—MOSS HART

■ ■ ■

If I have one vice, and I can call it nothing else, it is not to be able to say "no."

—ABRAHAM LINCOLN

■ ■ ■

No can be a hard word to say. It taps fears of not being liked, and, especially, of not being productive. Actually, by forcing us to become more focused, refusing to take on more tasks can make us more productive.

—RALPH KEYES,
TIMELOCK

EFFICIENCY

Simplicity is achieved by the efficiency of the processes that go in to creating it.

When Henry Ford was asked why he went to his executives' offices instead of having them come to his, he said: "I've found that I can leave the other fellow's office a lot quicker than I can get him to leave mine."

—E. E. EDGAR

■ ■ ■

While he was Vice President, Coolidge was visited by Channing Cox, his successor as governor of Massachusetts. Cox inquired how Coolidge had been able to see so many visitors a day and still leave the office at 5 p.m., whereas he himself often left as late as 9 p.m. "Why the difference?" Cox asked. "You talk back," said Coolidge.

—PAUL F. BOLLER, JR.,
PRESIDENTIAL ANECDOTES

■ ■ ■

On the nation's space-age program: "Our two greatest problems are gravity and paper work. We can lick gravity, but sometimes the paper work is overwhelming."

—DR. WERNHER VON BRAUN

■ ■ ■

Dr. Benjamin Spock, author of the *Common Sense Book of Baby and Child Care*, says that he once made a study of the features of newborn infants' faces to determine if they could show the baby's sex. "Today," says Dr. Spock, "I am convinced the older way of finding out is quicker."

—THE *INSIDER'S NEWSLETTER*

SQUANDERING TIME

As busy as people claim to be, often they could greatly simplify their life by not wasting time on non-essentials—particularly in front of the television screen.

Dost thou love life? Then do not squander Time, for that's the stuff Life is made of.

—BENJAMIN FRANKLIN

■ ■ ■

From a letter to Ann Landers:

> In the house
> Of Mr. & Mrs. Spouse
> He and she
> Would watch TV,
> And never a word
> Between them was spoken
> Until the day
> The set was broken.
> Then, "How do you do?"
> Said He to She.
> "I don't believe we've met."
> Spouse is my name.
> What's yours?" he asked.
> "Why, mine's the same!"
> Said She to He.
> "Do you suppose we could be . . . ?"
> But the set came suddenly right about
> And they never did find out.

■ ■ ■

We are always complaining that our days are few, and acting as though there would be no end to them.

—SENECA

■ ■ ■

The primary danger of the TV screen lies not so much in the behavior it produces as in the behavior it prevents.

—URIE BRONFENBRENNER
BREAKING THE TV HABIT
by JOAN ANDERSON WILKINS

■ ■ ■

If a man watches three football games in a row, he should be declared legally dead.

—ERMA BOMBECK

■ ■ ■

21

RENEWAL

An unhurried sense of time is in itself a form of wealth.
—BONNIE FRIEDMAN

After returning from Walden Pond, one of Henry David Thoreau's trademarks became frequent walks under the evening sky. At the end of one such twilight trek he wrote of "waiting on the hilltops for the sky to fall, that I might catch something." What Thoreau knew and what too many people today have forgotten is that the mind needs occasion to relax and renew itself—opportunity to stimulate the mind and refresh the body.

But in today's world, terms such as leisure, solitude, and relaxation have, in some cases, developed a pejorative connotation and the value of renewal has been diminished. The following stories, beginning with "Lesson of a Quiet Cove," however, remind us that we all need regular means and locations for finding refuge from the day-to-day storms and turbulences of life.

LESSON OF A QUIET COVE

William J. Buchanan

We had set up camp on the north shore of Skilak Lake, some twenty miles from where the murky glacier waters empty into Cook Inlet, off the west coast of Alaska's Kenai Peninsula. It was nearing midnight, but there was light that would remain throughout this summer night in 1968. A foil-wrapped salmon baked slowly on the grill. I glanced at my companion, Ed Gallant, on his knees at water's edge. He was extracting roe skeins from our day's catch and placing them on wax paper to dry. As I pondered the tranquil setting, I recalled the discordant events that had brought us here.

Six weeks before, newly promoted to lieutenant colonel, I had arrived at Elmendorf Air Force Base in Anchorage to assume duties as chief of the civilian engineering division of the Alaska Defense Communications Agency. I'd expected a demanding job, but was unprepared for the realities. The military command network in Alaska was a primitive mishmash of outdated components sprawling across a tremendous, often icebound area. Breakdowns were commonplace. Keeping this horse-and-buggy network operating was equivalent to maintaining a fleet of B-52s with baling wire and adhesive tape.

Deputy Chief Engineer Ed Gallant was my immediate subordinate. Fifty, of average height and robust build, he had a commendable record as the driving force of the engineering division. Yet our first encounters were stiff, newcomer sizing up old pro and vice versa.

That's how matters stood when, at the end of my second week, after frustrating days and sleepless nights, I called Gallant into my office. "Ed, there are still a dozen areas where a failure could prove disastrous in an emergency," I said, my voice betraying exasperation. "We've got to establish priorities."

He looked at me steadily for a few moments. "May I suggest priority one?"

"By all means."

"Go fishing."

"What!" I was incredulous.

"With me. This weekend. I promise you that when we return on Monday the priorities will be established."

It was preposterous. Yet something in his manner gave me pause. I shrugged. "Why not?"

As we took to the lake that Saturday, I found that I was enjoying myself. With the intuition of a dedicated outdoorsman, Ed led us to school after school of migrating red salmon. By camp time I had caught my limit. Still, I couldn't shake a nagging guilt about being there, instead of at my desk where so much remained to be done.

At water's edge Ed sprinkled some borax over the roe. After dinner I asked him about that. "Why the borax?'"

"Toughens the eggs. I'll freeze them when we get home. They'll make bait for—"

He dropped the sentence. Instinctively I said, "For next year."

It was a puzzling turn in the conversation. "I don't understand," I said.

He picked up a stick and poked the campfire back to life. "I've got malignant hypertension," he said. "It should have killed me a year ago." And he told me the story.

In 1960 he moved to Alaska to settle on the last unspoiled American frontier. He signed on with the Communications Agency. The job was a quagmire. An obsessed workaholic, he attempted to compensate for insufficient funds and lack of modern equipment by redoubling his own work load, putting in fifteen-hour days.

One night in the summer of 1966, alone at his desk, he suddenly couldn't read the blueprints. The blurred vision passed, and he said nothing about it. Then, two weeks later, he collapsed.

Tests revealed that he had severe high blood pressure. "I was given a choice: keep working and die in ninety days, or quit, take drugs, and maybe make it for a year.

"I agreed to the drugs," he continued. "But quit working? That would have killed me on the spot."

I managed to find my voice. "What did you do?"

He stood. "Come, I'll show you."

We were camped on the neck of a pear-shaped cove that penetrated two hundred yards into the woods. We walked inland to the cove's innermost point. Here, protected from wind and current, the waters were mirror-still.

Ed sat down on a fallen log and pointed. "Look carefully."

Just beneath the surface several huge salmon were swimming in snail-paced circles. Others were lying quietly on the shallow bottom, their only motion a slow, rhythmic fanning of gills and fins.

"When the doctors gave me that ultimatum two summers ago, I came here," Ed said. "I sat on this very log, trying to sort out my life. Then, for some reason, I began to watch the salmon. Not like before . . . but *really watch them.*" He turned and pointed outside the cove. "Look, out in the channel."

A swath of faintly rippled water revealed the upstream migration of thousands of salmon.

Ed said, "They're fresh from the sea, and strong. But tomorrow they'll reach the Russian River Falls. They'll make desperate leaps up the face of the falls. Some of them will be too spent to make it, and they'll be dashed back against the rocks below. And then, finally, they'll die from sheer exhaustion."

He returned his gaze to the salmon in the cove. "These are different. Some instinct has brought them to this quiet place. It's as if they know the falls are just ahead. Tomorrow they'll continue their migration, rested for whatever comes.

"It came to me that I was like those salmon out in the channel. Relentlessly forging ahead. At that moment I knew what I would do. I'd keep working, but when the pressures began to mount, I'd take time to come to the cove. That's how I've handled things since. How long can it last? I don't know. But I'm already a year older than the doctors said I'd ever be."

He turned and faced me. "Colonel, you're not the first person newly assigned up here to realize that we're operating a rickshaw system in the space age. You're not the first to swim constantly upstream against a stronger current."

Suddenly I realized what this outing was all about, what "priority one" really was.

"All right, Ed. What can we do?"

He smiled, relieved at my reaction. "I know the communications system up here like the back of my hand. I can handle the technical end of it. What I can't handle is the red tape. If you can keep the brass off our backs, the engineers and I will keep the system going."

And there on the banks of the cove we made a pact. From that weekend on, Ed handled the myriad day-to-day technical decisions, while I attended meetings, fielded nit-picking official queries, and placated ruffled egos. And I never hesitated to approve when Ed asked for time off to go to the cove.

Our pact was tested only once. Like most technologies, ours was entering the computer age. Directions came from Washington to convert our engineering orders to computer language. "It's absurd!" Ed said. "Our system doesn't require it. You must persuade headquarters to grant an exception."

I mulled over the matter for two days; then I called him into my office. "Ed, I'm going to overrule you on this," I said. "we may have to cope with an obsolete system, but that's no reason to foster obsolete engineers. They must adapt to the new methods. Their futures depend on it."

His jaw tightened. "As you wish," he said coolly, and left. For the remainder of that day our relationship was strained.

When I got to my office next morning. Ed was waiting for me. "I've been thinking over what you said—about the engineers. You're right, of course. About them having a future."

The next week, Ed devised a training program to nudge our engineers into the computer age. His success was plain when headquarters later requested a copy of his program to use as a guide for other commands.

As winter gripped Anchorage and sealed access to the Kenai Peninsula, Ed became restless. I often caught him gazing at a long-out-dated calendar on the wall behind his desk. It had an aerial photograph of Skidak Lake. Clearly visible on the north shore was the pear-shaped outline of the cove. "I must go back . . . at least once more," he would say.

But on Sunday afternoon, March 16, the duty officer called me. "Mr. Gallant has suffered a stroke."

I rushed to the base hospital. Ed lay unmoving, staring blankly at the ceiling. Then he saw me. His paralyzed left arm lay at his side, but he moved his right hand toward me and tried vainly to speak. I grasped the proffered hand. "It's all right, Ed. Don't try to talk."

He began to shift his gaze from me to the wall, and back again. After a while, I followed his eyes toward the wall. Suddenly his meaning came clear. I gave his hand a squeeze. "I'll be right back."

I drove to the agency and took down the old calendar. Then I returned to the hospital and taped it to the wall nearest his bed. He fixed his eyes on it, and at last he seemed at peace. And that's how he died, with his face turned toward that faded photograph of his beloved cove.

In the summer of 1970, my Alaska tour at an end, I returned to the cove one last time. The salmon were still there, resting for ordeals to come. As I watched I reflected on another night, when a wise and kindly man shared what he'd learned in this special place, a lesson that had sustained him in his darkest hours—the lesson of a quiet cove.

Everyone can benefit from places of refuge—personal quiet coves. And while I hope each of us has a favorite spot or two for more extensive retreats, we also need daily locations that are easily accessible. Some people find retreat in simply closing their eyes and meditating. Others find it while resting and listening to quiet music. Others through participating in physical activities, such as walking or playing sports. The location and method is not as important as the fact that we need to find ways to relax, refresh our minds, and restimulate our thinking.

————

Ed found his quiet cove for renewal. In the following story, a doctor prescribes that a patient search out renewal at a beach where he had happy memories from his youth. And he sent him there with four prescriptions.

THE DAY AT THE BEACH

Arthur Gordon

Not long ago I came to one of those bleak periods that many of us encounter from time to time, a sudden drastic dip in the graph of living when everything goes stale and flat, energy wanes, enthusiasm dies. The effect on my work was frightening. Every morning I would clench my teeth and mutter: "Today life will take on some of its old meaning. You've got to break through this thing. You've got to!"

But the barren days went by, and the paralysis grew worse. The time came when I knew I had to have help.

The man I turned to was a doctor. Not a psychiatrist, just a doctor. He was older than I, and under his surface gruffness lay great wisdom and compassion. "I don't know what's wrong," I told him miserably, "but I just seem to have come to a dead end. Can you help me?"

"I don't know," he said slowly. He made a tent of his fingers, and gazed at me thoughtfully for a long while. Then, abruptly, he asked, "Where were you happiest as a child?"

"As a child?" I echoed. "Why, at the beach, I suppose. We had a summer cottage there. We all loved it."

He looked out the window and watched the October leaves sifting down. "Are you capable of following instructions for a single day?"

"I think so," I said, ready to try anything.

"All right. Here's what I want you to do."

He told me to drive to the beach alone the following morning, arriving not later than nine o'clock. I could take some lunch, but I was not to read, write, listen to the radio, or talk to anyone. "In addition," he said, "I'll give you a prescription to be taken every three hours."

He tore off four prescription blanks, wrote a few words on each, folded them, numbered them and handed them to me. "Take these at nine, twelve, three, and six."

"Are you serious?" I asked.

He gave a short bark of a laugh. "You won't think I'm joking when you get my bill!"

The next morning, with little faith, I drove to the beach. It was lonely, all right. A northeaster was blowing; the sea looked gray and angry. I sat in the car, the whole day stretching emptily before me. Then I took out the first of the folded slips of paper. On it was written: *Listen carefully.*

I stared at the two words. *Why,* I thought, *the man must be mad. He had ruled out music and newscasts and human conversation. What else was there?*

I raised my head and I did listen. There were no sounds but the steady roar of the sea, the creaking cry of a gull, the drone of some aircraft high overhead. All these sounds were familiar.

I got out of the car. A gust of wind slammed the door with a sudden clap of sound. *Am I supposed,* I asked myself, *to listen carefully to things like that?*

I climbed a dune and looked out over the deserted beach. Here the sea bellowed so loudly that all other sounds were lost. And yet, I thought suddenly, there must be sounds beneath sounds—the soft rasp of drifting sand, the tiny wind-whisperings in the dune grasses—if the listener got close enough to hear them.

On an impulse I ducked down and, feeling faintly ridiculous, thrust my head into a clump of sea-wheat. Here I made a discovery: if you listen intently, there is a fractional moment in which everything seems to pause, wait. In that instant of stillness, the racing thoughts halt. For a moment, when you truly listen for something outside yourself, you have to silence the clamorous voices within. The mind rests.

I went back to the car and slid behind the wheel. *Listen carefully.* As I listened again to the deep growl of the sea, I found myself thinking about the immensity of it, the stupendous rhythms of it, the velvet trap it made for moonlight, the white-fanged fury of its storms.

I thought of the lessons it had taught us as children. A certain amount of patience: you can't hurry the tides. A great deal of respect: the sea does not suffer fools gladly. An awareness of the vast and mysterious interdependence of things: wind and tide and current, calm and squall and hurricane, all combining to determine the paths of the birds above and the fish below. And the cleanness of it all, with every beach swept twice a day by the great broom of the sea.

Sitting there, I realized I was thinking of things bigger than myself—and there was relief in that.

Even so, the morning passed slowly. The habit of hurling myself at a problem was so strong that I felt lost without it. Once, when I was wistfully eyeing the car radio, a phrase from Carlyle jumped into my head: "Silence is the element in which great things fashion themselves."

By noon the wind had polished the clouds out of the sky, and the sea had a hard, merry sparkle. I unfolded the second "prescription." And again I sat there, half amused and half exasperated. Three words this time: *Try reaching back.*

Back to what? To the past, obviously. But why, when all my worries concerned the present or the future?

I left the car and started tramping reflectively along the dunes. The doctor had sent me to the beach because it was a place of happy memories. Maybe *that* was what I was supposed to reach for: the wealth of happiness that lay half-forgotten behind me.

I found a sheltered place and lay down on the sun-warmed sand. When I tried to peer into the well of the past, the recollections that came to the surface were happy, but not very clear; the faces were faint and faraway, as if I had not thought of them in a long time.

I decided to experiment: to work on these vague impressions as a painter would—retouching the colors, strengthening the outlines. I would choose specific incidents and recapture as many details as possible. I would visualize people complete with dress and gestures. I would listen (carefully!) for the exact sound of their voices, the echo of their laughter.

The tide was going out now, but there was still thunder in the surf. So I chose to go back twenty years to the last fishing trip I made with my younger brother. (He died in the Pacific during World War II, and was buried in the Philippines.) I found now that if I closed my eyes and really tried, I could see him with amazing vividness, even the humor and eagerness in his eyes that far-off morning.

In fact, I could see it all: the ivory scimitar of beach where we were fishing, the eastern sky smeared with sunrise, the great rollers creaming in, stately and slow. I could feel the backwash swirl warm around my knees, see the sudden arc of my brother's rod as he struck a fish, hear his exultant yell. Piece by piece I rebuilt it, clear and unchanged under the transparent varnish of time. Then it was gone.

I sat up slowly. *Try reaching back.* Happy people were usually assured, confident people. If, then, you deliberately reached back and touched happiness, might there not be released little flashes of power, tiny sources of strength?

This second period of the day went more quickly. As the sun began its long slant down the sky, my mind ranged eagerly through the past, reliving some episodes, uncovering others that had been completely forgotten. For example, when I was around thirteen and my brother ten, Father had promised to take us to the circus. But at lunch there was a phone call: some urgent business required his attention downtown. We braced ourselves for disappointment. Then we heard him say, "No, I won't be down. It'll have to wait."

When he came back to the table, Mother smiled. "The circus keeps coming back, you know."

"I know," said Father. "But childhood doesn't."

Across all the years I remembered this, and knew from the sudden glow of warmth that no kindness is ever really wasted, or ever completely lost.

By three o'clock the tide was out; the sound of the waves was only a rhythmic whisper, like a giant breathing. I stayed in my sandy nest, feeling relaxed and content—and a little complacent. *The doctor's prescriptions,* I thought, *were easy to take.*

But I was not prepared for the next one. This time the three words were not a gentle suggestion. They sounded more like a command. *Re-examine your motives.*

My first reaction was purely defensive. *There's nothing wrong with my motives,* I said to myself. *I want to be successful—who doesn't? I want a certain amount of recognition—but so does everybody. I want more security than I've got—and why not?*

Maybe, said a small voice somewhere inside my head, *those motives aren't good enough. Maybe that's the reason the wheels have stopped going round.*

I picked up a handful of sand and let it stream between my fingers. In the past, whenever my work went well, there had always been something spontaneous about it, something uncontrived, something free. Lately it had been calculated, competent—and dead. Why? Because I had been looking past the job itself to the rewards I hoped it would bring. The work had ceased to be an end in itself; it had been merely a means to make money, pay bills. The sense of giving something, of helping people, of making a contribution, had been lost in a frantic clutch at security.

In a flash of certainty, I saw that if one's motives are wrong, nothing can be right. It makes no difference whether you are a mailman, a hairdresser, an insurance salesman, a housewife—whatever. As long as you feel you are serving others, you do the job well. When you are concerned only with helping yourself, you do it less well. This is a law as inexorable as gravity.

For a long time I sat there. Far out on the bar I heard the murmur of the surf change to a hollow roar as the tide turned. Behind me the spears of light were almost horizontal. My time at the beach had almost run out, and I felt a grudging admiration for the doctor and the "prescriptions" he had so casually and cunningly devised. I saw, now, that in them was a therapeutic progression that might well be of value to anyone facing any difficulty.

Listen carefully: To calm the frantic mind, slow it down, shift the focus from inner problems to outer things.

Try reaching back: Since the human mind can hold but one idea at a time, you blot out present worry when you touch the happinesses of the past.

Re-examine your motives: This was the hard core of the "treatment," this challenge to reappraise, to bring one's motives into alignment with one's capabilities and conscience. But the mind must be clear and receptive to do this—hence the six hours of quiet that went before.

The western sky was a blaze of crimson as I took out the last slip of paper. Six words this time. I walked slowly out on the beach. A few yards below high-water mark I stopped and read the words again: *Write your worries on the sand.*

I let the paper blow away, reached down and picked up a fragment of shell. Kneeling there under the vault of the sky, I wrote several words on the sand, one above the other.

Then I walked away, and I did not look back. I had written my troubles on the sand. And the tide was coming in.

No prescriptions fit all worries and stresses. But all of us need renewal. In such times, I encourage you to find a location filled with your own happy memories and try the remedies. First, listen. Where possible, listen to nature's soothing sounds. Listen to your deepest internal thoughts and desires, for in your heart are the most meaningful issues of your life. Think back to good times from your past. Focus on details including sights, sounds, and smells. Reflect on your deepest motives and examine if they are aligned with timeless principles and with who you want to become. Finally, try writing down two or three words or phrases that reflect stresses in your life and then toss them away, either figuratively or literally. Watch them disappear with the sands of time.

No, these steps will not make all your worries go away. But, if followed, they will help relax your body and mind, and put your soul in a better state to deal with stress.

While the two previous stories found renewal in a quiet cove and on the beach (or in the elevated skies), Nancy Blakey found her moments of renewal and joy all along the various side roads of her life.

LURE OF THE DETOUR

Nancy H. Blakey

Poet William Stafford once said that we are defined more by the detours and distractions in life than by the narrow road toward goals. I like this image. But then I am a highly distractible person.

Oh, I have goals like everybody else, and I get things done. But it is the crazy asides in a day that lead me to fruitful territory.

Like a good road trip. For my family this means one long and lazy detour after another—a saunter down back roads that eventually lead to the final destination. The lid is off time, and beyond every curve are possibilities. We stop at barn sales, inspect road kills, and buy the world's juiciest peaches at local fruit stands. And because we are unhurried, we talk.

It wasn't always this way for us. We discovered the lush side of road trips quite by accident—or by detour, you could say.

For years we made the nearly five-hundred-mile drive from our home in

Seattle to my parents' home in Boise in nine hours. We traveled the way most people do: the fastest, shortest, easiest route. Especially if my husband, Greg, couldn't come and I was alone with four noisy, restless kids who hate confinement and have strong opinions about everything.

Road trips felt risky, so I would drive fast, stopping only when I had to. I'd discipline the kids with my eye on the road and my arm waving into the far reaches of the car. We'd stick to the freeways. We'd count the hours and miles and arrive tired and cranky.

But then Banner was born.

Banner is our sheep. He was rejected by his mama days before a planned trip to Boise. I had two choices: Leave the lamb with my husband, who would have to take him to the office, feed him every two hours, and remember to change his diapers. Or take Banner to Boise with me. Greg made the decision for me.

That is how I found myself on the road with four kids, a baby lamb, five bikes, and nothing but my eternal optimism to see me through. We took the back roads out of sheer necessity. We had to stop every hour and let Banner shake out his long wobbly legs. The kids chased him and one another. They'd get back in the car breathless and energized, smelling fresh from the cold air.

We began to think of ourselves as weird in a wonderful sort of way. While the world was whizzing by, we were not. Instead of pushing through to Boise, in one shot, we stayed in a small motel in Baker, Oregon. This led in the morning to the discovery of a diner that served the most tender and fragrant cinnamon rolls we had ever eaten.

We explored side roads off side roads, surrendering to whim, like grasshopper-catching in waist high weeds. Even if we simply looked out the car windows at clothes flapping on a line, or baby pigs waddling after their mother, or the rise of a trout on an elbow of creek, it was better than the best ride down the freeway. Here was life. And new horizons.

We eventually arrived at my parents' doorstep astonishingly fresh and full of stories. It had taken us an extra five hours of road time, but heck, we used to spend five hours just recovering.

I grew brave—and a little giddy—with this venture. On the way home I looped through Idaho's panhandle to visit my grandmother. We paused at a hot spring I had raced past heedlessly for years. And I grew creative with my disciplining technique. On an empty stretch of road in eastern Washington, everyone started to bicker. I stopped the car, ordered all kids out, and told them to meet me up ahead. I drove about a mile, parked on the side, and read my book in sweet silence.

That trip with Banner opened our eyes to a world available to anyone reckless enough to idle and putter around. We discovered that we *can* stop at a river just because our toes are hot and the water is cold. The world *can* wait while we pull over to read historical markers along the road, imagining for one brief moment the courage and grit it took to survive a century and a half ago.

Some road trips are by necessity fast and straight. But it took a tiny black lamb to make me realize that a detour may uncover the best part of a journey—and the best part of yourself.

The world could benefit from more mothers (and fathers) like Nancy: people who recognize the value of a breath of fresh air and who also know how to expose their children to a wide range of vistas.

～

WRAP UP

Renewal is an amazing and very central component of nature. We see it not only in forests that replenish themselves following a fire, but also in our bodies, as our skin replaces itself on a regular basis, blood is replaced, and wounds mend. But as humans, we are not always as effective at applying the principle of renewal to our lives. Too often we let stress overtake us. Whether it be a trip to a quiet cove, a journey to a beach, or a trek along one of life's side routes, we all need to find ways to pace ourselves, enjoy some leisure, and catch a breath of fresh air. For even Everyday Greatness requires renewal.

REFLECTIONS

- Do you have a quiet cove where you can retreat from your immediate surroundings? Do you go there often enough?

- What "daily" quiet coves do you use as temporary getaways? Do you make time for leisurely activities such as meditation, walks, exercise, or reading to relax your mind?

- When was the last time you took time to *listen* to "outer" things in order to shift your focus from inner concerns? When was the last time you tried *reaching back* by focusing on happy moments of the past to blot out present worries? When was the last time you *re-examined your motives* to ensure that they are in alignment with your values and conscience? Do you ever *write your worries in the sand?* Do you have more things to write?

- On your day-to-day travels through life, do you take interesting side routes to discover the many enjoyments of life?

FURTHER INSIGHTS ON
Renewal

~

SETTING THE PACE

People who want to enjoy life over the long term must learn
to tame their schedules and pace themselves.

A friend of mine, a distinguished explorer who spent a couple of years among
the savages of the upper Amazon, once attempted a forced march through the
jungle. The party made extraordinary speed for the first two days, but on the
third morning, when it was time to start, my friend found all the natives sitting
on their haunches, looking very solemn and making no preparation to leave.

"They are waiting," the chief explained to my friend. "They cannot move
farther until their souls have caught up with their bodies."

I can think of no better illustration of our own plight today. Is there no
way of letting our souls, so to say, catch up with our bodies?

—JAMES TRUSLOW ADAMS,
THE TEMPO OF MODERN LIFE

■ ■ ■

Life is not a one-hundred-yard dash, but more a cross-country run. If we
sprint all the time, we not only fail to win the race, but never even last long
enough to reach the finish line.

—JOSEPH A. KENNEDY,
RELAX AND LIVE

■ ■ ■

In making a living today, many no longer leave room for life.

—JOSEPH R. SIZOO

■ ■ ■

If someone tells me, "I'm working ninety hours a week," I say, "You're doing something terribly wrong. I go skiing on the weekend. I go out on Friday. Make a list of twenty things that make you work ninety hours, and ten of them have to be nonsense."

—JACK WELCH

■ ■ ■

If you burn the candle at both ends, you may not be as bright as you think.

—HERBERT V. PROCHNOW

■ ■ ■

Over the years, many executives have said to me with pride: "Boy, I worked so hard last year that I didn't take any vacation." I always feel like responding; "You dummy. You mean to tell me that you can take responsibility for an eighty-million-dollar project and you can't plan two weeks out of the year to have some fun?"

—LEE IACOCCA,
IACOCCA

CALLING A TIME OUT

As we learned from the quiet cove, sometimes we need to call a recess in order to regroup and refocus on our priorities.

Every now and then, go away, take a little relaxation, because when you come back to your work, your judgment will be surer. To remain constantly at work will cause you to lose power of judgment. Go some distance away, because then the work appears smaller and more of it can be taken in at a glance, and a lack of harmony or proportion is more readily seen."

—LEONARDO DA VINCI

A holiday gives one a chance to look backward and forward, to reset oneself by an inner compass.

—MAY SARTON

Every human being needs a certain amount of time in which he can be peaceful. Peace may take the form of exercise or reading or any congenial occupation; but the one thing which must *not* be connected with it is a sense of obligation to do some particular thing at some particular time. I had two hundred letters waiting a few days ago and any amount of work which had to be done, and I deliberately spent two hours reading poetry.

—ELEANOR ROOSEVELT,
QUOTED IN THE *HOLLYWOOD REPORTER*

Sometimes the most urgent and vital thing you can possibly do is take a complete rest.

—ASHLEIGH BRILLIANT

Never be afraid to sit awhile and think.

—LORRAINE HANSBERRY

Enjoying the Detours

Often nature and life's little detours bring fresh air and a renewal of energy in ways no other activity can.

Oscar Wilde said, "Consistency is the last refuge of the unimaginative." So stop getting up at 6:05. Get up at 5:06. Walk a mile at dawn. Find a new way to drive to work. Study wildflowers. Read to the blind. Subscribe to an out-of-town paper. Canoe at midnight. Teach some kid the thing you do best. Listen to two hours of uninterrupted Mozart.

Leap out of that rut. Savor life. Remember, we pass this way only once.

—United Technologies Corp. message

■ ■ ■

I remember one long-ago November night when the last lamp had been blown out and everyone but Dad was asleep. Suddenly he jumped out of bed and rushed to the window. Then in a few moments he had everyone up.

"Outside!" he said. "Never mind dressing. Just throw a quilt around you. Quick!"

When we got outside all we could see was frost, coating everything with white fur, and the fat, smoky moon that lighted up a million diamonds.

"Listen!" he said.

Trying our best to silence chattering teeth, we strained our ears and looked skyward where he was looking. Yes, we could hear them now. Then we could see them. Wild geese flying across the moon.

"Must be a thousand of them," Dad said.

Afterward, as he pointed us back to the warmth of our beds, all he said was, "I think it was worth a minute of shivering."

Rather tragic it seems to me, that we have neither the time nor the inclination for that kind of fathering today. Tragic, too, that as the years roll by, there never seem to be any minutes in them anymore.

—H. Gordon Green

■ ■ ■

One spring morning I paused beside a park fountain to watch the spray diffuse sunlight into shimmering rainbows. A young mother, followed by a tiny blond girl, came hurrying along the path. When the child saw the fountain, she threw her arms wide. "Mommy, wait!" she cried. "See all the pretty colors!"

The mother reached for her daughter's hand. "Come on," she urged. "We'll miss our bus!" Then seeing the joy on the small face, she relented. "All right," she said. "There'll be another bus soon."

As she knelt with her arms around the child, joy filled the mother's face too—that rare and special joy of sharing something lovely with someone we love.

Since that day, I've found that the happiest, most observant, most creative children belong to families rich in rainbows shared.

—ALETHA JANE LINDSTROM

■ ■ ■

Architect Frank Lloyd Wright told how a lecture he received at the age of nine helped set his philosophy of life. An uncle, a stolid, no-nonsense type, had taken him for a long walk across a snow-covered field. At the far side, his uncle told him to look back at their two sets of tracks. "See, my boy," he said, "how your footprints go aimlessly back and forth from those trees, to the cattle, back to the fence and then over there where you were throwing sticks? But notice how my path comes straight across, directly to my goal. You should never forget this lesson!"

"And I never did," Wright said, grinning. "I determined right then not to miss most things in life, as my uncle had."

—JOHN KEASLER

■ ■ ■

Along with the peace and quiet of rural summers, the hammock seems to have vanished. Long ago, it was the symbol of rustic ease, comfort and modest luxury. Here one could lie on a drowsy afternoon, practically wallowing in indolence. Distant noises of bees, birds and farm activity had a lulling effect. Sleep came near. Anyone who indulged in this boneless, swaying relaxation was considered to be living the good life.

—DES MOINES REGISTER

BEING ALONE

Some of life's best moments are experienced in solitude. But you don't need a lengthy hermit adventure to find renewal, even short retreats provide refreshment.

A man must keep a little black shop where he can be himself without reserve. In solitude alone can he know true freedom.

—MONTAIGNE

■ ■ ■

If one sets aside time for a business appointment or shopping expedition, that time is accepted as inviolable. But if one says, "I cannot come because that is my hour to be alone," one is considered rude, egotistical, or strange. What commentary on our civilization.

—ANNE MORROW LINDBERGH,
GIFT FROM THE SEA

■ ■ ■

During the last days of World War II, President Harry Truman was asked how he managed to bear up so calmly under the stress and strain of the Presidency. His answer was, "I have a foxhole in my mind." He explained that, just as a soldier retreats into his foxhole for protection and respite, he periodically retired into his own "mental foxhole" where he allowed nothing to bother him.

—MAXWELL MALTS,
PSYCHOCYBERNETICS

■ ■ ■

Smart people spend time alone. They don't fill their days with appointments from 8 a.m. to 10 p.m., as many executives do. Inspiration is nurtured by activities like chopping wood, preparing dinner and reading to the kids. These activities soften the rigid pace of the day's pursuits and allow all our God-given intuition to work its unlogical magic.

—PHILIP K. HOWARD

FINDING RELIEF

There are many methods people use to banish stress. What
are some of yours?

Everything stress is, gardening is not. Stress is hurried and harried; gardening
has the pace of nature's season-long rhythms. Stress is feeling powerless and
victimized; gardening is control over both your food supply and your
immediate environment. As you garden, you are healed—body and mind,
heart and soul.

—WILLIAM GOTTLIEB,
ORGANIC GARDENING

■ ■ ■

"After a difficult day with the children," a young mother says, "I like to take
the car and go for a drive; I like to have something in my hands I can
control."

—LAWRENCE P. FITZGERALD

■ ■ ■

The best eraser in the world is a good night's sleep.

—O. A. BATTISTA

■ ■ ■

Give sorrow words. The grief that does not speak whispers the o'er-fraught
heart and bids it break.

—WILLIAM SHAKESPEARE

■ ■ ■

Those who think they have not time for bodily exercise will sooner or later
have to find time for illness.

—EDWARD STANLEY

■ ■ ■

On the Channel Island of Jersey, on a cliff overlooking the harbor, I came upon a worn, moss-covered bench. A century ago, when Victor Hugo was in exile, ill, persecuted by his beloved France, it was here that he climbed every evening and, gazing into the sunset, gave himself up to profound meditation, at the end of which he would rise and, selecting a pebble of varying size—sometimes small, at other times large—he would cast it into the water beneath. This behavior did not escape the notice of some children who played near-by, and one evening a little girl, bolder than the rest, pushed forward.

"Monsieur Hugo, why do you come here to throw these stones?"

The great writer was silent; then he smiled gravely.

"Not stones, my child. I am throwing self-pity into the sea."

—A. J. CRONIN

■ ■ ■

An early-morning walk is a blessing for the whole day.

—HENRY DAVID THOREAU

AFTERWORD

What a tremendous array of people this collection represents! People who, at various points of their lives, have made the choice to act, the choice of purpose, and the choice for principles.

So now the choice is yours. Will you make the three choices? Will Everyday Greatness become a more integral part of your life?

Again, life is not always easy. It hits like the waves of the ocean as one challenge rolls in after another. Amidst such a rush it seems to become more and more difficult even to pause long enough to reflect on our daily choices and what we want to do with the precious moments we call life. Yet making time for such pauses to clarify who we are and what we are about is so important to our progress as human beings.

Bill Tammeus vividly described the power of such pauses in a December 1989 entry:

> There is a special moment as the waves foam in. It occurs just at the instant that one wave has spent itself on the sand but, suspended, has not yet begun to be pulled back out to sea. For less than a second the waters stop churning and, through their clearness, I can see the ground beneath, see the rocks, the shells, the sand.
>
> Sometimes I think that's how much of a glimpse we are ever given of what is really going on in this life. We get a small clip of time as the forces that buffet us reach an occasional uneasy equilibrium. Then they retreat and the next wave smashes in and we lose that special momentary clarity.
>
> But while the clarity is there, while the action is suspended, calm, we should gather it in and store it deep within us so that when the next wave hits—and inevitably it will—we can keep our balance.

I hope this collection has provided such moments of clarity for you—moments when you could see clearly the potential that is within you. Moments when you were able to look beyond life's broken shells and swirling adversities, and see what a difference you can make in the lives of those around you. Cherish and hold on to such moments. Keep them at the forefront of your mind, so that when the buffeting waves of trivia and busyness crash in upon you, you can keep your sights elevated and focused on your highest dreams.

PUTTING PRINCIPLES INTO PRACTICE

My guess is that as you read through this collection some of the entries made little impact. Others you found clever and entertaining. But then there were a handful of insights that somehow snuck up on you and struck a quiet nerve that said, "This I need to do better." As you reflect on those insights, consider the following suggestions for getting the most from this book.

SUGGESTION #1: BEGIN WITH YOURSELF

I hope you share this collection with others. Indeed, I hope parents share the stories and principles with their children, employers with their employees, teachers with their students, and friends with their friends. But I firmly believe that the greatest value you can receive from this book will come as you first internalize and apply the principles to your own life. So open the gates to internal change and reflect first on those areas of your life where you feel the greatest need for improvement.

SUGGESTION #2: START BROAD, THEN FOCUS

Review this collection in its entirety to get a broad perspective on the principles and how they apply to you. Highlight favorite insights. Then, sort out two or three specific principles or insights that if applied better in your life will most directly help you achieve your dreams and potential. Work on those two or three areas for a while, then move on. Do resist the temptation to try to improve everything all at once.

SUGGESTION #3: ESTABLISH SPECIFIC, REALISTIC TARGETS

Set improvement goals that are not too hard and not too soft. Set time-frames that are not too far off and not too close. But be specific. Don't just say, "This week I will try to be more gentle," but rather determine specific ways you will be more gentle. In most cases it helps to set a specific time when you will try to be more gentle, such as dinnertime with your teens, bedtime with your toddlers, or performance review time with employees. Tremendous power comes from scheduling your plans and goals.

SUGGESTION #4: START SMALL, BUT GET STARTED

Too often when we experience impulses to make a greater contribution, the first thoughts that enter our minds are negative: *Oh, I am so busy, how could I possibly do more?* Or, *I don't have a wealth of talent or resources, so who am I to be of any value?* Some of us may even find ourselves wishing we had lived in an earlier era, thinking *I really could have been somebody if only I had been born in those days.* But the reality is that it does no good to waste time feeling inferior, harboring self-doubt, or wishing we lived in another time. These are our days and we must make the most of them if we want to feel at peace with who we are and what we are about. So start today and do something—if only a small thing, if only for one person.

SUGGESTION #5: SHARE WITH OTHERS

One of the best ways to learn a principle is to teach it. If you are a parent, for example, you may want to select one principle per week to teach and incorporate into the lives of your children. Share a story during a meal or at another convenient time, and then use the supporting quotes and anecdotes throughout the week to expand and reenforce the principle. Or, if you are a business leader you may want to find ways to integrate the principles into weekly meetings to stimulate team effectiveness. Just as there are individuals who possess Everyday Greatness, so there are teams and organizations that exhibit Everyday Greatness, particularly when compared to organizations and teams whose successes are so short lived. Whatever your role, trust your creativity in exploring ways to teach the principles found in this collection. You will learn the most.

SUGGESTION #6: BE PATIENT

This does not mean to go easy on yourself, because you do want to challenge yourself. But at the same time, do not get hung up on every little setback or mistake. Do not forget to give yourself credit for the good that you do. Self-growth is tender territory—it deserves time and respect. So work hard, make daily progress, and reward meaningful milestones. Remember, DeWitt and Lila Wallace left their legacy one quote, one story, and one edition at a time. They did not do it overnight or all at once. Likewise, Everyday Greatness is a way of living—a step-by-step daily opportunity—not a one-time event. So be patient with yourself, persevere, and it will happen.

I believe that each of these six suggestions will help you apply the principles contained in this collection. But I want to offer one final suggestion: Paint a mental picture, a visual image of yourself as a transition person. You will recall that in the Introduction I expressed hope that this collection would have three outcomes. First, I hoped you would find a sense of peace and enjoyment in your reading—a refuge from the storm, a haven of hope. Second, I hoped you would discover insights into how you personally could get a little more out of life, and give a little more. And I hope this collection has fulfilled those two goals for you.

But it is the third outcome that I truly hope will become a fixed image in your mind. It is the image of yourself becoming more of a transition person—a person who takes the negative or neutral that comes their way and turns it into something positive. See yourself as one who proactively searches out opportunities to make a meaningful contribution. As a person who not only fills his or her life with purpose, but helps others fill their lives with purpose as well. See yourself as a change catalyst. Commit yourself to becoming a light, not a judge; a model, not a critic.

Today's world needs people like you. So trust yourself. Trust the principles, and begin now. Make the choice to act. Make the choice of purpose. Make the choice for principles. As you do, may you never stop experiencing the inner peace and the personal satisfaction that come through living a life of Everyday Greatness.

ACKNOWLEDGMENTS

Of course there are many who deserve credit for their artistry and work in bringing together this collection. Much appreciation is extended to the Reader's Digest team of Jackie Leo, Harold Clarke, Sandy McCormick Hill, Marcia Rockwood, and Maureen Mackey for their hands-on involvement in putting the collection together, as well as Raimo Moysa, Chris Cavanaugh, and Eric Schrier for their encouragement and support of this project from its early stages. A particularly warm thanks is offered to Nancy Clark for her editorial prowess and patient capacity to please diverse interests. Furthermore, a heartfelt thanks goes to Boyd Craig of FranklinCovey Company for his integral contribution and leadership throughout the project, Julie Gillman for administrative and technical assistance, and my literary agent, Jan Miller, and her partner, Shannon Miser-Marven. Warm recognition is also extended to the publishing magic of Rutledge Hill Press, including the talents of Pamela Clements, Geoffrey Stone, Laura Troup, and Brian Mitchell. Finally, I express my deepest gratitude to my wife, Sandra, our children, their spouses, and all our grandchildren for their support and inspiration and for living lives of Everyday Greatness.

Notes

All the stories in this collection previously appeared in *Reader's Digest* magazine. The following contributors and publishers graciously granted permission to reprint material.

Stories

"The Cellist of Sarajevo" by Paul Sullivan from *Hope* (March/April 1996). Copyright © 1996 by Paul Sullivan.

"The Law of Unselfishness" by Fulton Oursler from *Christian Herald* (August 1946). Copyright © 1946 by Christian Herald Assn., Inc.

"The Boy Who Couldn't Read" by Tyler Currie from *The Washington Post Magazine* (February 23, 2003). Copyright © 2003 by Tyler Currie.

"Pope John Paul II" from *John Paul the Great*, Copyright © 2005 by Peggy Noonan. Published by Viking, a member of Penguin Group (USA) Inc.

"How Love Came Back" by Tom Anderson from *Guideposts* (August 1985). Copyright © 1985 by *Guideposts*.

"I Intend to Make It" by Betty Ford with Chris Chase from *The Times of My Life*, Copyright © 1978 by Betty Ford. Permission granted by William Morris Agency.

"Maya's Journey Home" by Maya Angelou from *I Know Why the Caged Bird Sings*, Copyright © 1969 and renewed 1997 by Maya Angelou. Published by Random House, Inc., (USA) and Virago Press (UK).

"The Man Who Said No to $1 Million" by Joseph V. Paterno and Bernard

Asbell from *Paterno: By the Book.* Copyright © 1989 by Joseph V. Paterno and Bernard Asbell. Reprinted by permission of Regina Ryan Publishing Enterprises, Inc.

"Catch of a Lifetime" by James P. Lenfesty from *The Minneapolis Star Tribune* (May 15, 1988). Copyright © 1988 by James P. Lenfesty

"Coming to My Senses" by Sarah Ban Breathnach from *Romancing the Ordinary,* Copyright © 2002 by Simple Abundance®, Inc. Published by the Simple Abundance Press/Scribner.

"A Lesson from the Mound" by Beth Mullally from *Times Herald-Record* (Sept 28, 1993). Copyright © 1993 by *Times-Herald-Record.*

"Where the Sun Spilled Gold" by Jaroldeen Edwards from *Things I Wish I'd Known Sooner,* Copyright © 1997 by Jaroldeen Edwards. Published by Pocket Books, a division of Simon & Schuster, Inc.

"Here's Johnny!" by Ed McMahon from *Here's Johnny!,* Copyright © 2005 by Ed McMahon. Published by Rutledge Hill Press.

"Johnny Lingo's Eight-Cow Wife" by Patricia McGerr from *Woman's Day* (November 1988). Copyright © 1988 by Patricia McGerr. Permission granted by Curtis Brown Ltd.

"Lend an Ear" by Roberta Israeloff from *Woman's Day* (July 13, 1999). Copyright © 1999 by Roberta Israeloff.

"It's About Time" by Noah Gilson from *Medical Economics* (March 22, 2002). Copyright © 2002 by Advanstar Communications, Inc.

"Crash Course" by Michael Collins from *Hot Lights, Cold Steel,* Copyright © 2005 by Michael J. Collins. Published by St. Martin's Press, Inc.

"Different Strokes" by Jeanne Marie Laskas from *The Washington Post Magazine* (March 12, 2000). Copyright © 2000 by Jeanne Marie Laskas.

"A Little Human Happiness" by Albert P. Hout from *The Lion* (May 1971). Copyright © 1971 by Lions International.

QUOTATIONS

About FranklinCovey

Mission Statement

We enable greatness in people and organizations everywhere.

FranklinCovey (NYSE:FC) is the global leader in effectiveness training, productivity tools and assessment services for organizations and individuals. FranklinCovey helps organizations succeed by unleashing the power of their workforce to focus and execute on their top priorities. Clients include 90 percent of the Fortune 100, more than 75 percent of the Fortune 500, thousands of small and mid-sized businesses, as well as numerous government entities and educational institutions. Organizations and individuals access FranklinCovey products and services through corporate training, licensed client facilitators, one-on-one coaching, public workshops, catalogs, more than 100 retail stores and www.franklincovey.com. FranklinCovey has nearly 1500 associates providing professional services and products in the United States and for thirty-seven international offices, serving more than 100 countries.

Programs and Services

xQ Survey and Debrief *(to help leaders assess their organization's "Execution Quotient")*

The 7 Habits of Highly Effective People workshop

The 7 Habits of Highly Effective Managers workshop

The 4 Disciplines of Execution work session

FOCUS: Achieving Your Highest Priorities workshop

The 4 Roles of Leadership workshop

The FranklinCovey Planning System

To learn more about FranklinCovey products and services, please call 1-888-868-1776 or 1-801-817-1776, or go to www.franklincovey.com.

ABOUT THE AUTHORS

STEPHEN R. COVEY is an internationally respected leadership authority, family expert, teacher, organizational consultant and author who has dedicated his life to teaching principle-centered living and leadership to build both families and organizations. He holds an MBA from Harvard and a doctorate from Brigham Young University, where he was a professor of organizational behavior and business management.

READER'S DIGEST magazine, part of The Reader's Digest Association, Inc., (NYSE: RDA) is published in twenty-one languages, in fifty editions, and reaches 80 million readers worldwide each month. The magazine celebrates the best of humanity and delivers a compelling mix of special reporting, humor, personal service and human-interest stories.

DAVID K. HATCH is a recognized consultant specialized in leadership and organizational effectiveness. His career has taken him to over thirty countries, where his assessment tools have benefited numerous Fortune 500 companies and over a half million leaders.

INDEX